VENOM

DE HAVILLAND VENOM AND SEA VENOM
THE COMPLETE HISTORY

DAVID WATKINS

Foreword by
Air Cdre Stuart McIntyre CBE, DFC, D.Com., FRAeS, RNZAF

SUTTON PUBLISHING

First published in 2003 by
Sutton Publishing Limited · Phoenix Mill
Thrupp · Stroud · Gloucestershire · GL5 2BU

British Library Cataloguing in Publication Data
A catalogue record for this book is available from the British Library.

ISBN 0-7509-3161-2

For Peggy

Classic head-on view of the Venom prototype, showing its highly polished metal surfaces. (*de Havilland*)

Typeset in 10/13 pt Sabon
Typesetting and origination by
Sutton Publishing Limited.
Printed and bound in England by
J.H. Haynes & Co. Ltd, Sparkford.

CONTENTS

FOREWORD

My introduction to the Venom FB.1 was not very encouraging. Having accepted the first aircraft on behalf of the squadron after what seemed an eternity of waiting, it came as something of an anticlimax to climb in before the assembled company, only to have the cartridge starter fail and to have to climb out to try another day. I confess to being quite disappointed when I first flew the Venom FB.1 on 5 May 1955. I'd done two tours on Vampires and had read of the astonishingly better performance of the Venom which allegedly included the ability to get to 40,000ft in seven minutes – but in the tropical temperatures of Singapore, the climb performance fell somewhat short of my expectations. However, it was satisfyingly faster and did rather live up to a description I read somewhere of being 'a Vampire with hair on its chest'. I was impressed that de Havilland's had at last got rid of the irritating 'spade grip' found on the Vampire and that the Venom's pistol grip provided an altogether much better way to control the machine. Also, one could see the instruments when one really needed to see them, i.e. while instrument flying – something to which the designers of the Vampire cockpit appeared to have given only passing thought. I was again surprised that the controls were much heavier than those of the delightful Vampire. The Venom had a serious deficiency in the air conditioning system which may well have been adequate in Europe but left a lot to be desired in the more demanding environment of the tropics. Overall, my first impressions were far from enthusiastic.

Nevertheless, as I became more familiar with the aeroplane I became a great enthusiast for it. The Venom's vices were fairly minor – it certainly didn't like spinning or, more to the point, recovering from spins. Its relatively benign behaviour when exceeding its critical Mach number could not possibly worry the most inexperienced pilot. It handled well at very high altitudes, being equally good at tree-top level, while the weapon load, although modest by today's standards, was certainly adequate for the squadron's tasks in the anti-terrorist role. It was a good weapons platform and capable of permitting quite respectable air-to-air scores using the 20mm cannon.

The Venom was a pilot's aircraft. Simple systems made it relatively easy to maintain and fly. I recall demonstrating the canopy closing system to a USAF F-100 pilot when we were based together at Don Muang airport (Bangkok). He was astonished and delighted to see that one could close the canopy with a simple winding handle. He commented: 'Gee! That's great! If our canopy won't close it usually means that the aircraft will be unserviceable for a week.' Having two of our colleagues eject from Venoms (through no inherent fault of the aircraft) also gave the rest of us confidence in the ejection seat while sincerely hoping we didn't have to put one to the test ourselves.

It is safe to say that those who flew the Venom enjoyed the experience and I can recall no one having a bad word to say about it – except for the air conditioner. I was privileged to fly it under operational conditions where it acquitted itself with honour. I am delighted that David Watkins has undertaken the task of recording the history of this fine aircraft.

Stuart McIntyre
May 2002

Stuart McIntyre had the distinction of carrying out the first operational strike in a Venom fighter when, on 6 May 1955, his squadron attacked a target north of Singapore during Operation 'Firedog' – the air campaign against the Communist terrorists in Malaya. Stuart was educated at Wellington College and joined the RNZAF as a cadet pilot in 1949. He graduated as a sergeant pilot in 1951 and served briefly with 4 (Territorial Air Force) Squadron at Taieri (Dunedin), flying P-51D Mustang fighter aircraft. The following year he was commissioned and joined 14 (F) Squadron RNZAF at Ohakea, which had recently been equipped with Vampire Mk.52s. The squadron was based at RAF Nicosia between 1952 and 1954, following which McIntyre was appointed deputy flight commander with 75 (F) Squadron at Ohakea and became leader of the first jet aerobatic squadron in New Zealand. Returning to 14 (F) Squadron in 1955 for a tour flying offensive operations against the terrorists in Malaya, he acted as squadron commander for several periods in the absence of any other flight commanders. On 1 May 1955 Stuart led the squadron's first 'Firedog' strike in Malaya, and during his two-year tour in Malaya he flew a total of forty-eight 'Firedog' and 'Smash Hit' sorties and was also a member of the squadron aerobatic display team. Between 1973 and 1977 Stuart commanded RNZAF Base Ohakea and was the driving force behind the formation of the Ohakea Museum, which later became a sub-unit of the RNZAF Museum. He returned to flying in 1960 as a flight commander with 14 (F) Squadron, operating Canberra B(I)12s, and was appointed its squadron commander two years later. Following his resignation from the RNZAF in 1983 to take up the position of Director of Civil Aviation, he also held other various consultant posts and in 1997 was awarded the 'Jean Batten Memorial Trophy' by the RAeS for his outstanding service to NZ Aviation. Stuart McIntyre currently lives in Wellington and is a consultant for the Massey University School of Aviation.

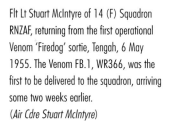

Flt Lt Stuart McIntyre of 14 (F) Squadron RNZAF, returning from the first operational Venom 'Firedog' sortie, Tengah, 6 May 1955. The Venom FB.1, WR366, was the first to be delivered to the squadron, arriving some two weeks earlier.
(Air Cdre Stuart McIntyre)

ACKNOWLEDGEMENTS

Compiling enough information to complete this book required the help of a great many people. I would therefore like to express my sincere gratitude to the following: Alan Allen, for kindly loaning me the various flight manuals and photographs, and for his well-informed advice on Venom survivors; Alan Roach, for his considerable knowledge regarding aircraft production at Chester and for patiently unravelling the complicated details of the various Venom contracts; Stuart McIntyre, for his support with the 'Firedog' operations in Malaya and his eager response to my many requests for photographs and information from New Zealand; Sqn Ldr Colin Richardson, to whom I am deeply indebted for kindly proofreading my manuscripts and meticulously preparing the various maps used in this book, for his extensive, personal knowledge of the Middle East and of Venom operations in Aden, Oman and during the Suez Crisis, and for his permission to use extracts from his personal account of the Jebel Akhdar War and his book *Masirah: Tales from a Desert Island*; and former DH test pilot John Wilson, for the loan of his personal notes and logbook of the Venom development programme.

Sincere thanks are also due to the following: my wife Anne, who patiently suffered the 'pangs' of yet another book, while at the same time reading for a PhD at 'Hogwart's Academy'; Audrey Edgeler, for putting aside her own history of Barnstaple pottery to read the manuscript; and Su Archard, for scouring the many back issues of the East Anglian newspapers for details of Venom crashes.

My gratitude is also extended to the following, who patiently and enthusiastically answered all my questions, generously loaned me their logbooks, scrapbooks and cuttings, and without whom this book would not be possible: Martin Anderberg; Cdr J.N.S. Anderson RN; Sam D'Arcy; Air Cdre Max Bacon; Cdr H.E.R. Bain RN; Marcus Bath, for his intelligent interpretation of my photographic requirements; Peter Biddiscombe; Qwilton Biel; Trevor Bland; Lt Cdr John Blunden RN; John Brady; Air Cdre Nelson Bright RNZAF; Tony Buttler, for his advice on fighter projects and specifications; Dan Carter; Colin Champ RAN, for his help with 808 Squadron RAN; Gp Capt Alastair Christie AFC, MRAeS; Ron Clear; David Clegg; Wg Cdr Tim Cohu; AVM Colin Coulthard CB, AFC & Bar, FRAeS; Ray Crompton; Comm R.M. Crosley DFC & Bar, RN; Air Cdre Bill Croydon; Geoff Cruickshank, for his constant support and for kindly supplying me with copies of the Venom record cards; Rod Dean, for his item on flying the Venom; Jeremy Dickson; Jean-Pierre Dubois, for the information on Sud-Est Aquilons; Cdr G.J.R. Elgar RN; Capt Curt E. Farley; Rob Faulkner RN; Santiago A. Flores; Mikael Forslund; Barry Gillingwater; Peter Goodwin, for his enthusiastic support and the generous loan of his photograph archive, which included the excellent colour slides of 8 Squadron; Tony Gronert; Lt Cdr John Hackett RN; Lt Cdr Jesse Hanks RN; John Hardcastle; Wg Cdr J.A. 'Harry' Harrison MRAeS; Gp Capt J.H. Hedger; Capt F. Hefford OBE, DSC, AFC, RN; Cdr Geoffrey Higgs AFC; Bob Hillman;

Wg Cdr Brian Hills; Gp Capt M.E. Hobson; Wg Cdr C.G. Jefford MBE, BA; Lt Cdr Len Jeyes RN; Roger Joel; Sqn Ldr H.D. Johnson; Capt Garvin Kable RAN; John Kendrick; Sam Key; Roy Kilburn; R.C.M. King; Wg Cdr Eric Knighton; Christoph Kugler; Dr F.T. Lane; Phil Langrill, for his permission to quote from his history of 8 Squadron; Roy Langstaff; Adm Sir Michael Layard KCB, CBE, RN; Sqn Ldr Tom Lecky-Thompson; Capt Ben Lewis; AM Ian Macfadyen CB, OBE, FRAeS; Major A.L. Mahmood; Sqn Ldr J.R. Maitland DFC (US); Gp Capt A.S. Mann DFC; Wg Cdr J.F. Manning AFC, ALCM; EV2 Sophie Marchione (PRO, Flotille 11F, Landivisau); P.R.E. 'Mac' McLeland; Lt Cdr S.A. Mearns DSC, RN; Sqn Ldr Brian Mercer AFC; Lt Cdr K.C.A. Monnery RN; Sqn Ldr Ray Morley; Patrick Mountain RN; Bob Myatt RN; Christian Noetzli, for his assistance with the Swiss Air Force: P.I. Normand AFC; Cdr S.G. Orr DSC, AFC, RN; Malcolm Payne; AVM L.W. Phipps CB, AFC, for permission to quote from his published article on Venom operations in the Middle East; Nigel Pittaway; AVM J.W. Price CBE; John Pugh; Lt Col Chris Pugsley DPhil., for permission to quote from his book *From Emergency to Confrontation: The NZ Armed Forces in Southeast Asia, 1949–1966*; Wg Cdr Robert Ramirez; Brig Gen A. Ramseyer, C-in-C Swiss Air Force; the late lamented John Rawlings; Clive Richards (MoD–AHB); Wg Cdr Hugh Rigg AFC, MRAeS; Luca G. Rivellino; Clive Rustin (ETPS Library); R.A. Scholefield; John Scrimshaw; AVM Sir John Severne KCVO, OBE, AFC, DL; Alan Simpson; Sqn Ldr Ian Small MBE; Richard Snell; Peter Squibbs; Brian St Clair; Chris Stace; Paul Stevenson RN; Gp Capt John Stocker MBE, MSc (219 Squadron Assce); John Sturgeon; Air Cdre Peter Thorne OBE, AFC & two Bars, FRAeS; Gp Capt A.F. Tucker DFC, RNZAF; Dave and Chris Van Liere; Gp Capt Geoff Wallingford RNZAF; Wg Cdr A.G. Walton RAF (11 Squadron); Lt Cdr Peter Walwyn RN; R.L. Ward; Sqn Ldr Joe Warne; Mike Waterhouse; Dave Watson; Capt R.J. Whitten RAN; Lew Willcox; Sqn Ldr Dave Williams MBE; Peter Williams; Lt Cdr John de Winton RN; Eric Young (145 Squadron Assce); and Roger Young.

My thanks also go to the many official establishments and organisations which made research material readily available: DERA Information Centre, DTEO Boscombe Down; DERA Farnborough; DTEO Llanbedr (Wendy Mills); DERA Pystock (Helen Gristwood); FAV-CLUB – The Venezuelan Air Force Fan Club (Richard Tovar); *The British Roundel* aviation research journal (Phil Spencer); The Fleet Air Arm Museum, RNAS Yeovilton (Gerry Shore); Fliegermuseum, Dubendorf (T. Bernhard); Kennet Aviation, Cranfield; Martin-Baker Ltd, Denham; RNZAF Museum, Christchurch (Matthew O'Sullivan); MARU, RNAS Lee-on-Solent (Lt Cdr McBallantyne and CPO Dave Pottle RN); OC 8 Squadron, RAF Waddington (Wg Cdr D.H. Johnson MA, BSc, RAF); OC 14 (F) Squadron RNZAF, Ohakea, and Flg Off Raymond Mudgeway; Public Record Office, Kew; RAF Historical Society; RAF Museum, Hendon; Service Historique de la Marine, Vincennes (Vincent Mollet); Source Classic Jet Flight, Bournemouth (Don Wood and Bernie Smith)

Finally, I have tried to include a representative selection from the many photographs that were made available to me for possible inclusion in this book. Although some were from official sources, many came from private collections where I could not always ascertain the identity of the original contributor. This proved to be particularly difficult where the photograph had been copied and passed on. I therefore hope that anyone who has not received the rightful credit will accept my sincere apologies.

David Watkins

INTRODUCTION

The de Havilland Venom has been largely overlooked by historians, who tend to dismiss it rather casually as an interim type that was used by the RAF and Royal Navy until a more suitable aircraft could be made available. It is also considered by some to have lived in the shadow of its more famous predecessor, and they have made disparaging remarks about it being merely the 'Son of Vampire'. However, from the many letters I received during the writing of this book from people associated with the aircraft, it is clear that there remains a genuine regard for the Venom, and that it is undoubtedly worthy of a more elevated place in the history books.

Despite a lively and impressive performance, it is true to say that the early Venoms had more than their fair share of development problems and they were never considered to be good aircraft until the advent of powered controls. In service, pilots generally regarded the Venom FB.1 as little more than a 're-worked' Vampire: fun to fly, but of little use in a war situation. The later marks of Venom, however, offered a significant improvement; with greater range at low level and hydraulically operated ailerons, they were much better operational aircraft. The Venom soon developed into an excellent air-to-ground platform, and was an example of an indifferent air defence fighter aircraft becoming a very good ground-attack aeroplane.

The original Venom FB.1 made its first official appearance in the middle of 1950. It had evolved from a proposed 'thin wing' production of the Vampire, powered by a Ghost engine and designed to Specification F.15/49, which called for an interim replacement for the Vampire until the problems with the early Hunters and Swifts could be resolved. In the initial stages of the Vampire's career de Havilland's realised that the airframe would have to be extensively modified to take advantage of the higher-powered turbo-jets then becoming available to improve performance and to raise the limiting Mach number. The Vampire, like its Meteor contemporary, was restricted in speed by its straight-wing design; the required increase in speed was obtained by installing the 5,000lb-thrust Ghost engine and completely redesigning the wings. The new wing had a thickness/chord ratio of 10 per cent (compared to 14 per cent for the Vampire), and a slightly swept leading edge to compensate for the heavier Ghost engine. To avoid the high cost of retooling, it was considered essential to use as many parts as possible from the Vampire, including the existing fuselage nacelle, booms and tail unit. Although initially designated as the Vampire FB.8, it soon became clear to the design team that the project had developed into an entirely new aircraft, and in September 1949 it was renamed Venom.

The design of the Venom was basically sensible, but it was chosen for the RAF against the advice of the Ministry of Supply, partly because it was thought that the aircraft was not strong enough for fighter duties. It was also selected before any proper flight-testing could be undertaken, and the subsequent problems found with its flight characteristics raised many doubts as to its performance effectiveness at high altitude. In 1952 a highly critical report published by the Controller Supplies (Aircraft) stated that the Venom suffered from rather violent high Mach number behaviour and stalling characteristics if the true Mach number of 0.9 was exceeded at heights above 40,000ft: worrying factors that could detract from its usefulness. The Royal Aircraft Establishment at Farnborough shared the opinion of the CS(A), confirming, following wind-tunnel tests on a scale model, that the problem of instability was outstanding – probably the worst that they had encountered.

Although there were those who expressed their doubts as to the future of the Venom project, there remained many who were impressed with the aircraft's potential. Several factors – a marked increase of speed and operational ceiling, combined with the fact that it could be in production within a few years – eventually persuaded the CS(A) to proceed with the contract, particularly because they believed that de Havilland's would press on with the design regardless, possibly with the intention of selling it to foreign air forces – in which event the RAF could face an aircraft superior to its own!

Because of the delays caused by its pro-tracted development and trials programme, the Venom fighter did not enter service until August 1952, gradually replacing the RAF's ground-attack Vampire squadrons in Germany, the Middle East and the Far East. Once in service, the aircraft was plagued with more problems: structural failures, mid-air fires and operating restrictions meant a series of modification programmes before it eventually went on to gain much praise for its excellent rate of climb and manoeuvrability.

The two-seat, radar-equipped variants also had problems, and suffered from a lack of thrust to balance the much higher operational weights. The entire tail unit of the Venom, which was based on the earlier Vampire NF.10 design, underwent many changes in an attempt to resolve its aerodynamic instability, including fin and rudder shapes, elevator area and trailing edge angle. Instead of the original tail unit of the Vampire night-fighter, an interim tailplane modification (incorporating dorsal fins similar to those on the Vampire trainer) became standard on most of the early Mk.2s delivered to the RAF. Eventually the fin and rudder were completely redesigned and fitted with reversed bullet fairings, which became the standard for all Venom aircraft; the result, if not perfect, at least rendered the handling and stability more acceptable.

With its crew of two, wartime radar equipment and standard armament of four 20mm cannon, the Venom night-fighter followed the standard RAF formula and, like the day-fighter version, it suffered from a lack of official interest. However, from its origins as a private venture it finally went into production ahead of the Venom FB.1 to bolster the RAF's inadequate night-fighter force.

It was with the Royal Navy that the Venom enjoyed slightly more success, with some 292 aircraft being produced as the Sea Venom and remaining in front-line service under various guises until 1966. As an all-weather carrier-borne strike aircraft, it provided the important transition from the piston-engined Sea Hornet to the advanced Sea Vixen. Adapted from the Venom night-fighter, it is worth recalling that the Sea Venom 20 went into service without ejection seats and with an obsolete AI Mk 10 radar. It was also regarded as falling slightly short of the usual naval standards when the early deck trials failed to show up the weaknesses in the deck hook; subsequent failures of the hook caused many serious accidents before a strengthening programme could be carried out. However, with the Sea Venom 21 and 22 the Fleet Air Arm was now equipped with a much better aircraft. Ejection seats, improved radar, powered ailerons, up-rated engine and a more efficient braking system ensured that it was able to withstand the rigours of carrier operations. The Sea Venom was adopted not only by the Royal Navy and the Royal Australian Navy, but also by the French Naval Air Arm, which was supplied with a considerable number built under licence as the Aquilon and used during ground-attack operations in Algeria and Tunisia.

At the height of its operational service the Venom fighter was considered a match for most of its contemporaries while, at a quoted price in 1953 of £23,425, it represented good value for money for potential overseas buyers. Although seven foreign air forces were eventually to operate the Venom or Sea Venom, an ambitious plan to build a large number of Venoms and Ghost engines under licence in Italy for its NATO partners in the 1950s was frustrated by political indecision, being finally blocked by the USA. Although lacking the production and export success of the Vampire, both France and Switzerland went ahead with their own plans to produce the Venom under licence – the last example of which remained in service until 1984. Some of these former Swiss aircraft can still be seen in the hands of private owners as 'Jet Warbirds'.

Although this book is largely concerned with the operational history of the aircraft, the Venom was also used in various aero-dynamic and equipment trials, culminating in the development of the Firestreak air-to-air missile. The Sea Venoms of 893 Squadron were tasked with the official service trials, successfully carrying out the first live firings over the Mediterranean in 1958. No history of the Venom would be complete, however, without examining the background to the various problems that beset its development; this I achieved by sifting through countless documents and flight-test reports stored in various repositories around the country.

As a ground-attack fighter the Venom was used with great effect by the RAF during the brief Suez campaign, for the 'Firedog' operations in Malaya, and in Aden and Oman, and it is probably true to say that it carried out more operational ground-attack sorties than any other RAF aircraft since the Second World War. It was during the Suez operation that the aircraft attracted the most attention and the relevant chapter in this book has been largely restricted to the role of the Venom and Sea Venom during this conflict. Although the contribution by the French Air Force and that of the other Allied strike aircraft during the conflict should not be overlooked, one could be forgiven for concluding that the RAF Venoms carried out all the ground-attack work. This is, of course, not the case. I hope that I will also be forgiven if I have inadvertently misspelt some of the place-names mentioned in this book, especially those in the Middle East and Malaya. Every available contemporary map was scrutinised in an effort to ensure accuracy, but any error must be laid firmly at my door.

'Then, Venom to thy Work . . .'

GLOSSARY OF TERMS AND ABBREVIATIONS

AA: Anti-Aircraft
A&AEE: Aeroplane and Armament
              Experimental Establishment
              (Boscombe Down)
AAM: Air-to-air Missile
ADDL: Aerodrome Dummy Deck
              Landings
AEO: Air Engineering Officer
AFDS: Air Fighting Development
              Squadron
AGL: Above Ground Level
AHU: Aircraft Holding Unit
AI: Airborne Interception
AOA: Angle of Attack
APC: Armament Practice Camp
ARS: Air Refuelling Squadron (USAF)
ASV: Air-to-surface-vessel (radar)
ATC: Air Traffic Control
AWF: All Weather Fighter (School)
AWI: Air Warfare Instructor
AWNW: All-Weather Night Wing (CFE)
AWS: All Weather School
AWW: All-Weather Wing (CFE)
CA: Certificate of Airworthiness
CAA: Civil Aviation Authority
CAP: Combat Air Patrol
CDEE: Chemical Defence Experimental
              Establishment (Porton Down)
CEPE: Central Experimental and Proving
              Establishment (Uplands, Canada)
CFE: Central Fighter Establishment
              (West Raynham)
CGS: Central Gunnery School
              (Leconfield)

c/n: Construction number
CS(A) :   Controller Supplies (Aircraft),
              Ministry of Supply
CSE: Central Signals Establishment
              (Watton)
CTP: Chief Test Pilot
DFGA: Day Fighter Ground Attack
DFLS: Day Fighter Leaders School
              (CFE)
DLT: Deck Landing Training
DMARD: Director of Military Aircraft
              Research and Design, Ministry
              of Supply
DOR(A):   Director of Operational
              Requirements (Air)
DTD: Director General of Technical
              Development, Ministry of
              Supply
EAF: Egyptian Air Force
ECM: Electronic Counter-Measures
EOKA: The National Organisation of
              Cypriot Fighters. (A terrorist
              group in Cyprus during the late
              1950s, seeking amalgamation
              with Greece.)
ETPS: Empire Test Pilots School
              (Farnborough)
FAA: Fleet Air Arm
F(AW):   Fighter (All-Weather)
FB: Fighter-bomber
FEAF: Far East Air Force
FTS: Flying Training School
FWS: Fighter Weapons School
GCA: Ground-Controlled Approach

GCI:	Ground-Controlled Interception
GGS:	Gyro Gun-Sight
HE:	High Explosive
ICAN:	International Committee on Air Navigation
IFF:	Identification Friend or Foe
IFR:	Instrument Flight Rules
IMN:	Indicated Mach Number
IRE:	Instrument Rating Examiner
IWM:	Imperial War Museum
JPT:	Jet pipe temperature
MEAF:	Middle East Air Force
MoS:	Ministry of Supply
MRLA:	Malayan Races Liberation Army
MTB:	Motor Torpedo-Boat
MU:	Maintenance Unit
NAE/NAD:	Naval Aircraft Establishment/Naval Air Department (RAE Farnborough and Bedford)
NAIRU:	Naval Air Radio Installation Unit
NAS:	Naval Air Section
NASU:	Naval Air Support Unit
NATO:	North Atlantic Treaty Organisation
NF:	Night-fighter
NTU:	Not taken up (usually applied to an airframe serial or code allocation)
OCU:	Operational Conversion Unit

PAI (QWI):	Pilot Attack Instructor (Qualified Weapons Instructor)
PEE:	Proof and Experimental Establishment (Shoeburyness)
RAAF:	Royal Australian Air Force
RAE:	Royal Aircraft Establishment (Boscombe Down)
RATO:	Rocket-assisted take-off
RDU:	Receipt and Dispatch Unit
RIDS:	Radar Interception Development Squadron (CFE)
RNAS:	Royal Naval Air Station
RNAY:	Royal Naval Air Yard
RNZAF:	Royal New Zealand Air Force
RP:	Rocket Projectile
RPM:	Revolutions per minute
RRAF:	Royal Rhodesian Air Force
SBAC:	Society of British Aircraft Constructors
SME:	Structures and Mechanical Engineering (Flight) (RAE)
SOC:	Struck off Charge
SP:	Senior Pilot
SSV:	Soft-skinned Vehicle
TAF:	Tactical Air Force
TDP:	Target Director Post
TRE:	Telecommunications Research Establishment (Defford)
USAF/USN:	United States Air Force/United States Navy
VHF:	Very High Frequency

CHAPTER ONE

VENOM FIGHTER DEVELOPMENT

Early in the development of de Havilland's first jet fighter design, the DH 100 Vampire, the company had made plans to replace the standard 3,000lb-thrust Goblin turbo-jet engine with the more powerful Halford H2 engine. The company's Engine Division had seen the potential of the Goblin engine and concluded that a new version, capable of producing at least 5,000lb thrust, would be required for future fighter development. The most direct method of achieving this increased thrust (without a major redesign of the engine) was to raise the maximum speed by providing a higher rate of mass airflow through the engine. This was obtained by increasing the diameter of the engine's single-sided centrifugal impeller from 31 to 36 in; this in turn raised the air mass flow from the 60lb/sec. of the Goblin to 88lb/sec. Under this arrangement an unusually high pressure ratio of 4.67:1 was also produced. One feature that contributed to the compactness of the new engine was the dimpling of the steel cone which allowed the combustion chamber 'cans' to be arranged close to the axis of the engine; this brought the overall diameter down to 53 in, only 3 in more than the Goblin; the number of combustion chambers was also reduced from sixteen to ten, with each chamber being fed by a coupled pair of diffuser outlets. The new engine weighed approximately 500lb more than the Goblin and, although initially called the Halford H2, in 1943 de Havilland's renamed its improved engine the Ghost.

Two prototype Ghost engines were built in 1944 and 1945; the second was subsequently redesigned to allow it to run at increased temperatures and so a give higher thrust rating. The construction of the Ghost resembled that of the Goblin in main essentials. The engine was built round a single rigid rotating component with bearings at the front and rear only, supported by a conical steel 'backbone' member, and with a compressor and diffuser casing in two sections to which the single-entry air intakes were attached. A spill-flow burner capable of producing a very fine atomised spray of fuel at altitude was also fitted, as was a Rotax twin breech, cartridge–operated turbo-starter system and a high-energy igniter system controlled by an automatic sequence operated from the cockpit.

In October 1945 a Ghost engine ran at 4,400lb thrust on the test stand and by December was developing its rated output at 5,000lb of static thrust. Unlike the Goblin, the Ghost was designed with an eye to civil as well as military needs, and in June 1948 it became the first British turbo-jet to attain full approval for civil operation with fare-paying passengers under Air Registration Board regulations. Early installations included the DH 106 Comet, a modified version of the Vampire and the SAAB J.29 jet fighter. Over 2,000 Ghost engines would eventually be built for the early Comet 1s as well as for the Venom and Sea Venom fighters for the RAF and Royal Navy, for the licence-built RM2 for Sweden, and for the Swiss Venoms and the French Aquilon naval fighters.

While the Vampire F.Mk.II and the proposed ground-attack Vampire F.Mk.IV would be fitted with Rolls-Royce Nene turbo-jets, de Havilland's announced that its latest designs – the Vampire Mk.7 (which was subsequently abandoned) and the FB.Mk.8 (which, it was suggested, would eventually replace the Vampire FB.5 ground-attack aircraft) would be fitted with Ghost engines. To take advantage of the increase in thrust required from the new engine and to raise the permissible Mach number, the company revealed that the Vampire FB.Mk.8 would feature a revised 'thin wing', with the thickness/chord ratio reduced from 14 to 10 per cent and a leading edge taper of 17 degrees 6 minutes. The concept of a swept and thinner wing section had been an integral feature of the DH 108 tail-less research aircraft, which had been designed and built to investigate the behaviour of the swept-wing design. Although all three prototype aircraft had been lost in flying accidents during the

Page from the company brochure, published in 1955.

trials programme, a great deal of important information had been gathered with regard to the development of the swept-wing layout to increase performance.

The British government showed little interest in de Havilland's latest project. However, on 23 March 1948 the Engine Division's modified Vampire TG278 (which had been used for the high-altitude development of the Ghost engine) established a new world height record of 59,446ft. Seizing the opportunity to exploit his new design (and no doubt influenced by the fact that the Air Ministry had decided to select the Gloster Meteor IV as the standard interceptor fighter for the RAF, thereby relegating the Vampire F.III to a less spectacular role), de Havilland's Chief Designer R.E. Bishop immediately forwarded the company's proposal for the 'Thin Wing Vampire' to the DMARD. In his letter Bishop remarked that his proposed Vampire F.Mk.8 differed from the earlier marks by having a thin wing, which would be stressed to carry underwing weapons and a jettisonable fuel tank at each tip. A Ghost 103 gas turbine engine producing 5,000lb of static thrust, new engine mounts and cowlings, redesigned air intakes and a strengthened tailplane were also features of the new design; the cockpit and canopy, however, would remain unchanged from the original design, as would the internal fuel capacity of 330 gallons. Bishop went on to confirm that a Vampire fitted with a Ghost engine had been undergoing a series of flight trials and that the limiting Mach number of the new fighter at altitude was expected to be at least 0.85 (585mph), compared with 0.79 for the Vampire. He also suggested that, since the operational requirement of the aircraft remained unchanged (i.e. as a single-seat interceptor fighter with the alternative role of a ground-attack fighter-bomber), the intention was to introduce the Vampire F.Mk.8 into service through modification action; Mod. 700 would incorporate all the changes from the Vampire FB.5. DMARD considered Bishop's design to be basically sensible, with no severe design or aero-dynamic problems, and further commented that if a decision was made to proceed with a prototype contract, production could begin within two or three years.

Bishop also sent a copy of the brochure to the Air Ministry, outlining the firm's develop-ment estimate. By June the CS(A) had responded by confirming its confidence in Bishop's proposal and advising that the decision to proceed with the new design should be taken. In a later memorandum the Air Ministry intimated that its decision was partly based on the fact that the company might possibly continue with the project regardless, with a view to selling the new aircraft to other countries.

On 1 October 1948 DMARD informed the company that a contract for two prototypes (which had by now been given the new type designation DH 112) had also been approved by the CS(A) against Specification Vampire 1/P/2 with Modification Vampire/700 installed. At the end of the month the contract was formally approved at a cost of £180,000, and two Vampire FB.5 airframes, VV612 and VV613, were allocated from the production line at Preston for conversion, with both aircraft ready for collection in early 1949. They were transferred to Hatfield in mid-February.

On 2 September 1949 the first prototype, VV612, took to the air from Hatfield, piloted by John Derry. Four days later the 'Thin Wing-type Vampire' was officially renamed the Venom and made its public debut at the SBAC air display at Farnborough. In a spectacular display of demonstration flying, John Derry put the prototype through its paces and thrilled the crowd with a succession of loops, slow rolls and his

Venom prototype — or Vampire FB.8 — VV612, undergoing ground checks at Hatfield prior to its first flight on 2 September 1949. (*Darryl Cott*)

trademark 'Derry Turn' – an inverted reverse turn. Until his tragic death in the DH 110 prototype at Farnborough a few years later, Derry was responsible for much of the test-flying of the Venom prototypes and was delighted at the aircraft's impressive performance with regard to general manoeuvrability at medium altitudes, climb rate and operational ceiling. He did express concern, however, about problems with aileron flutter, and the tendency for the aircraft to experience a violent wing drop in high-speed dives above Mach 0.84.

On 14 September 1949 Specification 15/49/P was issued to cover the design and construction of the 'Thin Wing Vampire to Operational Requirement 277', which was written around the aircraft to incorporate all the agreed modifications. The specification also called for wing-tip drop-tanks to be fitted and the tailplane to be strengthened; although an armament load of either two 500lb or two 1,000lb bombs or eight 60lb rockets was required, the installation of ejection seats was not considered essential. It concluded by saying that an initial order for 196 aircraft (sic) had already been placed. Two weeks after the specification had been issued, the decision to proceed with the Vampire F.Mk.8 – or 'Ghost Vampire' – was given by DOR(A) on the basis that it would replace the Vampire types at present in service with the RAF.

John Wilson, a contemporary of John Derry, joined de Havilland's as an experimental test pilot in 1948 and was initially concerned with the flight development programme of the Vampire series. He later became involved in the Venom project, beginning with the Venom prototype in January 1950, the Venom NF.2 – in which he made the first flight in August 1950 – and the Sea Venom NF.20 in April 1951. During the period to May 1956 he made a respectable 738 test-flights in Venom aircraft.

I spent many more hours flight-testing the Venom than I did the Vampire. The 'thin-wing Vampire' was a brute to develop and, apart from the Venom FB.4 with its powered ailerons, never became a good aircraft. The Venom wing was not really 'swept-back' as were the MiG-15 and F-86 Sabre: the planform being dictated more by the need to move the centre of pressure aft to accommodate the heavier Ghost engine.

During my first test-flight of VV612, I noted in my flight-test report that it was decided to carry out a combat climb to 50,000ft, during which longitudinal stability deteriorated with altitude, and at 45,000ft the lack of stability was the most noticeable characteristic of the flight. Levelling off at 50,000ft, speed was built up in a shallow dive to Mach .80, when dive brakes were extended. Tab flutter was noted of considerable amplitude, with some aileron movement. At Mach 0.842 nose-up trim change occurred with right wing drop, which was held up with aileron, while nose-up pitch was corrected with elevator to maintain the aircraft in compressibility. Aileron response at high Mach numbers was good, crisp but rather heavy. Two landings were made and a noticeable right wing low was noted when the flaps were fully down. Impressions of the test-flight were that, although the aircraft handled much more crisply than the Vampire, the stick force had increased and the feel of the wing decreased, especially at low level.

Following a period of company trials that included stability, flutter and high-altitude handling checks, VV612 was issued to the A&AEE at Boscombe Down in May 1950 for the official handling and stability trials. It was replaced at Hatfield by the second prototype, VV613, which took to the air for the first time on 23 July. By this time both aircraft were fitted with wing fences to reduce the spanwise airflow normally associated with swept wings, thereby avoiding tip stall. John Wilson again:

The second prototype Venom, VV613, during its trials programme. (*via Peter Goodwin*)

The first prototype Venom was later fitted with a metal canopy for pressure cabin trials. Wool tufts were added to evaluate the aerodynamic flow over the wing surfaces. (*MoD*)

I flew the prototype again in March 1950 to compare the handling characteristics following the addition of tailplane extensions, wing fences, new aileron torque tubes and re-balanced tabs. It was immediately obvious in the climb that there was a considerable increase in stick force stability, and although there was a tendency to 'Dutch Roll' at 40,000ft the aircraft still had positive stability – a marked improvement over the previous flight. At 45,000ft the aircraft was unstable at climb speed, deteriorating to a fair degree of instability at 48,000ft. On levelling off and increasing speed it was noticed that, at 0.75M and above 46,000ft the aircraft became stable, with stability increasing progressively with a Mach number up to 0.83M indicated. Increasing speed in the dive gave an unpleasant rapid and sudden nose-up pitch at approximately 0.86 Mach, which can hardly be called satisfactory, as there was no warning and a large positive acceleration. Misting and poor visibility limited the low-level handling, but it was immediately apparent that there was a great need for a 'g' suit. At 440 knots IAS there appeared to

be no great change of trim. Aileron response was crisper than before but the rate of roll at this speed was not very rapid.

On 8 July 1949 an initial production order for 200 Venom FB.1s – Contract no. 6/Acft/3627/CB.7(a) – was placed with de Havilland's, the funding for which had been authorised by the Treasury the previous March. Construction of the first order would be shared by the Hatfield, Chester and Ringway factories; Hatfield, however, was only to build the first sixteen Venom airframes because of its priority work on the Comet airliner, and the assembly line was soon switched to Chester. The first batch of aircraft was issued with the serial numbers WE255–WE483, with deliveries beginning in June 1951.

In December 1950 a second order for 85 Venom FB.1s was placed, followed by a further order for 400 aircraft in the following February. In a letter to the Air Council, the CS(A) confirmed that all orders for 1,159 (*sic*)

With an extended rear fuselage and enlarged tail bumpers, VV612 was modified for Ghost reheat trials and is seen here at the 1951 SBAC display at Farnborough. (*via Pat Dobbs*)

Venom fighters had been placed with both de Havilland's and the Bristol Aeroplane Company at Filton, and that by May 1954 the monthly production rate would be at a peak of 104 aircraft. The letter, however, pointed out that the Venom had been chosen before it was subjected to any rigorous flight-testing, and that it had been shown to possess some unacceptable characteristics that would introduce limitations in its role as a high-speed fighter aircraft. Doubts were also being expressed at this time as to the long-term future of the Venom following the decision not to produce the type under licence in Italy as NATO's standard fighter-bomber. This subsequently resulted in the production contracts being amended and the number of aircraft on order being reduced. In August 1953 the third order for 400 aircraft was cut back to 90, while orders for a further 461 Venoms placed with the Bristol Aeroplane Company were all cancelled.

Between May 1950 and September 1951 both VV612 and VV613 and the first production aircraft, WE255, were flight-tested at Boscombe Down, where subsequent reports confirmed the problems found during the company's early test programme and were highly critical of the Venom's characteristics. The major criticisms and recommendations included the following:

- The rate of roll was considered poor without tip-tanks and deplorable with them fitted. This was partly remedied in subsequent aircraft by increasing the span of the spring tabs.
- Longitudinal stability at high altitude was unsatisfactory; this was subsequently improved by a forward shift of the centre of gravity.
- Aileron tab 'buzz' was generated by the operation of the air brakes, which was associated with severe tip-tank oscillation. The report recommended that the ailerons should be re-rigged in the slightly 'up' position.
- The high Mach number characteristics were

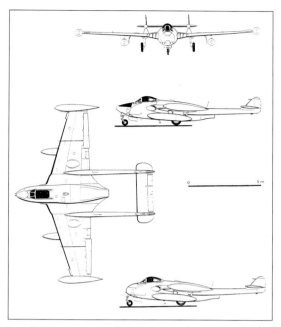

General arrangement drawing of Venom FB.1, also showing the modified nose of the Swiss version. (*Courtesy of the Swiss Air Force*)

also considered unsatisfactory because of a violent nose-up pitch at high and medium altitudes and rudder buffet at low altitudes. The latter was considered to be potentially dangerous: if the Mach number was increased sufficiently at high altitude then control of the aircraft would be lost owing to the almost simultaneous onset of aileron and elevator ineffectiveness. An investigation of ailerons with thickened trailing edges to improve their effectiveness at high Mach numbers had already begun and they would have to be, of necessity, power-operated. As an interim measure, until this system had been developed, several types of artificial warning for impending critical conditions were suggested: these included an audible warning, automatic operation of the air brakes or a stick shaker.

- Wing drop prior to the stall was excessive. Treating the wing surface with filler reduced this problem, though subsequent deterioration led to a more permanent filler being used and an improved basic wing shape being recommended.

- Airbrakes were insufficiently effective and caused aileron buffet.
- The absence of ejection seats was condemned.

In December 1950 VV612 was passed to de Havilland Engines at Hatfield to begin development flying of a Ghost engine fitted with reheat, following plans made by DOR(A) to install the system into the Venom night-fighter to improve its high-altitude performance. Earlier flight trials with a Vampire fitted with the system had shown that, within the limits of the tailpipe, such an engine was capable of giving up to 30 per cent thrust augmentation, thereby raising the static thrust to 6,700lb. In an attempt to control the area of the exit nozzle of the tailpipe to provide the desired turbine temperature and pressure conditions under both normal and augmented engine oper-ation, development was given over to both two-position and rectangular-type, fully variable nozzles. Trials had been originally carried out during 1949 with a similar system fitted to the Goblin engine of a Vampire (VV454), and had been continued when it was fitted to a Ghost the following year. To accommodate the reheat system the tailpipe of the Venom was extended and in this form the aircraft was exhibited for the first time at the 1951 Farnborough Display by test pilot Chris Beaumont. A contemporary report of its display concluded: 'When requiring thrust augmentation from this quite unobtrusively installed fitment, the pilot presses a button which operates the high-pressure fuel cock, and pushes a lever to ignite the extra fuel. The resulting noise is that of a gargantuan blowlamp, but the flame is less apparent than in earlier experimental installations.' In March 1952 the scheme to fit the Venom night-fighters with reheat was dropped, chiefly on the grounds of cost. By this time

VV612 was already nearing the end of its useful life. It did, however, make a final public appearance at Farnborough that same year and a further report subsequently recounted that:

This Venom FB.1, adapted for two-position DH afterburning, is silver finished and carries red bands on its wings outboard of the booms. Whereas on the reheat Venom last year the necessary modification appeared somewhat elementary, if not crude, the afterburner has now been faired into the nacelle with notable smoothness. The power boosting installation, incidentally, is primarily intended for the two-seater Venoms and Sea Venoms. R. Plenderleith was the demonstration pilot, and the most effective of his manoeuvres was his run-in with dive brakes extended, followed by retraction of the brakes and immediate opening up to full boosted power, with the afterburner glowing and emitting the characteristic cacophony.

In December 1954 VV612 was struck off charge and ended its days as a ground target on the firing ranges at Shoeburyness.

By April 1951 VV613 had been fitted with a modified tail unit and ailerons and was issued to the A&AEE for an assessment, but there was found to be no substantial improvement on the first prototype. The stalling and airbrake features criticised during the earlier trials persisted, with the additional characteristic of aileron tab 'buzz' at speeds above 390mph. Although the ailerons were found to be lighter, the rate of roll remained poor for an interceptor fighter, and the stalling characteristics of both aircraft were considered to be similar in that the stall was preceded by a starboard wing drop. Further trials with wing tanks fitted showed all the defects of the previous test: increased starboard wing drop prior to the stall and aileron tab 'buzz' producing a rapid oscillation of the tip-tank. The tanks also caused an appreciable reduction in the rate of

The first production Venom FB.1, WE255, pictured in May 1951 fitted with two 1,000lb bombs. This aircraft was responsible for the evaluation of underwing stores, together with the official armament trials at Boscombe Down. It was broken up at St Athan in May 1956. (*Alan Roach*)

roll and a slight reduction in the limiting Mach number. VV613 was to spend the next two years at Hatfield on a programme to remedy the problem of wing drop and aileron tab flutter, before being relegated in August 1953 for use as an instructional airframe at RNAS Arbroath.

In July 1951 the first production Venom, WE255, was flown to Boscombe Down to join the test programme on a series of gunnery trials. Before its release, de Havilland's had carried out a number of modifications in an attempt to rectify the problems found with the second prototype. The aileron tab 'buzz' and associated tip-tank movement, together with the tendency for wing drop during landing, were partially cured by rigging the ailerons in the 'up'

position and using a filler to smooth the surface of the port wing tip. These refinements were nevertheless still considered unacceptable, and the gunnery trials were subsequently discontinued when the high Mach number characteristics of the aircraft were thought to be potentially dangerous between 30,000ft and 40,000ft because of the magnitude of the nose-up pitch. Uncontrollable wing dropping at high altitude still occurred, and the use of filler on certain parts of the wing surfaces was also criticised.

During the first half of 1952 further tests with four early production aircraft (WE257, WE258, WE259 and WE260) to investigate the variations in the stalling and high Mach characteristics of individual aircraft resulted in a number of recommendations that

Venom FB.1 WE260 was used for power aileron control development. Later designated an FB.4, it continued with the trials, together with carriage of plastic pylon fuel tanks, during 1954. (de Havilland)

included the fitting of wing-tip slats to improve the stalling characteristics and the installation of a 'stick shaker' to indicate an impending stall. As a longer-term measure more effective power-assisted controls were required in the hope that flight to even higher Mach numbers would be possible and the loss of control eliminated. Corresponding handling trials conducted with the first two aircraft (WE257 and WE258) to be fitted with production-type 78-gallon wing-tip tanks proved to be satisfactory and they were subsequently recommended for service use.

Between July 1951 and August 1952 the Venom's official gunnery acceptance trials were carried out at Boscombe Down, using three aircraft, WE255, WE258 and WE259. Following an intensive air-firing programme, during which 117 sorties were flown and over 55,000 rounds fired in a variety of operational conditions, the installation was cleared for service use. Rocket-firing trials were also completed at the same time, with eight 3in, 60lb RPs carried on both conventional rails and in double-tier stowage under each of the wings. Two aircraft (WE258 and WE259) had Mod. 227 incorporated, which removed the trailing edge strip from the

rudder and rudder tab; this improved the lateral and directional characteristics during the tests but did not appear to affect the oscillatory stability. Dives from various levels were carried out during the tests and it was found that, except at high Mach numbers, the carriage of the RPs did not affect the handling characteristics of the aircraft. Nor did the carriage of the wing-tip tanks affect the launching or firing of the RPs. The only major criticism of the aircraft in the rocket-firing role was of the excessively heavy elevator stick forces at low altitude, which tendency prevented full advantage being taken of the attainable airspeeds.

The armament trials programme received a slight setback on 25 November 1952 when one of the Venoms (WE258), while returning from a bomb-handling sortie at Porton, collided with a Vickers Valetta in the circuit at Boscombe Down. Although the passengers and crew of the transport aircraft were uninjured, the pilot of the Venom, Sqn Ldr C.G. Clark, was unfortunately killed.

During the summer of 1952 a number of refinements were made to WE272 in an attempt to improve the stalling characteristics of the Venom. These included: Mod. 241, to introduce 10lb lead balance weights in the nose of the wing-tip tanks to eliminate wing-tip tank oscillation; Mod. 242, to install small, fixed wing-tip slats inboard of the tip-tanks to improve the stalling characteristics of the aircraft; and Mod. 251, to replace the round trailing edge strip of the aileron spring tabs with a flat section strip to eliminate aileron tab 'buzz'. Following a series of aileron flutter tests at Hatfield, the aircraft was then flown to Boscombe Down in August 1952 where, over the next eight months, further handling tests were carried out to evaluate the modifications. The subsequent report concluded that they had proved highly successful on this particular aircraft but that simultaneous tests carried out with another, similarly modified, aircraft had shown that the original handling characteristics still occurred and that further work with power-operated flying controls was essential.

Ejection Seats

One constant demand throughout the Venom's development trials was for the fitting of an ejection seat, but this proved to be a source of numerous problems for the design team at de Havilland's. As far back as 1946 preliminary studies had shown that such a seat could not be installed into a standard Vampire cockpit without considerable alterations to the cockpit and airframe structure, so the requirement had been temporarily dropped. By May 1950 the Martin-Baker Company had redesigned their basic ejection seat structure and successfully fitted it into a Vampire fuselage at their factory at Denham. To confirm that the cockpit arrangements were suitable for the Venom, a further Vampire (VZ835) was allocated to the trials programme and modified to represent an operational aircraft. A meeting held at Hatfield the following January discussed the various alterations

made to the MB.1E seat, which included modifications to the seat guide rails, the fitting of a shorter stroke jack and the inclusion of special foot rails owing to the proximity of the control column torque link. The face of the headrest pad should also be brought forward. Further requirements included an increase in the travel of the footrest tubes to ensure that the pilot's thighs were protected during ejection and the possible provision for head armour.

In January 1953 WE315 was delivered to Christchurch and became the first Venom to be fitted with an ejection seat, remaining with the company as a trials aircraft until late 1955. By this time, however, Mod. 80 had been introduced onto the assembly lines. This provided for the installation of either Martin-Baker 1F or 2F ejection seats into production aircraft. Although basically similar in design, the Mk.1F was a manual release seat,

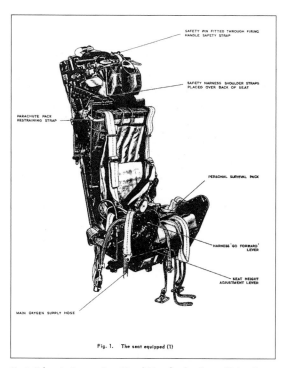

Fig. 1. The seat equipped (1)

Martin-Baker ejection seat Type 1F and 2F, as fitted to Venom FB.1 and FB.4 aircraft. (*Martin-Baker*)

whereas the Mk.2F automatically released the pilot from the seat and opened his parachute. This would only happen at an altitude of 10,000ft or less, where a barostat would allow an automatic time cycle barostat to start. This delayed separation from the seat for five seconds to allow the seat to slow down before the shock of parachute opening. This delay was later (under Mod. 205) decreased to three seconds to reduce the minimum height for safe ejection. Deliveries of the first Venom aircraft to be fitted with ejection seats began in early 1954.

A total of 375 Venom FB.1s and a further 18 Venom FB.50s (the export version sold to Italy and Iraq) were eventually built, with the last pair – WR308 and WR310 – being delivered in May 1955. A further 126 FB.1s were built under licence in Switzerland, together with 24 FB.1Rs for use in the reconnaissance role.

THE VENOM FB.4

One of the chief criticisms made by the A&AEE during the earlier tests carried out on the Venom was the loss of elevator and aileron control at high Mach numbers. The main problem was considered to be the aircraft's flying controls. These were connected to the control surfaces by cable circuits that stretched as the speed of the aircraft increased and prevented the ailerons from achieving their full travel. Redesigning the trailing edge of the ailerons had helped to improve their effectiveness at high Mach numbers, while the fitting of spring tabs to the elevator and ailerons reduced the heavy stick forces; it was clear, however, that power-operated controls would also be needed.

In February 1952 a production Venom FB.1, WE260, was flown to Hurn where it

Venom FB.4 WR413 was built at Hatfield and delivered to the RAF in March 1955. It was to serve exclusively in the Middle East with 6 and 208 Squadrons, and was struck off charge in March 1960. (*Darryl Cott*)

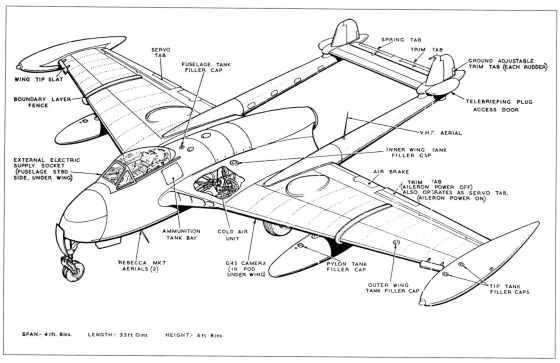

SERVO TAB

FUSELAGE TANK FILLER CAP

SPRING TAB

TRIM TAB

GROUND ADJUSTABLE TRIM TAB (EACH RUDDER)

WING TIP SLAT

BOUNDARY LAYER FENCE

TELEBRIEFING PLUG ACCESS DOOR

V.H.F. AERIAL

INNER WING TANK FILLER CAP

EXTERNAL ELECTRIC SUPPLY SOCKET (FUSELAGE STBD. SIDE, UNDER WING)

AIR BRAKE

TRIM TAB (AILERON POWER OFF) ALSO OPERATES AS SERVO TAB, (AILERON POWER ON)

AMMUNITION TANK BAY

COLD AIR UNIT

REBECCA MK7 AERIALS (2)

G·45 CAMERA (IN POD UNDER WING)

PYLON TANK FILLER CAP

OUTER WING TANK FILLER CAP

TIP TANK FILLER CAPS

SPAN:- 41ft. 8ins.   LENGTH:- 33ft 0ins.   HEIGHT:- 6ft 8ins.

Cutaway drawing of a Venom FB.4. (*de Havilland*)

was fitted with a new tail unit and power-operated ailerons of a larger chord. Hydraulically operated servodyne units were mounted on the rear spars of the main plane, the body of which was attached to the ailerons by an adjustable connecting rod. No aerodynamic loads were fed back to the control column so an adjustable spring strut unit was also incorporated in the system to give artificial 'feel' to the pilot while the ailerons were in 'Power'. In the event of a hydraulic power failure, the system automatically changed over to 'Manual' control. Manual or powered aileron control could be selected in flight by means of a control valve on the pilot's instrument panel close to the cockpit floor. If the hydraulic pump failed, resulting in a pressure drop, an additional audio warning sounded in the

pilot's earphones. The work to modify the aircraft was covered under Mod. 371.

Although the work on the system was briefly interrupted in April 1952 when the aircraft was flown to Boscombe Down for trials of the 'stick shaker' installation, it returned to Hatfield in June for further flight development work of the power controls. The following year it was flown back to the A&AEE for a preliminary assessment of the system, which concluded that the power-operated ailerons improved the high-altitude high Mach number characteristics of the aircraft by making the wing drop controllable, and that the rate of roll was also enhanced. It was also noted that the aileron spring tab 'buzz' and the associated wing-tip tank oscillations previously noted during the earlier trials of the Venom 1 had been eliminated.

With the number of modifications required for the standard airframe, the designation Venom FB.4 was selected for the improved version of the fighter. All design work was transferred to Christchurch, and in the autumn of 1953 a Venom FB.1, WE381, was taken from the production line at Chester and flown to Christchurch for conversion to the prototype FB.4. Although it retained the Ghost 103 engine, the tail unit was completely revised: to prevent excessive yaw and possible rudder locking at low speeds the height of the rudder was slightly increased and its shape altered to give a more flattened appearance. Additional rear 'bullet' fairings were also fitted at the fin/tailplane junction to improve handling by reducing elevator and rudder buffeting at high Mach numbers. The fins were removed from the wing-tip tanks, and additional 80-gallon streamlined fuel tanks could be mounted on pylons under the wings. Hydraulically

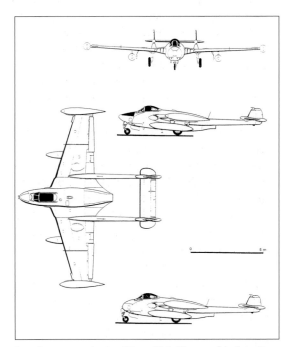

General arrangement drawing of Venom FB.4. (*Courtesy of the Swiss Air Force*)

operated flying controls were fitted as standard, as were Martin-Baker Mk.2F ejection seats. The prototype first flew on 29 December 1953 and was retained at Hurn for trials work until the following May, when it was flown to the A&AEE for the official handling trials. Although the preliminary trials found that the power controls did improve lateral control at high Mach numbers, they also revealed an excessive stick force at low altitude on this particular aircraft and it was returned to the company for further investigation.

The CS(A) decided to proceed with the new system, having already given its approval for work to begin on installing power-operated ailerons in the Venom FB.1, Venom NF.3 and the Sea Venom FAW.21 during the previous April:

Flight trials of the Venom FB.1 with power-operated ailerons at de Havilland's by company and A&AEE pilots have proved so successful that we have agreed that they should be fitted as soon as possible. The system has not, however, proved entirely satisfactory but we understand that the firm proposes to introduce an elevator with a wider chord on the Venom 3 to take advantage of the increase in critical Mach number. It is also proposed to fit electrical trim tabs and new elevators and ailerons.

In October 1954 WE381 was transferred to Boscombe Down for the CA release trials and further handling tests with 80-gallon pylon drop-tanks, its place on the company's trials and development programme at Hatfield being taken by another Venom FB.4, WR406. The A&AEE report was favourable towards the changes introduced in the FB.4, which resulted in an improvement in the handling qualities when compared to the earlier FB.1. The power-operated ailerons were seen to reduce the aileron forces and improve the rate of roll, while the high Mach number characteristics were now relatively mild and the severe wing drop experienced on the FB.1 was no longer present. Apart from certain criticisms made of the cockpit arrangement, the worst feature of the aircraft was considered to be the heavy elevator forces required to manoeuvre at low altitude. This criticism was particularly serious in view of the type's role as a ground-attack aircraft, in that it left very little room for error in judging the height of recovery and could lead to pilot fatigue. Since the emergency facilities in the event of a hydraulic failure were also considered to be unsatisfactory it was suggested that the possible introduction of a variable gear aileron system similar to that fitted on the Sea Venom FAW.21 should be examined.

No new contract was placed for the construction of the improved FB.4 variant, as they were all built from an original order for 400 Venom FB.1s placed in February 1951, which was subsequently amended in May 1954 to authorise 150 aircraft (WR374–WR564) to be completed as FB.4s. The work to build the aircraft was distributed between Hatfield (51 aircraft), Chester (51), Marshall's of Cambridge (33) and Fairey Aviation at Ringway (15). Deliveries were made between October 1954 and April 1956, with the first RAF squadrons in Germany receiving the type in July 1955, followed by further units in the Middle East and Far East. A total of twelve RAF squadrons eventually operated the Venom FB.4 until June 1962, when it was finally withdrawn from service.

In addition, twenty-two aircraft were sold to Venezuela in July 1955 under the export designation Venom FB.54. A further hundred airframes were built under licence at Emmen in 1956 for the Swiss Air Force and, through a constant modification and mid-life update programme, would remain in operational service until June 1984.

CONSTRUCTION

The construction of the Venom was similar to that of the Vampire. The fuselage or nacelle was basically a wooden structure of oval cross-section, constructed as right- and left-hand shells joined on the vertical centre-line, using two skins of moulded plywood separated by spacer shells of balsa. The fuselage halves were joined on a special alignment rig, where they were then clamped together to maintain the correct contour prior to final jointing. A protective envelope of Madapolam was then applied to the outer surface of the fuselage. Bulkhead no. 2 formed the cockpit rear wall, upon which were secured panels of armour plate, while the Ghost engine picked up on a four-point tubular mounting at the rear of bulkhead no. 4, aft of the main fuel tank. This bulkhead was regarded as the stress base upon which the whole airframe was built, its diaphragm being fashioned from heavy gauge light alloy sheet (which also functioned as the engine fire wall) in which suitable orifices were provided to accommodate the dual air-intake ducts feeding the engine compressor.

The wings were of orthodox metal construction, incorporating the air-intake ducts at the inboard leading edge. Tubular metal members transmitted wing bending loads across the nacelle between the main wing attachment points, which were located at the rear bulkhead; false-spar pick-up points at a lighter bulkhead forward of the main fuel tank took mainly drag loads. Stressed Alclad skinning was used to complete the mainplane structure, which was flush-riveted to the spars and rib flanges. The ailerons and rudders were constructed and skinned with stressed Alclad, while the flaps and dive brakes were hinged at the false spar of the inboard portion of the mainplanes. Tubular tail booms lifted the tail surfaces clear of jet interference; by removing the need for a long fuselage, this enabled the length of the tail pipe to be kept down to the most efficient figure.

The main undercarriage assemblies retracted outwards into wells in the under-surface of the wings, and to accommodate the thinner, high-pressure tyres a bulged fairing section (or blister) was attached to the upper surface of the wing. The nose-wheel assembly was mounted on a triangular, tubular steel structure attached to the forward face of the armoured plate at no. 1 bulkhead of the fuselage.

A pneumatic system was incorporated for the operation of the main undercarriage wheel brakes and pilots' anti-'g' system, air for which was supplied by a compressor mounted on the engine. Nine fuel tanks installed in the wings and fuselage provided a total capacity of 342 gallons, the main fuselage tank being situated within the fuselage between bulkheads nos 3 and 4. In addition fuel could also be carried in two light alloy wing-tip drop-tanks, each of 78 gallons capacity, and also in two light alloy underwing drop-tanks, each of 80 gallons capacity, thereby raising the total to 658 gallons.

For high-altitude flying the cabin was sealed and pressurised, with the automatically regulated air supplied from the engine impeller casing. The original fixed seat for the pilot in the cockpit of the fighter version was replaced by a Martin-Baker ejection seat, enclosed within a jettisonable, single-skin Perspex canopy and a windscreen with a bullet-proof centre panel.

TRIALS AIRCRAFT

VV612: Originally built at English Electric at Samlesbury, Preston, as a Vampire FB.5 with a Goblin 2 engine s/n A620828, it was allocated to DH Hatfield as a complete and finished aircraft on 20 January 1949, for use as a basis for the DH Vampire FB.8 sub-type. The major changes to the Vampire design required that the aircraft would be renamed the DH 112 Venom FB.1. Conversion took place in the experimental department at Hatfield and the aircraft made its first flight on 2 September 1949. The aircraft was engaged on development flying at Hatfield before transfer to the A&AEE at Boscombe Down between May and September 1950 for handling and stability trials. Following the aircraft's return to Hatfield the engine was modified to incorporate a simple afterburning system and the aircraft was displayed at the SBAC show at Farnborough in 1951 and 1952. The aircraft continued with development flying at Hatfield until it was SOC and issued to the PEE Shoeburyness on 17 December 1954 as a test piece.

VV613: Also originally built as a Vampire FB.5 at Preston, this aircraft was flown to Hatfield on 17 February 1949 and joined VV612 for conversion into the second Venom prototype. It was first flown on 23 July 1950. Following earlier problems with the flying controls of VV612, the aircraft underwent extensive modifications in the area of the ailerons and tailplane and was sent to Boscombe Down in April 1951 for trials. By January 1953 the wings had been modified with new profiles at Hatfield and the aircraft resumed its trials programme. On 14 August 1953 it was delivered by air to RNAS Culdrose for use as a Class 2 instructional airframe and was allocated the serial number A2327.

WE255: This aircraft was flown to Boscombe Down in June 1951 to continue the earlier company trials of external stores, and for the associated armament trials. It was badly damaged in October 1951 and returned to Hatfield, where it was passed to the Engine Division in December 1952 for flight development of the Ghost 103 and 104 engines. From January to August 1954 it was used at Boscombe for clearance trials of the no. 12 rocket launcher and was then transferred to the RRE at Defford for target duties. In February 1955 the fuselage was relegated for use as a Ground Instructional (GI) airframe, designated 7187M, at Cosford and St Athan until May 1956, when it was scrapped.

WE256: It carried out handling trials with underwing drop-tanks and the trial installation of a refrigerator unit at Hatfield and Hurn until September 1952, when it was passed to the A&AEE for hood-jettison tests in the blower tunnel. These trials were continued at Hurn from December 1952 to June 1954, when it returned to Boscombe Down for preparation for tropical trials at Idris in Libya. With the completion of these trials, it went back to Hurn in February 1955 and was reallocated for use as a GI airframe at St Athan as 7228M the following July. The airframe was scrapped in May 1956.

WE257: This aircraft was flown from Hatfield to the A&AEE in January 1952 for brief handling trials of the fuel system, including that of the compartmented 80-gallon wing-tip tanks, and for official spinning trials. It was then passed to the RAF Handling Squadron at Manby in April 1952 for preparation of the Handling Notes. It ended its days as GI airframe 7133M at Halton and was scrapped in December 1959.

WE258: Flown to the A&AEE in February 1952 for armament trials with various bomb and rocket installations, on 25 November 1952 this aircraft was involved in a fatal mid-air collision with a Valetta transport aircraft, 2 miles west of Boscombe Down. The pilot was killed.

WE259: From January 1952 until July 1954 this machine was used by the A&AEE for the armament clearance trials of a variety of bomb-loads and rocket installations, until being withdrawn for use as GI airframe 7157M at St Athan and Kirkham. It was struck off charge in December 1955.

WE260: This aircraft was delivered to Hurn in February 1952 for development of powered controls and improved ailerons and elevators. Transferred to A&AEE in April for tests of a prototype stick-shaker installation, it was flown to Hatfield the following June to continue development work on powered controls. Trials of the control system were carried out at the A&AEE at various periods between July and October 1953, when it was returned to Hatfield for further modifications to the elevator and rudder. The aircraft was designated as a prototype FB.4 and following a brief assessment at the CFE in October 1953 it was returned to the A&AEE for a continuation of the flight trials. Further development of the power controls was carried out at Hurn from November 1953 to May 1954, during which time it was demonstrated to representatives from Norway and the French Navy, after which it returned to the CFE for further assessment. In August 1954 it underwent an investigation of the fuel vent outlet on the underside of the fuselage, followed by trials of the new plastic pylon fuel tanks. Returning to the A&AEE in May 1955 it was used for toxic weapon trials on behalf of Porton Down. Placed into storage at 48MU Hawarden in September 1956, it was eventually sold for scrap.

WE262: This aircraft was used at Hurn for the trial installation of various modifications, including an assessment of a redesigned instrument panel and tip-tank trials from April 1952 until August 1953, when it was flown to 22MU Silloth for storage. It ended its days as GI airframe 7134M at Halton.

WE265: Following preparation for simulated rocket interceptor trials at Hurn in May 1952, this aircraft was transferred to West Raynham for service trials on behalf of the CS(A). The aircraft was officially transferred to the CFE in November 1952 to continue these trials, which involved three FB.1s (WE265, WE275 and WE313) and an NF.2 (WL818).

WE266: This aircraft was allocated for cold-weather trials at the CEPE's Climatic Department at Namao in Canada between July 1952 and May 1953. In March 1954 the airframe was dispatched to Marshall's of Cambridge following a serious fire, but repair was found to be not economic and the remains were transferred by road to Halton in August 1955 for use as GI airframe 7211M.

WE267: This aircraft went to the Armament Flight at RAE Farnborough in May 1952 for development and dive-bombing trials of 1,000lb bombs fitted with fixed fin tails and a practice bomb pylon adaptor. In November 1954 it was transferred to the Armament Flight at A&AEE for clearance trials of VT-fused bombs. On 6 December 1954 the fuselage and tailplane were badly damaged when the canopy detached in flight at high speed and it was subsequently declared a write-off. It was passed to Cranwell in February 1955 as GI airframe 7190M.

WE268: This machine was used for the development trials of Ghost 103, 104 and, later, 105 engines at Hatfield from June 1952. From March 1957 until February 1958 it was used for engine thrust reversal tests until finally being transferred to the RAE at Farnborough for structural fatigue tests.

WE269: This aircraft carried out tests with AVTAG fuel at Christchurch in July 1952, followed by hot-weather trials at Khartoum on behalf of the A&AEE. Remaining with the establishment, it later undertook armament trials from June 1954 until July 1956, when it was finally passed to 27MU Shawbury for storage and eventual scrapping.

WE272: This machine was flown by the A&AEE from September 1952 until May 1953 for handling tests of the various modifications to eliminate aileron flutter and to improve behaviour at low speeds. It was eventually issued to 58MU Honington Exhibition Pool and was allocated the GI airframe number 7358M.

WE275: This was allotted for high-altitude development flight trials in July 1952, and on 7 November that year John Wilson's logbook records that the aircraft was flown to 52,500ft during a sortie that lasted just over an hour. The aircraft's subsequent career was similar to that of WE265. It was delivered to the CFE in December 1952 for simulated rocket interceptor trials and two years later it was flown to 29MU High Ercall, where it was struck off charge and ended its days at Shoeburyness.

WE279: This was used by the Folland aircraft company at Chilbolton between September 1952 and November 1955 for development trials of an air-to-air rocket battery installation and rocket development trials. It went to RNAS Gosport as GI airframe A2399, after which it was burnt at Chivenor in 1959 and its remains later dumped at Yeovilton.

WE280: This aircraft went to Hatfield in September 1952 and was flown to Emmen by production test pilot George Thornton, for use as a demonstration aircraft for the Swiss Air Force. It was subsequently transferred to

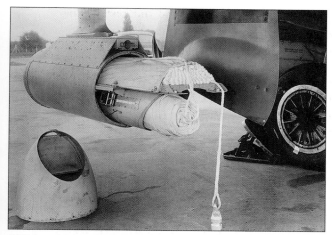

RFD high-speed target-towing equipment fitted to the underwing containers of Venom FB.1 WE361 at the RAE in May 1955. (*DERA*)

Following trials of the underwing banner targets at Farnborough, WE361 was withdrawn in July 1958 and ended its days being used for fatigue tests in May 1959. (*DERA*)

A&AEE for handling trials with bombs from January until March 1953, when it was transferred to Hurn for an investigation of rogue characteristics discovered during the tests.

WE281: This aircraft was displayed at the Farnborough Air Show by John Wilson in September 1952. Between November 1952 and July 1953 it was flown on various aerodynamic trials before being passed to 22MU Silloth and eventual issue to the RAF.

WE308: Following service with the CGS and FWS at Leconfield, this machine was passed to the RAE Farnborough for an assessment of the fatigue life of a fighter aircraft. It was struck off charge for scrap on 17 July 1958.

WE310: This aircraft was sent to RAE Bedford in November 1956 for tests with the airfield emergency barrier on behalf of the Hunting Percival Aircraft Co. It went to 71MU Bicester as scrap in November 1957.

WE315: This was the first production aircraft to be fitted with an ejection seat at Christchurch in January 1953. It was used for

pylon and wing-tip tank jettison trials at the A&AEE between April 1953 and February 1954. It was retained by the company for development trials until January 1956, when it was passed to 27MU Shawbury as GI airframe 7363M. It was eventually burnt on a fire dump at Andover.

WE361: This machine was used for installation and handling trials of target-towing equipment between June 1953 and July 1954, the work being sub-contracted to Marshall's of Cambridge. It was transferred to A&AEE for drag-launching trials with 30ft-long nylon net banner targets, before being passed to the RAE's SME Flight in January 1956 for further tests with various air-launched containers for banner targets and associated techniques. It was returned to Marshall's in March 1956 for modifications to the target-towing equipment and transferred to Christchurch the following September for clearance trials of the new plastic tip-tanks. It was eventually struck off charge in February 1958 and used for fatigue testing at Farnborough.

WE381: Modified with power-operated controls at Christchurch, this became the prototype Venom FB.4, making its first flight as such on 29 December 1953. It was transferred to the A&AEE in August 1954 for brief handling trials before being flown to Hurn for various trials, including fuel flow and fuel freezing tests for the official clearance of the 80-gallon pylon drop-tanks, together with wing flight strain tests. Sent to 27MU Shawbury in July 1957, it ended up on the dump at Farnborough.

WE455: Not a trials aircraft *per se*, this machine was delivered to Christchurch from 16 Squadron, based at Celle, in February 1956 to investigate alleged engine flame-outs at altitude. The following May it was downgraded to GI airframe 7352M and transferred to the FWS at Leconfield.

WE468: This aircraft was loaned to the A&AEE between January and March 1954 for flight trials to investigate complaints of heavy control forces.

WE471: Following a service career with the CGS and FWS, this machine was issued to the RAE in May 1957 for wing fatigue tests. It was struck off charge in December 1957 and scrapped.

WE479: This aircraft was sent to Hatfield in February 1954 for investigations into the lightening of stick force loads. It was transferred to the A&AEE the following May for a variety of trials, including stick force

measurements and armament trials, including that of the three-tier RP installation. In April 1955 it was flown to 29MU High Ercall for disposal.

WK422: This aircraft was briefly used by the A&AEE between June and September 1954 for the clearance trials of a rocket-launcher installation.

WK430: This machine was issued to RAE Farnborough in November 1956 for an assessment of the fatigue life of fighter aircraft. It was struck off charge in July 1958 and scrapped.

WR370: This aircraft was issued to de Havilland's at Hatfield in February 1954 for aerodynamic tests before being transferred to A&AEE the following August for rocket trials. It went to 29MU High Ercall in April 1955.

WR406: This aircraft was sent to A&AEE in October 1954 as a replacement for WE381 and was used for the Venom FB.4 acceptance trials, including that of CA Release handling trials and handling tests of the 80-gallon pylon drop-tanks.

WR407: This aircraft was used for the evaluation of powered aileron controls and handling trials of 80-gallon pylon drop-tanks at the A&AEE between October 1954 and March 1955.

CHAPTER TWO

VENOMS WITH THE SECOND TACTICAL AIR FORCE – AND ASSOCIATED PROBLEMS

Deliveries to the RAF began in February 1952, with WE257 being issued to the Handling Squadron at Manby. Two months later, on 21 April, the CFE (AFDS) became the first unit to operate the Venom FB.1 when WE263 was delivered to West Raynham by de Havilland's production test pilot George Thornton. Tasked with the operational evaluation of the Venom, the AFDS received two further aircraft (WE261 and WE264) during May, which allowed the tactical trials programme to get under way. By late 1952 the first part of the report of the CFE's trials, which evaluated the Venom's performance as an interceptor fighter, was published. It called to attention a structural weakness in the wings of the aircraft and expressed disappointment that ejection seats had not

Venom FB.1s of the CFE (AFDS) at 28,000ft over a cloud-covered Norfolk countryside. These aircraft are being flown without wing-tip fuel tanks. (*MoD*)

Three of 11 Squadron's Venom FB.1s, flown by Sqn Ldr Seaton DFC and Flt Lts Tanner and Chandler, 16 September 1952. The red wing bands denote performance limitations. (*Squadron Collection*)

been fitted to the early examples, despite Martin-Baker's successful installation trials during May 1950.

The report of the second phase of the CFE's trials programme was published in January 1954. This phase assessed the Venom's suitability for ground-attack and the report concluded that, owing to its larger fin and rudder surface, there was less tendency to 'snake' when flown within the speed range of the Vampire. The report also mentioned that (with practice) the Venom provided accuracy as a gun platform because of the greater acceleration in the dive, firing time was somewhat shorter and the stick force on pull out was far heavier.

In July 1952 two Venoms of the AFDS were flown to Wunstorf by Wg Cdr Bobby Oxspring DSO, DFC, and Sqn Ldr Peter

Vaughan Fowler DSO, DFC, to provide familiarisation flights for the pilots of 11 Squadron – the first operational unit to fly the type. Commanded by Sqn Ldr D.H. Seaton DFC, the squadron began its conversion from Vampire FB.5s on 1 August, with the delivery of Venom FB.1 WE271 from 22MU Silloth. A second Venom (WE274) arrived two weeks later and by mid-September the squadron had sufficient aircraft on strength to take part in Exercise 'Hold Fast', which was held in conjunction with the major NATO exercise, 'Mainbrace'. The squadron's role during the exercise was to amass as much information as possible on operational and other characteristics of the Venom so that the behaviour of the type in full squadron service could be assessed. For the purpose of the exercise the squadron was again joined by two Venoms from the CFE, flown by Sqn Ldr Fowler and Flt Lt Cherry Kearton, which were primarily used in the interceptor role.

In early October the squadron was again committed to a major RAF Fighter Command exercise, called 'Ardent'. The sixth and largest exercise since the war, it was designed to test UK defences against air attacks and the Venoms, drawn from both 11 Squadron and the CFE, were employed on both sides in the fighter and bomber role. The exercise was the first big test for the CFE's Venoms, which operated three aircraft from West Raynham as high-level interceptors. During the four-day exercise the Venoms flew 33 sorties, in the course of which 52 attacking aircraft were claimed as 'destroyed'; of these, 26 aircraft were claimed on 11 October when large formations of 'enemy' bombers and fighters were intercepted over the North Sea.

On 4 and 5 October four Venoms from 11 Squadron made the round trip to attack targets in the UK and encountered stiff opposition from defending fighters when, on at least one occasion, they were intercepted by up to thirty-six F-86 Sabres! AVM John Price flew Venoms with 11 and 98 Squadrons:

The Venom was a delight to fly, but the thin wings necessitated thin wheels with a much higher tyre pressure than that normal in the 1950s; indeed, I doubt if similar pressures have been used very often on an aircraft. We later had red bands painted on the wings to remind us that the aircraft were restricted to 6g – which seemed a dreadful limitation as all other RAF fighters were then cleared to 10g.

On 12 October 1952 I flew in Exercise 'Ardent', which entailed a two-hour sortie from Wunstorf 'attacking' London at 50,000ft. I remember the interceptors, including some early F-86 Sabres, falling away as they just couldn't get up to us – a good demonstration of the Venom's range and height capability, although we couldn't do much at that altitude apart from admire the view!

Once in service, further problems with the Venom soon began to manifest themselves, and de Havilland's experimental test pilot John Wilson was sent to Wunstorf in July 1952 to investigate comments made by 11 Squadron pilots during their work-up period. The main criticisms were that the stick force was too high (with any form of 'stick-shaker' being considered undesirable), the tyres did not give the desired life, and that anti-'g' equipment should be installed and made operational as soon as possible. John Wilson's report concluded:

The squadron is rightly insistent that the Venom is unsuitable for GCA approaches at the lowest minima and that modified cockpit presentation of the blind flying panel, as set up at Christchurch, must be incorporated in all aircraft before they can be termed as operational.

Climbing out of Wunstorf in May 1953, this is Venom FB.1 WE305 of 11 Squadron, minus wing-tip tanks. (*MoD*)

A Venom FB.1 of 5 Squadron at Wunstorf, soon after the unit fully converted from Vampires in 1953. (*via John Rawlings*)

The squadron is making the utmost use of the aircraft and piling up the hours as fast as serviceability will allow. Although, to date, the serviceability has not been bad and there are several unmistakable signs that it will <u>not</u> improve with further flying.

Bag tanks are just starting to leak – we have no cure for this other than lengthy and difficult tank changes.

The first aircraft (WE271, with 50 flying hours to date) has developed a lot of loose rivets and skin tears around the dive brakes; it is limited to 400 knots until a repair scheme is carried out.

Cold-air units are not standing up to continued operation; two out of three have failed so far and spares are not available.

John Wilson's report went on to criticise the poor standard of aircraft arriving at Wunstorf, blaming 'unskilled fiddling' after

they had left the Chester plant. This included inaccurately adjusted engine generators (which were set to cut in at 6,000rpm instead of 2,600rpm) and governors, as well as cable tensions being set too low; this latter defect caused the ailerons on WE274 to seize up during a roll, which might have ended in disaster but for the strength of the pilot, who managed to break the rib that was fouling the cable tensioner. Other points noted that the G4F compass was not considered suitable for night flying, an unpredictable stick movement emanated from the elevator spring tab and the standard of effective cockpit lighting was variable.

Once operational, 11 Squadron was tasked by HQ 2nd TAF to carry out the official, intensive Venom flying trials. These trials involved flying 300 hours as quickly as possible to gather data concerning servicing

A fine air-to-air photograph of Venom FB.1s of 98 Squadron, Fassberg, in 1954. The aircraft in the no. 2 position (WE377) was being flown by John Severne on 1 November 1954 when it suffered an in-flight fire. Luckily the pilot was successfully able to bring it back to Fassberg. (*Brian Sharman*)

procedures, maintenance and turn-round times, spares consumption, the pattern and frequency of unserviceabilities etc., so that procedures could be validated and manpower scales and skills, spares holdings and flying rates could be established. On the flying side the squadron was asked to evaluate the Venom in the day-fighter/ground-attack role to gain the maximum experience of its flying characteristics under operational conditions, and the pilots flew a variety of sorties, including low-level, air-to-ground gunnery, formation and night-flying.

Phase 'A' of the trials began on 4 August 1952, with eight Venom pre-Mod. 51 aircraft (i.e., subject to an operational restriction of 6g). During this phase 1,146 sorties were flown to provide pilot familiarisation and to give experience in high-altitude operations. This was followed by Phase 'B', which started on 5 January 1953 and employed eight fully operational aircraft with Venom Mod. 51 embodied, flying a further 1,163 sorties under closely simulated operational conditions. The flying task was scheduled to cover 500 hours at Wunstorf and a further 250 hours at the APC at Sylt, which included 471 firing and rocket sorties on the ranges.

With the completion of the trials on 16 April 1953, following the squadron's return from Sylt, numerous criticisms and recommendations appeared in the official report. The engines were virtually unacceptable in their present state of modifications, and their removal every 500 hours for combustion assembly servicing was an overly expensive operation. The discharge of black smoke during the cartridge starts needed to be reduced. A reduction in the number of stoppages with new guns was considered necessary, and a reliable system of hot air to prevent them freezing at altitude was required. The efficiency of the dive brakes had to be improved, particularly at high level, and some thought given to the installation of power controls; the present manual elevator trim should be replaced by an electric one with a control button on the stick; and expendable tip- and drop-tanks should be designed as soon as possible. On the positive side, the Venom was found to be a steadier gun and rocket platform than the Vampire during the weapons phase at Sylt. Astonishingly, one point in the report that went virtually ignored was the brief mention of 'minor cracks' (sic) in the lower mainplane and in the vicinity of the undercarriage wheel cut-outs; inexplicably, no recommendations were made for a long-term rectification or modification programme for this.

Together with John Cunningham, John Wilson returned to Wunstorf in October 1952 to assess the Venom as a potential high-altitude reconnaissance aircraft that could overfly eastern Europe at altitudes above 50,000ft. These flights were all made without tip-tanks, cannon, armour plate, and such luxuries as lighting equipment and radios. A pressure jerkin was worn and, apart from tightness around the ears and difficulty in clearing the sinuses during descent, the Venom was found to be quite pleasant to fly.

Two aircraft (WE265 and WE275) were involved, using take-off power throughout climb and level flight to attain an altitude of 52,500ft – although it was considered that if the climb were prolonged to the point where the fuel load was down to 100 gallons and the high-altitude temperature was well below ICAN, the aircraft could reach 54,000ft and possibly 55,000ft. Stability in the manoeuvre fell to zero at 45,000ft and only very limited manoeuvres were possible at 52,500ft. These flights showed clearly that without a substantial increase in thrust the single-seat Venom would not have the range, altitude capability or manoeuvrability to avoid interception by Russian aircraft. The possibility of extending the wingspan, as was done on the Vampire for the World Altitude Record

(60,000ft) during March 1948, was not considered practical within the time scale and available design department effort.

For the purpose of the assessment, it is believed that at least one of the aircraft (WE275) was painted with a cerulean blue fuselage and tail booms and allegedly made several high-altitude reconnaissance flights over eastern Europe while operating from Wunstorf. However, ex-2nd TAF pilots remain sceptical with regard to these flights, as a lack of range for strategic reconnaissance and the inability to navigate with any accuracy at extreme altitudes would have made them both technically and operationally unlikely.

Deliveries of Venoms to 123 Wing at Wunstorf continued during November 1952 with 5 Squadron (Sqn Ldr E.V. Daw AFC) followed by 266 Squadron (Sqn Ldr C.W. Coulthard) in April 1953. Next to equip was 121 Wing at Fassberg, with 14 Squadron (Sqn Ldr J.T. Lawrence) in May 1953, 98

Squadron (Sqn Ldr J.H. Smith-Carington AFC) in August and 118 Squadron (Sqn Ldr H.A. Asker DFC, DFM) in September.

In May 1953 266 Squadron was declared operational and accepted an invitation to renew its traditional link with Rhodesia by attending the Cecil Rhodes centenary celebrations in Salisbury, Rhodesia. Therefore on 29 May Sqn Ldr Colin Coulthard led twelve Venoms and their support crews off on Operation 'Long Trek One' from Wunstorf, flying via Istres, Luqa, El Adem, Fayid, Wadi Halfa, Khartoum, Juba, Entebbe, Tabora and Lusaka (where the squadron aerobatic team performed for the Northern Rhodesian Air Force), arriving at New Salisbury on 8 June. Eight squadron Venoms opened their display with various high and low demonstrations, before the crowd was entertained with an exhibition of formation flying by Sqn Ldr Coulthard, Flt Lts Taylor and Stowell and Plt Off McLeland. The squadron participated in the Air Rally and was entertained by the

For two years, from April 1953 to October 1955, 266 Squadron was the 2nd TAF's premier aerobatic team. Members of the team, depicted here in 1954, included Flt Lt Bob Kendall, Flg Off Tom Gribble, Flg Off Bert Cann and Flg Off Peter McCleland. (*Peter McCleland*)

Southern Rhodesian Air Force before departing on the return journey on 17 June, arriving back at base eight days later.

Following its return to Wunstorf, the squadron immediately contributed four aircraft for the massive static display at Odiham on 5 July 1953 as part of the Queen's Review of the RAF. Twenty-four Venoms of the Wunstorf Wing, drawn from 5 and 11 Squadrons, temporarily operating from Wattisham and led by Sqn Ldr C.S. West and Wg Cdr J.T. Shaw respectively, took part in the impressive flypast of RAF and Commonwealth aircraft. Also taking part were four CFE Venoms fitted with smoke devices and led by Wg Cdr H.A.C. Bird-Wilson, which inscribed 'ER' and 'VIVAT' in 5-mile-long letters on several occasions during the event.

For the rest of 1953 266 Squadron was kept busy with operational training, Exercise 'Coronet' in July and Exercise 'Momentum' in August, and a trip to Sylt for weapons training. The following year (November 1954) the squadron was awarded the Duncan Trophy, which was competed for annually by the 2nd TAF squadrons during their Armament Practice Camp at Sylt.

Peter 'Mac' McLeland joined 266 Squadron in November 1952 direct from training. For the next four years he was a member of the squadron aerobatic team as well as the squadron PAI:

We began to re-equip with Venoms on 1 April 1953 and had a pressing need to be up to full strength before we took them to Rhodesia for the Rhodes Centenary Celebrations the following

A formation landing at Wunstorf by four Venom FB.1s of 266 Squadron. Tip-tanks are either yellow or green to denote the respective flights. (*John Rawlings*)

The 'Winged Crusader's Shield' squadron markings and the blue Fassberg flash can be seen on the nose of this Venom FB.1 of 14 Squadron in December 1952. (*Sam D'Arcy*)

May. We were the last of the three squadrons on the Wing to re-equip and, as the company couldn't supply them fast enough, we had to 'pinch' them from 5 Squadron; this squadron was already having more than its fair share of teething problems, having lost six aircraft and four pilots over a nine-month period. Operation 'Long Trek' was a fantastic achievement, with only the CO, Sqn Ldr Colin Coulthard, experienced enough to undertake the massive planning task involved; the positioning of fuel being an immense problem.

I believe that 266 Squadron was the first to win the Duncan Trophy under the new rules. Since 1949 the competition was restricted to day-fighter squadrons in Fighter Command and Germany and was awarded to the unit that had made the greatest contribution to flight safety over a twelve-month period. In 1952 the rules were modified and the trophy was awarded annually to the 2nd

TAF fighter squadron that achieved the highest air-to-air gunnery scores while attending the APC at Sylt. No. 118 Squadron was beaten into second place, with 11 Squadron a close third. We were very proud to win the trophy, especially as were the young 'sprog' squadron. All the other Venom squadrons had been established longer than we had and that meant that they had experienced a higher turnover of pilots. We had all joined together when the squadron re-formed in 1952 and gained our experience at the same time. We didn't have the disadvantage of having to continually train new chaps, so in 1954 we were still there and fortunate to win the competition; I don't think any other Venom squadron was awarded the trophy. This was because of the advances in sighting and equipment that were coming in at the time. We had to use a 'pegged' range with the Venom, but the later development

Venom FB.1 WE401 served with 16 Squadron at Celle from January 1954 until April 1957. Note the black and yellow bands around the tail boom, the badge on the nose and the unusual practice of duplicating the airframe serial number on the tip-tank. (*Squadron Collection*)

of 'Radar Ranging' put the standards up above those obtainable in the Venom. Our average score was 16.9 per cent – mine was 19.8 per cent! I was the squadron PAI and was lucky enough to be awarded the Queen's Commendation the following year for my weapons training and as a member of the formation aerobatic team.

In February 1954, as the first Venoms fitted with Martin-Baker ejection seats were delivered to the Fassberg Wing, 139 Wing at Celle also began to re-equip: 16 Squadron (Sqn Ldr R.U.P. de Burgh) and 94 Squadron (Sqn Ldr A.W. Bower DFC) receiving the type in January, followed by 145 Squadron (Sqn Ldr F.A. Johnson DFC) in March. In an interview during February 1954 the Commanding Officer of 11 Squadron, Sqn Ldr D.H. Seaton DFC stated:

The Venom is a very popular aircraft, both as an interceptor and as a ground-attack aircraft, and could be thought of as a compromise between the load-carrying Thunderjet and the transonic Sabre; at heights above 35,000ft it has hardly an equal.

The rate of climb is a great advance on the Vampire it is replacing. The military Ghost with bifurcated intakes gives about 4,850lb thrust and, in spite of its greater all-up weight, [the Venom] has a considerably better take-off than its predecessor. The cartridge starter and Dowty fuel system with self-contained control unit are also praiseworthy. The Venom climbs at an exceptional rate and angle, and is highly manoeuvrable.

Following 145 Squadron's conversion from Vampires in early 1954, the problems with the 2nd TAF's Venoms began to compound themselves, and during the first couple of months the aircraft were repeatedly grounded for modifications and minor defects, including splitting flaps, movement of the intake trunks and chafing of the pitot heads. These problems, however, were minor compared to a more destructive malaise which affected the early Venoms: in July 1953 a CFE Venom (WE261) had broken up during a rocket attack on the Holbeach ranges, resulting in the death of the pilot. A subsequent Board of Inquiry investigation determined the primary cause of the accident to be a failure in the port wing at a point between ribs 4 and 5, at the outboard corner of the undercarriage cut-out.

A month after the accident an urgent signal was dispatched to all Venom units warning them of the possibility of skin cracking and instructing them to relieve any sharp corners found. At the same time the MoS issued orders for immediate inspection and incorporation of Mod. 206, which provided for a reinforcing plate to strengthen the affected area. During the subsequent inspection programme undertaken by the engineers on the Venom squadrons, serious cracks were discovered: on 12 August 11 Squadron uncovered its first defect and a week later a further five aircraft were found to be suffering from the same problem. An immediate directive was issued ordering the remaining Venom aircraft to have their tip-tanks removed and red bands temporarily applied to the wings to indicate that they were subject to an operational flying restriction of 6g.

Brian Pettit joined 14 Squadron at Fassberg in May 1953:

The flying on the squadron was quite varied. Our task was primarily ground-attack, so we spent most of the time at low level. There were designated low-flying areas, and most were joined by corridors. We had a weapons range within a few miles of Fassberg, and a left-hand pattern in

Photographed at the top of a loop from a Vampire trainer in 1957, the Venom FB.1s of 94 Squadron's aerobatic team feature maroon and silver tip-tanks. The team comprised Sqn Ldr Heywood, Flt Lt Evans, and Flg Offs Stock and Smillie. (*Squadron Collection*)

The remains of the port wing of CFE Venom WE261 after its catastrophic structural failure during rocket practice on the Holbeach ranges in July 1953. The wreckage was transported to Farnborough for investigation. (*DERA*)

the range usually took us over the edge of the airfield. We had regular practice with rockets and 20mm cannon, and later dive-bombing. We used to get up to four sorties with four rockets each out of one fuel load, and an engine running re-arm was normal. We also had an air defence commitment and regular trips to Sylt to practise air-to-air firing.

Our first Venoms were delivered in June 1953 and had broad red bands painted around the wings to indicate the 'g' limitation. As the Venom's cockpit layout and controls were almost identical to the Vampire's, our conversion comprised merely being handed a copy of the Pilot's Notes. It handled very well but was heavy on the elevator at half speed, and if you went into a steep dive at high level you could achieve Mach 0.87 – but then had no elevator control until you reached the

thicker air where the speed dropped to below Mach 0.84 and it was possible to level out again. The Venom also had much bigger flaps than the Vampire which were joined around the booms, and these enabled much easier speed control on the final approach, plus superb aerodynamic braking on the runway.

There were quite a few unexplained – or unacceptably explained – crashes at that time and if it wasn't proved otherwise they were attributed to pilot error! Our problems started with cracks appearing in the wing roots very soon after we received the new aircraft, culminating with a wing folding and falling off Flg Off Sam D'Arcy's aircraft as he was pulling out of a dive-bombing attack on the Fassberg range during March 1954. These incidents resulted in the squadron's Venoms being grounded for a while, and we were reissued with eight Vampires to keep us in the air. In fact, we were operating both types simultaneously for about six months.

Despite its early problems Sam D'Arcy still considered the Venom to be his favourite aircraft. During August 1953 the engine failed while he was returning from an aerobatics exercise and he was forced to put his Venom (WE304) down in a potato field near Visselhovede. Seven months later he became the first RAF pilot to eject from a Venom when the starboard wing failed during a bombing attack on the Fassberg range:

On 23 March 1954 I was detailed to carry out a high-level dive-bombing exercise in Venom

WE368. It was a Friday evening on a gin-clear spring day and it was my fifth range sortie of the day and the last sortie from Fassberg. After take-off I loosened my shoulder seat straps and moved forward in the seat into the firing position in order to feel as free as possible and to be able to get close to the sight.

The range officer was Don Headley from 14 Squadron, who cleared me for the first dive. After climbing to 17,000ft over the ranges, I rolled into a seventy-degree dive. Having dropped my first 25lb bomb, I started to pull out at about 8,500ft and 450kts, when suddenly the stick gave way, and I lost control. The aircraft as far as I could visualise went into some mad gyrations, which I had never before experienced. According to ground observers it was on fire, a mass of flames, and beginning to disintegrate.

The starboard mainplane of Venom FB.1 WE368 of 14 Squadron following the catastrophic failure during a bombing attack on the Fassberg ranges on 23 March 1954. (*Sam D'Arcy*)

To me, in the cockpit, it seemed like the end. Vaguely seeing the ground approaching rapidly, I remember thinking that soon I would be hitting the ground hard. Remembering the ejection seat I reached up above my head and pulled the blind down hard. Nothing seemed to happen, so I automatically gave another jerk forward of my head.

My next recollection was streaking through the air, face downwards in the seat. Immediately, and virtually unthinkingly, I released the seat harness, which caused me to roll forward in the seat. Without waiting, I pulled the parachute 'D' ring and I think I saw the 'chute beginning to develop over my left shoulder. I remember at this stage being with my right arm outstretched, holding the 'D' ring in my hand, thinking that something had broken or gone wrong. Almost immediately I felt a gentle jolt. Looking up I saw the final part of my parachute development; it looked very small. Looking down, the ground appeared very close, and I prepared myself for landing, but did not, I think, put my hands above my head on the lift webs. In a very short time, not more than ten seconds, I hit the ground on both feet and fell on to my right side; debris was falling all around me, including a large section of the burning wing.

I immediately got up to try my limbs and found, to my surprise, that everything was serviceable – with the exception of my pipe, for my first thought was to have a smoke.

When I ejected, I did not carry out any of the preparatory drill that was advised; the canopy was not jettisoned; my straps were loose; and my feet on the rudder pedals.

Sam D'Arcy's successful ejection from the Venom had involved a large element of luck. He was also fortunate to have had an aircraft with a fully operational Martin-Baker 1F ejector seat fitted, albeit a manual version. This meant that he had to jettison the canopy, pull the handle and then, once clear of the aircraft, undo his seat harness, push himself out of the seat, and finally pull the 'D' ring to deploy his parachute. He had actually hit the ground as his parachute was deploying, but his only injury was a cut hand, sustained as he smashed through the canopy, having rightly calculated that he had too little time to jettison it.

His ejection was particularly encouraging for other Venom pilots, especially following a similar but fatal accident at West Raynham and further unexplained incidents within the 2nd TAF Venom Wings. Not all the squadron pilots were enthusiastic about flying in aircraft fitted with ejection seats, and many of the older pilots allegedly regarded the device with apprehension. Stories of malfunctions were numerous. In an accident at Wunstorf Flg Off Cross of 14 Squadron had been involuntarily ejected from his Venom during a particularly heavy landing, which had been sufficient to operate the seat; this had done little to inspire confidence in the escape mechanism. Ultimately it was claimed that some pilots refused to fly with one of the 'new gadgets' beneath them, or even flew without removing the safety pin, preferring instead to take their chances of baling out in the conventional manner if necessary.

Sam D'Arcy's Venom broke up because of a fatigue fracture of the no. 2 wing rib, which caused the failure of the rear spar. All Venom aircraft were immediately grounded and the resulting investigation showed evidence of similar problems in the majority of them. These structural failures were eventually cured by fixing strengthening plates under the wings where 'sharp-cornered holes' between the air brake and undercarriage apertures had initiated the cracks, and subsequently led to the break-up of the aircraft.

Inexplicable mid-air fires on the early aircraft likewise caused a number of fatal accidents, and pilots were given strict orders to eject in the event of a fire because the flames tended to burn through the elevator

Northern Germany.
(*Colin Richardson*)

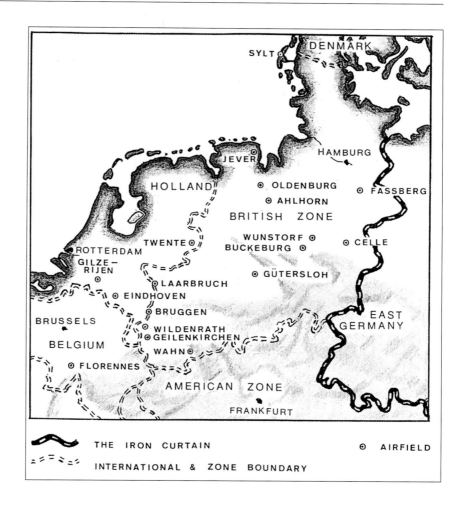

cables running through the engine bay. The mid-air fires came to a head on 20 March 1953 when a Venom of 5 Squadron (WE271) stalled on final approach to Fassberg, following a fire in the engine bay, with tragic results. An investigation concluded that the fire had been most intense in the starboard side of the airframe, with rib no. 1 being completely burnt out, and attributed its origin to the vicinity of the engine turbine shroud ring.

AVM Sir John Severne was a flight commander with 98 Squadron at Fassberg. In November 1954 he suffered a similar in-flight fire; his subsequent prompt actions enabled the aircraft to be saved for investigation, for

which he was awarded the Air Force Cross:

On 1 November 1954 I was authorised to carry out a general handling sortie in Venom FB.1 WE377, which included ground-control approaches and aerobatics. The weather was perfect with a cloudless sky. I have always been a very enthusiastic aerobatic pilot and on this occasion, after I had burnt off some fuel with some GCA-type approaches, I climbed to 10,000ft and commenced a loop over the airfield. I decided to hold the aircraft inverted at the top of the loop, but before I had time to roll out, there was a bang and smoke entered the cockpit through the air conditioning system; at the same time the fire warning light came on.

A formation break over Wunstorf by four Venom FB.4s of 266 Squadron in September 1954. (*Air Cdre Bill Croydon*)

After carrying out the fire drills, which obviously included shutting down the engine, I thought of George Schofield who had been one of the pilots in my flight and who had been killed only a few days beforehand when his Venom [WE365, on 27 October 1954] had caught fire. I was overwhelmed with a conviction that, as George's flight commander, my fire had been 'given' to me to try to solve the problem. I was certain that I had to disobey the order to eject and that I must land the aircraft at Fassberg, which I could see clearly below me. All the pilots regularly practised forced landings and setting up this one did not present any difficulty. I decided to jettison the tip-tanks and I remember watching the port tank roll inwards in the wing-tip vortex as the tank disappeared rearwards. I decided to land on the grass, wheels up, so that I could get out of the aircraft as soon as possible.

The fire engine was waiting for me and was alongside as I climbed out. I helped the firemen undo the engine panels and we found the engine was still smouldering. I directed them to use dry powder rather than foam so as to preserve as much of the evidence as possible.

After landing, the first thing I did was to brief the other pilots in the crew room on the incident. I emphasised the point that I had disobeyed orders and that under no circumstances were they to attempt a forced landing themselves. While I was doing this, the Wing Commander Flying came in and gave me a hell of a 'rocket', but finished with a smile on his face and said 'But well done!' I discovered that he had been airborne at the same time and had heard what was going on over the RT. He knew he should have ordered me to eject, but had kept quiet because he sensed what I was trying to do.

My squadron commander subsequently questioned my decision to land wheels-up on the grass; he pointed out that had I landed normally the underside of the aircraft would not have been damaged, such damage as there was might have hindered the investigation.

The accident investigators at Fassberg were interested in the fact that the fire had started while the aircraft was inverted, and a complete Venom fuel system was subsequently constructed in one of the hangars to recreate the circumstances. It was soon discovered that under certain conditions of low or zero 'g', fuel vented into an air scoop that cooled the engine turbine shroud ring. By reducing the air pressure driving the fuel from the tip-tanks and drilling drain holes in the top of the engine cowling, the problem could be resolved.

The following year the problem of in-flight fires returned to plague the Venom pilots. On the first day of 145 Squadron's summer detachment to the air-firing camp at Sylt in July 1955 the first section of aircraft had departed for an early morning sortie on the ranges. Within a short space of time the news was received that two Venoms had crashed after fires allegedly broke out in the vicinity of the gun bay; one aircraft (WK469) had been abandoned 2 miles south of the airfield at Tinnum, the other (WK480) had come down near Hornum. Luckily both pilots, Flg Offs John Price and Gordon Winspear, had been safely recovered and taken by helicopter to hospital.

Venom FB.4 WR441 was built at Chester and served with 11 Squadron from August 1955 until October 1957. The favourite mount of Flg Off Chris Golds, its tip-tank markings are black and yellow. (*Sqn Ldr Chris Golds*)

John Price had remained on the ranges longer than planned that morning to improve his firing scores, and began to indulge in some aerobatics while waiting on a fifteen-minute stand-off to the north of the island. As he pulled into his final vertical roll, smoke began to fill the cockpit and the fire warning light came on. Carrying out all the correct emergency procedures did not resolve the problem so, following a brief emergency call before the standby VHF set failed, he pointed the Venom out to sea and ejected. The descent by parachute went well until he hit the ground, when he unfortunately broke his ankle.

Geoff Winspear also had a lucky escape. His fire burnt through the control cables running through the engine bay and he was forced to abandon his Venom when he got no response from his flying controls. After ejecting, he ended up face down in the sea, being dragged along by his parachute in the high wind; he was fortunate to be rescued by the prompt actions of a German tourist.

An examination of the remaining squadron Venoms revealed that many of them showed scorch-marks inside the gun bays, and it was concluded that the main fuel tank atmospheric dump valve had been trapped when the gun bay doors were refitted. Instead of venting to the atmosphere under conditions of negative 'g', the fuel was leaking into the gun bay and when a flashback from one of the guns occurred a fire was almost inevitable. The subsequent introduction of Venom Mod. 947 called for an improved design for fuel venting and consisted of extending the vent pipe with a metal end piece; subsequent pre-flight inspections included a physical check to ensure that the vent pipe protruded through the gun door aperture. John Price was later to remark, rather sarcastically, that the Venom was 'the only aircraft you had to goose before you got it going!'

By this time the Venom was considered much more than 'a Vampire with hairs on its chest', and it quickly proved itself more than a match for most of its 2nd TAF contemporaries, being also ideal for ground-attack work. Although the pattern of training changed very little after re-equipping from the Vampire, i.e. ground-attack and day-fighter, the incidence and altitude of upper air work increased, with cine and battle-flight sorties regularly taking place at 40,000ft plus.

Given their proximity to the East German border, the Venom squadrons were also considered to be fully mobile, with crews, equipment and vehicles being in a state of instant response and redeployment once the aircraft had been 'scrambled'. This state of readiness was frequently tested through regular 'battle-flight' duties and NATO exercises, with the squadrons operating from a variety of airfields and under 'combat' conditions. On one occasion in September 1954 the Venoms of 139 Wing (16, 94 and 145 Squadrons) were deployed to the new NATO strip at Norvenich to take part in Exercise 'Battle Royal'; camouflaged and self-supporting, the Venoms provided close and general support for the ground forces. The CO of 145 Squadron, Sqn Ldr 'Ted' Johnson DFC, was later to comment on these operations:

Redeployment exercises were tough on domestic life because we never knew when one would be sprung on us, but they were challenging and exciting. For weeks at a time we would be deployed to an airfield offering little else but runways, dispersal revetments for the aircraft, fuel and ammunition stocks. The rest was up to us. Invariably on these occasions we would be required to operate intensively in a mock battle situation that tested our ability to operate effectively under such spartan conditions. We tangled many times with the F-86s of the Bruggen Wing during 'Battle Royal' and were getting quite a superiority complex. In manoeuvring, the Venom was all over the Sabre 'like a tent', and, if a Sabre broke, a Venom could 'follow straight through' without trouble.

The 2nd TAF Venom squadrons were also keen to demonstrate their formation aerobatics skills, which had been acquired and perfected during their Vampire period. No. 11 Squadron's team was the first to be formed in November 1952, led by Sqn Ldr Seaton; following its first display at Gutersloh in March 1953, it went on to provide excellent shows at both Madrid in May and Kloten in Switzerland the following August. In April 1953 266 Squadron was selected to make up the 2nd TAF's premier aerobatic team. Formed and led by Sqn Ldr Colin Coulthard, the original team members also comprised Flt Lt John Taylor, Flg Off Pete Stowell and Plt Off 'Mac' McLeland, and they soon became a major attraction at events both in the UK and on the continent. By 1954 the team line-up had changed slightly, with displays at Newton, Thornaby and Ahlhorn, followed by Fassberg, Ypenburg, Auxerre, Tours and Perpignan in 1955. The team was disbanded in October 1955. Some of the other 2nd TAF Venom units also maintained an aerobatic team, including 94 Squadron. Their team got off to a tragic start in July 1954 when two aircraft collided during a formation loop; both aircraft crashed close to Celle and one pilot, Sgt O'Shaughnessy, was killed.

During July 1955 the improved Venom FB.4 was issued to 123 Wing at Wunstorf, with 266 Squadron being the first to receive the type, closely followed by 5 and 11 Squadrons during August; 94 Squadron at Celle also operated a handful of Venom FB.4s alongside its FB.1s from March to September 1957, when it was finally disbanded.

Venom FB.1s of 145 Squadron at Celle. The squadron converted from Vampires between March and September 1954. (*Wg Cdr Brian Hills MBE*)

A group photograph of 145 Squadron at Celle on 15 October 1957, prior to the unit's last Venoms being flown to Butzweilerhof for disposal. The aircrew include Flg Off Winspear, Flg Off Schooling, Wg Cdr Don Kingaby (OC Fly Wing), Flg Off Fanner, Flg Off Wickham, Flg Off Lewis, Flg Off Paterson, Flt Lt Hills and Flg Off Knapp. (*Wg Cdr Brian Hills MBE*)

Although the Fassberg units (14, 98, and 118 Squadrons) converted to Hunter F.4s during the spring of 1955, the remaining 2nd TAF Venom units soldiered on with their FB.1s until late 1957, when they were also disbanded as a consequence of the Defence Review. Among the last was 145 Squadron, which flew its final Venom sortie on 15 October 1957. Flt Lt Brian Hills led a formation of nine aircraft from Celle to Butzweilerhof, whereupon the fully service-able aircraft were winched over a fence – and unceremoniously dropped onto a scrapheap!

Many other 2nd TAF Venoms suffered a similar fate to those of 145 Squadron, and the final few months for the remaining units were occupied with a mixture of low-level exercises with the army, high-level work providing training for the major radar sites in Germany and the Low Countries, and tactical exercises with other NATO air forces. One of these exercises included a detachment to Schleswigland in northern Germany in September 1957 for Exercise 'Brown Jug', which involved other 2nd TAF wings and the Danish defence forces. The week-long exercise at the 'bare base' proved interesting for all concerned, and it was unfortunate that on the last day (24 September) 11 Squadron lost an aircraft (WR426) when it stalled at high-speed during a simulated rocket attack. It spun in at Arnoje, Denmark, killing the South African pilot.

On 14 November 1957 123 Wing was able to put twenty-one Venoms into the air for a final flypast, and the following day the last Venom units in Germany, 11 and 266 Squadrons at Wunstorf, were disbanded. For many pilots their last flight in a Venom was to Butzweilerhof, where the aircraft were broken up. Some former 2nd TAF Venom FB.4s were reprieved and returned to the UK for further use later with 8 Squadron in Aden. On 13 December 1957 the final Venom (WR433 of 11 Squadron) was ferried from Germany to 22MU Silloth, bringing an end to five years of a valuable contribution to the collective defence of western Europe.

SERVICE IN THE UK

It is interesting to note that single-seat Venoms were never operated by the regular units of RAF Fighter Command or by Flying Training Command, although one example was evaluated by 5FTS at Oakington during the summer of 1956 as a replacement for its ageing Vampire 5s. Complete with camou-

flage and training bands, WE305 was intensively flown by the unit's Wing Commander Flying over a two-day period, following which he declared it to be 'too advanced' for student pilots!

The principal UK operator was the Central Gunnery School (CGS) at Leconfield, where the Trials Flight was issued with FB.1s for training-role evaluation during February 1954. Deliveries to the Ground-Attack Flight soon followed, enabling the first training course to begin in September. In a course lasting some three months, experienced front-line fighter pilots received training with the CGS to become weapons instructors for operational squadrons and were awarded the flying category Pilot Attack Instructor (PAI).

PAI courses were divided into three phases, with the Venom being used for the third, ground-attack phase. This covered rocketing,

Simultaneous start-up by Venom FB.4s of 5 Squadron at Wunstorf for their disbandment flypast over the bases of Sundern, Gutersloh, Buckeburg and Wunstorf on 11 October 1957. (*Flight*)

Venom FB.1 WE348, belonging to Wunstorf's Wing Leader, Wg Cdr J.T. Shaw, pictured at Tangmere in June 1953 in connection with the forthcoming RAF Coronation Review. It force-landed at Wattisham soon after this photograph was taken and was out of service for five months, being later passed to 5 Squadron. (*via Geoff Cruickshank*)

using a 3in rocket with a concrete head; air-to-ground firing with 20mm cannon and low-level bombing with 25lb practice bombs. The Venoms were armed with either four rockets and 500 rounds of 20mm cannon or four practice bombs, and this matched the alternative delivery styles current at the time: a 30-degree dive for rockets and gunnery and low-level/level-flight delivery for bombs.

During its relatively short time at Leconfield, the Venom FB.1 excelled in the ground-attack weapons-training role, and was such a good weapons platform that very high

degrees of accuracy were regularly achieved with all three armaments. The aircraft usually flew with internal fuel only, as there was no need for tip-tanks as the ground-attack range at Cowden, south of Hornsea, was just five minutes' flying time from Leconfield.

In November 1954 the unit was transferred to RAF Fighter Command and was renamed the Fighter Weapons School in the following January. It continued to operate Venoms until October 1957, when the school was disbanded as part of the government's defence cuts.

CHAPTER THREE

MIDDLE EAST OPERATIONS

For many years before the Second World War, the RAF's policy in the Middle East had been to develop and maintain airborne 'colonial policing' as a highly effective alternative to the use of land forces to support the rule of law. Historically, Arab tribes were hostile both to one another and to any governing authority that tried to keep them apart, and this unrest became a permanent feature of the wild and mountainous desert on the borders of the Aden Protectorate and Yemen, and within the Protectorate itself.

RAF operations in the Middle East began shortly after the First World War. The RAF presence safeguarded the air bases granted by Right of Treaty with new independent kingdoms in return for an undertaking tko defend them against external aggression, and in turn allowed the RAF to police its own interests.

By the mid-1950s RAF units in the eastern Mediterranean were spread over a vast and sometimes hostile area, being usually located on the UK-to-Far East communications route. Under the aegis of Middle East Command, Air Headquarters Malta controlled the routes to the east while Air Headquarters Levant in Cyprus was responsible for the airspace over the Mediterranean. In Egypt the security of the Suez Canal was of paramount importance, and in order to secure the rights of navigation along it six RAF stations were located on a small strip of land on the western side of the Canal Zone, which included Deversoir, Fayid, Kabrit and Shallufa. Further south, HQ British Forces Aden was tasked with the protection of the oil-shipping lanes between the Persian Gulf and the Red Sea, and operated as a peace-

A ground-attack aircraft in its element. A Venom FB.1 of 6 Squadron makes a low pass during Exercise 'Down Under' at Mafraq in March 1955. (*Gp Capt Mike Hobson*)

keeping force between the dissident Arab factions.

Despite the strategic importance of the Middle East to Britain's interests, the RAF's post-Second World War retrenchment had reduced its size to nine fighter squadrons, equipped with Spitfires, Tempests and Beaufighters. In July 1948 these obsolete fighters were gradually replaced by Vampire jet fighters, which for the next seven years formed the backbone of the Middle East theatre forces, equipping seven operational ground-attack and fighter squadrons.

By 1952 a replacement for the MEAF's Vampires was already being considered, and in the autumn of that year a Venom FB.1 (WE269) from Boscombe Down was dispatched to the TEU at Khartoum for hotweather trials. The following August the aircraft was damaged during a landing accident at Khartoum and was replaced by another A&AEE Venom, WE256, which successfully completed the trials of the ACRE 9 cooling unit and the evaluation of an improved water separator.

In March 1953 two Venoms from the CFE at West Raynham flew out to Deversoir to take part in Exercise 'Session', a three-day operation during which the entire air defence organisation of the Suez Canal Zone was brought into action against mass raids by Cyprus-based RAF and Commonwealth intruders. During one such raid the two CFE Venoms successfully intercepted a formation of RNZAF Vampires acting as high-altitude bombers. They were also reported to have achieved favourable results in combating low-level raids carried out by Lincolns, Varsities and Vampires, and the exercise was seen as an important means of evaluating the fighter development and tactics of the Venom in a hot climate.

On 11 February 1954 the first three Venom FB.1s for the MEAF (WE428, WE465 and WE466) were delivered to 6 Squadron (Sqn Ldr E.J. 'Red' Roberts) at Amman in Jordan to replace its Vampire FB.9s. Six more Venoms were issued to the squadron during the following month, enabling the last of its Vampires to be withdrawn by the end of May. Once operational, the squadron moved to Habbaniya in Iraq in June 1954, joining 73 Squadron (Sqn Ldr P.H.P. 'Black' Roberts) which was still flying Vampire FB.9s but began to re-equip with Venom FB.1s during July. The squadron's work-up period was hampered by temporary operating restrictions, which limited the Venom's usefulness. Furthermore the incorporation of a series of urgent modifications meant that several aircraft were temporarily grounded until the work could be undertaken; therefore, to ensure continuity, the squadron Vampires were retained for longer than had originally been planned.

Following a detachment with 77 Squadron RAAF in Korea, Alastair Christie joined 6 Squadron in July 1952. He recalls the period when the unit was re-equipped with Venoms:

The squadron deployed from Habbaniya in January 1954, with Vampire FB.9s, to the (then) new military/civil airfield at Amman, where it remained for six months. In February conversion to the Venom FB.1 started, with my first sortie on 20 February in WE428.

The CO, Sqn Ldr E.J. Roberts, had previously gained an enviable reputation as a test pilot with 'A' Squadron at the A&AEE, Boscombe Down. He had the test pilot's almost obsessive attention to detail and careful preparation for flight. He set up a five-exercise conversion programme which each pilot performed and he personally supervised the initial (first solo) flight briefings of each pilot. The exercises covered general handling, aerobatics, close and battle formations, simulated weapons sorties and circuit work. For three months the squadron operated the Venom FB.1 alongside the Vampire FB.9; the bulk of the weapons work was done on the Vampire. The one outstanding never-to-be-forgotten experience in the conversion programme was the high Mach number dive from around 42,000ft. The aircraft was rolled over into a vertical dive and at around M 0.86 the flying controls were useless with no response from the aircraft to the control movements. They remained in that 'exciting' state until the Mach number reduced as a consequence of entering warmer air. Gradually some 'feel' came back into the controls, so that by 12–15,000ft the aircraft was once more under control. This was a manoeuvre practised regularly thereafter! We returned to Habbaniya to rejoin 73 Squadron in 128 (Tactical) Wing by the end of 1954, by which time both squadrons had been fully converted.

The high-altitude capability of the Venom also gave reason for concern when a team from the Aviation Medicine Branch at Farnborough visited Habbaniya. They were surprised to learn that the crews were flying at high altitudes without pressure breathing equipment and were not equipped with the air-ventilated suit (AVS). The AVS had been developed in 1950 in an attempt to produce body cooling by the evaporation of sweat from the skin and consisted of a lightweight nylon liner with plastic tubing distributed throughout and connected, via the cockpit cold-air unit, to the engine compressor. Brief trials, which began with 6 Squadron in September 1955, involved set periods flying at low level. The suit proved unpopular with the squadron pilots, but the crews did adopt the pressure waistcoat for a short period; triggered by a barometric switch in the event of depressurisation, this would inflate around the pilot's chest and help oxygen to pass into

Three of 6 Squadron's Venom FB.1s (WE435, WE453 and WE454) over Amman, Jordan, on 21 February 1955. This formation was probably the squadron's aerobatic team, led by Flt Lt Mike Hobson. (*via John Rawlings*)

the bloodstream during a rapid descent to a safe altitude. By late 1955 a pressure mask was eventually introduced for Venom pilots at Habbaniya, although crews in Cyprus and Aden continued to operate with the old economiser unit.

The rise of Arab nationalism in 1951 and the signing of the Anglo-Egyptian Agreement three years later resulted in the gradual British withdrawal from the Canal Zone. On 15 September 1954 32 Squadron (Sqn Ldr A.H.W. Gilchrist DFC) moved down from Deversoir to Kabrit where, with the arrival of WE456 and WK498 the following month, it began to convert to Venom FB.1s. Early problems hampered the conversion; there were flying restrictions because of in-flight fires and all the aircraft were temporarily grounded to allow for urgent modifications to be made to the aileron hinge bracket. This meant that the squadron had to retain its Vampires longer than planned to remain operational. In January 1955 32 Squadron (nicknamed 'The Genuine Bedouins' because of the constant moves) flew down to its new base at Shaibah in Iraq and began an intense period of weapons training. Shaibah was not considered a popular posting and it was a welcome relief for the squadron to go to Nicosia in August for a period of live firing at the APC. Unfortunately the detachment was not without incident. On 13 September a Venom (WK497) crashed on take-off during a rehearsal for the Battle of Britain flypast, killing the pilot. In October 1955 Shaibah was handed over to the Iraqi Air Force and

Shrouded in smoke following its cartridge start, this is Venom FB.1 WE354 of 32 Squadron at Ta Kali in 1956. The markings on the tail booms are blue and white. (*Peter Goodwin*)

Pilots of 20 and 249 Squadrons gather for an informal group photograph in front of their aircraft following a period of affiliation training at Amman in June 1955. They are (from left to right): Tony Gronert, Doug Dallison, 'Curly' Hancock, visitor, visitor, Andy Anderson, visitor with 'Rab' Butler behind, Leighton Fletcher, visitor, Peter Cock, Keith Duro, the squadron adjutant and Geoff Leach. (*Tony Gronert*)

the squadron transferred to Ta Kali in Malta, where the facilities were found to be much better than those encountered in Egypt or Iraq.

In October 1954 249 Squadron (Sqn Ldr E.C. Gough) also moved from Deversoir to its new base at Amman and began to re-equip with Venoms, the first of which (WK472 and WK495) were delivered on 8 October. A less-than-happy 'honeymoon period' with minor incidents and technical problems culminated in the temporary grounding of the Venoms following a spate of mid-air fires and the loss, on 19 October, of WR307, which was abandoned in a spin during an aerobatic sortie, 14 miles east of Mafraq. The pilot, Flg Off Peter Cock, suffered severe injuries to his back during the ejection. It was March 1955 before the last of the squadron Vampires was ferried back to the UK.

During June 1955 249 Squadron hosted two detachments of F-86 Sabres from the 2nd TAF in Germany, which flew in from Cyprus to exercise with the Venoms. Squadron pilots recall outclimbing and outmanoeuvring the RAF Sabres with ease. In August the squadron was visited by six Hunter F.1s of the DFLS, led by Wg Cdr Scott-Vos, as part

of the unit's Middle East tour to evaluate current fighter operations and tactics. The Venoms were again given the opportunity to 'mix it' with four of the Hunters in a high-level engagement, during which the squadron 'more than held its own'. The Hunter visit was a lesson in the discipline of operating the Venom correctly, especially when the combat was drawn down to low level and evasion tactics were employed to reduce the speed of their opponents.

Tom Lecky-Thompson joined 249 Squadron in July 1955 and offers his views on the comparison between the Venom and the Hunter during these air combat manoeuvres (ACM) exercises:

The Venom could out-manoeuvre and out-turn the Hunter with ease, the difference between the two in ACM being the optimum speeds for Max rate and Min radius turns. Also the Hunter had a 'combat' flap to improve its performance. It was not until the CFE visit that this was brought home to us. Both operators had to be disciplined enough to stay in the regime where their aircraft operated best. We would try to 'sucker' the Hunters into following us through a roll-over and pull through to the 'deck', and as we used ground height as a base level you can imagine the odd rather shaken Hunter chap realising as he got near the vertical that he could not follow. It was due to people like our Flight Commanders – Jimmy Birnie, John Tetley and Charlie Slade – that all of us young chaps got educated and stayed alive, a fact borne out in that we never lost anyone in low-level ACM.

In common with the other operational MEAF Venom fighter units, 6 Squadron at Habbaniya was a mobile squadron, which meant that each of the two flights had its own aircraft, groundcrew and motor vehicles, and could be sent on detachment to operate autonomously. 'Shiny Six' had the proud and unique distinction of being the only RAF squadron to have two Royal Standards: the Squadron Standard, complete with battle honours, and also the personal Standard of King Abdullah of Transjordan, which had been presented in recognition of its service to his country and the close links that were forged with the Royal Jordanian Air Force when 6 Squadron was based in Amman. In keeping with its role as a ground-attack squadron, a considerable amount of time was spent on weapons training, with air-to-air firing on the Karbala range against a 30ft banner towed by a Meteor T.7, and air-to-ground, dive-bombing and rocket-firing on the Markab range. The rest of the flying programme consisted of high- and low-level battle formation, simulated strikes, navigational cross-country exercises and individual continuation training, including aerobatics, night-flying and exercises with the army. As a flamboyant touch of one-upmanship, on most Saturday mornings the squadron flew a '6' formation over the airfield – with twelve aircraft forming the figure six – as it was considered unlikely that its sister squadron could produce enough aircraft to fly a '73' formation.

Flt Lt Mike Hobson joined 6 Squadron at Habbaniya in June 1954 as 'B' Flight Commander, and he soon settled into an agreeable work and social routine. Situated 55 miles from Baghdad, Habbaniya was magnificently appointed: air-conditioned buildings, tree-lined boulevards, a golf course, playing fields, a fine swimming pool and a sailing club made it an impressive and unique station. Mike Hobson's delight at being stationed there was to be short-lived, however. Following a simulated strike on the village of Haditha, he belly-landed a Venom (WK474) belonging to his Wing Commander Flying.

A few months later Mike Hobson was witness to an unfortunate incident when 73 Squadron found itself in the unhappy position of losing an entire formation of aircraft. He picks up the story:

On 23 December 1954 I was leading a formation of four aircraft on a high-level battle formation exercise, interspersed with cine attacks on each other in pairs. Just as our fuel state was beginning to indicate that it was time to return to base, I received a call informing me that a fog (a most unusual condition at Habbaniya) was approaching the airfield and that we were to return and land as soon as possible. The only other aircraft airborne, apart from some local traffic, were two sections of four from 73 Squadron, and these had also been recalled. In about ten minutes I was close enough to call base to tell them that I was positioning the formation for a straight-in approach and would be landing as two pairs, each in close formation, and I instructed my no. 3 to drop back with no. 4 to a suitable distance behind me. I then heard the leader of 73 Squadron's Blue Section checking in and saying that he would be about one minute behind us. As we lined up on the approach I could see the grey mass of fog sweeping towards the airfield from the far side at an alarming rate, and it was with considerable relief that I touched down, knowing that my following pair would also be able to make it behind me before the oncoming cloud of swirling mist met us at the end of our landing run and immediately engulfed the whole

FB.1s WK434 and WE423 of 73 Squadron airborne from Habbaniya in April 1955. (*via John Rawlings*)

of the airfield. The leading pair of 73 Squadron's Blue Section succeeded in landing behind us, but nos 3 and 4 overshot as the airfield was no longer visible, and I then heard the leader of their Green Section announcing that they were climbing up through the fog as it was impossible to land. The Plateau Airfield was also, of course, now enveloped in fog. We taxied back to dispersal with some difficulty but were aided by the airfield lighting which had been switched on, and as soon as I had jumped out of the aircraft I dashed over to Air Traffic Control, and on entering the Local Control Room was just in time to hear the Green Section leader's voice announcing 'Canopies, canopies, GO!' as all four of his formation jettisoned their canopies and then ejected, still in battle formation. The remaining pair of Blue Section had managed to retain sight of the desert and force-landed on the sand.

Although Flg Offs Mike Elliot (Blue 1) and Mike Sparrow (Blue 2) were able to land safely at base, the four pilots of Green Section, Flg Offs 'Jimpy' Annand (Green 1, WK490), Dave Wyborn (Green 2, WE480), 'Red' Crane (Green 3, WR315) and Geoff Taylor (Green 4, WR274), were forced to eject 12–15 miles north of Habbaniya. They took shelter under a canopy made from one of their parachutes, supported by the cannon retrieved from one of the crashed aircraft, but they were quickly found by the Desert Rescue Team. It took considerably longer, however, to locate the other two pilots, Flg Offs 'Chris' Doggett (Blue 3, WK493) and Mike Bevin (Blue 4, WR289), who had set course for Baghdad and force-landed in a field near Khadimain after finding a gap in the cloud. All six aircraft were complete write-offs.

49

Shortly after crash-landing the boss's Venom at Habbaniya in October 1954, Mike Hobson's bruised confidence received a boost when he was selected to lead a flight of the squadron's Venoms down to South Africa. Periodically, a Middle East squadron was required to test the rapid deployment of aircraft and the navigation services along the Cape-to-Middle East short-range ferry route. Code-named Exercise 'Quick Return', the flights had the added purpose of checking the refuelling facilities and continuing suitability of airfields, as well as providing an opportunity for liaison with the South African and Royal Rhodesian Air Forces. Up to the end of 1954 five 'Quick Returns' had been flown, and it was considered appropriate that 6 Squadron should fly the sixth. It would be the first time that RAF Venoms had travelled as far south as Cape Town, previous 'Quick Returns' having never extended beyond Swartkopf.

It was further decided that the squadron should 'show the flag' all the way down the African continent by giving formation aerobatic displays. They were due to leave for Cape Town in May 1955 and Mike Hobson was given the task of forming a team – the 'Four Aces' – and developing a display routine as soon as possible. Appropriate symbols were painted on the aircraft and flying helmets, and flying practice with the team members – Mike himself, with Flg Offs Bill Page, Stewart Graham and Bob Woodhouse – began in October 1954. Their first public display was put on for HRH the Prince Regent of Iraq in February 1955.

The 6 Squadron aerobatic team – 'The Four Aces' – at Swartkopf, South Africa, during Exercise 'Quick Return 6' on 2 June 1955. Left to right: Flg Off Stewart Graham, Flt Lt Mike Hobson and Flg Off Bill Page. (*Gp Capt Mike Hobson*)

Venom FB.1s (and a Vampire T.11) of 73 Squadron being refuelled at Habbaniya during March 1955. Note the asbestos blanket used to protect the tailplane during start-up. (*Wg Cdr J.F. Manning AFC*)

On Whit Sunday 29 May 1955 the team set off on the first leg to Amman, accompanied by a Valetta transport aircraft of 114 Squadron carrying the support equipment and groundcrew. The following morning the team flew down to Wadi Halfa, where an after-flight inspection revealed a cracked undercarriage radius rod on one of the Venoms; this reduced the team numbers to three. Further stops at Khartoum, Entebbe, Tabora, New Salisbury Airport and Swartkopf enabled the team to give a series of displays to enthusiastic onlookers. The final stage of the flight down to the Cape took them to the Vampire OCU and gunnery school at Langebaanweg, where the team members were given a tremendous reception. Between bouts of hospitality, the team provided a further series of displays. Sub-

sequently the pilots were pleased to learn that they had beaten the unofficial record for the Cape to Pretoria flight (678 nautical miles), previously held by a Vampire of the South African Air Force in 1 hour and 32 minutes, by some nine minutes.

The team returned to Habbaniya on 12 June, with the three Venoms having each flown 31½ hours and given thirteen formation aerobatic displays during a journey of 11,141 miles. 'Quick Return Six' had been a worthwhile and rewarding exercise for all concerned; training methods were shared and good publicity won for the RAF.

The success of the trip to South Africa undoubtedly convinced Air HQ that the RAF should provide a daily item at the Royal Agricultural Show in Mitchell Park, Nairobi, during September 1955, and that item should be the 6 Squadron aerobatic team. Departing on 24 September, with Flg Off Vince Stewart replacing Stewart Graham and accompanied by the 'Boss', Sqn Ldr Peter Ellis DFC, the team received a rapturous ovation during the three-day event and received a cup for the most outstanding show item of the year. The return flight to Amman was completed on 4 October.

The squadron returned from an APC at Cyprus on 12 December 1955, during which it was able to break two MEAF records, with the award of the Lloyd Trophy for the best all-round efficiency and the Imshi Mason trophy for the best weapons results.

With the termination of the Anglo-Iraqi Treaty in April 1955 and the subsequent withdrawal of British forces from Habbaniya, 73 Squadron (now commanded by Sqn Ldr J.F. Manning AFC, who had taken over the squadron in the previous February) became the first RAF unit to move to Nicosia in Cyprus on 2 May, replacing 14(F) Squadron RNZAF, which had earlier transferred to Singapore. In June the squadron was detached to Malta for three weeks for the annual defence exercise with French Air Force Mistral fighters against the aircraft of the American 6th Fleet. In October 1955 a further detachment was made to Amman in order to relieve 249 Squadron, which had flown to Nicosia for a period of live weapons training.

The arrival of 73 Squadron at Nicosia in May 1955 had coincided with the resurgence of Greek nationalism on the island, and on 27 November 1955 a state of emergency was declared following a campaign of violence by the Greek Cypriot terrorist group EOKA, seeking 'Enosis' (union with Greece). Murders of British military and civilian personnel led to a period of increased tension on the island, with extra security measures against terrorist attacks being imposed at military bases, including Nicosia and Akrotiri. The sabotage of aircraft, especially during the Suez operations when the bases were crowded with aircraft, also continued to be a major threat, with four Canberra aircraft and one Hunter being destroyed by EOKA bombs between November 1956 and November 1957.

It was discovered that the terrorist groups were receiving weapons and materiel reinforcements from Greece; they were delivered by a series of caiques, landing clandestinely along the north coast of the island. These fairly small sailing vessels appeared, to all intents and purposes, to be harmless fishing boats. Nevertheless in late 1955 73 Squadron flew a number of shipping sweeps, 'Caique patrols', in search of these vessels until the Royal Navy took over the task of patrolling the waters around Cyprus.

Archbishop Makarios, the chief religious leader on the island, supported the EOKA movement, blatantly allowing his monasteries to be used by the leader of the terrorist group, Col Georgios Grivas, as headquarters and supply depots; the most important of these was Kykko monastery in the Troodos mountains. On 16 June 1956 the Venoms of 73 Squadron were placed on readiness armed with rockets and 1,000lb bombs for an attack on the position. Although the strike was cancelled, units of the security forces subsequently captured the monastery, seizing a large hoard of weapons and equipment.

The campaign of violence in Cyprus continued until 1958 when, following negotiations between the Greek, Turkish and British governments, the demand for Enosis was abandoned. In return, the British government agreed to relinquish its sovereignty over the island, except for those bases necessary for its military needs. During the four-year armed struggle the EOKA movement had been responsible for the death or serious injury of over 1,500 people.

On 13 June 1955 the first batch of three Venom FB.4s (WR408, WR475 and WR483)

One of the first photographs to be taken of 6 Squadron's Venom FB.4s, this is WR476, flown by Flt Lt Mike Hobson, on 19 July 1955. The aircraft had been delivered to the squadron the previous month. (*Gp Capt Mike Hobson*)

was delivered to 6 Squadron at Habbaniya. The squadron had completed its changeover by July, coinciding with the beginning of 249 Squadron's gradual re-equipment with FB.4s. In April 1956 6 Squadron left Habbaniya and moved to its new base at Akrotiri in Cyprus.

In the summer of 1956 the political situation in the Middle East deteriorated, following the nationalisation of the Suez Canal by Egypt's President Nasser. (The role played by the MEAF Venoms in this conflict are recorded more fully in the next chapter, 'The Suez Crisis'.) The final withdrawal of British forces from the Suez Canal area in June 1956 placed an increased importance on Amman and Mafraq in Jordan as alternative operational airfields for the RAF. The sudden decision to transfer 32 Squadron to Amman from Malta in September 1956 to replace 249

Squadron because of the worsening situation in the Middle East was also seen as a precautionary measure to defend the airfield against a possible Israeli incursion following the Egyptian action to nationalise the Suez Canal. The move was to cause serious difficulties as Jordan continued to expect the British government to fulfil its obligations under the Anglo-Jordan Treaty to take action against the increasing cross-border raids. As the Suez crisis escalated it became clear that the British forces in Jordan were in an untenable situation.

Squadron routine continued with weapons training on the ranges. A detachment of Hunters was flown in from Nicosia for a programme of PI's with 32 Squadron, but by this time anti-British feelings in Amman had developed into rioting and as the situation worsened the personnel were confined to base. During this difficult period a Venom (WR337) was lost in a fatal accident on 22 October when it stalled and crashed on the final approach to Queen Alia airfield at Amman, killing Flg Off Chris Richmond.

The Suez crisis continued to escalate and on 29 October 32 Squadron was ordered to move up to Mafraq, where its presence created more hostility. No flying was possible during the first two weeks of November as the station was under virtual siege, with trenches and barbed-wire fences being positioned around the squadron dispersal. Throughout December the station faced further rioting, sabotage and looting by some members of the Jordanian army, although 19 LAA Wing of the RAF Regiment and the arrival of 109 Field Battery of the Royal

Artillery from Cyprus strengthened the station's defences. The operational restrictions placed on the squadron, including being placed on 24-hour standby and with two aircraft constantly at five minutes' readiness, disrupted the normal training programme and made its position more tenuous. By the end of the year Sqn Ldr Gilchrist was succeeded as CO by Sqn Ldr G.D. Sutcliffe, and in January 1957 32 Squadron finally left Jordan for Akrotiri as part of the RAF withdrawal from the region.

In early 1957 the first Canberra B.2 bombers were delivered to Cyprus and were gradually issued to the three Venom squadrons at Akrotiri. The first to re-equip was 32 Squadron in January, followed by 73 Squadron in March and 6 Squadron in June. On 1 March 1957 a formation of twenty-

A neat line of Venom FB.1s of 249 Squadron during the AOC's Inspection at Amman in May 1955. The squadron markings on the tail booms are yellow and blue diagonal stripes, while the yellow tip-tanks have either red or blue flashes to indicate the respective flights. (*Tony Gronert*)

eight aircraft drawn from the Akrotiri Venom Wing made a farewell flypast over Cyprus, led by Wg Cdr J.C. Button DSO, DFC (whose aircraft had one tip-tank painted black and the other white to distinguish him from the other squadrons). This was followed on 13 June by a flypast of eight Venoms, ten Canberras and six Hunters, which made up the Queen's Birthday Formation as they flew over the Trooping of the Colour at Nicosia.

On 29 June 1957, the last day of Venom flying at Akrotiri, twelve aircraft of 6 Squadron proudly flew in a '6' formation over Nicosia, Limassol, Episcopi and Akrotiri, before being officially grounded.

The remaining Venom unit, 249 Squadron, had left Cyprus for El Adem in March 1957, and moved again to Eastleigh in Kenya during July that year, maintaining a temporary detachment at Sharjah for anti-terrorist operations in Oman. Mike Waterhouse joined 249 Squadron in July 1955:

After the Suez crisis, 249 Squadron remained at Akrotiri until early March 1957. Then, being a mobile unit and the aviation nomads of the Middle East, we were ordered to move to El Adem. Although we were officially based at El Adem until mid-July, half of our flying was carried out at Ta Kali (Malta) – mainly to hone our skills at air-to-air firing on a towed flag. Although basically a ground-attack squadron we had to be ready for everything. In fact, in June 1957 it was put to good use during the NATO exercise 'Rosie Rosie' when we 'attacked' Cyprus, which was being defended by Hunter squadrons.

On 13 July we moved again, this time to Eastleigh. We were not sorry to leave El Adem, but there was more excitement on the way when Flg Off Roy Waite's aircraft [WR398] suffered a hydraulic failure and he had to belly-land at Nicosia.

Operations in Oman began on 28 July and continued until 1 October, when the detachment was recalled. My return to Sharjah from Kenya on 29 September 1957 coincided with the death of Flg Off Dave Elford in a flying accident, which was a sad day for the squadron. It was also at about this time that we heard that we were to be re-equipped with Canberra bombers and a new 249 Squadron was to be formed; this was not what we wanted to hear.

The end came on 15 October 1957 when, following a final formation flypast, it was disbanded as a Venom ground-attack unit and re-formed the following day as a Canberra squadron at Akrotiri.

ACTION IN ADEN AND THE YEMEN

As the longest-serving squadron in the Middle East, 8 Squadron (Sqn Ldr A.J. Houston), based at Khormaksar in Aden, began to convert from Vampire FB.9s to Venom FB.1s in March 1955. This squadron had been responsible for the internal security of the region since 1920, and had been permanently based in Aden since 1946 with a succession of fighter and ground-attack aircraft, whose air power was employed to support the rule of law. The strategy and tactics of 'colonial policing' devised by the RAF before the Second World War in the Western Aden Protectorate, northern Iraq and the North-West Frontier Province of India had been greatly expanded and developed, and the offensive/air-to-ground-attack component of air power had become a dominant element in maintaining order, often in conjunction with the ground forces.

As the protecting power in Aden, the British would order a dissenting tribe to surrender a quantity of arms and/or Maria Theresa dollars (the silver currency of the interior). If the demand was ignored the tribal area would be 'proscribed' and the tribesmen would be safe in their villages, though no outside movement was allowed. It was assumed that everyone understood the rules and little damage was done in a proscribed area. Periodically, the Venoms would arrive to check, and any people or animals outside the villages would be strafed. When dissidents in an area to the east of the Western Aden Protectorate ambushed an Aden to Al Khabr convoy in October 1958, an area of 100 square miles was proscribed. The villagers seemed not to understand the implications, for when three pairs of Venoms later went to investigate the area they found life being conducted as normal in one valley about 5 miles long. During the ensuing attack the Venoms were responsible for the deaths of 600 goats, 8 camels, 2 cows and a villager. The devastation would have been worse but for the dust from the attack which obscured visibility over the target area.

Periodic disturbances in the wild and mountainous borders of the Aden Protectorate and Yemen were aggravated by inflammatory propaganda and the supply of arms from Egypt to the marauding tribes in the Yemen, who raided villages and forts inside the Protectorate border. Despite a British treaty of friendship with the Iman of Yemen, the proposed federation of the Western Aden Protectorate's sheikhdoms provoked the Yemeni's mistrust and jealousy, resulting in an increase of cross-border raids.

Air support had proved to be effective and was called upon for a variety of situations including border incursions from Yemen, cross-border retaliation when British forces came under mortar attack, armed attack on up-country convoys, as well as the containment of outside-inspired action. Aircraft were also called upon to operate in the deterrent role, flying blatantly and repeatedly over areas where trouble might be brewing ('flag-waving'), or on airborne standby along the route of a convoy en-route to an up-country destination ('cab-rank'). A pair of aircraft armed with rockets and 20mm cannon remained on permanent standby at Khormaksar from dawn to dusk daily.

In May 1955 one flight of 8 Squadron had converted to Venoms and was declared operational, carrying out its first strike when a rebel target in the Wadi Mirria was bombed. In most cases air strikes against rebel positions were coordinated and controlled by a squadron pilot acting as Air Liaison Officer (ALO) with the ground forces, equipped with a VHF radio. The following July six Venoms flew some eighty sorties when the squadron bombed the Wadi Hatib during an operation to relieve the government fort at Robat.

The following October 8 Squadron began to re-equip with Venom FB.4s after the arrival of five aircraft (WR446, WR477, WR487, WR526 and WR528) from the UK, and by the end of November had completed its conversion.

Throughout January 1956 the squadron was kept fully occupied with further air strikes against rebels in the Wadi Hatib, led by the infamous Salim Ali Mauer, described as the 'arch enemy of 8 Squadron'. In one devastating attack by the Venoms several members of the gang were either killed or injured, including Ali Mauer. Later in the month the squadron's formation aerobatic team flew down to Uganda to take part in the first Kampala Trade & Agricultural Show; during their four-day visit, they were able to give four displays. The Kenya Air Show at Kitale on 7 and 8 January was considered the most ambitious ever attempted in East Africa, with civil airlines, flying clubs, charter companies and RAF units all working together to produce a splendid flying display. Three Venoms from 8 Squadron led by Sqn Ldr Houston gave an impeccable display of formation flying, concluding their performance with a spectacular 'ding' – a very fast dive over the airfield, breaking away at right angles to the leader.

The warning flag on the nose of Venom FB.4 WR399 of 8 Squadron indicates that it is armed. (*via R.L. Ward*)

By May the squadron's Venoms had been cleared to fire rockets and guns with the under-wing fuel-tanks fitted. These tanks were originally designed for ferrying only, but clearance to use them on operations increased the Venom's radius of action by 100 miles; allowing for five minutes' flying at full power at low level, the Venom FB.4s could now attack targets at up to 360 miles range. The most immediate benefit was that a request for air support on the Saudi Arabian border north of the Wadi Hadramaut could now be carried out without having a detachment at Riyan. The disadvantage of having these fuel-tanks was that the Venoms could not carry bombs, as these used the same pylons.

There followed what was to be a relatively quiet period for the squadron, with a trip to Habbaniya for ten days of air firing and a visit by fourteen SAAB Safirs of the Imperial Ethiopian Air Force being the main highlights. In February 1956 Sqn Ldr Houston was replaced as CO of the squadron by Sqn Ldr H.D. Johnson DFC, who in turn was

replaced by Sqn Ldr C.I. Blyth DFC, AFC, in the following July when Johnson was flown back to the UK for surgery to an old leg wound.

In July 1956 73 Squadron was detached to Khormaksar to replace 8 Squadron, which had transferred to Cyprus for its annual APC; the first section of four aircraft was led by the CO, Sqn Ldr J.F. Manning AFC, on 21 July, the remaining sections each following a day apart. After an initial period of familiarisation (spent on sector recces, simulated low-level strikes and exercises with HMS *Kenya*), the squadron went into action for the first time on 30 August when two waves of Venoms attacked Arab dwellings at Al Jalela with rockets and cannon fire in reprisal for the murder of a local dignitary. Further armed strikes in support of the Lincoln bombers of 1426 Flight to dislodge the rebel Halmain tribesmen in the Boran area continued throughout late September and October. Targets included caves believed to be used as dissident hideouts. On 5 October

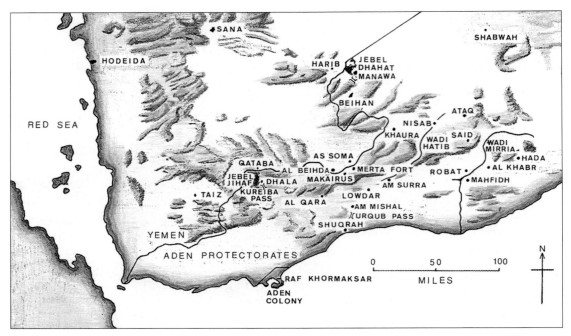

The Gulf of Aden. (*Colin Richardson*)

1956 8 Squadron moved to Akrotiri to join 6 and 249 Squadrons in anticipation of the Suez operations. Throughout the Suez crisis 73 Squadron flew defence patrols along the Yemen border, to counter the possibility of bombing attacks by Egyptian aircraft that had arrived in the area during early November. On 8 December the squadron carried out its last operational strike when four aircraft carrying rockets cleared a blocked pass at Khaura. The squadron returned to Akrotiri on 21 December 1956 and immediately took over the Venom FB.4s and associated ground equipment left behind by 8 Squadron.

Following 8 Squadron's return from Cyprus in December 1956, attacks against the Yemeni-occupied areas of Saudaniya and Hadhaiya were carried out throughout January and February 1957, with houses and wells being especially targeted. On 11 February, following a warning that the village would be attacked, the squadron's Venoms struck at the village of Danaba following its continual use as a base for raids by Yemeni tribesmen and the ambush of a security patrol of the Queen's Own Cameron Highlanders in the Kureiba Pass. During a difficult six-hour operation the village's thick-walled stone houses were destroyed in a series of attacks, during which the Venoms fired seventy-two rockets in nineteen sorties. Further support operations in late February for the beleaguered Government Guard post at Lazarak was followed by a three-day operation near Huzarak in early March, when a proscribed area was attacked by twenty-eight Venoms, killing villagers and animals. The damage inflicted by the attacks was not all one-sided, as Flg Off Peter Goodwin discovered when his Venom (WR363) took several hits from small arms fire during a low-level attack south of Dhala. The rifle rounds caused considerable damage to the fuel-tank, jet pipe, air brake and starboard rocket rail of the Venom, and although he was able to return safely to base the aircraft was subsequently written off as beyond repair.

Also in March it was decided to clear the Aden–Dhala road of dissidents and their fortifications. This road was the main route for the large resupply convoys for the Aden Protectorate Levies (APL) garrison at Dhala, which had come under fire from the rebel tribesmen taking cover in sangars (circular emplacements of rock). With a combined air strike involving twelve Venoms, four Shackletons, two Meteors and a helicopter, Operation 'Zipper' was mounted to demolish these strongholds. During the brief action 8 Squadron flew some eighty-two ground-attack sorties.

On 9 April the squadron returned to Lazarak, where herds of camels and goats were spotted inside the proscribed area. During the ensuing attack by six Venoms, led by Sqn Ldr Blyth, one of the leading aircraft (WR357) failed to clear high ground and struck the slope of a hill about a mile south of Lazarak, killing Flg Off Wally Price. An attempt to recover his body by helicopter was hampered by rebel fire and proved unsuccessful.

Ground-attacks against rebel positions continued throughout the rest of 1957, with most of the action taking place in the border areas. Yemeni infiltration near Beihan and the subsequent establishment of positions on the top of the Jebel Dhahat in September resulted in a request for a squadron strike, after which the APL recaptured the mountain, climbing from Manawa in the north and Tamra in the south. The squadron also destroyed a fort in the Eastern Aden Protectorate near Ruadha.

In December continual looting of the caravans and convoys on the Lowdar–Shuqrah road compelled the APL to start a military convoy from each end, meeting in the middle at a roadblock in the Urqub Pass. Code-named Operation 'Muggah', fifty-one sorties were flown by the Venoms against rebel snipers in

the pass. Also in December Sqn Ldr George Elliott assumed command of the squadron, transferring from 6 Squadron at Akrotiri following its re-equipment with Canberras.

On 10 January 1958 Yemeni troops occupied the ruined fort of Dhimra near the Yemeni town of As Soma and began to fire upon an APL convoy from across the border with a 20mm gun. In such circumstances authorised air strikes – or Operation 'Counter Battery' – were carried out across the border against Yemeni positions that had been firing into the Protectorate. A pair of Venoms was scrambled and carried out a 'flag-wave', beating up Dhimra fort to intimidate the Yemenis. The action proved ineffective, and the Yemenis continued to fire over the border after the Venoms had left the area. Two more pairs of Venoms flew up and attacked the fort with rockets. One of the rockets fired by Flg Off Colin Richardson knocked the top off the tower, killing thirteen Yemeni gunners. After the Venoms had departed, the Government Guard emerged from Merta Fort and went across the border in pursuit of the survivors, killing four of the rebels during a brief exchange of fire. A further 'Counter Battery' action by the squadron Venoms near Qataba later in the month saw Yemeni guns being rocketed following a mortar attack on ground forces at Sana Fort.

The requirement for photography and reconnaissance was initially carried out by a detachment of Meteor FR.9s of 208 Squadron from Malta. However, following the re-equipment of 208 Squadron with Hunters in January 1958, four Meteor FR.9s and five pilots were transferred to Khormaksar and became C Flight of 8 Squadron; together with an eventual strength of twenty Venoms and two Vampire trainers, this was to become the largest operational fighter squadron in the BFAP, and probably the whole RAF. Most of the squadron pilots came from disbanded Venom units and led a

In May 1958 8 Squadron's Venoms attacked anti-aircraft positions located at the barracks in the Yemeni town of Qataba.
(*Courtesy OC 8 Squadron*)

mobile life, spending only a third of their time at Khormaksar, the remainder being spent on detachment at Sharjah or up-country with the army on ALO duties.

In January 1958 1 Squadron of the Royal Rhodesian Air Force arrived from Salisbury with its Vampire FB.9s for a period of duty in support of 8 Squadron. Operations began on 21 January, with armed strikes on Al Khabr and the Jebel Dhahat being carried out until late March, when the squadron returned to Rhodesia. The following August the Vampires returned to Aden and took on the majority of 8 Squadron's operational commitments. Operations began on 15 August when a combined force provided cab-rank patrols close to the Yemen border. Further strikes continued throughout the month and on 6 September a combined force of Venoms and Vampires provided air support for a Dhala convoy that had come under fire. A total of 114 rockets and a large quantity of 20mm cannon were fired during the operation, resulting in the deaths of thirty-two Yemenis.

In April 1958 the Yemenis had managed to subvert the leading sheikhs on the Jebel Jihaf, a large mountain in Protectorate territory behind the town of Dhala. On top of the Jebel Jihaf was the Government Guard fort of As Sabir, which was targeted by the dissident sheikhs who had been given rifles and ammunition from the nearby Yemeni garrison town of Qataba. On 22 April the area's Assistant Political Adviser, Mr Fitzroy-Somerset, went to investigate a complaint from a tribesman of kidnap and murder. He and his escort were ambushed and forced to take refuge in the fort at As Sabir. The following day 8 Squadron's Venoms flew eleven sorties in support of an APL relief column, killing two rebels; the ground forces found Mr Fitzroy-Somerset trapped inside the fort. On 28 April the Venoms flew twenty-nine sorties to provide cover for the air and ground operations, followed by a further twenty sorties two days later during the final stages of the relief of the fort by the Kings Shropshire Light Infantry. A strike on the rebel headquarters near the village of Al Rukba later in the day brought an end to the brief action.

On 6 May an APL patrol from Dhala came under fire from sangars at the foot of the

Jebel Jihaf. The Venoms were called in to attack the rebel positions but came under fire from anti-aircraft guns located at the barracks in the Yemeni town of Qataba. The squadron had long awaited an opportunity to attack this splendid target, and a devastating rocket strike by the Venoms destroyed most of the guns, while fuel and ammunition exploded and burnt within the building. By the end of the day the target was severely damaged. The following day a further thirteen sorties completed the operation despite intense enemy fire which damaged at least two of the aircraft.

The following month the terrorist leader Mohammed Aidrus took refuge in his large manor house near Al Qara following a series of bomb outrages in the Aden colony. On 16 June two Venoms dropped leaflets on this virtually inaccessible house in the Lower Yaffa district to warn the occupants that it would be attacked. The leaflets were carried between the ribs of

the Venoms' split flaps. Early the following morning Sqn Ldr Elliott fired the first rocket during an attack that lasted until midday, by which time the manor house had been reduced to knee-high rubble. Over the following two days the squadron destroyed individual houses in the nearby villages of Falasan and Sharyan. The houses belonged to active supporters of Mohammed Aidrus and pinpoint accuracy was required to avoid damaging neighbouring houses as far as possible.

On 1 July 1958 two houses belonging to dissident sheikhs in the villages of Qa'ashan and Ukaima were destroyed in a rocket attack. While rocketing a house in Ukaima, Flt Lt Colin Richardson's Venom (WR375) was hit three times by ground fire, with one round piercing the main fuselage fuel-tank and causing fuel to pour out onto the engine. Colin quickly returned to base, by which time 100 gallons of fuel had been lost; despite a safe landing, the aircraft was

On 22 August 1957 a ricochet hit Flt Lt Dave Foster's Venom FB.4 WR550, and he was forced to make an emergency landing on the weapons range at Khormaksar. The cockpit section broke away and he was fortunate to escape uninjured as he was dragged backwards, still sitting in the ejection seat. The following July he was shot down and killed in the Beihan area. (*Peter Goodwin*)

The terraced valleys and the rebel stronghold of Al Qara in the Western Aden Protectorate, photographed from a Shackleton of 37 Squadron in January 1958. The large 'manor house' in the village was destroyed by a concentrated rocket attack in June 1958. (*Geoff Corlett*)

subsequently categorised as scrap and struck off charge.

Separating the town of Beihan in the Aden Protectorate and the Yemeni garrison town of Harib is a large mountain called the Jebel Dhahat, upon which were positioned detachments of the APL used for observation. On the night of 7 July the APL came under fire from the Yemenis and 8 Squadron was ordered to mount a 'Counter Battery' sortie the following morning. At 07.15 hours the first pair of Venoms, flown by Flt Lts Dave Foster and Sam Key, got airborne and they were directed on to an area of scrub where a 12.7mm heavy machine-gun was positioned. The leader, Dave Foster, made two passes to identify the target and began his attack, by

which time all the other guns in the area had opened up at him. He failed to recover from his attack and the Venom (WR503) flew into the ground in Yemeni territory, leaving Sam Key to return to base; Dave Foster's body was eventually returned five days later after the threat of severe reprisals.

As a result of this loss, a further nineteen sorties were flown by the squadron, attacking gun positions around the town of Harib. Following a two-week lull in activity, the Yemenis began to fire again upon the APL positions on the Jebel Dhahat from a fort close to the border, which was subjected to a coordinated attack by two pairs of Venoms.

The next month two more Venoms (WR481 and WR541) were written off after a mid-air collision on the Khormaksar range; Flg Off Rod Jude was killed when he failed to eject, but Flg Off Ian Morgan was able to safely return to base despite extensive damage to the wing of his aircraft. Rod Jude's failure to eject was caused by a badly corroded ejection seat handle, which was impossible to pull out of its housing. It was subsequently discovered that a number of the squadron's aircraft also suffered the same fault.

AIR OPERATIONS IN OMAN

If activity for 8 Squadron appeared to be intense in Aden, developments elsewhere in the Arabian Peninsula also stretched the reserves of the unit when, following an armed rebellion in the region of Jebel Akhdar, it was called upon to support the beleaguered Sultan of Muscat and Oman. The Sultanate of

Muscat and Oman lay to the east and north of the Aden Protectorate. In 1955 there was an insurrection in the mountainous interior of the country but the Sultan easily quelled it. However, the rebel leaders were not imprisoned and continued to work towards an armed rebellion to establish independence for the interior. The rebel leaders were Talib bin Ali, his brother Ghalib (who was appointed Imam of Oman by his brother) and Sheikh Suleiman of the Jebel Akhdar region. The leading activists were able to move to Saudi Arabia and spent almost two years forming and recruiting the Omani Liberation Army (OLA) and planning an armed rebellion in central Oman in the region of Jebel Akhdar.

The leading activists returned home from Saudi Arabia in 1957, and rumours of unrest soon reached the Sultan. He sent part of his small army to investigate, and it received an

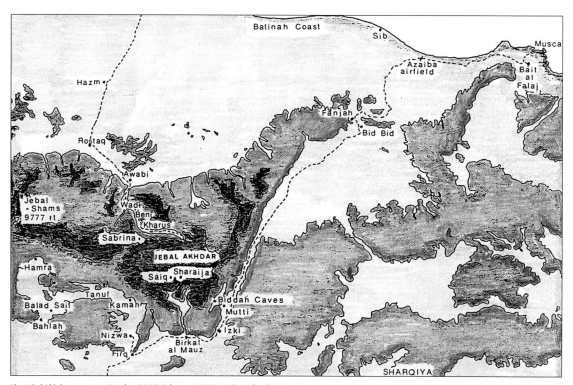

The Jebel Akhdar campaign, October 1957–February 1959. (*Colin Richardson*)

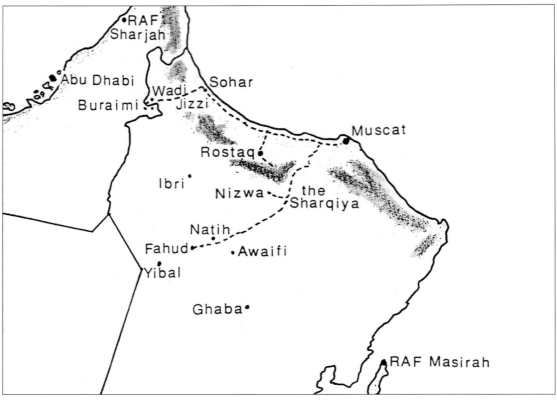

Muscat and Oman. (*Colin Richardson*)

exceedingly bloody nose at the village of Balad Sait. The few survivors moved to the oil company camp at Fahud and licked their wounds. It was clear that the Sultan had lost control of the Jebel Akhdar region. The Sultan called on the British government for help and on 20 July 1957 four Venoms of 8 Squadron were quickly moved to Sharjah, some 200 miles to the north-west of the Jebel. To support the operation Shackletons and Beverleys were detached to nearby Bahrein, while British troops and armoured cars from Aden joined the Trucial Oman Scouts (TOS) at Sharjah and moved south to Fahud. Sharjah was far from ideal as an operating base, with poor accommodation and facilities. The runway was a strip of rolled sand, which caused huge dust clouds as the

aircraft took off, and two strips were required to maintain operations, one for landing and one for take-off.

The Venom air strikes began on 24 July with the forts of Izki, Nizwa and Tanuf being rocketed on successive days, with ten or twelve sorties against each fort. The attacks were only a partial success. Nizwa withstood an air strike by four Venoms which fired 48 rockets and 7,000 rounds of 20mm cannon – but only succeeded in cratering the thick walls of the big fort. On 27 July a further six Venoms from 249 Squadron arrived at Sharjah from Eastleigh, and two days later all six aircraft, led by Sqn Ldr 'Jock' Maitland, together with the four Venoms of 8 Squadron, attacked the fort at Birkat al Mauz, 5 miles west of Izki. The nearest houses were a short distance away, and a leaflet warning preceded the attack. Pilots reported 'considerable damage' to the walls of the fort.

Continued attacks on the fortified towers at Firq and Bakhla over the next few days failed to dislodge the rebels and it was a daring night attack by the Cameronians on 6 August, supported by bombing and rocket attacks by Shackletons and Venoms, which eventually secured the area at the foot of the Jebel on its southern side. This forced the rebel leaders and their followers to retreat into the stronghold of the Jebel. On 11 August the rebel headquarters at Nizwa surrendered without resistance to government forces.

Flt Lt Mike Waterhouse and Flg Off Dave Williams of 249 Squadron both recall the move to Sharjah and subsequent operations:

The flexibility of the Venom, and 249 Squadron's ability to move rapidly within the Middle East, was put to the test during the summer of 1957. At the time 8 Squadron was involved in new troubles in Oman, and also the perennial problem in Yemen, so probably having us near to Aden would serve as a useful back-up squadron and in a better location to assist. We flew from El Adem to Habbaniya on 9 July, to Aden the following day, finally arriving at Eastleigh, via Hargeisa (British Somalia) on 13 July. Having hardly arrived in Kenya we were then redeployed back to Aden, where we briefly attached to 8 Squadron, before continuing to Sharjah on 25 July. The Venom was minimally equipped with navigational aids; consequently the long cross-country flights were accomplished through careful map reading.

Sharjah in those days was nothing more than a desert airstrip comprising two parallel runways, which were alternated daily allowing a primitive watering and rolling of the runway not in use. Having settled in, the squadron pilots were flown over the area in a Shackleton to familiarise them with the terrain.

On 28 July Sqn Ldr Jock Maitland and three pilots carried out our first recce of the area. The following morning two sections of Venoms

The fort at Birkat al Mauz in the south-east corner of the Jebel Akhdar in 1957. Despite being subjected to heavy rocket attacks by the Venoms of 8 and 249 Squadrons, the outside walls show minimal damage. (*Peter Goodwin*)

attacked the fort at Birkat al Mauz with rockets. The only thing that sticks in our minds about the attack was the size of the walls surrounding the fort which, with four 60lb rockets, was not too difficult to hit, and with four aircraft aiming at the same area it was possible to breach a large hole.

Operations continued until 27 September, with further attacks on the rebel strongholds of Firq, Nizwa and Birklan. Despite a few aircraft being damaged by ricochets, the detachment was considered a success.

With order virtually restored by late September the British troops withdrew and the Venom detachments were able to return to their bases. No. 249 Squadron flew back to Eastleigh on 1 October, having flown a total of 242 operational sorties in support of the Sultan's forces for the loss of one Venom (WR381). It had failed to recover from a simulated rocket attack on an airfield installation at Sharjah on 9 September, killing the pilot, Flg Off Dave Elford.

The next part of the campaign ran sporadically for over a year from October 1957. Although 8 Squadron had returned to Khormaksar, the detachment was recalled to Sharjah on 20 October when four Venoms were used for a firepower demonstration on an unoccupied peak close to the rebels on the 6,000ft plateau of the Jebel Akhdar. For just over a week further demonstration rocket attacks on the peak proved ineffective and the Venoms returned to Aden on 5 November. Shackletons and Venoms then operated over the whole area of the Jebel but paying particular attention to the central plateau, disrupting water supplies and destroying crops, attacking anything that moved in the area, and generally making life unbearable for the rebels and local inhabitants so that a surrender would be forced. None of these actions proved successful, however, and in spite of the miserable conditions the rebel force remained defiant.

On 15 November the Sultan's army was again reinforced by the TOS for an attempted invasion of the Jebel Akhdar, and seven Venoms led by Sqn Ldr 'Joe' Blyth were sent to Sharjah to provide cover. Despite successful rocket and strafing attacks against targets on top of the Jebel, the ground forces' plan to advance up the Wadi Kamah was frustrated when they came under opposition from rebel snipers and were reluctantly forced to withdraw.

After an absence of a few months a new Venom detachment of three aircraft was sent to Sharjah in March 1958. Confident that their position on the Jebel Akhdar was secure, the rebels had laid land-mines to within 200 yd of the Muscat Armed Forces camp at Firq. About twenty vehicles had been blown up, and the first targets for the Venoms were the groups of huts thought to be used by the mining parties. On the first day of operations the three Venoms fired 66 rockets and over 4,500 rounds of ammunition. Following a further period of monotonous inactivity the Venoms were eventually called up when some rebels were caught in the open after an ambush as they tried to escape up the Jebel north of Nizwa. Four days later there was another ambush, this time at Muti, where a steep-sided wadi ran into the Jebel. The TOS were pinned down and the Venoms were scrambled to support the Ferret armoured cars sent to rescue them. On arrival the Venoms killed eight rebels and went on to attack some huts on the side of the Jebel, where a further fifteen rebels were killed.

Two more Venoms joined the original three at Sharjah but the rate of attrition soon gave cause for concern to those aware of the dwindling number of replacement Venoms: on 29 March 1958 one aircraft (WR563) flown by Flt Lt Colin Richardson was written off when the starboard main undercarriage leg collapsed on landing; on 5 May Flg Off Dennis Batchelor was killed during an

A detachment of 8 Squadron's Venoms being prepared for operations at Sharjah, 1958 or 1959. (*Courtesy OC 8 Squadron*)

unexplained accident while air-testing WR533; and on 30 August Flt Lt Owen Watkinson was also killed when his Venom (WR552) flew into the plateau near the village of Sharaijah while strafing animals. Corrosion also took its toll of the aircraft, and the scrap compound at Sharjah contained an extraordinary number of expired Venoms.

Two weeks after the loss of Owen Watkinson there was another fatal crash at Sharjah when one of the Venoms (WR442) being flown back to Aden for an overdue servicing dived into the ground soon after take-off. The remaining squadron Venoms were immediately grounded while a Board of Inquiry tried to discover the cause of the accident. It eventually concluded that a flapping ammunition access panel had distracted the pilot, Flg Off Paul Edwards, who had then inadvertently stalled the aircraft as he attempted to recover to Sharjah. While the Venoms remained temporarily grounded, operations against the rebels were carried out during September with Sea Venoms and Sea Hawks from HMS *Bulwark*, and there was no further participation by 8 Squadron for nearly a month.

The Venom detachments continued flying throughout the summer of 1958, their primary aim being to deny food to the rebels.

Known ambush positions were also attacked, together with a valley known as the Inner Circle, which lay behind the first ridge of the Jebel around its south-east corner.

At the end of October four Venoms returned to Sharjah for a brief detachment, led by the Squadron Commander, Sqn Ldr George Elliott. Soon after his arrival he surprised the rebels by leading a night attack guided by the lights of their campfires – which was also a surprise for the detachment pilots, as they were not trained for night attacks! Following this attack the rebels negotiated for a truce, which they used to replace their losses and regroup. After a two-week lull in the fighting it came as no surprise when their peace terms were considered as unacceptable.

For a time there was also some doubt whether the Venoms could continue to use Sharjah after the sheikh came under pressure from Cairo to evict the British forces from the area. Masirah was considered as an alternative. Eventually, however, despite the poor state of the sand runways, Sharjah continued to be used for the final, short and decisive phase of the campaign.

The approaching cool weather of the winter provided an opportunity to take the Jebel from the rebels when the Sultan's forces, the TOS and D Squadron SAS, which had been secretly flown in from Malaya, began mounting patrols and probing attacks from several directions. On 28 November 8 Squadron was ordered to send a detachment to Sharjah as soon as possible to support the attacks, and by the following morning five Venoms were in place under the command of Flt Lt Colin Richardson.

An extraordinary picture of two Venom FB.4s of 8 Squadron at Sharjah following an overnight rainstorm in 1957. The wheels of the cyclist show the extent of the flooding. Both aircraft are armed. (*Peter Goodwin*)

The initial attack met fierce resistance from the rebels. A rebel cave was identified and rocketed by the Venoms, killing twenty of the defenders. There were further fierce, hard-fought battles against a well-armed and well-trained enemy as the SAS scaled the Jebel. When the weather permitted the Venoms continued to target positions on the plateau and on two nearby rounded hills at Aqbat al Dhufar – known colloquially as 'Sabrina', after the well-endowed contemporary actress! On 6 and 7 January 1959 the Venoms killed approximately seventeen rebels during a series of dusk strikes on this enemy position. The weather was wet, dark and stormy at the 8,000ft ridge, and it was miserably cold for the troops.

Heavy storms and flooding at Sharjah throughout December 1958 and early January 1959 made operations very difficult to maintain and eventually resulted in a temporary grounding of the aircraft. Briefly moving to Masirah in order to remain operational, the detachment returned to Sharjah on 19 January to find a further five Venoms had arrived from Aden, increasing the strength to ten aircraft for the final offensive assault on the Jebel Akhdar, planned for 25–6 January.

At the same time D Squadron SAS had been joined by A Squadron Life Guards and Arab troops for a surprise night attack on the rebels' position on the 6,000ft plateau. The assault went well and the Venoms quickly silenced any further resistance with a coordinated dawn attack. The air strikes continued, and after the arrival of the Muscat Regiment on the plateau two days later the remaining rebels surrendered, their leaders having already made good their escape to Saudi Arabia. The occupation of the plateau was the first time that an organised army had penetrated the Jebel since the Persians in the tenth century.

On 24 February 1959 the Venom detachment finally returned to Aden. The Jebel Akhdar campaign had demonstrated the capability of air power, and throughout the eighteen-month campaign 8 Squadron had flown 1,315 operational sorties. It had also fired 3,800 rockets and 271,000 rounds of ammunition, which was remarkable considering that the whole operation was merely an extension to 8 Squadron's main area of operations in the Aden Protectorate. Talib's terrorist campaign finally collapsed in 1962 with the development of the Sultan's intelligence network and the seizure of arm caches by his security forces.

Operations by the Venoms throughout the Arabian Peninsula are summed up by AVM Les Phipps, a former flight commander and PAI (QWI) with 8 Squadron at Khormaksar between January 1958 and April 1959:

After Suez and by December 1956 8 Squadron was back in Aden, where it was soon to become the only remaining Venom squadron in the Middle East. The others were progressively re-equipped with Canberras to form a four-squadron light bomber wing at Akrotiri; the last of these units was 249 Squadron, by then stationed at Eastleigh, which finally retired its single-seaters in October 1957. By that time the impact of the Duncan Sandys' White Paper on Defence was making itself felt and the last six Venom squadrons in Germany had all been disbanded before the year was out.

As the post-Suez unrest in Arabia intensified, 8 Squadron became fully extended with operations from its Khormaksar base in Aden. It then became additionally extended with operations in the Sultanate of Muscat and Oman in the north, where the Sultan called for British support to suppress outside-inspired attempts to depose him and his government.

The squadron establishment of sixteen aircraft was quickly increased to eighteen as events in the central part of Oman, about one thousand miles to the north-east, began to unfold and extend the squadron's commitments beyond the Protectorate. For most of the 1957–9 period of operations across the Arabian Peninsula the aircraft strength was in fact higher – at around twenty Venoms. For this sizeable squadron, constantly engaged in armed operations, the aircraft engineering task was enormous. It included a special programme to combat general deterioration from corrosion and other effects of high heat, high humidity and a salt-laden atmosphere. Battle-damage repair was also frequently necessary. But regardless of the engineering effort, few of the fleet were able to successfully pass Major Servicing at 700 hours. Aircraft life was therefore fixed at a very short 750 hours, after which the airframe and sometimes the engine were withdrawn from service. This seemingly depressing state of affairs was acceptable because more Venoms were available. Although FEAF squadrons still needed to be maintained, more than half of the 150 Venom FB.4s built had been delivered direct to the Middle East and the survivors of these, plus a few hand-me-downs from the disbanded Wunstorf Wing, provided ample stocks from which to sustain 8 Squadron until a replacement type could be maintained. Interestingly, at least sixty-five FB.4s were on charge to 8 Squadron at one time or another. To take advantage of the kinder climate, some of the surplus Venoms were held at Eastleigh where, from early 1959, 142 Squadron was established to fly some of them.

For flying in the Western Aden Protectorate the FB.4 flew with the normal Venom operating configuration of wing-tanks. For deployment away from Aden, and while in northern Oman, they flew with additional fuel in underwing tanks. Armament during operations consisted of 3in rockets with 60lb high-explosive warheads plus four fully loaded 20mm cannon.

During the Sharjah-based operations, 8 Squadron aimed to maintain an effective detachment strength of at least four aircraft. To achieve this, replacement aircraft were frequently required from Aden. Serviceability at Sharjah was very poor, for the most part owing to the debilitating effect of the climate on hydraulics, electrics and fuel systems. All servicing and re-arming was done in the open – there were no hangars, just one canvas shelter under which a Venom might sit for extended work. There was also a depressing site at the edge of the airfield where the remains of Venoms which had crashed or were otherwise beyond repair were left to the elements.

Aircraft operated with a maximum fuel load and carried four or eight 60lb rockets and 800 rounds of 20mm cannon. Sortie length was up to 1 hour and 40 minutes, and executing an attack manoeuvre required careful handling skills and sharp judgement; the very curved trajectory of the 3in rocket needed 30 degrees and 600 yd for accuracy, and this could lead the unwary to an excitingly close proximity with the ground during the pull-out. Several aircraft also suffered damage from ricochets or from enemy fire.

Operationally the Venom was a first-class aircraft for the job it had to do. By mid-1950s standards it had a sparkling performance and impressive operational capability. It could achieve 535 knots at low level, it was highly manoeuvrable, a good weapons platform, could climb to 50,000ft, and with underwing tanks for deployment its range was nearly 1,000 miles.

The successful Venoms might have continued longer in service with 8 Squadron were it not for the debilitating effect of the operating conditions, and the fact that they were constantly flown in armed action, mostly at low level and very frequently to the limits.

By mid-1958 a replacement for the Venom was urgently required. To conserve the airframe hours of the remaining aircraft, it had already been decided to restrict the flying to eighteen hours per aircraft per month. HQ British Forces Arabian Peninsula in Aden had also been able to persuade the Air Ministry to lay on a competitive evaluation project to find a new ground-attack aircraft, which would involve three contrasting aircraft types: the Hawker Hunter, the Folland Gnat lightweight fighter and the Hunting Jet Provost trainer. Under the aegis of 8 Squadron, the Venom Replacement Evaluation Trial was established at Khormaksar, led by Wg Cdr Colin Coulthard of the Central Fighter Establishment. While the two Hunters were flown direct from West Raynham by Colin Coulthard and Bill Bedford, the Gnat and Jet Provost were flown out to Aden in a Beverley transport aircraft and reassembled for the trials, which ran from 14 to 17 August 1958. Although it was thought at one stage that the Gnat might be adopted, the Hunter eventually emerged as the clear winner of the trial and an order was placed for the conversion of a number of Hunter F.Mk.6s for tropical trials.

The month of October 1958 opened in spectacular style with a full-blooded sand-storm at Khormaksar, which arrived after only six minutes' warning. Later in the month an area north of Mahfidh was proscribed following the ambush of a convoy of the Hadramaut Bedouin Legion in a pass between Al Kabr and Hada. Although the rebels had retreated to their inaccessible homes in the hills, a strike by three pairs of Venoms accounted for a large number of their animals, which were not permitted outside the villages in a proscribed area.

The early part of 1959 was taken up with air activity in response to increased Yemeni attacks in the Protectorate. During March the Al Kabr area was proscribed over a period of four days and was attacked by four pairs of Venoms. On 13 April command of the squadron was handed over to Sqn Ldr Rex Knight, and during the latter part of the month further unrest brought a brief but intense period of action for 8 Squadron when Al Bubakr bin Farid and his supporting tribesmen attempted to usurp the Sultan of the Upper Aulaqi sheikhdom. Security forces were sent out to capture Bubakr bin Farid, the principal leader of the

dissidents, but they were unsuccessful when the rebels took shelter in the hills near Said.

At the beginning of May the area around Said was proscribed and was subjected to continuous attacks by 8 Squadron Venoms in an attempt to dislodge the tribesmen. Further attacks on animals, villages, water holes and sangars continued into mid-June, when a two-day strike operation on a house in As Surra, which was being used as a base for rebel operations, was attacked and destroyed with rockets and cannon after a leaflet drop.

On 5 June six Venoms led by the CO left for a goodwill visit to the Imperial Ethiopian Air Force. This was in return for the visit of the Ethiopians some three years earlier, and following a flypast over Addis Ababa the aircraft landed at Harar Meda. During the stream landing Flt Lt Dave Riley overshot, but subsequently won the acclaim of the local press for his 'quick thinking and gallantry in saving the lives of his brother officers'! The detachment was later inspected by his Imperial Majesty Haile Selassie, following which four Venoms laid on a firepower demonstration against the hulks of two SAAB 17A light bombers; 16 rockets and over 2,000 rounds of ammunition were fired at the targets during the event. The show was brought to a close by Dave Riley, who carried out a display of solo aerobatics.

Just before the Ethiopian visit a change was made to the squadron markings in the form of an arrowhead in the squadron's colours on the nose of the aircraft. This had been devised by Sqn Ldr George Elliott and replaced the fishtailed coloured bands previously carried on the Venoms' tailbooms.

Following the visit to Ethiopia, intelligence reports located the presence of dissident tribesmen massing at Al Beihda just inside Yemen. No. 8 Squadron was at once ordered to attack the houses of the rebels as a warning to the population, and the Meteors of the Fighter Recce Flight dropped leaflets one hour before the attack, advising the locals to clear the area. The message was either misunderstood or ignored, and instead of leaving the area the population gathered in strategic areas to watch the show, while the remainder took up firing positions, rifles at the ready, to await the Venoms.

By mid-morning on 15 June the first house in Dhir Surra (just inside the Protectorate) had been reduced to rubble and attacks had started against the second target. By this time the Venoms had come under return fire from the rebels, which proved effective and hit three of the attacking aircraft; Flg Off Doug Bebbington (WR473) returned to Khormaksar desperately short of fuel because of a punctured wing-tank, while Flt Lt John Morris (WR438) was wounded in the left arm and had severe problems with his engine throttle control.

Tactics were now revised; instead of single rockets being fired during the attack, the aircraft were loaded with eight rockets which were fired, where possible, in a single salvo. The 20mm cannon were fired on entry to the rocket dive to deter any return fire. The remaining houses were later destroyed without any further damage to the aircraft, and on completion of the operation the squadron received the following signal from HQ BFAP: 'Secret: From Upper Yaffa Town Planning Authority. Many thanks for splendid work on our slum clearance scheme in Dhir Surra. Have other clearance projects in hand. Would be grateful for any assistance.'

On 1 August C Flight and its Meteor FR.9s became an independent unit, the 'Arabian Protectorate Reconnaissance Flight'. A further ninety-two operational sorties were flown throughout the month by the squadron's Venoms in the Said area in support of the APL's efforts to drive out Bubakr bin Farid's tribesmen and to move the seat of government from Said to Museinah, 6 miles to the west.

A general strike and the declaration of a state of emergency throughout September to November caused increased tension within the Aden colony. Despite the station being placed on a state of alert, the air strikes continued against Bubakr bin Farid's tribesmen, which had now split into smaller groups taking refuge in caves in the Wadis Karar, Adze and Hatib. With the support of the Vampires of 1 Squadron RRAF, which had returned to Aden on detachment for the third time in October 1959, the caves were attacked by the Venoms using rockets. These assaults were followed up with further strikes on suspected rebel positions in the south-west portion of the proscribed area.

By January 1960 local support for the rebel tribesmen was beginning to wane, and the continuous offensive by the RAF and units of the APL was to cause their eventual surrender. On 18 January 8 Squadron carried out its last Venom operations when two aircraft flown by Flt Lt Alex Brown and Flg Off John Dowling carried out a 'flag-wave' over Wadi Farah, near the Said proscribed area. This was followed by a final sortie flown by Flt Lt Mike Merrett and Flg Off 'Buster' Webb.

During almost five years of operations in the Aden Protectorate, the Venoms of 8 Squadron had flown over 2,500 operational sorties in the most gruelling of conditions. Frequently maligned as being out of date, the Venom was considered a pilot's aircraft and could do, and did, more than might have been expected of it at that time. With the exception of ferry flights to Eastleigh, all Venom flying ceased on 23 January, when the squadron was declared non-operational until the Hunter conversion programme was completed. By the middle of February 1960 the last of the squadron Venoms (or 'Steam Chickens') had been withdrawn.

In January 1960 8 Squadron began to convert to Hunter FGA.9s and had completely re-equipped with the type within a space of a few weeks. This left 142 Squadron as the only Venom unit in the British Forces Arabian Peninsula (BFAP). The squadron had previously operated as a bomber unit during the Second World War and it was originally intended that it would re-form with eight Venom FB.4s at Khormaksar under the command of Sqn Ldr Robert Ramirez. However, because of the lack of suitable accommodation and the work planned for the runway at Khormaksar, the Air Ministry decided to establish the squadron at Eastleigh, Nairobi. In January 1959 the CO and Flt Lt 'Mac' McLeland were dispatched to Eastleigh to collect two Venoms and return to Khormaksar, where a selection of pilots from the UK squadrons had assembled to begin their conversion. Following a short familiarisation period, the cadre unit transferred to Eastleigh and officially re-formed on 1 February 1959. It was intended that after a six-month work-up to operational status 142 Squadron would return to Khormaksar to rejoin 8 Squadron. Tim Cohu joined 142 Squadron in January 1959 after flying Hunters with 92 Squadron in the UK:

No. 142 Squadron was formed as a back-up to 24 Brigade and 8 Squadron, which had been actively engaged in the Oman during the 1950s. The CO, Bob Ramirez, sat down with the personnel people in the UK to assemble a balanced bunch of pilots, and in January 1959 we arrived at Khormaksar, where 8 Squadron was based, to begin our conversion and work-up period. Since most of us had been flying smart shiny Hunters in the UK it was quite a shock to see what years of exposure to sun and sand could do to fighter aircraft. But despite their tatty appearance 8 Squadron's Venoms had a very high serviceability rate.

We converted to the Venom using two or three of our own aircraft, which happened to be at Khormaksar and were allocated to 142

Squadron. On 23 January we all flew to Eastleigh on scheduled transport and collected the bulk of our complement of Venoms, which were in storage there as 8 Squadron's reserve. We were also originally short of pilots with Venom experience and only 'Mac' McLeland had flown them before in Germany, but Sam Key and Roy Morris from 8 Squadron were later posted to the squadron to smooth our transition to operational status.

For the next two months the squadron trained in Kenya, operating from the dirt runway at Eastleigh and using the large empty areas of the Rift Valley for low-flying and ground-attack training. However, 142 Squadron's existence was to be short-lived. On 31 March 1959 208 (Hunter) Squadron based in Cyprus was disbanded as part of the current reorganisation within the RAF and its numberplate transferred to 142 Squadron at Eastleigh, where, on the following day it was officially re-formed, still with Venom FB.4s.

Two months later, on 17 June, 208 Squadron flew down to RRAF Thornhill in Southern Rhodesia to carry out live weapon practice with rockets and cannon on the Kutanga range. This firing phase was followed by a tour of the Federation of Rhodesia and Nyasaland, with visits to Livingstone, Lusaka, Bulawayo and Salisbury, before the squadron returned to Eastleigh on 7 July.

Within a week of returning to Kenya, the squadron detached six of its Venoms to Bahrain and Khormaksar to participate in Exercise 'Mad Dog' with elements of the Trucial Oman Scouts (TOS) and with the aircraft carrier, HMS *Albion*. Led by the CO, Sqn Ldr Robert Ramirez, the detachment was most successful and demonstrated that it could transfer to an operational area some 2,500 miles away in forty-eight hours. During the detachment a section of aircraft operating from Sharjah attacked targets in the Jebel Danna and Jebel Akhdar areas with rockets

A formation of Venom FB.4s from 208 Squadron near Mount Kilimanjaro, September 1959. The 'club' or 'spade' card markings on the tip-tanks were applied to differentiate between the two flights. (*Peter McCleland*)

A composite photograph of the nine-aircraft formation loop achieved by 208 Squadron's Venoms on 22 December 1959. (*Sam Key*)

The end of the line? Following service with 5, 266 and 8 Squadrons, Venom FB.4 WR493 briefly served as a reserve aircraft with 208 Squadron at Eastleigh until it was struck off charge in March 1960 and dumped on the airfield. This photograph was taken in July 1963, before it was placed on the camp gate for display. (*Ray Deacon*)

and cannon fire. The following month the squadron also exercised in the Northern Frontier Province of Kenya with elements of the SAS during Exercise 'Sandstorm'.

In August 1959 208 Squadron was designated the official aerobatic team of the BFAP, having been in existence since the previous April with team members comprising the CO and Flt Lts Sam Key, George Ord and 'Mac' McLeland, who was also the team's solo display pilot. The team's first official display at Zanzibar for the Sultan's 82nd birthday was followed by various trade fairs and air rallies in Kenya and Uganda. To comply with the squadron tradition decreeing that whenever it was re-equipped with a different type of aircraft eight of them should be looped in close formation, on 21 December 1959 the eight-aircraft formation looped with the aerobatic team as the nucleus. The next day the squadron went one better in a glorious act

of showmanship by adding a ninth aircraft to its formation loop!

On 4 January 1960 six Venoms were flown to Bahrein and Sharjah to maintain a three-month detachment. During the following weeks the squadron took part in a variety of exercises that included coordinated attacks on the frigate HMS *Loch Fyne*, and further simulated strikes on the Jebel Danna and Jebel Akhdar as well as sector reconnaissance flights for the TOS; these last sorties included 'Camel Recces' where coastal camel trains suspected of carrying explosives were particularly sought.

On 21 March 1960 the squadron carried out a mass flypast of all its aircraft over Eastleigh, following which the remaining aircraft were flown to Khormaksar to be broken up and sold locally as scrap. A week later (on 28 March) the squadron disbanded as a Venom unit, the aircrew returning to the UK to collect their new Hunter FGA.9s from Stradishall.

CHAPTER FOUR

THE SUEZ CRISIS

The Suez Canal was the vital link between Britain and its interests in both the Middle East and the Far East, and was operated by the Suez Canal Company from which Britain and France took a large share of the revenue as joint shareholders. In November 1954 Col Gamal Abdel Nasser was elected President of Egypt following the overthrow of King Farouk some two years earlier. Nasser was seen as a leader of Arab nationalism, with an agenda to rid his country of the colonial domination of European powers. One of his priorities was the construction of the Aswan High Dam, which would harness the waters of the Nile to generate electricity and create fertile farmland. The project would cost a billion dollars and the World Bank had promised a loan if America and Britain also provided funds. Nasser's politics, however, made his backers uneasy. He had purchased a large number of MiG-15 and MiG-17 fighters, Il-28 bombers and a quantity of tanks from Czechoslovakia during 1955, and had allowed the Soviet Union to establish a presence in the country. He had also promised to reverse the Egyptian defeat by the Israelis in the war of 1948. Fearing that Egypt was moving into the Eastern Bloc, in July 1956 President Dwight Eisenhower and his Secretary of State, John Foster Dulles, withdrew funding of the Aswan Dam with the excuse that the Egyptian economy was unsound, thus making the investment too risky; Britain and the World Bank quickly followed suit.

Nasser's response was immediate. On 26 July he nationalised the Suez Canal and seized its assets – the income from which would be used to finance the Aswan High Dam project. The British Prime Minister Sir Anthony Eden saw this action as a declaration of war, which threatened his country's position in the Middle East. Joint military planning with the French began in August 1956; meanwhile, military reservists were recalled and a large task force assembled to undertake the first Allied invasion since the Second World War.

In October 1956 French representatives secretly met with their opposite numbers and proposed a plan in which the Israelis would attack Egypt on a predetermined date, following which the British and French would call for a cease-fire. Israel had to be seen to be attacking the Suez Canal, which would be used as the basis for British and French intervention.

On 29 October the Israelis invaded Egypt on the pretext of throwing back the Egyptian forces which threatened their border, and seizing control of the Sinai Peninsula. The attack was made by 400 paratroopers in the Mitla Pass, 30 miles east of Suez. The British and French governments immediately issued a 12-hour ultimatum to both countries to withdraw their forces; Egypt refused to obey the conditions of the ultimatum and the Allies began the first moves to destroy the Egyptian Air Force.

Britain and France mobilised their forces for a coordinated assault on Egypt, code-named Operation 'Musketeer'. Such military action was considered necessary to oust Nasser and restore a government that would

The Nile Delta and the Suez Canal. (*Colin Richardson*)

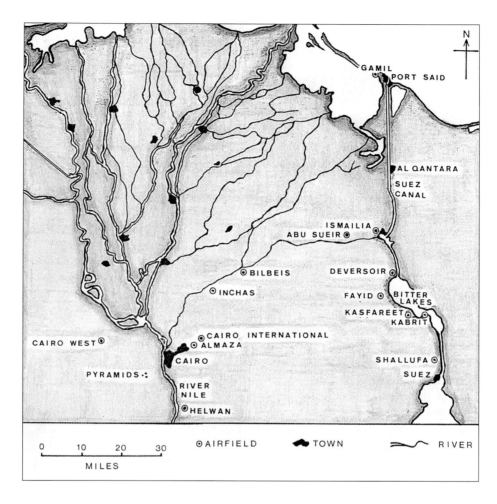

be more sympathetic to the West. With the political complications in the Middle East, Cyprus was considered to be the only base in the eastern Mediterranean able to offer a reasonable security of tenure for air operations; its two principal airfields at Akrotiri and Nicosia were some 250 miles from the centre of the Suez Canal, or 35–40 minutes' flying time for a jet aircraft.

Akrotiri was a completely new and large military airfield, which was officially opened in October 1955. It was still under construction the following April when the Venoms of 6 Squadron (Sqn Ldr P.C. Ellis DFC) arrived from Habbaniya to join the Meteors of 13 Squadron. The airfield still

lacked the facilities for operational units and 6 Squadron's buildings consisted of a few huts and a large tent, with the airmen being accommodated in Cawood prefabricated semi-detached buildings. The situation had barely improved the following August/ September when 8 Squadron (Sqn Ldr C.I. Blyth DFC, AFC) and 249 Squadron (Sqn Ldr J.R. Maitland DFC (US)) flew in to make up the Venom Strike Wing, totalling some forty-seven aircraft.

Other fighter squadrons in the area included the Venom FB.1s of 32 Squadron (Sqn Ldr A.H.W. Gilchrist DFC), which had moved from Malta to Amman in August 1956 as a precautionary measure to defend

Jordan against any possible incursion, under the Anglo/Jordanian treaty. Meanwhile, 73 Squadron (Sqn Ldr J.F. Manning, AFC) found itself 'stranded' at Khormaksar, having flown there in July 1956 to relieve 8 Squadron, which had departed to Nicosia for its APC.

Operational training began almost immediately, with the Venoms' 20mm cannon being 'spread harmonised' to maximise the effect of the rounds. The main features of the training included high-angle rocketing, air-to-air firing, ground-attack exercises with a ground-control team and low-level attacks on the island's key military positions. There was also valuable training with the Royal Artillery's L70 anti-aircraft guns, of which there were over sixty at Akrotiri alone.

At the outbreak of hostilities the Egyptian Air Force (EAF) was the largest air force in the Middle East with an estimated strength of 168 jet fighters (mainly MiG-15s, Vampires and Meteors), 49 Il-28 'Beagle' jet bombers, and some 200 piston-engined transport, training and communications aircraft. The effectiveness of the EAF was, however, untested, and a shortage of experienced crews and technicians was considered to limit its operational usefulness.

The air attacks against Egypt would be divided into three phases:

Phase 1: Neutralisation of airfields, which included the destruction of enemy aircraft on the ground and in the air. The RAF would attack its former bases in the Canal Zone, including Abu Sueir, Deversoir, Fayid, Kabrit, Kasfareet and Shallufa, while the Royal Navy would concentrate on those in the Nile Delta at Cairo West, Cairo International, Almaza, Inchas, Bilbeis and Dekheila.

Phase 2: Air attacks against armour, mechanised vehicles and all forms of army support.

Phase 3: Close support for the parachute drop and joint assault on Port Said.

Most of the crews at Akrotiri were aware of the build-up of the strike force. Flt Lt J.A. 'Harry' Harrison was the senior flight commander with 6 Squadron:

Two things stick in my mind which indicated to me that operations were imminent: these were the reinforcement of all three Venom squadrons with a few additional pilots (three, I think), and French Mystere fighters staging through Akrotiri on their way to Israel. The world had been told that there was collusion. The month before Suez could be said to have been a work-up period. We carried out rocket-firing, air-to-ground firing, air-to-air firing, high-level combat training, low-level strikes and army cooperation training. We did not combine training with any other units, although armament training was considered a regular part of every week on the squadron.

The build-up of Allied aircraft continued, and on the eve of operations Akrotiri was filled to capacity with RAF units operating Venoms, Hunters, PR Canberras and Meteor night-fighters. In addition there were a further three French fighter and reconnaissance squadrons flying Republic F-84F Thunderstreaks and RF-84F Thunderflashes. In total, there were 115 aircraft. At Nicosia were seven RAF Canberra bomber units detached from the UK, while at nearby Tymbou airfield ten RAF and French transport units were at readiness. Added to this the Malta Bomber Wing at Luqa and Hal Far comprised Valiants, Canberras and Shackletons from the UK, together with Hunter and Meteor fighters based at Takali.

Flg Off Tony Gronert of 249 Squadron recalled:

We had a feeling of frustration at the massive build-up taking place. It was generally thought that we were ready operationally from the time we had arrived in Cyprus and that we had no doubts about our ability to achieve air supremacy in a

The Carrier Air Group of HMS *Eagle*, November 1956. Visible on the flight deck are the Sea Venom 21s of 892 and 893 Squadrons, the Sea Hawks of 897 and 899 Squadrons, the Wyverns of 830 Squadron and the Skyraiders of A Flight, 849 Squadron. (*FAA Museum*)

couple of days. During October the Venom Wing was flying a large number of 'Alert Patrol' sorties, with security at the base tightened up considerably. The aircraft had 'invasion' markings painted on and all squadron insignia were removed. Another change which removed our identity was the use of 'Mission Numbers' instead of the squadron callsign.

In the Mediterranean the squadrons embarked on the Fleet Air Arm's strike carrier HMS *Albion*, which had completed six weeks of intensive working-up when she sailed from Malta on 29 October and joined HMS *Eagle* and *Bulwark*. The three carriers,

together with two Royal Navy Commando carriers, proceeded towards the eastern Mediterranean and by 31 October they were about 150 miles off the Nile Delta. *Bulwark*'s Air Group comprised three Sea Hawk squadrons, while *Albion*'s Air Group consisted of two Sea Hawk squadrons and the Sea Venom FAW.21s of 809 Squadron (Lt Cdr R.A. Shilcock). Embarked on *Eagle* were two Sea Hawk and one Wyvern squadron, together with two Sea Venom units, 892 Squadron (Lt Cdr M.H.J. Petrie) and 893 Squadron (Lt Cdr M.W. Henley DSC). This gave a total of 107 aircraft at sea, including 25 Sea Venoms.

Lt John de Winton was a pilot with 809 Squadron on board HMS *Albion*:

No. 809 Squadron embarked in HMS *Albion* in the Channel on 15 September. The ship sailed direct to the Med and we started flying as we approached and passed Gibraltar. We remained embarked until 12 October and continued flying and exercising, often in company with *Eagle* and *Bulwark*. Exercises included a major 'Musketeer' rehearsal between 2 and 6 October with much close air support and forward air controller practice. No. 809 disembarked to Hal Far from 12 to 23 October and continued flying. After re-embarking on 23 October we remained in the Malta area for a few days and sailed to the eastern Mediterranean. Much of the time was spent in preparing for war and painting the aircraft with yellow and black stripes.

The CO of 249 Squadron was the Korean War veteran Sqn Ldr J.R. 'Jock' Maitland:

In June 1956 I set off in my Proctor (G-AKYP) to take command of 249 Squadron, which was based in Amman. All went well until I reached Mersa Matruh in Western Egypt, where I was detained and roughly treated by one individual, who was convinced that I was a spy. The Air Attaché in Cairo eventually secured my release after three days.

Among us all was a certainty that war with Egypt would come soon and we worked to get the maximum numbers of aircraft serviceable and to put in as much range practice as possible. Our squadron was brought up to mobile standards and the dispersal was filled with ambulances, fire engines, water carriers and trucks.

Two squadrons of French RF-84Fs arrived on 31 October; highly efficient, tents and all. Awkward items, like liquid oxygen and rocket-assisted take-off gear, were included, along with their own photographic aircraft and facilities to process the results. They put us to shame, and if they had controlled the operation we would have occupied the Canal Zone before world opinion turned against us.

Operation 'Musketeer' officially began on 31 October when RAF and French reconnaissance aircraft took photographs of Egyptian airfields. This was followed by an attack on Cairo International by Canberra and Valiant bombers during the night. On 1 November British and French ship- and shore-based fighters launched their attack on the four bombed Egyptian airfields, while five more in the Canal Zone were strafed and bombed. The assault opened up soon after daybreak when two sections of four aircraft from 6 Squadron took off from Akrotiri to make the first strike by RAF Venom aircraft against Egypt. The first section was led by the squadron's commanding officer, Sqn Ldr Peter Ellis. 'Harry' Harrison led the second section: 'I led the first strike against Fayid and Abu Sueir. We arrived over the target at 0604 hours and our eight rockets per aircraft were fired into the hangars and MiG fighters, with our front guns being used to destroy the Meteors.'

Air Marshal Sir David Harcourt-Smith was a Flight Lieutenant with 8 Squadron: 'I flew two sorties on 1 November, the first against Fayid and Abu Sueir airfields and the second against Kabrit airfield. In all cases the primary target was the destruction of the Egyptian Air Force and in particular the MiG-15s. Most of the aircraft were either in hangars – they left the doors open and you could see bits of the MiGs – or they were camouflaged out in the open.'

Two sections from 249 Squadron, led by Sqn Ldr 'Jock' Maitland and Flt Lt Doug Dallison, were dispatched against Fayid and Abu Sueir. At least six MiGs and a number of transport aircraft were destroyed in a surprise rocket attack. Sqn Ldr 'Jock' Maitland recalled: 'The nerves of the Venom Wing at Akrotiri were taut with anticipation.

Formation of 249 Squadron Venom FB.4s (including WR431 and WR499) over the Troodos Mountains in Cyprus for the squadron's 1956 Christmas card. The Suez markings applied to the tail-booms are already beginning to fade. (*Tony Gronert*)

Although we were given orders to attack El Arish on the Israeli–Egyptian border at dawn on 1 November the mission was cancelled and we subsequently flew a strike against Kabrit and Kasfareet, where we destroyed MiG fighters and damaged the hangars.'

Tony Gronert flew as No. 3 in the section led by Flt Lt Dallison: 'We were the first section off, with our target being the MiG-15 base at Kabrit. We all had a good strike on aircraft parked neatly in lines on the dispersal area. Following our rocket attack we flew on to Abu Sueir where we attacked further MiGs and motor transport targets. It appeared that the Egyptian Air Force was completely taken by surprise and at that time had made no attempt to hide or disperse its aircraft, though some that survived were very skilfully hidden in sunken blister hangars.' Later that afternoon the same section attacked Abu Sueir with rockets and Fayid with 20mm cannon fire. Tony Gronert destroyed a Meteor during the second attack. Flt Lt Mike Waterhouse and Flg Off Tom Lecky-Thompson went on to strafe and rocket the airfields at Fayid, Kasfareet and Kabrit, destroying at least six MiGs and a Vampire trainer.

At 0520 hours four Sea Venoms of 809 Squadron, led by Lt Cdr Shilcock and

accompanied by four Sea Hawks of 802 Squadron, were launched from HMS *Albion*; their target was the airfield of Almaza, 6 miles east of Cairo, where MiG-15s and Il-28s were attacked with rockets and 20mm cannon, as were the hangars adjoining the runway. The mass naval assault launched during the morning from the carriers *Eagle*, *Bulwark* and *Albion* against the airfields of Cairo West, Almaza and Inchas was considered successful, with at least fifty-eight EAF aircraft destroyed. The opposition proved almost negligible: the only EAF fighter seen was a MiG-15 on 'finals' at Almaza, and only lack of fuel prevented Lt Davidson of 809 Squadron from attacking it. The strikes continued throughout the day on a 1 hour 5 minute cycle, and only light and inaccurate flak was encountered from AA defences around the airfields. The 'one pass and away' principle was adhered to strictly at first until it was realised that the opposition was non-existent in places. At Bilbeis there was no defence at all and about a hundred training aircraft were found scattered around the airfield. The attacking navy fighters circled in a continuous racetrack pattern until a shortage of fuel or ammunition forced them to return to HMS *Albion*.

Lt Nigel Anderdon of 893 Squadron flew thirteen sorties during the six-day conflict, during which he destroyed five aircraft and damaged a further four. During his first sortie on 1 November he attacked Cairo West, with Sub Lt Walsh as his Observer:

We had two aircraft hit by Egyptian fire. I got a very small piece of shrapnel in my starboard wing on my very first strike. It seemed a big bang, but did no real damage. I felt annoyed though, and when I saw four Vampires being serviced at the end of a big hangar I was determined to get my own back. I fired over 700 rounds in one burst, firing from about 2½ miles in to 200 yd. Three Vampires caught fire and bits came off the fourth.

Lt John de Winton remarked: 'My logbook shows that my first sortie was a CAP [Combat Air Patrol] for the Task Force from 0635 to 0750 hours. My second sortie from 0845 to 1000 hours was an attack on Inchas airfield to strafe aircraft on the ground, during which I was able to claim a MiG-15.'

Lt John Hackett was the Senior Observer of 809 Squadron: 'The squadron launched the first strike for the Fleet Air Arm, when we attacked Almaza at 0601 hours. I flew as observer to the CO, Lt Cdr Ron Shilcock, in Sea Venom XG670 and we were able to damage five MiG-15s. Three subsequent missions during the day were flown as CAPs.'

Harry Harrison got into a skirmish with two unidentified aircraft:

We were returning from the first strike at high level (at least 35,000ft) and in battle formation when my no. 2 [Flg Off Bryan Hurn] called 'Two MiGs turning in'. I immediately called 'Break into them', and as a light Venom turns very quickly we soon found ourselves behind and getting close. We were ready to fire and I had started to range my gunsight on one of them. At this stage they were obviously very surprised and both rolled and went

straight down, probably supersonic. As they turned, American markings could be seen very clearly, and we identified them as Grumman F9F-8 Cougars once we had returned to base. It turned out that we had overflown the American Sixth Fleet on our way from the target.

In the afternoon I led another four-aircraft strike against Abu Sueir and Kabrit, and this time we destroyed more MiGs. No effort had been made by the Egyptians to disperse their aircraft, which made it easy to line up an attack and destroy several aircraft in one pass. Most were fully fuelled and lit up very quickly when hit by our 20mm explosive rounds.

The last RAF Venom strike of the day was against Abu Sueir and Kabrit, where 6 Squadron found a large number of MiG-15s still intact. Seven of the Egyptian fighters were destroyed in the ensuing rocket attack at Abu Sueir, and a further four at Kabrit. Harry Harrison recalled: 'I led a section of four aircraft on a strike on Abu Sueir and then on to Kabrit. We destroyed quite a few of the dispersed MiGs – probably between six and nine. Several anti-aircraft guns fired at us and I took one out on my second dive with two rockets. Other sandbagged gun positions were attacked by others in my section using either rockets and guns, with good effect.'

Photo-reconnaissance reports confirmed that the first 24 hours of operations had caused extensive damage to EAF runways and hangars. The three RAF Venom squadrons had flown 104 sorties and jointly claimed 59 EAF aircraft, together with 11 probables and 37 damaged. Individual claims for all the FAA Sea Venom squadrons are not available. However, the total FAA claims for the day were put at 80 aircraft destroyed, 9 probables and 85 damaged. The squadron diary for 892 Squadron records that some twenty-one sorties were flown during the day, either as CAP or as strikes against Cairo

A Venom FB.4 of 8 Squadron returns to Akrotiri after a sortie over Egypt, 2 November 1956. It carries the code letter B, but the serial is obliterated by the 'Suez stripes'. (*8 Squadron*)

West, Almaza and Bilbeis, during which four MiGs, four Harvards, two Lancasters and an Il-28 were destroyed, plus another six aircraft damaged.

Following further overnight raids by RAF Valiants and Canberras against EAF bases, the RAF Venom Wing was again airborne from Akrotiri at 0515 hours for the first of the next day's strikes. Throughout the early part of the day 6 Squadron flew three ground-attack operations against Shallufa, Kabrit and Abu Sueir, claiming one MiG-15 destroyed and a further six damaged. Hangars, buildings and soft-skinned vehicles (SSVs) were also strafed with cannon fire.

Two sections of Venoms from 8 Squadron, led by Sqn Ldr Blyth and Flt Lt Harcourt-Smith, were also able to make dawn attacks on Abu Sueir, Fayid and Kabrit, where many

of the dispersed aircraft were destroyed by cannon fire. No opposition was met from the EAF.

Meanwhile, 249 Squadron enjoyed similar success in their attacks against the airfields at Abu Sueir, Fayid and Kabrit, strafing and destroying MiG, Meteor and Vampire fighters, and bringing to forty-four the number of aircraft destroyed during the morning's strikes by the RAF. Tony Gronert again: 'Because of the lack of resistance from the ground, we were starting to diversify our targets. The first sortie was similar to the first day with an attack on Kabrit and Abu Sueir, where I was able to claim two MiGs and a Proctor. The second sortie was an armed recce between Deversoir, Geneifa and Fayid, where I possibly destroyed a tank and bowser.'

Inchas airfield under attack by the Sea Venoms of 809 Squadron, November 1956. The runways appear to have been hit, as do some of the concrete revetments. (*Lt Cdr John Hackett RN*)

The Sea Venoms of 809 Squadron were also active when they came to Action Stations at dawn and attacked Inchas airfield with four aircraft at 0559 hours. There was little sign of life and no aircraft were observed so the squadron opened fire on the control tower and hangars. Almaza was also attacked by two Sea Venoms, destroying a number of MiGs and Vampires. Four Sea Venoms of 892 Squadron made attacks on Cairo West and Bilbeis, claiming three Harvard trainers, a Chipmunk and a Fury – Lt Anderdon claimed the Chipmunk and one Harvard. As soon as it became apparent that the EAF posed no real threat to the Task Force, most of 809's efforts were directed towards ground-attacks against shore targets, and 'cab-rank' patrols where aircraft could be called down to attack individual targets.

Convinced that the EAF had been effectively destroyed, part of the Allied air effort was switched by mid-morning from the airfields to a large military transit camp at Huckstep near Almaza in the Nile Delta, where a number of tanks and military vehicles were destroyed in the face of intense and accurate AA fire. An attack by seven Venoms of 6 Squadron almost turned into a disaster because the intelligence briefing before the action was hopelessly inadequate. The crews had been assured that Huckstep would be poorly defended. As it was an important target it was decided that the Venoms would fire four of their rockets during the first dive, then regroup and return to fire the other four rockets from another direction. They arrived over the target at 10.25 hours and the first run went according to plan. However, after reforming for the second attack the Venoms were met by heavy AA and small-arms fire, which forced them to dive to ground level and make good their escape at high speed. Although all seven aircraft were able to return to base, three were hit, including one with a damaged wing and another with a hole in the rudder. Several tanks and SSVs were claimed as destroyed during the action.

Further attacks by French Air Force F-84s and sections of rocket-armed Venoms from 8 and 249 Squadrons against Huckstep Camp were continued until mid-afternoon, and further damage was inflicted against the tanks and military vehicles.

The last two missions for the day were strikes against Kabrit and Abu Sueir by 6 Squadron, where five MiG-15s, a Harvard and a FIAT trainer were claimed as destroyed. A little earlier, at 1700 hours, a combined attack by Sea Venoms from 892

and 893 Squadrons led by Lt Cdr Henley was launched from HMS *Eagle* against Almaza, where a MiG, a Vampire, a Spitfire and a Commando transport aircraft were destroyed. The Sea Venoms made their first attack against selected targets which were widely dispersed on the airfield. Re-forming to carry out their second attack, the fighters encountered opposition from 40mm Bofors anti-aircraft fire. Lt Cdr Wilcox was at 500ft when his Sea Venom (WW281) was hit in the vicinity of the gun bay by flak, rendering the hydraulics useless. Lew Wilcox escaped with just a minor cut on his right arm, but his navigator, Flg Off Bob Olding, suffered multiple shrapnel wounds in both legs. With no hydraulic power, Wilcox was forced to make an emergency belly-landing on the carrier. Following urgent treatment in the carrier's sick bay, Olding was flown to Cyprus where he unfortunately developed gangrene, requiring the amputation of one leg

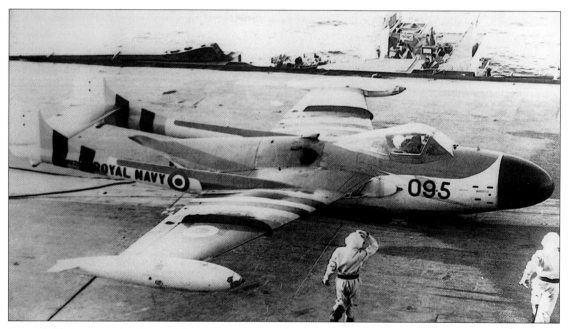

Damaged by flak during an attack on Almaza airfield, Sea Venom 21 WW281 of 893 Squadron was obliged to carry out a wheels-up landing on HMS *Eagle* on 2 November 1956. The navigator, Flt Lt R.C. Olding, was seriously injured by shrapnel during the attack. (*Royal Navy*)

above the knee to save his life. Both Wilcox and Olding were later awarded the DSC. Astonishingly, Olding subsequently continued his flying career with an artificial leg and eventually retired from the RAF in 1984 as a group captain.

Throughout that day 892 Squadron flew twenty sorties, either as CAP or as strikes against the airfields, claiming eight aircraft and a radar station destroyed. There had been no resistance during the attacks.

On 3 November it was officially announced that the Allied air offensive had virtually destroyed the EAF as an effective force. All Egyptian airfields had been seriously damaged and the aircraft destroyed. HMS *Albion* withdrew to replenish at sea, leaving the Sea Venoms of 892 and 893 Squadrons to concentrate on attacks against Almaza and Cairo West, where a variety of former British aircraft were strafed. Claims were submitted for Chipmunks, Meteors, Spitfires, Furies and Lancasters, together with a number of Dakotas, Harvards and MiG fighters.

The RAF Venom Strike Force's missions were switched from armed strikes on airfield targets to armed reconnaissance in specified areas. Targets were becoming increasingly difficult to find, but a strike by 6 Squadron against Kabrit claimed the only intact MiG. A further strike by a second section led by Sqn Ldr Peter Ellis strafed and destroyed two Meteor F.8s at Fayid, together with two Sherman armoured personnel carriers (APCs). Flg Off Colin Richardson described what happened:

I was not operational when the operations started, but I made such a nuisance of myself that my flight commander took me along. Although I had done some rocketing I had never fired the cannons at ground targets. My very first air-to-ground firing was on an Egyptian Meteor F.8 at Fayid. When we landed back at base the 'Boss', Sqn Ldr Peter Ellis, saw me getting out of the aircraft and made for

my flight commander and had a few words with him. Then the Boss came across to me and said: 'Colin, we can't have non-operational pilots doing this sort of thing. You're operational!'

I noted in my logbook that our target was some kind of tank park and that I destroyed a Sherman APC. I think that they were our own tanks and APCs stored in the Canal Zone, but we didn't want the Egyptians to get hold of them and use them against us.

During an armed reconnaissance sortie to the Deversoir area during the morning by a section of 249 Squadron Venoms, led by Flt Lt Tam Syme, the Venoms strafed and rocketed fuel bowsers, a tank transporter and some trucks. A further dawn reconnaissance sortie between al-Qantara and Ismailia by a section from 8 Squadron led by Flt Lt Doug Cater flew at low level to avoid the intense flak. As the aircraft turned along the road, 2 miles south of Ismailia, to select their targets, one of the Venoms (WR505) suddenly erupted in a ball of flame and cartwheeled into the ground. The pilot, Flt Lt A.E. 'Ted' Sheehan, a war reinforcement pilot, who had previously flown Venoms with 5 Squadron in Germany and had participated in the Royal Review flypast at Odiham in July 1953, was killed instantly. It is not clear whether the Venom was hit by flak.

The day's air action by the Venom Strike Wing ended with forty-eight sorties flown, during which fourteen EAF aircraft were claimed as destroyed, together with a large number of enemy tanks and vehicles. No. 8 Squadron flew thirty-two sorties, during which 94 rockets and over 6,000 rounds of 20mm ammunition were fired. In return, several of the Venoms returned to Akrotiri with flak damage, which was quickly repaired through the ingenuity of the hard-working groundcrews.

On 4 November the air assault was switched from bombing to cannon and rocket attacks on radar installations, coastal guns and AA batteries as a prelude to the Allied military landings. HMS *Albion* returned to station during the early hours of the morning, and then it was the turn of *Eagle* to be withdrawn for replenishment. An early morning attack against Cairo International by Sea Hawks and a section of Sea Venoms from 809 Squadron encountered some unexpected flak. John de Winton recalled: 'I was one of four 809 Squadron Sea Venoms on the early morning attack on Cairo International. We were getting a bit careless and there was more flak than we expected. We circled the airfield at about 4,000ft and someone else reported seeing flak bursts getting closer and closer to my tail, of which I was unaware. We made at least two low-level strafing runs over the airfield.' At 0700 hours two further sections of 809 Squadron's Sea Venoms were scrambled to locate three Egyptian E-Boats that had been harassing the naval Task Force north of the Nile Delta. The CAP leader had identified the three boats in a rapidly dispersing morning sea fog some 30 miles off Alexandria, and the 809 Squadron aircraft were joined by a section of Sea Hawks for the strike. Two of the boats were sunk during the ensuing rocket and cannon attack, and the third was damaged, although it was allowed to pick up survivors and return to Alexandria.

No. 6 Squadron flew fourteen operational sorties throughout the day. Attacks were made against the airfields at Abu Sueir and Gamil, where a MiG-15 and Vampire trainer were destroyed. Radar installation sites near Gamil airfield were also attacked and put out of action. Just before midday a third, long-range, mission was mounted to destroy tanks in a large army camp at Giza, a few miles south-west of the great pyramids. Fitted with underwing tanks, the Venoms had enough range (365nm) to reach the target, but it was considered prudent to shut down for refuelling

on the end of the runway immediately before take-off. Despite all the planning the attack was largely abortive, with the first aircraft being unable to fire its rockets and the pilot of the second failing to find the tanks, which had been hidden among some tents. The second pair misjudged their pull-up point, so no rockets were fired during the mission, although several SSVs were strafed by cannon fire. The last mission of the day was led by the B Flight Commander, Flt Lt Alan Keys, when more tarpaulin-covered tanks at Huckstep were attacked with rockets and cannon fire. The target area was shrouded in smoke following an earlier attack by French Thunderstreaks, and the Venoms were met by light but accurate AA fire. Several aircraft were slightly damaged, including the Venom flown by Flg Off Joe Daniels – who subsequently found pieces of the front axle of an SSV embedded in his port wing!

Both 8 and 249 Squadrons were also busy, attacking gun emplacements and armoured vehicles. Flg Off Richard Hadlow of 8 Squadron was a member of a section that attacked gun emplacements at al-Raswa, led by the CO: 'We arrived over the target at 0830 and I was hit in the wing by flak. It caused little damage, but entered the wing tip so as to trigger the tip-tank jettison mechanism – thus I lost the tank. Had this happened at the southern end of the Canal I would have run out of fuel on the way back, but it happened over Port Said and I just made it.'

At 0715 on 5 November 600 British paratroopers were dropped at El Gamil airfield during a fifteen-minute operation; their objectives were to storm the control tower and eliminate the enemy from the perimeters of the airfield. They were sup-ported by a further 500 French paratroopers who were dropped at nearby Port Faud. With top cover provided by RAF Hunters, the force encountered no air opposition and only a little flak as the RAF Valetta and Hastings transport aircraft went in at 600ft.

Air support for the landings began at 0655 when the Venoms of 6 Squadron attacked airfield buildings at Gamil; the lack of any significant military targets had meant a change of tactics for the squadron, and the strike included a rocket attack on the control tower by Sqn Ldr Ellis. The tower was left in flames. Colin Richardson recalled:

I was in the last formation of Venoms at Gamil airfield before the paratroopers arrived. My logbook shows that we left ten minutes before the paratroopers dropped on to it, and I remember seeing the transport aircraft on their way in as we were returning to Akrotiri. We needed to damage anti-aircraft gun emplacements, etc., but I think that they may have already been destroyed, and I remember putting a rocket into the Air Traffic Control tower. But we were not allowed to fire on the beach huts, which were owned by the Egyptian civilians. This was a mistake because they contained Egyptian soldiers who fired on our soldiers, or so I was told.

The squadron's third mission of the day involved an attack on a convoy of troop lorries about 25 miles from the coast, heading north across the desert towards the Port Said area. Sixteen of the lorries were destroyed in the ensuing attack.

Tanks, vehicles and gun positions on the mole at Port Said were also targeted by 8 and 249 Squadrons, the latter having flown eight flak suppression sorties before the arrival of the transport aircraft. A total of twenty sorties were flown by the Venom Strike Wing throughout the morning, including attacks by 8 Squadron on Shallufa, Kabrit and Kasfareet, followed by an armed recon-naissance of the Ismailia/al-Qantara area.

During the night the Carrier Strike Force had sailed to a position some 40 or 50 miles to the north of Port Said, and all possible aircraft were employed on cab-rank missions in support of the parachute drop, while the necessary CAP was also maintained. At least three attacks on targets that were holding up the advance of the paratroopers were made by the rocket-armed Sea Venoms of 809 Squadron, the aircraft being talked down onto the targets by teams of air controllers who had parachuted in with the Commandos. No. 809 Squadron, led by Lt Cdr Ron Shilcock, went into action at 0720, when a tank dug into the ground outside a hospital was destroyed. John Hackett's logbook recorded the day's events: 'Four Cab-ranks flown between 0730 and 1620 – six Sea Venoms every two hours; RP and 20mm. Attacked dug-in tanks with RPs, mortar positions, trucks (flamer) and troops.'

The seventeen sorties flown by 892 Squadron during the day included strikes against Almaza (where two MiG-15s were destroyed), cab-rank sorties for army support and CAP or armed reconnaissances. Two moored MTBs were also attacked, with one claimed as destroyed and the other left on fire.

Further strikes during the evening by 8 Squadron against Huckstep Camp and an armed reconnaissance by 249 Squadron meant that the Venoms had to return to Akrotiri in the dark. Many had been damaged during the day's action (mainly by flying debris and ricochets from the ground attacks), and once again the crews toiled throughout the night to have the aircraft serviceable for the following morning's work.

On the day the paratroopers were dropped at El Gamil airfield the Soviet Union threatened military intervention to restore peace in the area. The possibility of nuclear attack could not be ruled out. Eisenhower himself was opposed to the military action, and refused to back the Allies. He also felt personally betrayed by Eden and was instrumental in the United States' blocking of Britain's application to the International Monetary Fund for drawing rights to ease its economic problems.

The United Nations was under pressure from the American and Russian governments to secure an immediate cease-fire. There was little alternative but to order a cessation of hostilities at midnight the following day. However, despite the impending cease-fire, it was decided that the Allied paratroopers would be unable to capture Port Said without the planned landing by Commandos the following morning. Thus at 0215 hours on 6 November the pilots of the three Venom squadrons at Akrotiri were awakened by a loudspeaker van that instructed them to report to the Wing Operations briefing room. The assembled crews were informed by the station commander that an attack had been ordered to eliminate a group of guns in concrete emplacements on the west mole breakwater in Port Said, and that a maximum effort was required from them immediately. Although it was appreciated that the attack would only, at best, do superficial damage, there was a possibility that the guns could be used against the Allied fleet during the invasion. The Venom attacks would therefore have the effect of either driving the Egyptian gunners away or keeping their heads down.

Taking off in darkness the thirty-one Venoms were confronted by a large cumulonimbus cloud over the airfield, extending to 40,000ft, with violent lightning, heavy rain and extreme turbulence. In the absence of Sqn Ldr Ellis, whose aircraft went unserviceable on start up, Sqn Ldr Maitland of 249 Squadron took over as master bomber, calling in each section of aircraft in turn to avoid the possibility of collision with so many aircraft over the target area in the half-light. It is thought that only half of the rockets from the strike actually hit the eight gun emplacements on the breakwater, although the later sea-borne assault encountered no firing from these positions. Harry Harrison again:

I was instructed to lead the strike, with 8 and 249 Squadrons following behind. Weather conditions on take-off were atrocious with a very large thunderstorm right over the airfield. If it had not been important for the strike to take place at or before dawn, I am sure that the whole thing would have been delayed. The climb-out in pitch darkness – except when broken by vivid lightning which then made it appear even darker – in severe turbulence and the frightening clatter of heavy rain or hail on the aircraft was one of the most memorable ten minutes in my 20,000 hours of flying. It was made all the more difficult by the fact that the aircraft were very heavy with full fuel and eight rockets. I arrived out of the cloud with my four aircraft still in formation but most sections had lost at least one or two and some were split completely into single aircraft. In the meantime, Sqn Ldr Ellis had taken off in a spare aircraft and by flying flat out had managed to arrive over the target and had taken over his directing duties for the remaining sections.

Several pilots also reported being shadowed by a MiG fighter. Their sightings were confirmed by Flg Off Nigel Budd of 6 Squadron who spotted the fighter over Gamil after the strike on the mole. Instead of the expected Egyptian roundels, the MiG was carrying the red Russian star; although Budd was within 500 yd of the fighter when he gave chase and was able to fire a long burst at it, the Russian fighter was well out of range and accelerated away to the east.

Tony Gronert's section arrived over the Port Said area at first light and encountered some determined resistance:

There were a couple of smallish guns which were taken out without any trouble and we did a sweep along the beach to where the paratroops had established positions at Port Said airfield. I had not had the opportunity to fire my rockets owing to the fact that there were no targets in the vicinity, so I brought them home with me. When we arrived back at base the groundcrew found that my aircraft had been hit by small-arms fire and they gave me a piece of shrapnel taken from near my foot. They also found that the electric cable to my rockets had been severed by a bullet, so I could not have fired them even if I had wanted to.

Flg Off Dave Williams of 249 Squadron remembered:

The weather in the Cyprus area and en route to Egypt was poor to say the least. My main memory is of flying tight formation on the leader with the only reference point being my navigation light illuminating the tip-tank of his Venom. It was dark, wet and stormy so to lose sight meant that you were on your own, in the cloud, with upwards of thirty Venoms in close proximity. We attacked the gun installations at Port Said and met some stiff resistance. Unbeknown to me at the time, the underside of my Venom was hit by shrapnel, which penetrated the lower engine cowl and pierced a burner can.

The seaborne assault on Port Said by the Royal Marines of 40 and 42 Commandos went ahead at 0545 and the town was occupied following brief but stiff resistance; their orders were to join up with the paratroopers and secure the Suez Canal. The Sea Venom squadrons were detailed to carry out cab-rank sorties over the beachhead, with the first being launched by 809 Squadron from *Albion* at 0615. *Bulwarks*' catapults were not serviceable until 0900, which prevented the first four Sea Venoms from getting airborne for their patrol over the beaches until 0910. Further patrols during the day included an armed recce to Port Said and Ismailia, where several tanks and SSVs were strafed, and a search was carried out for a

pilot who had ejected in the desert near al-Qantara.

No. 892 Squadron flew sixteen sorties throughout the day, during which a MTB at Ras Ada Biya and a number of Bren gun carriers at al-Kirsh Camp were destroyed. Meanwhile, 893 Squadron attacked Almaza, following which claims were submitted for a Meteor, a Harvard and two Furies. Nigel Anderdon put in a claim for one of the Furies; earlier in the day he was involved in the attack on the mole breakwater: 'We eventually became a bit blasé about the AA guns because "Nobby" Hall called me as his no. 2 to fly high over the target [the gun on the end of the Suez breakwater], while he strafed from the back. I did a large barrel roll at about 600ft, dropping the nose on to the target. "Nobby" came in low, the results of his strafing attack causing a large explosion in the gun revetment. I strafed for luck, but I don't think there was much left by then.'

The RAF Venom Strike Force was also engaged in armed reconnaissance sorties, attacking road and rail traffic in the al-Qantara/Ismailia area. A suspected ammunition dump in a wire compound at al-Qantara camp was strafed by Flg Off Colin Richardson of 6 Squadron – and it immediately erupted as boxes of landmines exploded. Colin Richardson's last trip of the day included a rocket attack on a steam locomotive pulling a passenger train towards the Canal Zone; it was suspected of carrying soldiers. Both 8 and 249 Squadrons were similarly engaged on attacking targets of opportunity, including fuel bowsers, vehicles and ammunition dumps.

At 2359 hours on 6 November the Anglo-French forces called a cease-fire, and for many at Akrotiri the next few days were spent on maintenance or on stand-by. The Carrier Strike Force (especially the Sea Venoms of 809 Squadron) was still carrying out occasional armed reconnaissance patrols over the Port Said area. The ensuing period proved to be rather an anticlimax for the crews, who felt annoyed at not being allowed to complete the operation. Despite their losses, morale in the squadrons remained high, with some finding time for reflection and self-analysis. Sqn Ldr Maitland:

The squadron pilots gathered at Akrotiri must have constituted one of the most experienced teams ever brought together in peacetime, with superb standards of gunnery and rocketry. The more senior pilots were on anything up to their fourth or fifth tour on fighter squadrons.

We had three days to destroy the Egyptian Air Force, an insult to a wing such as ours against inexperienced opposition. By the second day we were circling airfields at low level trying to find MiGs. We lost no aircraft and destroyed the EAF on the ground in a day. We felt no animosity towards them, and catching their trucks on the Cairo road we always flew over to let everyone get clear before opening fire.

Between 6 and 29 November negotiations took place to replace the Allied troops with a UN Emergency Force. Meanwhile, the British and French forces occupied positions on the banks of the Suez Canal, and ships of the Task Force lay at anchor in the approaches to Port Said. In a show of force to deter any form of attack, the Sea Venoms continued to mount CAPs or armed reconnaissance patrols over the area.

Although strongly disputed by the Egyptian authorities, the initial British estimates for the number of EAF aircraft destroyed or damaged by air attack were put at 229 destroyed, 24 probables and 239 damaged by the Venoms and F-84s from Akrotiri, the Fleet Air Arm aircraft and the RAF bombing attacks. Those destroyed included 104 MiG-15s, 11 Meteors, 30

Vampires, 26 Il-28s, and 63 training or support aircraft (this figure includes an unspecified number of Fury ground-attack aircraft that had been earlier placed into store). During the six days of operations the Venoms were credited with 101 enemy aircraft destroyed, 12 probables and 16 damaged. The Akrotiri Venom Strike Wing had flown 94 missions, involving some 396 sorties.

It is known that many of the aircraft supplied to the EAF from Russia had been flown to safety in neighbouring Syria and Saudi Arabia before the crisis, and of the large number of MiG fighters reported as destroyed during the operation AM Sir David Harcourt-Smith comments: 'There are conflicting views of how successful the attacks against the aircraft parked on the airfields were. Pilots at the time reported a high strike rate, and with the benefit of hindsight there was a fair number of decoy MiGs on the airfields. The fact that a large number of aircraft had been flown out to other bases and that MiGs were not seen during the five days of operations seems to suggest that some of the successes were against these decoys.'

While decoy aircraft were certainly deployed on the Egyptian airfields, another RAF pilot offers a different opinion as to the number of claims submitted during the ground-attack operations: 'I do not recall seeing any decoys at airfields we attacked, and it is quite apparent what is a real aircraft when attacking in the ground-attack role, particularly when the fuel tanks explode after being hit by HE rounds. It is possible, however, that some of the claims later in the week were for aircraft that had already been destroyed and were attacked again because there was nothing else to target.'

Squadron claims taken from the Operational Record Books are as follows:

Unit	Destroyed	Probables	Damaged	Sorties	20mm	Rockets
6 Squadron	28	0	21	128	32,720	491
8 Squadron	43	6	30	134	34,920	490
249 Squadron	30	6	15	134	20,947	430

With the exception of 892 Squadron, individual squadron claims are not available for the Fleet Air Arm's Sea Venoms. However, the total sorties flown by the carrier-based squadrons are as follows:

Carrier	Sorties Flown	Destroyed	Probables	Damaged
HMS *Bulwark*	Figures not available	33	6	65
HMS *Eagle*	621	59	6	48
HMS *Albion*	415	36	0	60

For the sake of continuity, the total number of operational sorties flown by 892 Squadron during the period are:

1 November: 21 sorties as CAP or strikes; 11 aircraft destroyed and 6 damaged.
2 November: 20 sorties as CAP or strikes; 10 aircraft destroyed and 1 damaged.
3 November: 20 sorties as CAP or strikes; 6 aircraft destroyed, plus 1 radar station.
4 November: Carrier withdrawn for replenishment.
5 November: 17 sorties as CAP or strikes; 2 aircraft destroyed, plus 2 MTB.
6 November: 16 sorties as CAP or strikes; 1 MTB destroyed, plus 5 Bren gun carriers.

In addition, 809 Squadron claimed twenty-two EAF aircraft as destroyed or damaged on the ground, two E-boats sunk and another damaged, together with a large number of vehicles also destroyed during ground-attacks.

The crisis had raised real fears of a Third World War; it divided Britain and ended in humiliation and failure. Several lessons had been learnt, however, and the operation highlighted the speed, mobility and flexibility of the carrier-borne attack force. This was due to a combination of three factors: the short range from ship to target (which gave a longer time over target); the quick aircraft turn-rounds; and the continuous pressure that could be applied with the three carriers flying a staggered operating cycle. (This was in contrast to the periodic peak efforts of the long-range RAF aircraft.)

The effectiveness of the Allied air attacks was also demonstrated, and although the strike operations carried out by the Sea Hawks, Sea Venoms and Wyverns should not be overlooked, the brunt of the ground attacks fell to the RAF Venoms. Fitted with tip-tanks, under wing drop-tanks and a full armament load, the Venoms were able to reach all of their targets from Akrotiri – including those at the very southern end of the canal – and still have enough time at ground level to complete their attacks. Rockets were confirmed as the best weapon for attacks on hard targets that cannon shells would not penetrate, such as tanks, whereas 20mm cannon was the best weapon against SSVs and aircraft. Rounds carried were both high explosive and incendiary.

Most of the 6 Squadron pilots who took part in the Suez operation are depicted in this photograph, taken at Akrotiri on 27 November 1956. They are (from left to right): Nigel Budd, Dougie Lang, Brian Clinch, Steve Palmer, Len Morgan, Dave Stuart, Sedge Norris, Bryan Hurn, Sqn Ldr George Elliott, Harry Harrison, Roy Duggins and Alan Keys. The two dogs, Tangy and Rusty, did not take part in any of the operations! (*Colin Richardson*)

On 7 November HMS *Eagle* returned to Malta for repairs. A structural failure in her starboard catapult during late October had meant that she had operated throughout the crisis with only one fully serviceable catapult. *Bulwark* and *Albion* remained on station until 29 November, when they also returned to Malta; the squadrons disembarked to Hal Far three days later. Following an air defence exercise against the RAF fighter squadrons at Akrotiri, the carriers and their air groups returned to Port Said in mid-December to cover the evacuation of Port Said. Code-named Exercise 'Harridan', the withdrawal of troops began on 19 December, with the Sea Venoms providing combat air patrols over the fleet in case of a final air threat. With E-Day on 22 December and the last troops safely out, the carriers disembarked at Malta two days later.

On 17 December 1956 the 8 Squadron crews returned to Khormaksar by courtesy of RAF Transport Command, because of the ban on fighter aircraft flying over Arab countries; their Venom 4s were left behind for 73 Squadron, which returned from Aden four days later.

While 8 Squadron continued its anti-terrorist operations in the Aden Protectorate, 32 Squadron also returned from Mafraq as part of the major changes to the MEAF Venom Wing when, between January and August 1957, the four fighter squadrons – 6, 32, 73 and 249 – re-equipped with English Electric Canberra light bombers.

SUEZ 1956 –
A VENOM GROUND-ATTACK SORTIE

What was it like to fly an operational sortie in a Venom? Colin Richardson was a young first tourist on 6 Squadron at Akrotiri in November 1956, and was not yet operational when the Suez operation started. In 1957 he put together his recollections, allowing us to share the excitement and apprehension of his first sortie when he attacked the Egyptian airfield at Kabrit and a tank park.

During the first few days of the Suez operations I was a frustrated bystander while the operational pilots destroyed the Egyptian MiG-15s on the ground. I made a real nuisance of myself to my flight commander, Harry Harrison, pestering him to take me on an operational trip. On the third day of the operations, he suddenly announced: 'I've got you down for a trip today. You're number two to me on a four ship.' And there was my name on the board. Great!

We pile into a Landrover and drive to the operations tent. A full briefing on the task, issue of gold coins and check the rest of the escape kit, and then back to the squadron. We buckle on our revolvers as the flight leader briefs us: 'Well, you know what it's all about, it's the tank park until we get bored. Then we'll look round for anything interesting, including the airfield, which is our secondary. All procedures SOP, and remember it's radio silence until we get there. So keep your mouths shut and your eyes open. OK, let's go!'

We sign out in the books and walk out to the four Venoms. I wonder what it's going to be like. What if a fuel tank is punctured or the engine damaged? It would be desperate to eject over Egypt. I wonder what they would do to you? It might happen. On the other hand it might not. It's too late to worry now.

That's my aircraft, 'George' in the recently superseded phonetic alphabet. It has eight 60lb rockets under the wings, and a red flag askew in the nose-wheel door to show that the guns are armed – all four 20mm cannons. The squadron markings have been removed. Instead there are black and yellow stripes round the tail booms and wings, standing out from the drab camouflage paint. All the Allied aircraft have these markings. A quick inspection of the aircraft and everything looks normal. The oleos look a bit flat, but with a full war load and full underwing tanks it's hardly surprising. I'm glad it's my own aircraft. It's getting old and dirty, but for some reason it's still one of the fastest on the squadron. Let's not have any of your stupid electrical fires today, George, and don't let me down. We want to get back, don't we?

One of the other pilots takes a photo of me just before I get into the cockpit. That's supposed to be bad luck, isn't it? Then into the cockpit. Connect the 'g' suit and 'sex suit', helmet on and plugged in, pin out and the pre-start checks. There is the start signal from the lead aircraft. Press the start button. Acrid black smoke and the roar of rushing gas. The engine has lit up and all the gauges read normal. The radio crackles: 'Foxtrot Delta 137, check in.' 'Two,' I say. 'Three' and 'Four' say the others. 'All fives,' says the leader. 'Foxtrot Delta 137, taxi.' I wave away the chocks as ATC gives clearance.

We taxi out in turn. Not too close now, and a bit sideways from the exhaust of the aircraft in front. Careful with the trigger. Coming up to the runway threshold, and there are our armourers. Up alongside no. 1 and brake to a halt. Hands up on the windscreen while the armourers plug in the rocket pig-tails. Thumbs up from everybody, canopies closed and taxi on to the runway alongside the flight leader. At the wind-up signal from no. 1 I open the throttle and give him the thumbs up. 'Forward Chop' signal comes from no. 1, so wheelbrakes off and we accelerate together down the runway. The other pair will follow in a few seconds. I lift into the air with the leader. Squeeze the brake lever and then select undercarriage up. I turn away into battle formation, flaps up and check the gauges. There is the other pair drawing up abreast on the other side and several hundred yd away. So far, so good. Cyprus slips astern. It's sea now until Egypt.

Egypt! What we are doing is still almost unbelievable. I never thought we would actually do it. This is not a normal training sortie. This is the real thing. The heavily loaded aircraft claw their way up through the thin bright air. The

Flg Off Colin Richardson of 6 Squadron, Akrotiri, November 1956. (*Colin Richardson*)

leader is levelling off now, but there is a long way to go. I ease out a bit further to get a better view behind. That's my job now. I am a pair of eyes searching the sky behind the other pair. That's them, two black specks suspended in the glare. They depend on me. If they are bounced by MiGs it's my fault. Check the MiG's wingspan is set on the gyro gunsight, guns/RP selector to 'Guns', oxygen check and everything seems OK. Keep looking behind!

There is Egypt and the Canal. We are letting down now. This is when it is most difficult to look behind. As we let down the arid landscape expands in front of us. The other pair is slipping in behind us now for low-level battle formation. I ease back to be a little bit behind the leader and to one side. And now we are down, skimming along the ground. All around us is alien territory and everything is enemy except for the leader and the pair behind. Look all round, and don't fly into the sand. Christ! No. 1 is low. Should be there soon. The leader pulls up abruptly and I follow. We are there. And there are rows of tanks just like the photograph in the ops

tent. They are our tanks in storage, but we don't want the Egyptians to use them against us. With 72ft on the gunsight, range set to MRP and guns/RP to Rockets. No. 1 is rolling in now. Leave it a bit longer, and now I pull round and dive down behind him. I select Salvo. The bottom diamond on that tank in the middle. Steady now, and uncage the gyro. Wait till no. 1 is out of the way, I don't want to hit him. His rockets snake down and he pulls away to one side. Drift that diamond a touch left. Fireballs explode alongside my tank. Never mind the leader's rockets – concentrate. Right . . . NOW. There is a sharp roar and a glimpse of white smoke. The rockets are away. I press the button again and the other four rockets are on their way. Don't wait to see them strike, pull round and get low. Where the hell is no. 1? Ah, there he is. Get up with him again. What now?

Leader's voice: '137 four, what did it look like?'

'Good. All on target.'

'Flak?'

'Wouldn't chuckle. They had woken up by the time I came in.'

95

'Roger. We won't make a second pass. Anyone got any rockets left?'

'Three still has four.'

'Poke them into a hangar at the secondary. We are going there.'

'Roger.'

Three and four are catching up nicely and everything is tidy. Select 'Guns' and check round the cockpit. All readings are normal. Look round the sky for MiGs. And Israelis. Here's the airfield ahead. No. 1 pulls up and I stay with him while looking at the airfield as it drops away in front of the port wing. Looks like most of the MiGs are burnt out. There is a single-seat Meteor in front of the air traffic control, and a car is driving away from it. I'll take it. The lead aircraft has picked something off to the left. I roll in and put the fixed cross just above the Meteor. A bit of bank needed for the crosswind. Everything steady . . . NOW. The whole aircraft shudders as the four cannon fire. This is the first time I have fired all four guns, and the first time I have fired at anything on the ground. The white cross dances on the Meteor. Suddenly there are twinkling lights on the ground, a little short but creeping up on the Meteor. The shells are hitting now. Half a second more. That's it, stop firing and pull away. Open the throttle and catch up with the leader. I glance over my shoulder. Three and four are curving in behind us. The Meteor is burning and there is smoke drifting from a hangar.

No. 1's voice again: 'Four from leader, any flak?'

'Nope, negative flak.'

'There's a fuel tanker on the road down there. We'll take him. There's not much left on the airfield. The tanker is driving like hell.'

There he is. The leader fires on him and the tanker stops in the sand. I open fire and the shells creep over the tanker. It does not burn until our second time round. Thick black smoke. It must be some kind of oil, not fuel.

'Three fired out.'

'Roger,' says no. 1. '137, let's get the hell out of here.'

Quite right. It's like wasps round a rotten plum. We have been here too long. I still have a few shells left in case we are intercepted. Which one is the leader? That must be him making off north. Full bore to catch him up, and very low round the AA battery at Ismailia. The others are behind somewhere. Yes, here they come. Funny to see ships in the middle of the desert – you can't see the canal itself from this low. I wonder what they think about all this. They seemed to have stopped anyway. Not stopped – hove to, isn't that what ships do? For Christ's sake stop dreaming and think about what you are doing. My fuel! I can't get home with that much! It must be slow feed from the underwing tanks. It's got to be, or I will be sitting in a dinghy in the middle of the Mediterranean. Stop worrying and look behind or we won't get as far as the sea. There's Port Said. There's a big fire there. Lots of smoke. It must be storage tanks. Does no. 1 have to fly *quite* so low? Dangerous. Good, here's the sea.

Safely out to sea and the leader is climbing. Oxygen OK and out into battle formation. No, other side you fool, three and four are this side. No. 1 will probably take us up to 30,000ft on the way home so long as we don't trail. Internal tanks filling up now that we are no longer full throttle at low level. Looks like there is enough fuel to get home.

Levelling off now. DME locked on to the Cyprus beacon. That must be it under the yellow haze on the horizon. Hell, I'm stiff. Looking forward to a cup of coffee and a cigarette. Ah. It looks like no. 1 is letting down. He is taking us straight to the keyhole, which is the laid-down entry point that shows we are not hostile. Through the keyhole and there is Akrotiri. What a target it would make. There must be over a hundred aircraft down there, including the French. Let's make a smart break and landing. The lead aircraft breaks sharply on to the downwind leg. Three seconds. Now crisp with the bank and pull round with the leader on the horizon. Throttle back and airbrakes out. Keep him level. Undercarriage down and three green lights. Test the wheelbrakes. Airbrakes in and flaps down, and follow him round not too close. He's landing left, so I go to the right on the runway centre line. Grease it on to the runway. Keep the nose up, up, up. Now nose-wheel down and reasonable braking. Good. Now, flaps up and follow the lead Venom into the squadron dispersal. There's the marshaller, waving me up beside the leader. Cut the engine and switch everything off. The ground crew put the ejection seat pin in to make the seat safe. I climb stiffly out of the cockpit and take off the tight helmet. That's better. A lot better. Legs feel a bit shaky. 'No Chief, the guns are not fired out. Everything serviceable.' When no one is looking I give George a pat on the nose and walk back towards the tent.

Coffee finished, we go to the ops tent for the debrief and hand in the sovereigns before they find their way into the coffee swindle.

It was all over. But there would be others on following days.

Colin Richardson joined 6 Squadron at Akrotiri in May 1956 and flew four operational sorties during the brief Suez crisis. He later joined 8 Squadron at Khormaksar, and between July 1957 and March 1959 carried out a further 108 strikes against rebel tribesmen in the Aden Protectorate and Oman. This was followed by tours of instructing at Cranwell and the Pakistan Air Force College, then by a stint of fighter reconnaissance in Germany, and yet more instructing at Leeming and Cranwell. He left the RAF in 1973 and joined the Sultan of Oman's Air Force as a contract ground-attack pilot during the Dhofar War in southern Oman, where he amassed another 214 strikes against Communist insurgents. After a short spell at headquarters, he returned to the instructing role again, this time for eleven years on Strikemasters at Masirah.

CHAPTER FIVE

'FIREDOG' OPERATIONS IN MALAYA

Following the Second World War the British reoccupied Malaya and in April 1946 introduced the Malayan Union with a more centralised government and equal voting rights for all races. However, the Malayan Union was immediately unpopular and throughout 1947 and 1948 there were many Communist-inspired strikes. In June 1948 the former Malayan Peoples' Anti-Japanese Army was reactivated following legislation to prevent strikes and rioting, and was renamed the Malayan Peoples' Anti-British Army. To continue the armed struggle the Chinese Communists in Malaya returned to jungle warfare, a strategy in which they had gained much experience during their campaign against the Japanese during the Second World War.

Provoked by the Communist Party's General Secretary, Chin Peng, rioting continued and on 17 June 1948 a state of emergency was proclaimed. The following month the Communist Party was declared illegal, and on 23 July Operation 'Firedog' – the air campaign against the Communist terrorists (CTs) in Malaya – began. It would continue to run for another twelve years, until July 1960.

The topographical features of Malaya – mountains and deep valleys, all covered with dense tropical jungle – meant that aircraft were required to play a predominant part in the campaign, both by engaging in direct air strikes on the enemy and by providing vital air logistic support to the ground forces. As intelligence reports disclosed the locations of CT forces in the Malayan jungle, army troops were deployed and strike operations were mounted as required by Headquarters FEAF. The pre-planned bombing, strafing and rocket attacks against the jungle hideouts by units of the RAF, Royal Navy and Commonwealth air forces were all labelled 'Firedog' operations, and although the bombing had only a limited effect on the terrorists the campaign did mean that the CTs were constantly harassed, driving them into prepared ambush positions. A request for air support against opportunity targets resulted in immediate response operations – code-named 'Smash Hits' – which were undertaken by standby airmen and groundcrews who were available 24 hours a day.

In 1948 the RAF in Malaya had eight operational squadrons, based at Changi, Seletar and Tengah on Singapore Island, and at Kuala Lumpur in the west of Malaya. Two of these squadrons, nos 28 and 60, flew Spitfire FR.18s, while 45 and 84 Squadrons were still operating the Beaufighter TF.10. In August 1949 the Tempest IIs of 33 Squadron arrived from Gutersloh to reinforce the RAF's ground-attack operations following the departure of 84 Squadron to Habbaniya to re-equip with Brigands and 28 Squadron to Hong Kong because of Chinese unrest in the area.

Towards the end of the following year preparations were made to equip 60 Squadron at Tengah with Vampire FB.5s. By February 1951 the squadron had completed its conversion and was able to carry out the first jet strike against CT hideouts in April. The next year the squadron was re-equipped with 'tropicalised' Vampire FB.9s. Also based at Tengah was 14 (Fighter) Squadron RNZAF, which had arrived from Cyprus in April 1955. Commanded by Sqn Ldr N.H. Bright, the squadron had transferred from Ohakea to Nicosia in October 1952 and operated as part of the Commonwealth Strategic Reserve (CSR) in Cyprus and the Canal Zone, flying Vampires hired from the RAF. In 1954 the New Zealand government responded again to Britain's request for a contribution to the CSR in the Far East by agreeing to send 14 (NZ) Squadron from Cyprus to Singapore. On 10 April 1955 the squadron completed its move to Tengah and was accommodated in the former 45 Squadron dispersal on the north-west side of the runway. Because of the shortage of available aircraft, the squadron was obliged to compromise with an assortment of ex-RAF Vampire FB.9s and T.11s instead of the expected establishment of sixteen Venom FB.1s.

In April 1955 both 14 (NZ) Squadron and 60 Squadron began to receive their first Venoms: on 24 April 14 (NZ) Squadron was issued with one aircraft (WR366), while 60 Squadron picked up another two (WR365 and WK437) from Seletar. By September 60 Squadron had received its full complement of sixteen Venoms, although it was not until March 1956 that 14 (NZ) Squadron was up to strength. Both units continued to operate Vampires during the intervening period.

There was keen inter-squadron rivalry to carry out the first 'Firedog' strike with a Venom. Eventually the honours went to 14 (NZ) Squadron, which was declared operational on 1 May 1955 following an attack on a CT position by five Vampires.

A fine formation of Venom FB.1s of B Flight, 14 (F) Squadron RNZAF, led by Flt Lt Stuart McIntyre, over the western end of Singapore Island. The aircraft carry the pre-September 1956 squadron markings of red and white checks on the rudders. (*RNZAF Official*)

Five days later a Venom (WR366) flown by Flt Lt Stuart McIntyre and a further four squadron Vampires carried out a rocket attack on a suspected CT position in the Labis area, 75 miles north of Singapore; this particular strike was believed to be the first time a Venom had been used on active service operations. On 14 July two Venoms from 60 Squadron, flown by Flt Lt Terry Kearns and Pt Off John Pusey, took part in a mixed formation strike with two Vampires in the Mount Okil area.

Stuart McIntyre was a flight commander with 14 (NZ) Squadron between 1955 and 1957. He had already completed a tour with the squadron in Cyprus and was subsequently awarded the DFC for operations during the Malayan Emergency. He said: 'The real rivalry between the two squadrons was to be first to use the Venom on operations. 60 Squadron had a silver Vampire model that had been presented by de Havilland's for being the first squadron to use the Vampire on operations and we badly wanted a silver Venom. Unhappily the generosity of the company did not extend to the Commonwealth and 14 Squadron merely received an acknowledgement of the fact, which the company promised to include in its records.'

Commanded by Sqn Ldr D.C. Lovell DFC, AFC, 60 Squadron completed its work-up with the new Venom aircraft in July 1955 and carried out its first Venom-only strike on 26 July when three aircraft, flown by Flt Lt Brian Mercer, Flt Lt Pete Cornish and Flg Off 'Willie' Alcock, attacked a target in the North Segamat area, dropping six bombs and firing over a thousand rounds of ammunition.

In a typical 'Firedog' sortie, attacks against CT positions in the jungle were made by up to three sections of four Venoms, each carrying 600 rounds of 20mm cannon ammunition and either two 1,000lb bombs – twice the previous capability of the Vampire – or eight 3in rockets with 60lb HE heads.

A long-burning flare dropped from a very low level onto the jungle canopy by an Army Air Corps Auster – or 'Marker John' – indicated the precise target. The Venom squadron's original dive-bombing technique was the steep glide delivery method favoured by the Middle East Venom units, but they later adopted 60-degree dive-bombing from 8,000ft down to 4,000ft, resulting in an average accuracy of 35 yd.

In addition to 'Firedog' operations the Venom fighter squadrons were also responsible for the air defence of Singapore and were trained to meet both a medium- and high-level bomber threat. Routine squadron training included simulated low-level strikes, rocketing and air-to-ground firing at the China Rock range off the south-eastern tip of Malaya, individual level bombing and 60-degree dive-bombing at the Raffles Light range south of Singapore, high-level battle formations and practice interceptions. The squadrons also retained a few Vampire T.11s, which were used for continuation and instrument training, together with the occasional strike sortie.

On 22–3 May 1955 Exercise 'Joss Stick VII' was held at Tengah, with 14 (NZ) and 60 Squadrons' Vampires and Venoms providing the air defence of Singapore against bombing raids by an attacking 'enemy' force consisting of three B.29 Superfortresses of the 81st ARS (USAF), three Lincolns of 1 (B) Squadron RAAF and Canberras of 101 Squadron from Butterworth. 'Joss Stick' exercises had begun in 1953 and were now a regular feature of the squadrons' training programme, with regular detachments of SEATO squadrons combining to carry out long-range air defence exercises in the Far East.

An increase in a request for air attacks throughout June was attributed to the number of urgent operations coming within the Venoms' radius of action inside Johore, mostly in the swamp area to the east of Kulai

Venom FB.1 WR353 of 45 Squadron over paddy fields east of Butterworth. The squadron markings consisted of a white dumb-bell on a red rectangle, while the flying camel insignia on the tip-tanks is just visible. (*via Wg Cdr C.G. Jefford*)

and in the Kluang and Kota Tinggi areas. The majority of 14 (NZ) Squadron's sorties were still being flown with Vampires because of a protracted re-equipment programme and a lack of suitable tradesmen. Aircraft service-ability was also a problem because of the poor condition of the replacement Venoms, and by the end of the year the squadron was reduced to a handful of aircraft and had to suffer the indignity of borrowing aircraft from 60 Squadron to maintain operations; this inevitably led to much friendly banter from 60 Squadron and 'Aircraft for Hire' signs appeared around Tengah.

Further north at Butterworth, in Malaya's western region, 45 Squadron also began to re-equip with Venoms. Butterworth was used as an advanced operational base for missions in northern Malaya and for periodic APC detachments, where rocketry, gunnery and practice bombing was conducted at the Song Song range off the coast north of Penang

Island. In late 1955 the RAAF began a massive three-year expansion programme at the airfield, which enabled it to be used by the RAAF component of the CSR for offensive operations against the CTs operating in northern Malaya and along the Malay–Thai border.

No. 45 Squadron had considerable experience of 'Firedog' operations. They had flown their first strike in August 1948 and had been successively equipped with a variety of aircraft types, including Beaufighters, Brigands and Hornets. In March 1955 the squadron was transferred from Tengah to Butterworth and briefly amalgamated with 33 Squadron during the conversion of their Hornet crews to jets. The following August the squadron was issued with a quantity of Vampire FB.9s, pending re-equipment with Venom FB.1s, the first four of which (WK486, WR346, WR359 and WR369) were delivered in September. Work-up training began under the command of Sqn Ldr V.K. Jacobs.

In September 1955 a three-month amnesty was called by the Malayan government following the country's first democratic elections, during which period air operations were suspended and Communist activity declined. However, on 3 December 1955, in response to an increase of terrorist attacks in Johore following the breakdown of truce talks, the first post-amnesty strike was mounted by two sections of 60 Squadron in support of the 1st Northern Rhodesian Regiment against a target in the Kluang area.

By December 1955 doubts had been expressed by the RAE as to the Venom's chances of surviving the pull-out from a dive-bombing attack if one of its bombs were to hang up. It was considered that continued stress on the wings over a period of time under operational conditions could lead to a failure of the wing attachment points. Also, there was a possibility of debris being thrown into the flight path of the aircraft during recovery from a 60-degree dive, so a temporary ban was placed on such attacks until another method could be devised. To overcome this embargo, a level bombing technique was developed for the two Venom squadrons at Tengah. Sections of four aircraft flew towards the general target area in box formation, the leader flying exactly level at 2,000ft AGL (the minimum safe height for bomb blast) and at 260 knots. The leader would then adjust his track to take the formation directly over the flare previously dropped by the Auster, and would aim his bombs at the target using the fixed cross of the gyro gunsight (GGS); the 'sight' was calibrated by tilting the GGS sunshield so that the projected image of the fixed cross and the ring appeared to touch the nose of the aircraft. The whole section then released their bombs on the leader's countdown. This seemingly crude sighting method was actually very effective: 60 Squadron's average on the Raffles range was under 25 yd for dropping smoke and flash practice bombs. After weapon impact the aircraft would go into a loose line astern formation and would then strafe the target individually with their 20mm cannon. RP attacks were made in a similar fashion to the gun attacks, although the dive angle was steeper to accommodate the greater range of release and the large gravity drop of the projectile. The level bombing technique was considered to have two advantages: cloud cover was less likely to restrict strikes; and pattern bombing was judged to be more likely to achieve kills than simply hitting clearings with pin-point accuracy. It also proved suitable to the Malayan terrain and weather, but called for accurate flying and lacked the excitement normally associated with dive-bombing operations.

During January 1956 'Joss Stick IX' found the three Venom squadrons carrying out defensive sorties against B.29, Lincoln and Canberra bombers; although many of the interceptions against the big bombers were considered successful, the Canberras proved elusive with their ability to fly higher and faster. A further seventeen 'Firedog' sorties were also completed during the month. On 2 January 45 Squadron was able to mount its first Venom strike. This morning attack on a suspected terrorist camp in the Bongsu Forest Reserve by Flt Lt J.J. 'Jimmy' Connors was a combined operation with the squadron's Vampires to prepare for the Royal Australian Regiment's first patrol in Malaya.

Although one aircraft had been lost in a take-off accident during the previous month, by February 1956 45 Squadron had fourteen Venoms on strength and was able to carry out four strikes. On 10 February the squadron's Vampires again attacked the Bongsu Forest Reserve, with another strike on a small clearing near the Thai border on the 22nd; while on the 24th and 25th targets near Ipoh and Bacing were also bombed. The last three of these strikes were carried out in

Venom FB.1 WE470 of 14 (F) Squadron RNZAF, flown by Flt Lt Stuart McIntyre, drops its 1,000lb bombs on a terrorist target in the Malayan jungle during a 'Firedog' sortie. (*via Mark Lenton*)

company with the Canberra bombers of 12 Squadron from Butterworth.

Both 14 (NZ) and 60 Squadrons were also busy during February 1956, flying twenty-one 'Firedog' sorties against identified guerrilla camps. On 22 February a large-scale strike in conjunction with Operation 'Kingly Pile' involved the bombing of a CT position in the Kluang area of central Johore, the base of Goh Peng Tuan, commander of the 7th Independent Platoon MRLA. The camp was first bombed by Lincolns of 1 (B) Squadron RAAF from Tengah and Canberras of 12 Squadron. Twelve Venoms from 60 Squadron, led by Sqn Ldr Philips, and seven Venoms from 14 (NZ) Squadron, led by Sqn Ldr Nelson Bright, then completed the task with rockets and cannon fire. During the

attack, in which 46 rockets and 6,362 rounds of 20mm cannon were fired, fourteen CTs were killed, including Goh Peng Tuan himself. It was later considered that this particular attack, in which a handful of pilots on attachment from 28 Squadron also took part to gain operational experience, was the most effective of the emergency.

Also in February (on the 15th) a joint squadron comprising five Venoms from 14 (NZ) Squadron and twelve from 60 Squadron flew to Don Muang, near Bangkok, to take part in a SEATO exercise called 'Firmlink'. This was 14 (NZ) Squadron's first full-scale, long-range and mobility exercise since leaving Cyprus, and both squadrons operated throughout the demonstration with a huge variety of transport and fighter aircraft drawn

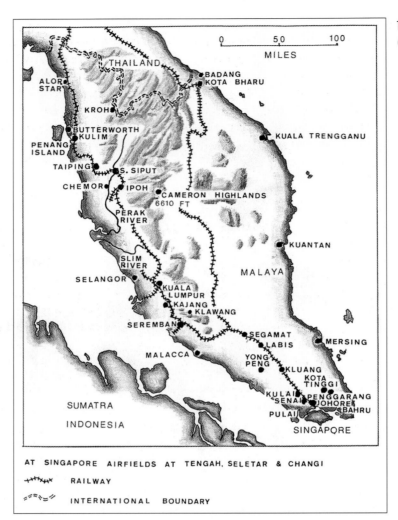

The Malay Peninsula.
(*Colin Richardson*)

from seven nations, including F-84 Thunderjets of the USAF and F-8F Bearcats and T-33 Shooting Stars of the Royal Thai Air Force. Before their return to Tengah on the 17th, both squadrons were also able to include spirited displays by their respective aerobatic teams, which – as the compilers of the ORBs for both units subsequently reported – 'Stole the Show'. A ten-minute display of formation aerobatics by the 14 (NZ) Squadron team led by Sqn Ldr Nelson Bright, together with an individual display by Flt Lt 'Clarry' Berryman, is said to have 'completed the best fighter display of the

exercise'. Also performing was the team from 60 Squadron, led by Flt Lt Brian Mercer (who later commanded 92 Squadron and led the Blue Diamonds premier aerobatic team flying Hunter F.6s during the 1961/1962 seasons) and consisting of Flg Offs John Pusey, Dave Ryles and Bob Johnson. This was the first official display by the squadron's Venom team, which had been formed the previous October by Brian Mercer. He comments:

The formation display at Bangkok was a great success. The Americans were rather disgruntled that we stole the show with our little team. They had moved in a vast quantity of staff, and apart from the hosts of transport aircraft and paratroopers they also had a squadron of F-84s from Okinawa. Having seen our practice they decided that they had better try this formation aerobatic stuff themselves. To do this without previous practice was brave but foolish and they came very close to disaster.

Two large-scale exercises were held during March 1956. Between 5 and 10 March Exercise 'Welcome' found 14 (NZ) and 60 Squadrons operating as part of the defensive force against determined attacks by carrier-based Sea Hawks, Sea Venoms and Gannets. Thirty-eight sorties were flown by 60 Squadron at Tengah, while a further five aircraft were detached to Kuala Lumpur where fourteen sorties were flown, during which fifteen Sea Hawks were claimed in return for one Venom 'shot down'. Brian Mercer recalls the exercise:

I led the five Venom aircraft detached to Kuala Lumpur, where I flew four sorties on 9 March, landing back at Tengah after the fourth sortie. We had a terrific dogfight with the Sea Hawks from HMS *Albion* and *Centaur* in the misty dawn at low-level in the Kuala Lumpur area. I recall a camera gun film of mine that showed a Sea Hawk firmly in my sight as we belted along the Johore Straits, very low, between two moored Sunderland flying boats. The next shot showed the same Sea Hawk and one of the Tengah hangars – again at low level!

The pace of squadron activity showed no respite, and this exercise was quickly followed by 'Joss Stick X' during 15–18 March, another naval cooperation exercise and several 'Firedog' strikes in the Labis area.

During April no strike operations were flown by the Tengah Venom Wing although 45 Squadron at Butterworth managed to mount a strike on the 23rd, when six aircraft, led by the new CO, Sqn Ldr G.S. Cooper, bombed a target in the Senai area. Although April was a relatively quiet month operationally, on 4 April 14 (NZ) Squadron suffered its first serious flying accident when Flg Off Ian Ferguson crashed into rubber trees at Lim Chu Kang Road following engine trouble during a practice overshoot. Ferguson was lucky to escape unscathed before the aircraft (WR272) burst into flames and was destroyed. Two weeks later Plt Off Tom Evans was forced to belly-land his aircraft (WE370) at Tengah after the undercarriage failed to lower and his engine flamed out. Although the aircraft was later declared a write-off, Evans was unhurt.

June was a very good period for all three squadrons, with 165 'Firedog' sorties flown. The largest strike of the month was a combined operation on the 18th against a camp near Kluang that contained fifteen terrorists. The attack was code-named Operation 'Canterbury'. Eight aircraft from 14 (NZ) Squadron led by Flt Lt Stuart McIntyre, followed by eight aircraft from 60 Squadron led by Flt Lt David Blucke, took off at 0745 hours, and were joined over the target area by a further six Venoms from 45 Squadron, led by Sqn Ldr Cooper, and six Canberras of 9 Squadron from Butterworth. Following a successful bombing run by six Lincolns of 1 Squadron RAAF, the attack by the twenty-two Venoms was described as a most impressive sight, with a visible shock wave going through the jungle. Three days later eight Venoms from 14 (NZ) Squadron and nine Venoms from 60 Squadron also bombed a target at Seremban. The month was rounded off with further strikes in the Kluang area and a flypast over Sembawang, comprising sixteen Venoms, three Canberras and five Lincolns, for delegates to the SEATO Military Conference.

On 24 July a period of unfortunate flying accidents involving 45 Squadron's Venoms since re-equipment was climaxed by the loss of WE373, which broke up in mid-air during a low-level run and crashed into the sea near Yen Kedah. The pilot, Flg Off Hobson, was killed. Fortunately, this would be the only fatality during the squadron's two-year association with the Venom.

The following month two more of 45 Squadron's aircraft were lost. Flg Off Dave Proctor crashed on take-off at Butterworth on 6 August, while on 21 August Flg Off Brockson was forced to abandon his take-off and overshot the runway, the Venom ending up in the sea. Both pilots were uninjured.

The next few weeks involved routine training for the Venom squadrons, with practice sessions for the aerobatic teams, sector and naval cooperation exercises, and a practice ground-attack operation against the disused airfield at Mersing, heavily defended by an RAF Regiment squadron. On 9 August an afternoon search carried out by six aircraft from 45 Squadron for a missing Auster in the Kroh area proved unsuccessful. Word was later received, however, that the pilot and his passenger were safe, having walked into Kroh airfield following a forced landing in the jungle.

On 9 September twelve Venoms drawn from 14 (NZ) and 60 Squadrons were ordered to attack a target in the Slim River area. Following an initial run by 60 Squadron, the aircraft from 14 (NZ) Squadron were approaching the target when an over-enthusiastic ground party reported that they had accidentally moved too far forward and were themselves now in the target area. The Venoms had to abort their attack and withdrew to Kuala Lumpur, where they subsequently learnt that a Malay soldier had been injured during the earlier strafing run.

The annual Battle of Britain celebrations at Kuala Lumpur on 15 September were marked by a flypast of forty-two aircraft, including twenty-seven Venoms drawn from the three squadrons, nine helicopters, three Austers and three Pioneers. Later in the day, in spite of very rough weather conditions over Changi, the aerobatic team from 14 (NZ) Squadron, comprising Flt Lt Stuart McIntyre and Flg Offs Colin Rudd, Mayne Hawkins and Barry Flavell, carried out a very polished display.

On 13 October 45 Squadron responded, at rather short notice, to a request to fly down to Tengah to take part in a strike operation. Four aircraft (and a reserve), led by the CO, left Butterworth at 1100 hours and two hours later were part of a combined attack, comprising five Lincolns, sixteen Venoms and a Sunderland, bombing a terrorist camp in the Kluang area. The squadron was able to return to Butterworth by early evening.

On 23 October six aircraft of 60 Squadron were detached to Saigon for a flypast and formation aerobatic displays as part of the celebrations of the first anniversary of the founding of the Republic of Vietnam, and they flew in a mass formation with forty USAF aircraft on the 26th. The following day the aerobatic team, led by Flt Lt Brian Mercer and comprising Sqn Ldr Alan Jenkins, Flt Lt Bob Price and Flg Off John Pusey, gave two displays over the Saigon River and the destroyer HMAS *Anzac*, which was carrying the Vietnamese president. Brian Mercer recalled: 'The display over the middle of Saigon was very exciting. The late and lamented President Diem was watching from the bridge of an Australian destroyer, which was moored in the Saigon River opposite the main street. We finished off with a "bomb burst" over the destroyer and my line after that was straight up the main street. Very, very low and fast. It was most exhilarating. You couldn't do that over London!' Returning to Tengah on the 28th, the team found that riots had broken out in Singapore and the crews had been dispersed to provide armed guards to protect military installations. No flying was carried out until 31 October when, despite the ongoing emergency, the curfew hours were extended and no more incidents were reported.

On 26 October, following the murder of a rubber estate manager and two special constables at Sungei Siput, 45 Squadron was called into action. An Auster later spotted the terrorists floating on a raft in the Perak River, and six Venoms led by Sqn Ldr Cooper carried out a strafing attack on the dense cultivation bordering the river, where the CTs were believed to be heading.

For the rest of the year operations began to decrease in number as the security forces gained the upper hand, although a strike on a CT transit camp in the Chickus Forest Reserve was mounted on 9 November, followed by a bombing operation at Kluang on the 12th and a further attack in the Kulai area of Johore on the 16th.

During 1956 a total of 460 'Firedog' sorties were flown by the three Venom squadrons, but by early 1957 active operations began to decline as the terrorists were pushed further into the jungle. Most of eastern Malaya was now declared 'white', and by the time the country had gained its independence on 31 August 1957 the majority of strikes were against targets at Perak in the north-west and Johore in the south. This reduction in air operations resulted in only 98 'Firedog' sorties being flown by the three squadrons until the end of April. On 24 January three aircraft from 60 Squadron led by Flt Lt Mercer took part in a dusk strike in the Kajang area, while 45 Squadron flew five strikes between 10 and 26 January. During this last strike two waves of four Venoms attacked a terrorist clearing in the Slim River area using the bombs distributor setting, which delayed the release of the second bomb for a fraction of a second to lengthen the 'kill zone' from about 90 to 180 yd. The target disappeared completely as the first wave of bombs exploded, leaving the Auster unable to find anything to mark for the second wave.

During the first quarter of the year the Venom squadrons had flown just over 5,200 hours, losing five aircraft in flying accidents. On 23 April Flg Off Alcock of 60 Squadron struck a parked Land Rover with the starboard wing of his Venom (WE399) during a night take-off; although 'Willie' Alcock was unhurt, the two occupants of the vehicle were killed. Six days later Flt Lt Mike Palmer of 14 (NZ) Squadron was leading a section of four Venoms on a low-level sortie over the Johore Bahru when his engine failed. After climbing for height, Mike Palmer achieved the distinction of being the first pilot to eject from a RNZAF aircraft (WR282) and was rescued from his dinghy by a police launch soon after entering the water in the Straits of Johore.

On 18 April, using the Target Director Post (TDP) technique, 14 (NZ) Squadron was able to mount its first strike for several months when a suspected CT hideout in the Kulai area was bombed. This method involved close control by ground radar to a point for the bomb drop, with the command to drop being given by a ground controller. Brian Mercer again: 'TDP was otherwise known as Forward Radar Control Post, and its main use was at night with the RAAF Lincolns. I asked why we couldn't be used at night and the reply from HQ FEAF was that fighters couldn't formate at night. So, one night I led a formation of 12 Venoms, with all their lights on, on several runs over Changi and the Senior Officers' Mess at Fairy Point. Not a word was said!'

Also on 17 April 45 Squadron took part in Exercise 'Tradewind' at Butterworth, when seventeen sorties were flown defending Butterworth against attacks by RAN Gannets from HMAS *Melbourne*. The 'enemy' aircraft were all intercepted 30 miles from base, much to the delight of the crews who later witnessed the Gannets being chased by the squadron's Venoms over Butterworth as the Australians pressed on with their attacks.

During April 1957 60 Squadron began to re-equip with Venom FB.4s when two aircraft

'The last Venom FB.1 starts up.' With its characteristic plume of smoke, WR365 of 60 Squadron makes a dramatic exit from Tengah on 30 July 1957. The squadron had begun to re-equip with Venom FB.4s in the previous April. (*Wg Cdr Hugh Rigg*)

(WR558 and WR564) were passed to the unit from Seletar. By 7 May the squadron had received a sufficient number of FB.4s to enable it to carry out the type's first strike when Flt Lt Mercer flew WR564 as part of an eight aircraft TDP strike against a target in the Klawang area, in company with four Venoms of 14 (NZ) Squadron and the Lincolns of 1 (B) Squadron RAAF. By the end of July the last of the FB.1s had been withdrawn, having taken part in a final strike on 18 June against a target in the Kulai area.

Between February and April 1957 60 Squadron had seen little operational activity. Two strikes were carried out by the squadron in the Kota Tinggi and Layang Layang areas at the end of April as part of a harassing operation, together with an attack by seven Venoms of 45 Squadron against a party of CTs crossing the border into Thailand at Kulim.

Taking advantage of the reduction in air strikes, 45 Squadron was also able to form an aerobatic team and prepare for its only display of the year, at the opening of Brunei airport in May. The team was led by Flt Lt Bob Baff, and comprised Flt Lts W.E. 'Wally' Close, John Barrett and Flg Off K.R. 'Curt' Curtis, with the solo display carried out by the CO, Sqn Ldr Geoff Cooper. Operating from Lubuan, the team's faultless display before the Sultan of Brunei on 8 May was well received, and was later described by the local press and onlookers as 'impressive'.

May was taken up with further harassing operations at Kota Tinggi and in Johore, a few miles east of Changi. The main attacks were directed towards Teng Fook Loong, the leader of 3 Platoon MRLA, who was eventually killed during a bombing raid by RAAF Lincolns later in the month. The highlight for the New Zealand squadron during the month was, however, a return to Bangkok on 29 May for the army cooperation exercise 'Firmlink' in collaboration with units of the USAF and Royal Thai Air Force. Over the next three days the six Venoms flew a

Venom FB.1 WK428 of 14 (F) Squadron RNZAF is flown over Changi airfield by the CO, Sqn Ldr Fred Tucker, in October 1956. The aircraft carries practice rockets and the post-September 1956 markings of a white Kiwi on a black rudder. (*RNZAF Museum*)

series of ground-attack exercises in support of the F-100 Super Sabres of the USAF, with T-33s of the Royal Thai Air Force acting as the 'enemy'. The detachment was slightly marred when Flg Off Trevor Bland suffered an engine surge on take-off, which caused his Venom (WE420) to overshoot into a large ditch.

Throughout July 1957 the Venom squadrons flew only sixty-eight operational 'Firedog' sorties, but all were considered to be significant as they kept the pressure on the groups of terrorists withdrawing towards the Thai border. Three strikes flown by 14 (NZ) Squadron in the Kluang and Kota Tinggi areas (which included a target occupied by thirty CTs of the South Johore Regional Committee) and a dawn strike by six aircraft of 60 Squadron on a terrorist camp, 15 miles north-east of Kulai on the 28th, were followed by two strikes carried out by 45 Squadron on the 5th and 19th.

Also in July 45 Squadron was told that its Venoms would be gradually withdrawn while a new air echelon was to be formed in the UK with Canberra light bombers. This new unit would eventually be based at Tengah. As the squadron prepared to run down, its operational commitment also diminished, with only three strikes tasked for the period July–September. The most notable of these strikes was on 7 July when, as part of Operation 'Eagle Swoop', the banks of a mountain stream north of Kroh on the Thai border were rocketed and strafed by eight Venoms in order to drive the terrorists away from their source of water and towards the waiting ground forces.

The month was marred by a further series of accidents: on 3 July Flg Off Geoffrey Hubbard of 14 (NZ) Squadron was forced to eject from his Venom (WE409) at 5,000ft over the Malayan jungle after entering an uncontrollable spin. A helicopter later picked him up from the edge of the jungle near Batu Pahat. Five days later Flg Off J.D. 'Abe' Lincoln of 60 Squadron was lost. He was taking part in a formation take-off at Tengah, while flying as no. 2 to Sqn Ldr Jenkins, when his Venom (WK471) stalled and crashed inverted into a block of airmen's married quarters. 'Abe' Lincoln was killed instantly, together with the wives of two RAF sergeants and a one-year-old child.

In spite of their operational commitments, which included a sector exercise on 23 August when Tengah was 'attacked' by RAF Meteors and RAAF Lincolns, the Venom squadrons were still occasionally called upon to provide aerobatic demonstrations and flypasts; one such occasion was on 1 September 1957 when six Venoms of 14 (NZ) Squadron took part in a flypast over the review of Federation Forces at Kuala Lumpur to mark Malaya's independence, forming the letter 'M' with six RAAF Canberras to signify *Merdeka* (Malay for 'Independence').

Despite the confirmation that it was also to re-equip with Canberra bombers in the near future, 14 (NZ) Squadron continued to launch air strikes against CT targets, especially from Butterworth, where the squadron was occasionally deployed to carry out strikes in the northern areas of Malaya. Other live air strikes included two TDP bombing attacks on 24 September by two Lincolns and eight Venoms in Negri Sembilam State. No. 60 Squadron was also very active, with eight strikes flown against targets at Kulai and around Ipoh during November.

In November 1957 45 Squadron carried out its last operational Venom strikes of the Malayan Emergency. On 4 November five aircraft led by Flg Off Brian St Clair bombed a suspected CT camp in the hills near Sungei Siput, 2 miles west of Chemor. Brian St Clair flew with both 45 and 60 Squadrons:

We dropped 1,000lb bombs using the 45 Squadron 'bombsight', which was exclusive to the squadron and was first used in May 1956 to overcome the embargo on Venom dive-bombing operations.

The technique involved the use of a chinagraph line drawn from the bottom of the windscreen, 42 nautical miles long on the 1/1,000,000 scale. When the top of this line coincided with another mark in the centre of the GGS sunscreen, and provided we were flying level at 2000ft AGL and at 283 knots IAS, bomb release could achieve a mean point of impact within 50 yd. We then turned astern for strafing runs using 20mm cannon. I once saw a monkey fall out of a tree! No CTs – that was for sure.

A week later, on 11 November, the squadron flew its final 'Firedog' strike when four aircraft led by the CO, Sqn Ldr Geoff Cooper, dropped eight bombs and strafed a suspected terrorist camp in the Slim River area during an early morning attack.

On 15 November 45 Squadron carried out a flypast over Kuala Lumpur. This was followed by a farewell aerobatic demonstration by Sqn Ldr Geoff Cooper, Flt Lt Trevor Coplestone and Flg Offs 'Curt' Curtis and Brian St Clair. A few Venoms lingered on until December. By this time the squadron had re-equipped with Canberra B.2s at Coningsby, the first of which had been flown out to Tengah during the previous month. Some of the Venom pilots were fortunate enough to complete their operational tours by transferring to 60 Squadron.

November was also a busy month for the New Zealand squadron when it was detached to Butterworth on the 16th for Operation 'Striptease', its annual armament practice camp. For the next two weeks the squadron flew a record number of rocketing sorties against targets on the Song Song range – with the exception of the fourth day of the camp, when the owner of the islands, the Sultan of Kedah, decided to have a picnic close to the range and all firing for the day had to be abandoned!

Meanwhile, the aerobatic team of 60 Squadron was preparing for a visit to the

Venom FB.4 WR496 of the 60 Squadron aerobatic team departing Tengah for Manila on 13 December 1957. For the squadron's tour of the Far East, at least four aircraft were repainted in an all-over white colour scheme with red tip-tanks, rudders and serial numbers. (*AVM A.F. Jenkins via Sqn Ldr Joe Warne*)

Philippines, to take part in the Manila Air Display. With six aircraft (WR407, WR421, WR496, WR537, WR553 and WR564) repainted especially for the event in an all-white scheme with red rudders and tip-tanks, the team (Sqn Ldr Jenkins, John Barrett, Sam Toyne and Rick Howden) left Tengah on 13 December, accompanied by a Canberra to provide radio communications. Following a successful trip the team returned to Tengah five days later.

One strike was mounted during December when three aircraft from 60 Squadron and one from 14 (NZ) Squadron attacked a target in Johore. A further exercise scheduled for 13 December was cut short when two Canberra aircraft of 45 Squadron were involved in a mid-air collision while en route from the UK to Tengah, resulting in the loss of four of the

six crew members. The year had ended with a slight decrease in 'Firedog' sorties compared with the previous year, with 14 (NZ) Squadron flying 61 sorties, 45 Squadron 134 sorties and 60 Squadron 218 sorties.

January 1958 began with 14 (NZ) and 60 Squadrons bombing and strafing known terrorist camping areas for three successive days to discourage them from raiding villages at Penggarang, south-east of Kota Tinggi. By the end of the month 139 'Firedog' sorties had been flown by the two Venom squadrons, mostly in support of 99 Infantry Brigade.

February was a much quieter month for operations, with 60 Squadron departing to Butterworth for a period of air firing. The following month was more active when the unit was called upon to continue harassing attacks against the CTs in the Kota Tinggi,

111

Pilots of 60 Squadron are briefed at Tengah before departing on an operational strike in 1958. Left to right: Flg Off Rick Howden, Flg Off Doug Smith, Flg Off Hugh Rigg, Flg Off Pete Evans, Flt Lt Mick Rooney, Flg Off Sam Toyne and Flg Off Paul Evans. Paul Evans was killed soon after this photograph was taken when his 8 Squadron Venom crashed near Sharjah. (*Wg Cdr Hugh Rigg*)

Kluang and Yong Peng districts, with forty sorties being flown over a five-day period. The main targets for the strikes were suspected CT food dumps and resting places in thick jungle following a series of raids on small villages 20 miles south-east of Kota Tinggi. As well as discouraging the CTs from making similar raids, the strikes also served to boost the morale of the local villagers who were fearful of further visits.

By March 14 (NZ) Squadron had been officially told that it was to disband as a Venom unit the following May and re-equip with Canberra bombers. Operations would continue until then, however, and on 13 March six of the squadron's Venoms went into action again, together with a further six from 60 Squadron, after six CTs were spotted running along a beach after RAAF Lincolns had bombed a jungle target near Jasons Bay

on the east coast of Johore. After a delay caused by a heavy storm, a large area was strafed under the direction of an AOP Auster.

Large-scale combined operations in the Ipoh area at the end of March continued into April with the start of Operations 'Granite' and 'Tiger' in Johore, and the continuation of Operation 'Bintang' in support of 2 Federal Infantry Brigade and Operation 'Ginger', the large-scale harassment operation in support of 28 Commonwealth Infantry Brigade in the Chemor Hills, west of Ipoh. Strikes were made in the Yong Peng, Kluang and Penyam districts of Johore in order to assist ground forces in their efforts to eliminate the last of the CTs in this area and create a 'white' Johore. Fifty-four sorties were flown by 14 (NZ) Squadron, which included two strikes in the Yong Peng area on 13 April, while a further fifty sorties were mounted by 60 Squadron.

A detachment from 60 Squadron also operated from Butterworth in support of ground forces clearing out the last remnants of terrorist operations in the Chemor Hills, west of Ipoh. This area had already been subjected to heavy bombing by RAAF Lincolns, which had resulted in the CTs being driven from the deep jungle into the surrounding jungle; the squadron's task was to strike at targents in the central regions to discourage re-entry.

In April 1958 the Malayan Prime Minister, Tunku Abdul Rahman, was able to declare that a 2,720-square-mile area of Johore State was free of Communist terrorists and that a large number of 'hard-core' insurgents had given themselves up, including Hor Lung, the head of the terrorist organisation in South Malaya. It was also announced that the guerrilla army in the jungle 'badlands' of Perak State had been 'smashed', thereby bringing Operation 'Ginger' to a successful conclusion. Since its beginning in January 1957, 'Ginger' was considered the biggest single assault on CT strongholds since the fighting began in June 1948; it was responsible for the deaths of 150 bandits and the surrender of many more.

On 21 April 1958 a final detachment to Don Muang to take part in the SEATO exercise 'Vayubut' saw six Venoms of 14 (NZ) Squadron working with units of the USAF and Royal Thai Air Force in a series of simulated strikes against ground targets in northern Thailand. A flypast of all participants was held on 25 April and the squadron returned to Tengah the following day.

Following its return from Bangkok, the squadron was detached to Butterworth during mid-May for a final weekend of practice interceptions. While at Butterworth, Sqn Ldr Fred Tucker led the last squadron strike when a target in the Sungei Siput area was bombed and strafed on 12 May; during the operation he was accompanied by his three senior pilots, Flt Lts Mike Palmer and Barry Gordon and Flg Off Geoff Roud. Four days later Sqn Ldr Tucker led a farewell flypast, comprising ten Venoms and three Vampire trainers flying in a figure '14' formation over Tengah, Seletar, Changi and Singapore city. This was followed by a display of aerobatics over Singapore harbour by Flt Lts Barry Gordon, Mike Palmer and Geoff Wallingford, together with Flg Offs Neil Alston and Geoff Roud, before the last Venom touched down at 1100 hours.

The aerobatic team's display was the last commitment for the New Zealanders, reflecting that it was not only the final sortie flown by the squadron in the Far East but also the very last flight of an operational Venom FB.1. By 21 June 1958 the remaining aircraft had been flown to Seletar and the crews embarked for New Zealand, being replaced by 75 Squadron RNZAF, which took over as New Zealand's contribution to the CSR. The arrival of the Canberra B.2s and new crews at Tengah marked the end to three years of Venom operations for 14 (NZ) Squadron, which was also the last squadron in the Far East Air Force to fly Venom FB.1s. During this time its pilots had flown almost 600 Vampire and Venom operational sorties, had dropped over 500,000lb of bombs and had fired 1,523 rockets onto terrorist positions. The Venom's airframe life was 750 hours, and during its last twelve months of service the squadron had written off nineteen aircraft. Although nine Venoms had been lost in flying accidents, there had, fortunately, been no fatalities.

By mid-1958 air operations were virtually non-existent as the remaining terrorists were driven up to the Thai border or pinned down in central Johore. The CTs had taken refuge in Thailand as life was considered too dangerous for them in Malaya, and they were tolerated by the Thai government provided they discontinued their activities and

A formation of Venom FB.4s from 60 Squadron over Singapore Island. The squadron markings were black with a white lightning flash. (*via John Rawlings*)

restricted themselves to living in the jungle. Also, as Canberra bombers were increasingly used on 'Firedog' strikes the operational commitment for 60 Squadron declined. On 17 July a target near Pulai was bombed, but it was not until 3 September that a further nine operational sorties were flown against a target in the Ipoh area as part of Operation 'Bintang'.

On 8 December 1958, after a two-month break from operations, the squadron carried out its final 'Firedog' strike when two sections of Venoms bombed a target in the Rasa area of Selangor, near Kuala Lumpur, led by Sqn Ldr Smart and Flt Lt Tony Neale. This particular strike brought an end to 60 Squadron's active operations in Malaya. Its pilots had flown 725 'Firedog' sorties since re-equipping with the Venom in July 1955.

Wing Commander Hugh Rigg served as a pilot officer with 60 Squadron between February 1957 and November 1959; during this time he flew sixteen operational 'Firedog' sorties:

Life on 60 Squadron in Singapore in the late 1950s was, quite simply, tremendous fun. Although we were at the end of the Imperial supply line, and flew obsolete Venom aircraft when all of us wanted to fly Hunters or Swifts, our role and theatre of operations more than made up for this.

We were a day-fighter/ground-attack squadron, responsible for the air defence of Singapore and Malaya, and air support of the ground forces in the area. Our monthly routine consisted of a fortnight's high-level battle formation and air combat training, followed by a week of air-to-air firing and a week of air-to-ground rocketing

(3in RPs) and bombing (25lb practice bombs). The high-level battle formation was sometimes done at 50,000ft (in retrospect somewhat foolhardy given the oxygen equipment in the Venom), and almost always ended in a dogfight, keenly contested and debriefed afterwards. The weaponry weeks were always flown intensively competitively, and one's scores, known by all, were a direct measure of one's skill. The programme was further spiced with practice long-range strikes on targets in the north of Malaya, exercises with the navy during which we flew simulated strikes against visiting aircraft carriers and ships, and deployments on armament practice camps to Butterworth in North Malaya, near Penang Island. The squadron also detached to Hong Kong in 1959, via Clark Field in the Philippines, and returned via Saigon in Vietnam.

Operational frisson came with strikes, using bombs, rockets and guns, against the communist terrorists in the jungle, of whom there were a significant number still at large. We worked hard too; two weekends a month we flew practice interceptions under the control of 61 Signals Unit radar controllers.

The weather was generally superb, but we learned to respect the tropical cumulo-nimbus, a potential killer. I once crept over the top of one at 55,000ft rather than fly through it to get back to Tengah, which says a lot for the high-altitude qualities of the Venom. I also recall a pair of 60 Squadron Venoms 'hacked' a pair of Australian Sabres who were foolish enough to stay and fight over their home base at Butterworth, much to their chagrin.

As an RAF operational aircraft aged, so it was deployed further from home, and the Far East Air Force was as far as you could get, Singapore first and then Hong Kong. None the less, the Venom did a good job; its range with eight 60lb rockets was 285 miles, which was ample for its role against the CTs in Malaya. Our bombing pattern was less than 30 yd, which would have been at least as good as the Lincolns and Canberras, and probably slightly better. Clearly we couldn't carry

as many weapons as the bombers, but a formation of four Venoms did drop eight bombs, which probably wasn't far short of each Canberra. The only real problem I actually recall with the Venom was that the damp used to get into the two 10-channel VHF radios at times, otherwise it was very good.

In early 1959 60 Squadron was informed that it was to become a night/all-weather unit equipped with Meteor night-fighters, and that the flying task was to be reduced in order to conserve the airframe hours of the remaining Venoms. On 27 February the squadron took its Venoms to Butterworth for a final APC, during which they achieved some impressive results. This was followed by its last overseas deployment on 16 April, when nine aircraft were flown to Hong Kong for the Queen's Birthday flypast. The flight to Hong Kong was made via Labuan and Clark Field, with the return flight staging through Saigon and Butterworth. Although one aircraft suffered fuel transfer problems on the Kai Tak–Saigon leg of the flight, the trip was a great success for all concerned and the aircraft were able to return on 1 May. Later in the month the squadron returned to Butterworth to take part in Exercise 'Bullfight', which was designed to test the air defence system of northern Malaya and Butterworth in particular; the 'enemy' this time was the Sea Hawks and Sea Venoms from HMS *Albion*.

Meanwhile, back in the UK, crews for a second 60 Squadron had assembled at Leeming and after a three-month refresher course flew the first of the Meteor NF.14s out to Tengah in October 1959. As more Meteors became available, the remaining Venoms were gradually withdrawn from service and flown to Seletar for scrapping. On 13 November 1959 the last of the FEAF's Venoms (WR417, WR497, WR537, WR539, WR540 and WR564) were flown to Hong Kong, led by Sqn Ldr M.C.N. Smart, where they were to form the basis of 28 Squadron's re-equipment programme.

The Venom had arrived in the Far East during the so-called 'Offensive Period' of the Malayan Emergency, during which there was an ongoing debate about the value of offensive air operations against CT ground targets, which increased as the guerrillas withdrew and dispersed into small groups in their deep jungle bases. The Venoms' arrival also coincided with a decline in requests for operational strikes as Canberras took over their role and the crisis drew to a close. During the three-and-a-half years of operations the three squadrons had flown a total of 1,414 Venom sorties, during which almost 1½ million tons of bombs had been dropped and a vast number of rockets and ammunition expended, in return for the loss of twenty-seven aircraft and two pilots killed in flying accidents. The damage caused and the number of terrorists killed during this period can only be estimated because of the very nature of the operations, but what is certain is that the effective use of air power ensured success on the ground. Without the air strikes, the ground forces might still have won, but it would have taken longer and might not have been so lasting.

VENOM 'FIREDOG' SORTIES FLOWN DURING THE PERIOD MAY 1955–DECEMBER 1958

Month	14 (F) Sqn RNZAF	45 Sqn	60 Sqn	Month	14 (F) Sqn RNZAF	45 Sqn	60 Sqn
May 1955	1	–	–	April 1957	–	4	27
June 1955	–	–	–	May 1957	4	11	34
July 1955	2	–	7	June 1957	4	20	18
August 1955	–	–	20	July 1957	24	38	6
September 1955	–	–	11	August 1957	–	8	7
October 1955	–	–	–	September 1957	8	–	12
November 1955	–	–	–	October 1957	16	8	–
December 1955	12	–	31	November 1957	–	9	84
January 1956	4	5	8	December 1957	1	–	3
February 1956	10	14	11	January 1958	68	–	71
March 1956	8	6	32	February 1958	4	–	–
April 1956	–	6	–	March 1958	82	–	42
May 1956	–	12	25	April 1958	54	–	50
June 1956	59	36	70	May 1958	4	–	36
July 1956	4	8	8	June 1958	–	–	9
August 1956	–	10	–	July 1958	–	–	16
September 1956	18	16	14	August 1958	–	–	4
October 1956	5	21	12	September 1958	–	–	9
November 1956	25	–	13	October 1958	–	–	–
December 1956	–	–	–	November 1958	–	–	–
January 1957	–	28	15	December 1958	–	–	8
February 1957	–	4	12				
March 1957	4	4	–	Totals	421	268	725

CHAPTER SIX

VENOMS IN THE FAR EAST: THE ROLE OF 28 SQUADRON

In May 1949, because of Chinese unrest on the border between Hong Kong and China, the Spitfires of 28 Squadron were transferred from Malaya to join 80 Squadron at Kai Tak. With the start of the Korean War in 1950 Hong Kong had become an essential base for air and maritime links and was itself threatened by the Chinese Communist forces along its northern border. Although Britain had come to the conclusion that the colony was militarily indefensible, it was nevertheless considered necessary 'to be seen to be taking' whatever measures were possible. The presence of Mao Tse-Tung's activists among the refugees from across the border posed the threat of civil unrest within Hong Kong: the obvious deterrent was a British presence.

The extreme shortage of space at Kai Tak obliged 28 Squadron to move in May 1950 to Sek Kong, a forward ('Bamboo Curtain') airstrip in the New Territories close to the Chinese border. A large army camp with primitive facilities, Sek Kong was situated in a narrow valley with the 3,100ft Mount Tai-

In September 1956 the legendary Group Captain Douglas Bader – who was by then Head of Aircraft Operations for the Shell Petroleum Company – paid a visit to 28 Squadron at Sek Kong to promote the film *Reach for the Sky*. To his left is the CO, Sqn Ldr Arthur Phillips. (*Andy Maitland*)

Mo-Shan overlooking its north-eastern approach; hemmed in on three sides by towering hills, the airfield's single strip runway made for some of the most difficult approaches ever encountered in service flying.

In January 1951 the squadron began to replace its Spitfire FR.18s with Vampire FB.5s and went back to Kai Tak for a few months to allow an extensive rebuilding programme to take place at Sek Kong. The squadron had returned to Sek Kong by the time it received the first of its Vampire FB.9s in February 1952, and eventually became Hong Kong's only resident day-fighter/ground-attack unit after the disbandment of 80 (Hornet) Squadron in 1955.

During February 1956 the Vampires were gradually exchanged for Venom FB.1s. The 2,000-mile ferry flight by the Vampires to Seletar, via Clark Field (Philippines), Labuan (North Borneo) and Kuching (Sarawak), returning with the Venoms by the same route, was a major operation. Few diversions were available for the convoys, and they were usually escorted by a Valetta to provide radio communications. To enable the squadron to continue training, the Venoms were ferried out four at a time, with the first aircraft (WE371, WE422, WK499 and WR305) being collected at Seletar on 23 February. Three days later, led by the CO, Sqn Ldr Arthur Phillips, the formation set off for the return flight, arriving at Sek Kong on 28 February. By the end of August a full complement of sixteen Venoms had been achieved but these aircraft had already seen service in the Middle East and Germany and so the work-up period was hindered by the discovery of stress cracks and the temporary enforcement of 'g' limitations for many of them.

Such was the terrain at Sek Kong that, regardless of wind direction, take-offs could only be made in one direction and landings in the reverse direction. The airfield had its own ATC, but once out of the circuit the aircraft were under the control of Hong Kong Approach. Considerable ingenuity had been shown during recovery and bad weather let-down procedures with the acquisition of a former army gun-laying radar unit, nick-named 'Zippy', which provided radar coverage up to 25–30 miles from the airfield. There could be no night flying at Sek Kong, and during the typhoon season (August to November) the aircraft were frequently returned to Kai Tak to take advantage of the protection offered by the large permanent hangars of the Hong Kong Aircraft Engineering Company.

Flying in the New Territories was somewhat restricted in area, and the squadron's routine usually comprised high-level battle formations, practice interceptions, exercises with army and navy units and formation flypasts as required. Daily 'armed recces' flown by the duty pair had the objectives of reporting on pirate junks and unusual activity in the Pearl Estuary, intercepting unidentified aircraft, and – perhaps uniquely – spotting for sharks around the more popular beaches.

Most forms of ground-attack were also practised, for which the Port Shelter firing range was ideally suited. Standards were well above average. Meteor training aircraft of the resident Station Flight were employed to tow the flags for air-to-air firing over the range situated toward the east of Hong Kong, but the proximity of the civilian airways meant this was restricted to low- and medium-altitude levels.

The squadron also made occasional detachments to Clark Field in the Philippines, where training was carried out with fighter units of the USAF. During one such encounter the Venoms acquitted themselves extremely well during a high-altitude dogfight against the latest F-100 Super Sabres; afterwards the American pilots were astonished to learn that their opponents' aircraft were partly made of wood! In May 1956 a squadron detachment was able to take part in Exercise 'Round Up', which was concluded with a combined flypast over Manila of sixty aircraft drawn from the four air forces taking part.

In September 1956 a squadron aerobatic team was formed to take part in that year's Battle of Britain display at Kai Tak, with Flt Lts John Hardcastle and Joe L'Estrange and Flg Offs Bill Croydon and Andy Maitland. Because of the location of the squadron there was little scope for suitable venues, and the next and only 'away' performance was in Manila in December 1956 where, during Philippine Aviation Week, the squadron stole the honours from teams from the American, Philippine and Chinese Nationalist Air Forces. The team maintained an erratic existence for the next couple of years, and by 1959 it was reduced

to three pilots (Flt Lts Thornton, Forse and Lewis).

On 14 May 1956 the squadron suffered an unfortunate and fatal accident. Flt Lt Tony Madden (WK423) retracted his undercarriage too soon after take-off, and sank back onto the runway. His no. 2, Flg Off Pete Dearn, immediately swung his aircraft (WK412) across the runway and climbed to port in an exaggerated nose-up attitude, which resulted in a stall and loss of control. The pilot was killed and three Chinese civilians were injured in the crash.

A further series of accidents during the first half of 1957, with four Venoms written off in six months, did not improve the squadron's flight safety record. On 25 February a recent arrival on the unit, Plt Off Stew Hailwood (WK499) failed to recover from a low-level

Flg Off Colin Coombes, Chinese junk-master Lo Ho and Flg Off Roger Joel during the presentation ceremony at Shaukiwan fish market, 17 May 1957. (*Roger Joel*)

The last three Venom FB.4s of 28 Squadron, WR537, WR540 and WR539, pictured over Kai Tak in 1962. (*Gp Capt A.S. Mann AFC*)

practice attack on HMS *Cockade* and crashed into the sea 7 miles west from Waglan Island.

Two months later Flg Off Colin Coombes (WE423) was blinded by the sun during a high-level crossover turn and lost sight of his leader; his subsequent error of judgement resulted in a collision that sliced off the nose section of Flg Off Roger Joel's Venom (WR299). Both pilots were able to eject before the Venoms crashed into the sea 15 miles south-east of Waglan Island. Roger Joel picks up the story:

On 25 April 1957, at approximately 1500 hours, I took off in a Venom FB.1 aircraft, WR299, flying as no. 3 in a formation of four aircraft. We were briefed to carry out practice interceptions at 30,000ft, and when we reached 20,000ft the formation split into two sections. I led my section as target for the first interception, climbing up to 30,000ft.

A successful interception was made and I was then instructed by the Controller to vector my section on a heading of 240 degrees. This entailed a turn to port of 80 degrees and necessitated my

no. 2, Colin Coombes, carrying out a normal cross-under turn. I called the turn and commenced turning with 45 degrees of bank. I saw Colin cross under to my starboard side, and his actions did not appear in any way dangerous.

My next recollection is of seeing Colin's aircraft appear right under my nose and I felt a heavy bang as we collided. The other aircraft immediately fell away to starboard after the collision, and it appeared to have lost its tailplane; my aircraft went into a spin to port. I immediately called 'White Leader, we have collided'.

The control column felt solid so I jettisoned the canopy just as I heard the formation leader call 'Bale out'. The canopy left the aircraft cleanly, but the slipstream snatched my right arm out of the cockpit when I raised my arms to eject. After a short struggle I managed to retrieve my arm and ejected normally.

I sensed whirling, and with no leg restraints my legs flailed, which tore the hamstring on my left leg. As the seat's emergency oxygen tube caught on something on the way out and ripped off, I very quickly passed out and only came round at 10,000ft when the automatic seat separation operated, leaving me hanging in the parachute. I then saw another parachute about 1,500ft below me, and saw two splashes in the sea. There was also a Chinese junk in the near vicinity.

The descent was quite uneventful, and at about 2,000ft I discarded my oxygen mask and at 1,000ft turned the parachute quick-release box. As my feet hit the water I struck the quick-release box and inflated my Mae West. The parachute fell away cleanly and then I inflated my dinghy and climbed in. About ten minutes later I was picked up by a boat and taken back to the junk. Approximately 75 minutes later I was transferred to the Air/Sea rescue launch and returned to Kai Tak.

Colin Coombes' Venom had lost a wing in the collision but following his ejection he was able to climb into his dinghy to await rescue. Both pilots were eventually retrieved from the South China Sea by the Chinese junk, and in recognition of his efforts the junk-master, Lo Ho, was later presented with a testimonial certificate, an enormous sack of rice and a cheque for HK$1,000 (£62 10*s*) at a colourful ceremony at a local fish market.

On 22 July the station commander, Group Captain A.J.M. Smyth, tried to get his aircraft (WE371) airborne too soon and subsequently stalled. His Venom collided with a flagpole after he decided to abandon

Parked in the RAF enclave at Kai Tak airport under the shadow of the Lion Rock, 28 Squadron prepares for the ceremonial flypast of the RAF's last operational Venom aircraft on 27 June 1962. Aircraft taking part include Venom FB.4 WR539, flown by the Station Commander, Gp Capt A.S. Mann DFC, a Hunter FGA.9 piloted by Squadron Commander, Sqn Ldr M.I. Stanway, a Hunter T.7 and a Vampire T.11 which acted as a 'camera ship'. (*RAF Kai Tak via John Rawlings*)

WR539, 28 Squadron's – and the RAF's – last Venom FB.4, on display at Kai Tak during 1963. Some thirteen years later it would be rescued and returned to the UK for eventual restoration. (*Sqn Ldr Joe Warne*)

the take-off, and eventually ran into some 3-ton trucks on the side of the runway, leaving the pilot to make a rapid departure before the ammunition exploded in an impressive display of pyrotechnics.

On 14 June 1957, following the infamous White Paper on Defence, the squadron returned to Kai Tak as part of the Far East economy cuts. Sek Kong was transferred to the army and relegated to the status of an emergency airfield. In December 1957 28 Squadron was drastically reduced in strength as part of the ongoing defence cuts, with many of the Venoms being returned to Seletar for disposal; the unit was retained in Hong Kong, however, in order to maintain 'a military presence' in the colony.

Facilities had greatly improved at Kai Tak, including the construction of an extension to the runway stretching into Kowloon Bay to meet the increased demands of both civil and military aircraft. Although it was not scheduled to be opened until September 1958, the new runway came into use prematurely on 31 August following the crash of an American C-54 Skymaster, which completely blocked the intersection. The civil authorities immediately agreed to open the

new runway, and while the pilot of the first scheduled aircraft – a Chinese Airlines DC.6 – went through his take-off checks on the threshold, Flt Lt 'Bill' Forse of 28 Squadron taxied past him and took off – thereby claiming the distinction of being the first aircraft to become airborne from the new runway! Two weeks later, on 12 September, the official opening of the runway by the Governor of Hong Kong was followed by a flying demonstration by the squadron's Venoms.

The squadron continued to operate with a handful of aircraft until the first two weeks of November 1959, which were devoted to the 'Venom Ferry'. This involved the collection, air testing and ferrying of replacement Venom FB.4s from 60 Squadron and RAF Seletar to Hong Kong. All six aircraft were received on 16 November and they immediately took part in Exercise 'Whizz Bang', a combined services firepower demonstration on the Port Shelter range with aircraft from HMS *Centaur*.

In addition to maintaining its primary role of security patrols and weather recces, the squadron was also involved in a further series of exercises with local army units, combining with the Sea Venoms of 894 Squadron from

HMS *Bulwark* and 805 Squadron of the Royal Australian Navy. In April 1962 Exercise 'High Noon' – designed to test the airfield defences – marked the end of the Venom's operational career with 28 Squadron and its gradual withdrawal from RAF service. On 20 May 1962 the first of the replacement Hunter FGA.9s arrived at Kai Tak from the UK. A third Hunter was delivered to the squadron on 12 June, on which day Flt Lt L'Anson carried out the Venom's last operational duty when he flew a local weather reconnaissance sortie.

On 27 June 1962 the withdrawal of the RAF's last operational Venom, WR539, was marked with a brief ceremonial flypast around the colony, piloted by Kai Tak's station commander and former squadron CO, Wg Cdr A.S. Mann DFC. The Venom was accompanied by a Hunter FGA.9 (flown by the CO, Sqn Ldr M.I. Stanway), a Hunter T.7 and a Vampire T.11 – which acted as a 'camera ship' for the occasion.

WR539 was struck off charge on 4 July and relegated to crash rescue training at Kai Tak. It fell into a state of disrepair until it was rescued by Flt Lt Bob Turner and members of the squadron, who refurbished it for static display as 8399M. In 1976 the airframe was transferred to Cosford for a proposed rebuild for the RAF Museum, but this project was abandoned because of the aircraft's poor condition and it was then sold to Visionair of Miami in April 1980 and placed into storage. Two years later it was passed to the Wales Air Museum at Cardiff Airport, and was acquired in October 1992 by the Mosquito Air Museum at Salisbury Hall. A major two-year restoration of the wooden fuselage pod was undertaken by the Gloucestershire Aviation Collection and it was returned to the renamed De Havilland Heritage Centre in December 2000 with the intention of restoring the aircraft to its original condition in the markings of 28 Squadron.

CHAPTER SEVEN

THE RAF'S VENOM NF.2

The rapid contraction of the postwar RAF left its night-fighter force sadly depleted, equipped with ageing Mosquito aircraft fitted with wartime AI Mk.10 radar. The absence of modern jet fighters was undoubtedly considered the weak link in the UK defences, especially in the face of the increasing threat of attacks by massed Russian bomber formations following the deterioration of East–West relations. Wartime experience had shown that two-seat night-fighters were essential, and if the night-fighter force were to remain effective until more suitable equipment became available then some form of stopgap would have to be introduced as soon as possible.

To meet the RAF's urgent requirement for a night-fighter, the Air Ministry issued two specifications in January 1947: F.43/46 for an interceptor fighter and F.44/46 for an interim, twin jet-engine all-weather fighter. Both designs were covered by Operational Requirement no. 227, which called for a two-seat, all-weather fighter, capable of 525 knots at 40,000ft and with an endurance of two hours. Armament should comprise four 30mm Aden guns, with the pilot and navigator seated in a tandem arrangement in a pressurised cockpit. Ejection seats would also be required.

Six companies submitted proposals. None fully met the RAF's requirements because of the lack of available design technology, but the Gloster Meteor NF.11 was eventually selected for use until a more suitable aircraft became available. After much alteration, in February 1948 the original requirement was replaced by F.4/48, which was issued to both Gloster Aircraft and de Havilland's. Two designs were subsequently tendered: the Gloster GA.5 and the de Havilland DH 110.

In April 1949 orders were placed with both companies for prototype aircraft for both the RAF and the Royal Navy, with production estimated by mid-1953. However, by the following November the effects of government budget restraints and policy changes resulted in a reduction of orders and created delays in the development programmes. The effects of these delays led the Royal Navy and RAF to consider adopting interim types, including the de Havilland Vampire and Venom night-fighters.

Early in 1948 de Havilland's had submitted their first proposal for a two-seat, night-fighter version of the Venom to replace the Vampire NF.10. The design would incorporate side-by-side seating in an enlarged fuselage nacelle, AI Mk.10 radar and a 4,850lb-thrust Ghost 103 engine. Although the Air Ministry had shown very little interest in the proposal, the company decided to build a prototype at its own expense, retaining as much as possible from the existing Vampire two-seat design. With the fuselage of a Vampire NF.10 (c/n 13004) as the basis for the Venom prototype, the slightly swept wings were structurally identical to those of the Venom fighter, except that the root end rib was altered to suit the new fuselage; boundary layer fences were also fitted to the top of the wings. The tail unit of the Vampire night-fighter was also retained, with its tall triangular fin and rudders. Also

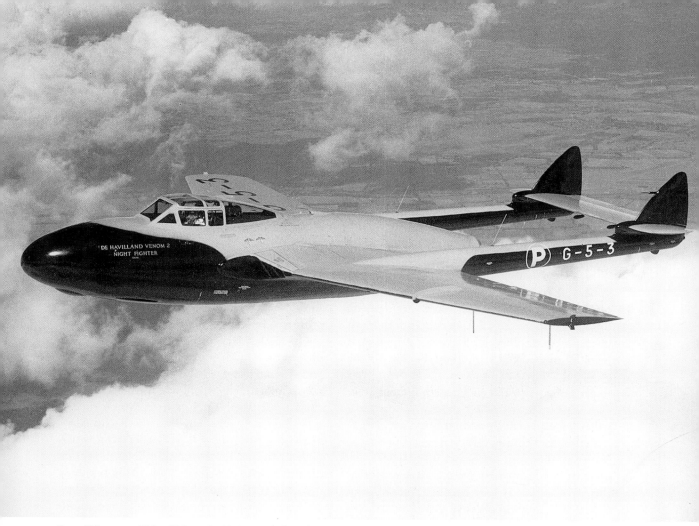

Venom NF.2 prototype G-5-3 on 18 September 1950, a month after its first flight. It carries its prototype and B class markings, together with the company stencilling on the nose. It is also, unusually, finished in the standard night bomber scheme of medium sea grey and black. (*Author's Collection*)

retained were the fuel system, undercarriage, dive brakes, the heavily framed canopy with an upward-hinging hatch for access, and the four 20mm Hispano cannons mounted in the floor of the nacelle.

Changes to the original Vampire fuselage design included the enlargement of the overall size of the nacelle to accommodate the pilot, navigator/radar observer and additional radio and radar equipment. The length of the fuselage was also increased from Bulkhead no. 2, to incorporate the AI Mk.10 search and navigational radar installation. The radar scanner and associated equipment was housed within a detachable plastic nose fairing, access to which was obtained by two

doors that were hinged to open outwards on both sides. Fuel was housed in nine tanks, permanently contained within the airframe structure; these comprised one rigid tank and four flexible bag tanks in each wing, providing a total internal capacity of 342 gallons. Additional fuel could be carried in a further 78-gallon tank mounted on each wing tip and two optional pylon-mounted 80-gallon drop-tanks.

As it was a private venture, the prototype (c/n 12001) was allocated a civil, Class-B registration, G-5-3, and made its first flight at Hatfield with John Wilson at the controls on 22 August 1950. Between then and January 1951 he continued to fly it on a variety of company trials, which included general handling, stability and flutter tests. Following his first three flights, which totalled about 1 hour 20 minutes of low altitude and general handling checks, he noted in his flight log that the aircraft was capable of 440 knots IAS at 5,000ft and at 9,000rpm. John Wilson went on to comment that the view from the cockpit was good under all conditions of flight but, as the speed increased, a general 'thundering' was audible in the cockpit that appeared to be coming from all round the canopy. He also noted that there was centring on the rudders at all speeds, and that an increase in stability with the long nose had resulted in marked trimming changes to the elevator. Further recommendations for improvements to the cockpit equipment were also suggested, including pressurisation via a galley pipe, which should be fitted as soon as possible as the aircraft was very prone to internal misting. In September 1950 the aircraft made its first public appearance at the SBAC show at Farnborough, where John Derry laid on an impressive demonstration of the type's low-level performance capabilities.

Although the Gloster GA.5 proposal was eventually chosen in preference to the DH 110 and was ordered by the RAF (as the Javelin), there were various delays in the programme. As a result of these setbacks, the Venom night-fighter soon attracted the attention of the Air Ministry. In June 1950 the DMARD suggested to the company that, although it was no longer interested in the Vampire night-fighter, it might possibly be interested in the Venom. However, no decision as to whether the aircraft would be adopted for the RAF could be taken until full official tests of the prototype had been carried out.

On 22 January 1951 the MoS bought the prototype Venom night-fighter for £130,000 and allocated it the military serial WP227. It was retained at Hatfield for further company trials until April 1951, during which time it was also briefly evaluated for the Royal Navy by a team from the A&AEE, following which it was flown to Boscombe Down for its official CS(A) clearance trials. This typically involved several months of handling, stability, stalling, high Mach numbers, spinning, radio and gunnery trials to clear the aircraft for

In January 1951 the MoS purchased the Venom night-fighter prototype for service evaluation and clearance trials. It was allocated the military serial WP227. (MoS)

The Venom NF.2 and Sea Venom FAW.20 production line at Chester in December 1952. The line on the right also contains a Venom FB.1, WE314, which was delivered to the CFE in March 1953. (*de Havilland*)

service use. During this period it would return to Hatfield at various times to be fitted with a new radome and an anti-spin parachute.

The conclusions of these preliminary handling trials were that the aircraft was pleasant to fly by day and night, but it was considered necessary to lighten the elevator forces and reduce the wing-dropping tendency prior to the stall when it was fitted with wing tanks. It was also suggested that the aircraft should be made less tiring to taxi, rudder travel should be restricted to eliminate rudder overbalance, and improvement in the rates of roll would be required if the aircraft were to fulfil its role as an all-weather fighter.

Simultaneous flight trials conducted at high Mach numbers showed the aircraft to be satisfactory at low and medium altitudes. The high-altitude characteristics were considered to be undesirable, however, and an improvement in aileron control and elevator effectiveness, together with more successful air brakes, would be required before the aircraft could be considered as acceptable. The report added that, should the urgent need for the Venom make it necessary to accept the aircraft pending a solution of the problem, it would be considered as acceptable at higher

altitudes up to the limits imposed by the company, i.e. 0.87IMN with the tanks off and 0.86IMN with the tanks on. In the event, the report further stressed that pilots should be adequately briefed about the behaviour of the aircraft at high Mach numbers to ensure that they fully realised the consequent operational limitations.

During the spring of 1951 a cockpit assessment of the Venom prototype was carried out, which noted that the cockpit of the aircraft was almost identical to that of the Vampire NF.10. Further observations in the report included the difficulty of entry and lack of room for the two crew members to strap in simultaneously. Although the seating position was comfortable and access to the flying controls and instruments was acceptable, the distortion through the curved roof panels should be eliminated.

The report's major criticism, however, was directed toward the inadequate escape facilities, with deep regret being expressed that ejection seats had not been fitted. It was suggested that every effort should be made to design and install a new canopy to improve the crew's chances of abandoning the aircraft in an emergency. In its response to this report de Havilland's noted that they were investigating possible designs for a new canopy – and also considering taking the radical step of introducing an escape hatch in the starboard side of the nose for the navigator!

The CS(A) clearance trials with WP227 continued until late 1953. In the meantime the aircraft's busy test career included flight development of the Ghost engine and the installation of a high Mach meter warning device (or stick-shaker). The experimental stick-shaker installation was fitted at Hurn in January 1952 and the aircraft was passed to the A&AEE for trials the following month, after which it was recommended that it should be fitted to Venom aircraft as soon as possible.

In September 1953 WP227 was relegated as an instructional airframe and passed to 1 Radio School at Locking as 7098M. It was finally struck off charge in December 1956 and scrapped.

In November 1950 the DOR began to complain that the lack of an operational requirement was holding up the placement of an order for the Venom night-fighter. As a result, on 29 November 1950 Specification F 108P for 'a prototype night-fighter for the RAF' was issued to cover the design and construction of the prototype, while on 21 December 1950 a contract for sixty Venom NF.2s was placed with the company at a cost of £2,047,500. Eight airframes (WL804–810 and WL812) were initially built at Hatfield, with the first aircraft, WL804, taking to the air on 4 March 1952. However, with factory space and available manpower being directed towards production of the Comet airliner, the remainder of the Venom contract was transferred to Chester, from where deliveries began the following December.

The production of the Venom was governed by Operational Requirement no. 265, dated 6 February 1951, which called for an interim night-fighter to cover the period prior to the production of the Gloster Javelin. The specification also stipulated that the aeroplane was to be fitted with a Ghost 103 engine and be capable of a speed of 435 knots, with an endurance at 30,000ft of at least two hours (after allowing for fifteen minutes of combat). Armament would comprise four 20mm cannon, with 700 rounds of ammunition. AI Mk.10 (SCR 720) radar and IFF equipment would be required, together with a G.4F compass and GEE Mk.3 (ARI 5816) navigation aid. A crew of two, comprising pilot and observer, would be seated in a pressure cabin. Amendments incorporated into the specification since its original issue included side-by-side seating instead of the staggered tandem arrangement. Moreover, although it would accept the AI Mk.10 radar in the short term, the aircraft should be tailored to accept the American APS.21 radar installation as soon as possible. Although there was no requirement for ejection seats to be fitted in the Venom night-fighter, the DMARD continued to express its desire for improved escape facilities but reluctantly accepted the fact that a major redesign of the cockpit layout would be required for the seats to be installed.

Pressed as to whether they would achieve the release date to the RAF (July 1952), de Havilland's admitted that they were still experiencing trouble with the Venom's high-speed handling characteristics. These included rudder dither and high-speed yaw, high stick forces, vibration at high Mach numbers, and 'trumpeting' of the gun blast tubes. There were also a considerable number of minor defects, many of which were suspected to be related to the fitting of a larger engine into what was basically a Vampire fuselage. As a consequence the aircraft was not expected to achieve its release date.

Anxious to get the type into service as soon as possible and to obtain the improvements they wanted without delaying production, on

15 July 1952 the DOR agreed a policy to introduce the aircraft in three stages:

Stage 1 (January 1952–September 1952): sixty aircraft would be accepted without any improvements.

Stage 2 (July 1952–May 1953): a further unspecified number of aircraft would be accepted with modified canopy to Mod. 170.

Stage 3 (May 1953–until final rundown): a new mark of night-fighter with all deficiencies made good would be in production by May 1953, in particular having ejection seats and APS.21 radar.

As a result of the issue of this DOR policy, a second order for a further 100 Venom NF.2s, which had been placed with the company in March 1951, was later revised to incorporate the Stage 2 interim modifications, while additional orders for 293 aircraft were amended or subsequently cancelled. The programme of modifications included:

Mod. 241: Balance weights in the wing-tip tanks to eliminate aileron tab flutter.

Mod. 242: Wing-tip slats to improve rear control stall.

Mod. 245: A sharp trailing edge to the rudder to cure the violent vibration at about Mach 0.80, which had caused the loss of Sea Venom WK376 in August 1952.

Mod. 247: Pilot-operated aileron trim tab.

A number of Venom NF.2s were actively engaged in the firm's test and development programme. The first production aircraft, WL804, had been retained by the company for gun port vibration and rudder dither trials, but had problems when the undercarriage retracted on landing in May 1952. The aircraft finally flew again in June, only to force-land at Hatfield the following September after suffering an engine failure. It was subsequently written off. The second production aircraft, WL805, was also retained at Hatfield and Christchurch for various trial installations from October 1952 until December 1954, when it was transferred to Marshall's to be fitted with a new canopy. WL806 was used for the official service release trials at Boscombe Down, following which it was fitted with a new tail assembly at Hurn in May 1953 and returned to the A&AEE for various trials involving the radar, gun and navigation installations. In late 1952

Built at Hatfield, the third production Venom NF.2, WL806, was responsible for official service release trials at Boscombe Down. It was later fitted with a new tail assembly and was used for various trials until ending its days as an instructional airframe at RNAS Bramcote. (MoS)

WL807 was fitted with a modified tail at Hurn. It was also adapted with an anti-spin parachute on the upper surface of the tailplane for the type's official handling and spinning trials, which were conducted at Boscombe Down between May and July 1953. It was sent to Marshall's in September 1954 for conversion to NF.2A standard.

Both WL808 and WL809 were to cause the manufacturers many problems during the trials carried out with the proposed wing-tip slats and tailplane modifications. WL808 was later used for engineering trials at the A&AEE, before issue to the de Havilland Engine Company at Hatfield in August 1953 for intensive flight development of the Ghost 104 engine. It was later converted to NF.2A standard. WL809 was issued to the A&AEE for handling trials, which were conducted between January and February 1953 but had to be abandoned when severe rudder overbalance was experienced. The aircraft was sent back to Hurn in April 1953 to be fitted with dorsal fins, and was later used in the development of aileron power boost and for the clearance trials of the Venom NF.3 tail assembly. It was fitted with a new canopy in late 1954 and eventually placed into store at Shawbury in March 1955.

WL810 was the first aircraft to be fitted with the new tail assembly and modified canopy. Between October 1952 and March 1954 it was used for the investigation and remedy of the high-speed yaw and for spinning trials with the new tail assembly at Hurn. WL811 was delivered from Chester in December 1952 for canopy trials at Christchurch, before transfer to Boscombe Down in April 1953 for blower tunnel tests. Fitted with a modified tailplane at Christchurch, the aircraft was returned to the A&AEE in September 1953 for further trials. Between November 1953 and January 1956 various trials with the new canopy, tail assembly and dive-brakes were carried out at Hurn. It was

eventually placed into store at Shawbury and scrapped in March 1958.

WL812 was issued to the de Havilland Engine Company in January 1953 for development trials of the Ghost 104 engine for the Sea Venom FAW.21 and the proposed Venom NF.5, but it suffered severe damage following an engine fire in February 1954. Further work with the aircraft consisted of engine development trials at Idris in 1956 and as a chase aircraft for a Canberra fitted with a DH Spectre rocket motor between June 1957 and January 1958. It was sold as scrap in January 1959.

Two aircraft, WL813 and WL820, were loaned to de Havilland Propellers at Hatfield between December 1952 and March 1959 for air trials of the Blue Jay/Firestreak air-to-air missile. WL813 was probably allocated the Class B Registration 'G-5-26' at some stage during the trials.

WL814 was allotted from Chester during December 1952 for flight trials and development of a large chord elevator at both Hatfield and the A&AEE to improve control at high Mach numbers. Further handling tests with new dorsal fins showed that although fin stalling had been eliminated, the spinning characteristics of the aeroplane were still unacceptable. The tail unit was redesigned with an extended top chord to the fin and rudder and fin-mounted pitot. It was also fitted with an anti-spin parachute. Returned to the A&AEE in 1954 for handling and spinning tests, it showed a marked improvement, though rates of roll still remained poor and lateral stick forces were higher than desirable. In November 1954 it was transferred to Marshall's for conversion to NF.2A standard.

Finally, WL831 was briefly used at Christchurch in August 1955 for the clearance trials of plastic tip-tanks, while WL857 was fitted with sophisticated instrumentation and painted in an overall yellow colour scheme for high-speed calibration checks of new aircraft at Boscombe Down between September 1953 and December 1958.

In January 1951 de Havilland's received the only export order for their Venom night-fighter when the Swedish government confirmed its intention to acquire a quantity of Venom J.33s (NF.51s) to replace its Mosquito night-fighters. The first thirty airframes were built to NF.2 standard at Ringway and Chester, and were fitted with Ghost engines built under licence by Svenska Flygmotor. Deliveries to Sweden were made between December 1952 and June 1954 – some eleven months before the RAF took delivery of its first Venom NF.2! A second order with Stage 2 modifications incorporated was delivered between December 1953 and August 1954.

INTO SERVICE – AT LAST!

On 6 May 1953 the Venom NF.2 was finally granted its CS(A) release, and five days later WL817 was flown to the RAF Handling Squadron at Manby for the compilation of the Pilots' Notes. Later in the month two more Venoms (WL816 and WL818) were issued to the CFE (AWW), based at West Raynham, to carry out the evaluation and development of night-fighter tactics. These trials at the CFE consisted of an all-weather performance evaluation conducted by WL816, while WL818 took part in a simulated rocket interceptor trial between August and October 1953.

On Wednesday 23 November 1953 23 Squadron (Sqn Ldr A.J. Jacomb-Hood DFC) at Coltishall became the first RAF squadron to be equipped with Venom night-fighters, with the delivery of four aircraft (WL819, WL823, WL828 and WL858) from the Maintenance Units at Hawarden and Shawbury. The squadron had developed a reputation as a skilled exponent in the art of

night-fighting, having been selected to become the first specialist offensive (intruder) squadron in November 1940. Equipped with successive aircraft types, including Havoc and Mosquito night-fighters, 23 Squadron entered the jet age in October 1951 when it began to exchange its Mosquito NF.36s for Vampire NF.10s. Deliveries of the new NF.2s continued, and the squadron became non-operational for a short time to convert from the Vampire NF.10. Despite a period of bad weather that hampered the task, most of the pilots had flown the new type before the end of the year.

On 29 December 1953 squadron morale was hit by the loss of Flg Off A. 'Soapy' Towle who was killed when he made a forced-landing near Tuxford, Notts, after collecting a new aircraft (WL829) from Hawarden. His was the squadron's first fatal accident following the conversion to Venoms. Sadly, however, he was not to be the last. On 21 January 1954 the commanding officer and his Nav/Rad, Flg Off A.E. Osbourne, were killed when their aircraft (WL828) dived out of cloud during a weather test and crashed in Reffley Wood near South Wooton, King's Lynn.

By March 1954 the squadron was able to commit a handful of Venoms for its first exercise, 'Magna Flux', during which twenty-three sorties were flown in return for thirty 'kills' and one 'probable'. The month was to end in tragedy when another squadron Venom (WL830) crashed into the sea off the Happisburgh lighthouse during a low-level night exercise. An extensive search by ships and the Cromer lifeboat failed to find the crew, Sgts P.B. Jackson and H. Drabble.

In early April a heavy schedule incorporating modifications to the flaps, following the discovery of a small crack beneath the butt joint in the upper wing skin of the Venom, meant that some of the aircraft were temporarily grounded until the problem could be

A pair of 23 Squadron Venom NF.2s (WL822 and WL826) up from Coltishall on 21 June 1954. The squadron would be the only operational unit to be equipped with the type. (*via 23 Squadron Association*)

rectified. Subsequent restrictions of an altitude limit of 10,000ft and a maximum speed of 455 knots were also briefly imposed on the RAF's Venom fleet until a minor modification – Mod. 281 – was introduced. This consisted of a small reinforcing plate riveted over the affected section at the rear of the undercarriage bay.

Noel 'Snowy' Davies flew both the Vampire NF.10 and Venom NF.2 with 23 Squadron:

About four pilots, including myself, attended the Venom handling course at Hatfield in December 1953. The aircraft seemed similar to the Vampire, but the differences were critical: the range/endurance was improved, so was the height and performance, but the radar was the same as the Vampire's with a range of around 4–10 miles. Occasionally, the pilot would see the target, even at night, before the Nav/Rad picked it up on his set!

I only flew the Venom NF.2, the earliest form. Our aircraft had been in store for many months, awaiting modifications demanded by the Air Ministry, and all suffered from 'fatigue-type' problems. Although cramped, the cockpit accommodation was adequate for most, the side-by-side seating being preferred to the tandem version in the Meteor. The aircraft also had very narrow wheels to fit in the thinner wings, and were kept at very high pressures, which sounded rough on landing.

During my last year with 23 Squadron, we lost ten men in ten months through flying accidents, including two commanding officers. Within a couple of years three more of my squadron contemporaries had been lost. A sad time.

Following long hours and much hard work by the groundcrews to get the aircraft serviceable again, a normal squadron training programme was eventually resumed with low-level 'Rat and Terrier' exercises, and practice interceptions up to 50,000ft, which revealed a marked improvement in performance over the earlier Vampires. Regular claims against aircraft such as USAF F-84 Thunderstreaks and B-45 Tornadoes also began to appear in the pilots' logbooks, although the Canberra bomber remained as difficult to intercept as ever. Seemingly confident in the Venom's capabilities, the new CO, Sqn Ldr P.S. Engelbach, was able to comment: 'The squadron has also been flying higher and faster, and with the introduction of 40,000ft as a normal height for interceptions, increasing to 48,000ft whenever the control system was able to do it, the squadron now considers itself the highest and fastest flying night/all weather squadron in the Royal Air Force.'

It was during this period that one of the squadron's flight commanders, Eric Knighton, with the help of London Zoo, devised the practice of allocating the names of venomous snakes to individual squadron aircraft. These names were applied in gold to the starboard side of the front fuselage and included:

A Flight: Adder, Boomslang, Cobra, Diamond Back, Echis, Fer-de-Lance, Gaboon, Hamadryad, Mamba, Naja, and RattleSnake.

B Flight: Sand Snake, Tic Polonga, Ular Sower, Viper, Whip Snake, Xenopeltis, and Yoperohobobo.

To complement the adoption of the names of poisonous snakes, the squadron's Vampire trainers were, in turn, given the names of anti-venoms: Ammonite, Antivenin and Snakestone.

A temporary lack of serviceable aircraft did not prevent the squadron taking part in Exercise 'Dividend' during July 1954, its first major Fighter Command exercise since re-equipping with the Venom. Although the first phase of the exercise was hampered by bad weather, the squadron flew nineteen day and eleven night sorties, claiming eighteen enemy aircraft 'destroyed' and a further two 'damaged'. Improved conditions during the second phase saw the Venoms flying forty-three day and forty-two night sorties, resulting in a further twenty-eight 'kills' and three 'damaged'.

Bob Myatt joined 23 Squadron in November 1954, and for the next three years he was not only a pilot but also OC Engineering:

At this time (1954) the RAF night-fighter force was equipped with only one Venom NF.2

squadron. The Javelin was behind schedule, and the greatest threat to the UK came from a mass daylight assault by Russian bomber formations. Bombers were regularly operating at heights upwards of 40,000ft, which the Meteors were unable to reach, and the new Canberra was proving difficult to catch.

The Venom NF.2 was hurried into RAF service and did not receive the attention it deserved. The maintenance units were also pressured to get the aircraft into service as soon as possible. Therefore, when in squadron service the aircrews were able to find many faults. Normally, a lot of the problems would be discovered and rectified during the service trials, but because of the indecent haste with which the Venom was pressed into squadron use – when it was flown regularly at .84M and at high altitude, and full use was made of airbrakes, flaps and undercarriage – cracks and other faults were found by the groundcrew. The designers worked hard to keep updating the Venom NF.2 to meet operational requirements, and quite a few modifications were undertaken to strengthen various operating surfaces, such as the flaps, undercarriage and tail unit.

The wing cracks were never too frightening and the aircraft were never grounded for more than a few days. I flew aircraft with obvious signs of cracks, and at no time did I feel nervous of operating the Venom NF.2 – in any weather. I personally liked the Venom NF.2, and can only recall pleasant flights in the type – despite an engine failure on one occasion at 53,750ft over the Friesian Islands!

However, 23 Squadron was destined to be the only RAF squadron equipped with Venom NF.2s. In August 1954 it took delivery of the first of the new Venom NF.2As; three months later the last of its NF.2s was passed to Marshall's of Cambridge for conversion to NF.2A standard. A few of the modified aircraft would see further squadron service; the rest would be put into storage and eventually join the others as they were reduced to scrap.

CHAPTER EIGHT

'AN IMPROVED VENOM': THE VENOM NF.2A

In January 1953 representatives from the MoS and de Havilland's met to discuss the suggested introduction of modifications to resolve the aerodynamic problems that had dogged the trials of the early Venom aircraft. The defects had included high-speed yaw, rudder dither, severe wing drop and the lack of adequate escape facilities for the crews. By the following July it was decided to incorporate the following:

- DH Mod. 170: a modified canopy to improve visibility and make it easier for the crew to vacate the cockpit in the event of an emergency. The single-piece, upward-opening canopy with a hydraulically powered jettison device and direct vision windscreen side panels was similar to those also being fitted to the Vampire trainers.
- DH Mod. 244: extended fin acorns at the rear of the tailplane to improve handling by reducing elevator and rudder buffeting at high Mach numbers.
- DH Mod. 372: dorsal fairing extensions similar to those fitted to Vampire T.11s to eliminate the fin stalling and rudder overbalance found on early production aircraft. This modification also involved a redesigned tail unit and incorporated the flat-topped fin and rudder of the Venom FB.4. The rudder also featured an extended horn balance, a thin trailing edge and a repositioned bottom rib to clear the new bullet fairings.

WL810 was the first Venom to be fitted with the new dorsal fairings, and in October 1952 it was transferred from Hatfield to Hurn for further investigation of high-speed yaw and for spinning trials. Three further aircraft (WL811, WL866 and WL868) were partially modified by de Havilland's, the first of which (WL811) was fitted with a new canopy at Christchurch in December 1952. Following blower tunnel tests at the A&AEE at Boscombe Down, it was returned to Christchurch in May 1953 to be fitted with dorsal fairings, where it replaced WL809.

Earlier production handling trials conducted with WL809 at Boscombe Down in December 1952 had shown severe rudder buffeting and overbalance, and the aircraft had been returned to Christchurch in March 1953 to be fitted with the new dorsal fairings. The following month the aircraft was sent back to the A&AEE for brief handling tests (together with a production Vampire trainer that had also been fitted with dorsal fins for evaluation at the same time). The subsequent trials showed that the dorsal fins and small increase in fin area helped to eliminate fin stall and rudder overbalance, but without affecting the aircraft's rate of roll; the modification was therefore considered to be acceptable provided that the spinning characteristics also proved to be satisfactory. In a memo to the MoS following these tests, the company stated that WL809 had been selected to 'act as a production standard for the modifications introduced for aerodynamic reasons', and proposed that WL815 and subsequent aircraft (i.e. those intended for direct delivery to the RAF) should be to this standard; earlier aircraft, on loan to the CS(A), would also be brought up to this standard before delivery to the service.

The spinning trials conducted at Boscombe Down with WL809 were subsequently found to be disappointing and further tests were carried out with WL814, which had been fully modified to incorporate the new fin and rudder and had been fitted with an anti-spin parachute at Christchurch in October 1953. The following April it was sent to Boscombe Down to extend the earlier handling and spinning trials previously completed with WL809, in which the rate of roll was found to be poor. Large stick forces were also required in order to obtain a reasonable aircraft response to the elevator on the final approach.

Air Cdre Peter Thorne was a test pilot with A Squadron A&AEE at Boscombe Down from 1952 to 1955. He occasionally flew both the Venom 1 and Venom 4, and in 1953 was appointed as the project pilot on the Venom NF.2:

My next full service release trial was the Venom NF.2 in early 1953. There had been some concern over the directional stability of the bulbous-nosed Vampire/Venom variants (the Vampire T.11 was in mid-evaluation for dorsal fillets) but the trials aircraft arrived with the standard Venom tail. The aircraft was a production Mk.2, WL807, fitted with full wing tanks for the purpose of the trial, which was for spinning from straight stalls.

Satisfactory in most aspects of flight it was deficient in directional stability and was returned to Christchurch for remedial action. It came back with dorsal fillets and the assurance that its directional stability was beyond reproach. During the spinning trial from 41,000ft the aircraft behaved normally until recovery action was taken

when, after rotation had nearly stopped, a violent sideslip to the right precipitated a runaway phase of rapid uncontrollable spins in alternate directions, with severe pitching between the vertical and 20–30 degrees past vertical. Order was finally restored, with horizontal flight regained at 17,000ft; Mach 1 and all 'g' limits had been exceeded on the way. Fortunately the aircraft was fully instrumented and had a wire recorder. It went back to the firm; a completely new tail was designed and fitted to Venom NF.3s and Sea Venoms, and the Venom NF.2 was limited for service use when released.

My personal report to the A Squadron Tech Office suggested that the violent sideslip at the normal point of recovery was caused by fin stalling, and that the subsequent uncommanded behaviour was a function of the fin stall, complicated later by the effects of compressibility. I see from my logbook that the service release trials of the Mk.2 were completed on WL814, with particular reference to high IMN handling.

Of the thirty-six main aircraft types and twenty variants flown during my tour with the A&AEE, the Venom 2 stands out in my memory as one of the least pleasant, though certainly it was more operationally effective than the Vampire NF.10 it replaced.

Meanwhile, an evaluation of the new canopy fitted to WL811 was carried out by the A&AEE between April and May 1953, and concluded that the redesign had resulted in considerable improvements in visibility, escape facilities, rudder dither and the incidence of 'hood roar', although criticism was made of the operation of the direct vision panel and of the heavy framework around the windscreen. By the following September the aircraft had been fitted with a fully modified tail assembly and was returned to Boscombe Down for an assessment of the canopy at a range of speeds higher than had been previously permitted; it was found to be satisfactory.

Further modified trials aircraft included:

WL806: Accepted as a representative airframe, it was flown to the A&AEE in September 1952 for radar, gunnery and service release trials. During the gunnery trials the proposed 'de-tuners' for curing gun-port problems – Mod. 289 – disintegrated and were replaced by an improved, strengthened version for further trials on WL809. The airframe was eventually downgraded for instructional use at RNAS Bramcote in May 1957.

WL807: Allocated for spinning trials, this aircraft later went to de Havilland Engines for flight development of the Ghost 104 engine, to Christchurch for further spinning trials and to Hatfield for hydraulic system tests.

With their clear-view cockpit canopies and revised fins and rudders, the modified aircraft continued to retain most of the equipment of the original Venom NF.2, including the 4,850lb-thrust Ghost 103 engine and AI Mk.10 radar. There was to be no official Air Ministry sanction for the modified aircraft, and in RAF service the variant was still referred to as the NF.2 or the 'modified Venom NF.2'. (The origin of the designation NF.2A is unclear but it was certainly being referred to as such in an article featured in an issue of *The Aeroplane* during December 1955. Therefore, to ensure continuity and to differentiate between the two versions, the designation NF.2A will continue to be used.) Although the modifications were still considered to be 'interim', it was decided to introduce the Venom NF.2A into RAF service as quickly as possible, and thirty airframes (WR779–808) – part of an original order for a hundred Venom NF.2s placed in February 1951 – were modified on the Chester and Hatfield assembly

A line-up of Venom NF.2As of 33 Squadron at Driffield. The nearest aircraft, WR794, was to spend its entire service career with the squadron, being withdrawn to 27MU in July 1957 and eventually scrapped. (*MoD*)

lines against Contract no. 6/ACFT/10129. Deliveries began in June 1954.

At least twenty-three Venom NF.2s had been fitted with the interim tailplane modification at Chester before delivery (including WL816, WL817, WL849, WL850, WL853, WL855, WL856, and WL859 to WL874), together with a further twenty-two aircraft which were brought up to full production standard at the Marshall's Engineering site at Waterbeach between June 1954 and July 1956. These aircraft included: WL805, WL807, WL808, WL809, WL814, WL815, WL818, WL819, WL821, WL822, WL824, WL825, WL826, WL827, WL831, WL845, WL846, WL847, WL851, WL852, WL854 and WL858.

Initial deliveries were to 23 Squadron (Sqn Ldr P.S. Englebach) at Coltishall, with the first, WR781, arriving on 19 August 1954. A further four aircraft had been delivered by the end of September, and the squadron was up to strength by mid-November as the last of the NF.2s was ferried away. Irritating minor problems with the new aircraft and a low serviceability record did not deter the squadron from taking part in exercise 'Battle Royal' during September, when four Canberras and a Lincoln bomber were claimed as 'destroyed' during eight sorties.

The new year got off to a bad start for the squadron when, on 15 February 1955, the CO and his navigator, Flg Off M.J. Wright, were killed when their Venom (WR781) hit a tree soon after take-off and crashed into a field at Rougham, Norfolk. Command of the squadron was temporarily passed to Sqn Ldr C.R. Winter DFC. In July 1955, following a reversion to the wartime policy of night-fighter units being led by an officer of wing commander rank, Sqn Ldr Winter was replaced by Wg Cdr A.N. Davies DSO, DFC. One of the new CO's first initiatives was to implement the 'Coltishall Experiment', where the squadron was split into three units, A and

B Flights (flying) and C Flight (engineering).

With an increase in the rate of serviceability, all twelve squadron Venoms were able to take part in a successful three-week armament programme at Acklington during May and June, which had been preceded by a squadron 'first' on 17 March, when a Valiant bomber had been intercepted at 47,500ft during a regular 'Bombex' exercise. Bob Myatt's earlier comments on the Venom NF.2s can be complemented by his opinions on the squadron and its new aircraft:

By the end of 1954 the aircraft serviceability and morale compared to other night-fighter units was low. The squadron had lost two commanding officers in quick succession, and it was not until the arrival of Wing Commander A.N. Davies and the introduction of the 'Coltishall Experiment' that the situation began to improve – even though the Venom was being called upon to fly faster and higher.

The new hood fitted to the Venom NF.2A (and NF.3) was extremely good and enabled us to operate at very low weather thresholds, and by the time I left the squadron the Venom operated well at 45,000ft and at maximum allowed airspeeds because time had been used sensibly and events didn't demand too much from us.

On 18 April 1955 a second squadron was formed when 253 Squadron (Wg Cdr P.J.S. Finlayson AFC) assembled at Waterbeach, having taken delivery of its first aircraft, WR808, two weeks earlier. Declared operational on 1 September, the squadron's first major exercise was 'Beware' at the end of the month when, during fifty sorties, thirty-nine Canberras and five B-45 Tornado bombers of the USAF were claimed as probably destroyed. The CO, however, was not entirely impressed with the Venom's radar equipment:

Exercise 'Beware' gave the squadron its first opportunity to find out how effectively the NF.2

WL873 was built at Chester as a NF.2 but was modified to NF.2A standard before delivery to 253 Squadron at Waterbeach in September 1955, where it was assigned to the CO, Wg Cdr P.J.S. Finlayson DFC. (*John Rawlings*)

would perform. In the long-term view the results were not too encouraging; quite plainly any sustained flying effort will develop an overpowering degree of [aircraft] unserviceability. The performance of the AI Mk.10 equipment varied enormously and proved to be 65 per cent effective throughout the exercise. This may be a respectable figure for the AI Mk.10 but is hardly a reputable prospect for the defence of the realm at night.

Despite the CO's doubts as to the effectiveness of the Venoms' radar equipment, the squadron continued to notch up more claims during 1956 when it took part in the usual round of Fighter Command exercises, and in January was a runner-up in that year's Ingpen Trophy competition at Acklington for the best night/all-weather squadron. During its two-and-a-half year association with the type, 253 Squadron lost only two aircraft: on 27 September 1956 WL832 dived into the

ground at night shortly after take-off during Exercise 'Stronghold', killing Flg Off O'Hare and Sgt O'Brien; two months later, on 21 November 1956, a tip-tank broke loose during an air-firing exercise and the aircraft (WR808) had to be abandoned following a loss of control. Fortunately, the crew, Flt Lts Mallett and Hodges, were uninjured.

During the autumn of 1955, while 23 Squadron was trading in its NF.2As for the Venom NF.3, two further squadrons were established at Driffield for the all-weather defence of Yorkshire and Lincolnshire. No. 219 Squadron (Wg Cdr R.A. Watts AFC) was formed on 5 September, receiving its first NF.2A the following week, and 33 Squadron (Wg Cdr R.C. Patrick DFC, AFC) on 1 November, after flying 'Firedog' ground-attack operations in Malaya with Tempest and Hornet fighters for the previous six years.

The majority of the crews selected for the night-fighter squadrons were normally serving on their first operational squadron, with the pilots receiving at least five hours of transition training in instrument flying and general handling in the Vampire T.11. The navigators were trained at an OCU on either Meteor NF.11s at Leeming (for the Venom NF.2 and NF.2As fitted with AI Mk.10 radar), or on Brigands and Meteor NF.14s at North Luffenham (for the Venom NF.3 fitted with AI Mk.21 radar).

It was not until April 1956 that 219 Squadron achieved its full establishment of sixteen Venoms. The following August it was able to detach six aircraft to Waterbeach for Exercise 'Fabulous'. A regular feature of squadron life for all the Venom night-fighter squadrons, this week-long detachment to either Waterbeach or Wattisham was considered as an operational commitment and required the aircraft to be fully armed and placed on readiness in the event of a scramble.

Ian Small was a navigator with 219 Squadron from November 1955 to July 1957, having previously flown Meteor night-fighters with 96 Squadron in Germany:

Many of the aircrew had been on Meteor NF.11s in Germany with me, and more or less came across en masse to 33 and 219 Squadrons when they re-formed with Venoms. The squadron routine included mutual air practices; low-level 'rat and terrier' exercises; air-to-air cine and live firings, usually on the range at Filey; a month of air-to-air firing at Acklington; a couple of weeks holding the Fighter Command operational standby at Waterbeach or Wattisham, known as Exercise 'Fabulous'; CIANO air defence exercises, which called for the Venoms to fly high-level profiles as targets for the radar defences and day-fighter squadrons; occasional sorties on 'freelance' practice interceptions looking for some unsuspecting Meteor/Canberra/Vampire to have a go at; and air tests and night-flying tests – in those

Photographs of the Venom NF.2As of 219 Squadron at Driffield are quite rare. This aircraft (WL872) is depicted at the ROC display at Church Fenton in August 1956 and wears the red and black squadron chevrons on the tail-booms. (*Eric Taylor*)

days it was usual to fly your own aircraft during the day prior to night flying to assess radar performance and tweak it up for the night sorties.

Serviceability was poor in the early days and I can remember waiting around for days for an aircraft. A good month's flying for an individual would be about 20 hours (13 day and 7 night) and this would be about twenty sorties. The Venom was quite a bit faster in the climb than the Meteor NF.11 and generally operated better at height. I enjoyed the side-by-side seating with the pilot, and, with fairly useless radar, two pairs of eyes looking out the front certainly helped. Pick-up range on the AI radar on another Venom was about 5 miles, which was unbelievably bad compared to today's standards. With the 20mm cannon mounted in the nose, air-to-air gunnery

scores were generally better than the Meteor NFs. On 219 Squadron we had a favourable accident record. I think that we had only one serious crash – which is not bad for a Venom squadron in the mid-1950s. On 3 May 1956 Johnny Galloway (in WL848) stalled in the circuit during his final approach on the south-west runway at Driffield, rolled over and went straight in. Both he and his Nav/Rad, Sgt Reice, were killed.

For the Battle of Britain 'At Home' Day celebrations held in September 1956, 33 Squadron sent five aircraft to various RAF stations to take part in the static exhibitions. It was originally intended that the squadron's aerobatic team should be represented at the displays. The four-man team had been

In 1956 Venom NF.2A WL826 was allocated for conversion as a high-speed navigation trainer to replace the RAF's Vampire NF(T).10s. The proposal was dropped the following year and the aircraft languished at Hawarden, where it was photographed in May 1958. Note the yellow training bands on the tail-booms. (*R.L. Ward*)

formed earlier in the year and was led by Sqn Ldr Caryl Gordon, a former personal pilot to HRH the Duke of Edinburgh, and consisted of Flt Lts Dunwoody, Morley and Wright. However, with negative 'g' restrictions being imposed on the Venom, the AOC 13 Group decided to reduce the number of aircraft in the team to three. His decision was quickly overruled by HQ Fighter Command, who imposed a complete ban on Venom aerobatics and cancelled their appearance, which effectively brought an end to all further Venom night-fighter displays.

The following month the squadron suffered its first fatal accident after re-forming. On 11 October Venom WR784 struck a tree and some high-tension cables soon after take-off from Driffield and dived into the ground, killing Flg Offs Northen and Curry.

In February 1956 46 Squadron at Odiham became the first operational unit to receive the Gloster Javelin all-weather fighter. Together with the drastic cuts contained within the 1957 White Paper on Defence, this marked the beginning of the gradual withdrawal of the Venom night-fighter from RAF service. Both 33 and 219 Squadrons were declared non-operational and disbanded

on 31 July. No. 253 Squadron remained operational until the end of July and was able to contribute most of its remaining aircraft to Exercise 'Vigilant', when forty-six 'enemy' aircraft were claimed. On 8 August the squadron carried out its last operational sortie when it put all of its aircraft into the air for the traditional farewell tour of local night-fighter stations. It was disbanded on 4 September 1957 and its Venoms were ferried away to Silloth. After a short period in storage at various MUs, the final Venom NF.2A airframe was sold for scrap in 1959. Sadly, not one example of the type has been preserved for posterity.

In 1956 one Venom airframe, WL826, was allocated for conversion to a high-speed navigation trainer type to replace the Vampire NF(T).10, currently serving with the RAF's Air Navigation Schools. It was delivered to 48MU Hawarden in May 1956 following its conversion to NF.2A standard. By June 1957, however, the proposal to modify Venom aircraft for use in the training role had been abandoned in favour of the Meteor NF(T).14, and although the Venom was seen at Hawarden in May 1958, during an RAeS 'Garden Party', it was struck off charge the following month and scrapped.

CHAPTER NINE

THE VENOM NF.3: THE ULTIMATE VENOM NIGHT-FIGHTER

The Venom NF.3 was the final all-weather variant to enter operational service with the RAF, and was publicly announced in April 1953. It was also the last of the postwar interim types to be produced, and incorporated the improvements developed during the aircraft's protracted trials programme and set down by the Air Ministry's earlier policy of getting the Venom into service as soon as possible. Although its contemporary, the Sea Venom FAW.21, went on to enjoy a comparatively longer service life with the Royal Navy, the RAF's night-fighter version suffered from a degree of financial restraint in its development costs owing to the proposed re-equipment of the all-weather fighter squadrons with the Gloster Javelin.

To improve the high-altitude interception capabilities of the Venom NF.3 and Sea Venom, it had been originally intended to install a Ghost engine fitted with a reheat system. Trials had begun in December 1950 when the first Venom prototype was fitted with an elementary, two-position reheat Ghost engine. In August 1952 the Air Ministry began to consider the possibility of fitting the system into Venom night-fighter aircraft and called for a comparison in performance with the Gloster Meteor NF.11. Subsequent trials had shown that there was little to choose between the two types other than in endurance, and that the fitting of reheat appeared to offer very little improvement in performance. It was further decided that, while an increase of thrust was necessary in order to give any appreciable advantage over the Meteor, at a development cost of about £2,100 per aircraft the installation made it very expensive; a reasonable compromise, however, could be obtained by introducing the up-rated Ghost 104 engine, capable of 4,950lb of thrust. The following March the proposal to install reheat was officially cancelled on the grounds of cost and the probable short service life of the aircraft.

In common with the earlier night-fighter variants, ejection seats were not fitted to the Venom NF.3. In September 1954 de Havilland's responded to an Air Ministry request to consider the possibility of having them installed and stated that the total cost to make the necessary alterations to the structure of the cockpit and retrospectively install the seats would be in the region of £5,225. The company also stated that it would not be possible to carry the GEE navigation aid and that a Rebecca 7 installation would have to be substituted. Although Martin-Baker lightweight ejection seats had been successfully fitted in the Sea Venom, the cockpit layout differed in the two types and the Air Ministry was asked to reconsider the installation as the useful life of the Venom NF.3 would be short. By October 1956 the plan was finally abandoned because of Fighter Command's current re-equipment programme with the Gloster Javelin.

WV928, the all-silver Venom NF.3 prototype, probably at Christchurch in 1953. Retaining the framed canopy and tail assembly of the Vampire night-fighter, it was responsible for most of the flight trials of the AI Mk.21 radar equipment. (*de Havilland*)

The Venom's original AI Mk.10 radar equipment was also replaced by the American Westinghouse AN/APS-57 installation, supplied through funding from the MDAP. Designated AI Mk.21 by the RAF, the forward-searching radar had a range of 15–20 miles, compared to the 6–10 miles of the AI Mk.10; the scanner and its associated equipment was housed in a new, completely symmetrical plastic radome, which was hinged upwards for easier access. The new radar was made available in September 1952, and the following month it was proposed that a prototype aircraft should be ordered for company and service trials of the equipment. Accordingly, WV928 was built at Christchurch under Contract no. 6/Acft/7006/

CB.7(a), retaining a framed canopy and the tall, pointed fin and rudders of the Vampire night-fighter. The initial flight was made at Hatfield on 22 February 1953 and the following June it was issued to the TRE at Defford, where flight trials of the APS-57/AI Mk.21 radar were carried out. WV928 was later transferred to the CFE for further development trials and was known to have taken part in Fighter Command's Exercise 'Momentum' in August 1953. At the end of its service life, WV928 was issued to RAF Cranwell in March 1955 as an instructional airframe.

Further improvements incorporated into the Venom NF.3 included powered flying controls, a Maxaret braking system to

Photographed on an early test flight in May 1954, this is the third production Venom NF.3, WX787. Built at Christchurch, it never entered squadron service, being used for development trials. It was eventually sold as scrap in April 1958. (*Darryl Cott*)

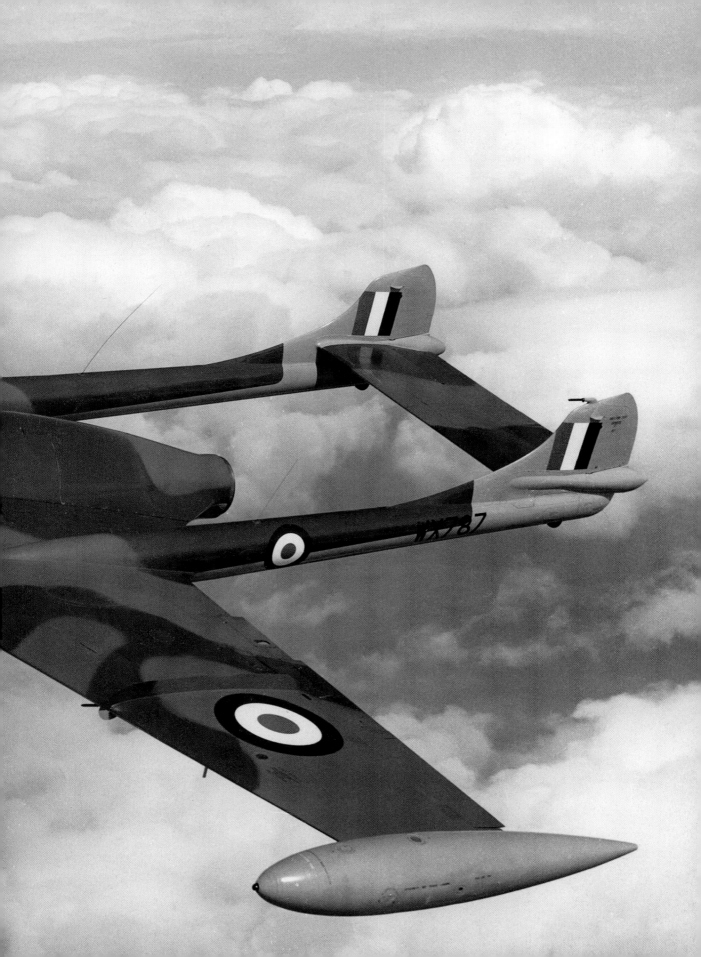

prevent the wheels locking during hard braking, a clear-view canopy fitted with a powered jettison device, and the removal of the original tailplane extensions outboard of the fins to improve the effectiveness of the rudders and elevator. Early flight trials carried out at Boscombe Down had shown the handling qualities of the NF.3 to be considerably better than those of previous Venoms. Up to the limiting Mach number the controls were found to be light and effective, and manual handling in conditions of poor visibility and turbulence was the only aspect for which the A&AEE could recommend any form of improvement. The higher all-up weight from the 13,838lb of the Venom NF.2 to 14,544lb, however, resulted in a deterioration in performance such that it would be scarcely considered adequate for dealing with contemporary bombers: the rate of climb was deemed to be poor – sixteen minutes to 40,000ft; operational altitude was barely above 40,000ft; and the usable Mach limit was 0.85 TMN. The report concluded that it was doubtful whether the increased effectiveness of the AI equipment carried in the NF.3 would offset the decreased performance.

Nevertheless, in July 1951 an initial production order for 123 aircraft was placed with de Havilland's, with the construction to be shared between Christchurch and Chester. However, following an alteration to the programme, some of the airframes produced at Chester were sent down to Hatfield as fully equipped kits for final assembly. A second order for thirty-four aircraft placed in September 1951 was later reduced to six. Final production of the 129 Venom NF.3s for the RAF was distributed between Chester (86 aircraft), Hatfield (23) and Christchurch (20), with deliveries between August 1953 and April 1956.

Initial allocations were to the Controller (Air) for various company trials and test programmes, the first production aircraft (WX785) being passed to de Havilland's at Christchurch on 17 September 1953. Between that date and November 1955 a further eighteen Venom NF.3s were allocated as trials aircraft. These included:

WX785: Issued to de Havilland's at Christchurch and in September 1953 made its first public appearance in the static park at the Farnborough Air Show. It was later used to evaluate the Venom cockpit layout until it was damaged in a landing accident in October 1953. Following repairs it was transferred to the A&AEE in June 1954 to test the strength of the nose radome during gun-firing trials. It was returned to Christchurch in May 1955 for further trials and passed into storage the following September.

WX786: Flown on type clearance trials at Christchurch between January and April 1954, when it was issued to the A&AEE for general and performance measurement trials. It went into storage at Hawarden in October 1955.

WX787: Used for engineering test work at Christchurch and the A&AEE between March 1954 and April 1955.

WX788: Allocated for spinning trials and fitted with a tail parachute.

WX789: Issued to the de Havilland Engine Co. at Hatfield in August 1954 for flight development of the Ghost 104 and 105 engines. In March 1958 it was briefly involved with photographic work during the flight test programme of Canberra WK163, which had been fitted with Viper turbo-jet engines. With the withdrawal of MoS financial support for the Ghost 105 development programme, WX789 was sold to de Havilland's in September 1958.

Venom NF.3 WX792 soon after delivery to the Handling Squadron at Manby in January 1955. Its service career would be brief and it was struck off charge in July 1957. The demarcation line of the camouflage applied to the upper surfaces of the fuselage is seen to advantage. (*MoS*)

WX790: Engaged in Maxaret brake handling tests at Christchurch, before being handed to the A&AEE in November 1954 for CA release approach and landing trials. Following the incorporation of various modifications at Hurn, it was passed back to Boscombe Down in June 1955 for engineering and Maxaret brake trials. It was returned to Christchurch in February 1956.

WX793: Briefly used for an investigation into cockpit icing at Christchurch between May and September 1956.

WX797: Employed on radar research trials at RRE Defford between October 1955 and August 1957.

WX799: Used for trial installation of various modifications at Christchurch from March

1955 until July 1957, when it was passed to 27MU Shawbury.

WX809: ARI 18006 clearance trials at CSE Watton between June and September 1955.

WX865: Operated by the RAE at Bedford between January 1956 and July 1962 on a variety of boundary layer research trials. These trials included buffet tests, and it was experimentally fitted with a wing-tip parachute in June 1960 to investigate the effects of wing-tip wake. It was struck off charge in July 1962 for use in apprentice training at Bedford.

WX874: Used in IFF 10 and ARI 18006 radio installation and radome strength trials at Christchurch until March 1956, when further flight trials of ARI 18006 were carried out by the A&AEE and CSE. It was passed to Shawbury in May 1957.

WX926: Used for the trial installation of Martin-Baker ejection seats at Christchurch between November 1955 and February 1957.

The Venom NF.3 obtained its CS(A) release in February 1955 and entered RAF service along the lines laid down by the standard procedure: one aircraft (WX792) was issued to the Handling Squadron at Manby in January 1955, and a further three (WX804, WX807 and WX808) were sent to the AWNW at West Raynham in the following June.

With the arrival of four aircraft (WX793, WX801, WX803 and WX841) on 5 July 1955, 141 Squadron (Sqn Ldr J.O. Dalley DFM) based at Coltishall became the first RAF squadron to re-equip with Venom NF.3s. The squadron had earlier converted from Mosquito NF.36s to Meteor NF.11s in September 1951. As more Venoms and their crews arrived at Coltishall they were joined by Brigand trainers from Colerne equipped with AI Mk.21 radar to provide conversion training for the navigators. Throughout the month of June some 200 navigator hours were flown by the 'Brigand Circus', with the squadron's Meteors being used as targets.

Also based at Coltishall was 23 Squadron (Wg Cdr A.N. Davies DSO, DFC), which began its conversion from Venom NF.2As in November. Once operational, the two squadrons devoted alternate weeks to day and night flying; a typical day's work for the Coltishall Wing included cross-country and air-to-air gunnery exercises, GCA, formation and instrument flying, as well as ground-vectored interceptions, usually against another squadron Venom. The Coltishall Wing's first major air defence exercise, 'Beware', was held between 23 September and 2 October 1955, during which it was joined by two Javelin FAW.1s from the All-Weather Wing of the CFE at West Raynham on service-test evaluation trials. The figures for the three units during the exercise were:

Unit	Sorties Flown	Possible Kill	Damaged
23 Squadron	98	100	1
141 Squadron	104	114	8
CFE	53	47	0

In October 1955 Sqn Ldr Joe Dalley was succeeded by Wg Cdr P.L. Chilton DSO, DFC, AFC. In one of the outgoing CO's monthly reports, he wrote: 'The Venom is a good deal harder to fly than the Meteor NF.11 – particularly say, above 25,000ft – and is harder to produce a satisfying cine exercise (where a reasonable angle-off is required, together with a realistic opening range). No air-to-air firing has been carried out due to the damaging effect on the radomes.' Some aircrew regarded these comments as a little harsh, especially considering that the Venom had a slight operational advantage over the Meteor and was fitted with powered ailerons. It was also difficult for former aircrew to recall any actual damage to nose radomes occurring, although there was genuine concern among them following evaluation trials carried out by the CFE, when some incidents had been reported.

Despite success for 141 Squadron during Exercise 'Fabulous' in November 1955, when two B-45 Tornado bombers and one F-84F Thunderstreak fighter of the USAF were claimed, together with five Canberra bombers during a 'Bombex' exercise, aircraft serviceability remained a great problem. The seven aircraft available at the beginning of December were reduced to only three by the end of the month. The situation was also reflected in the flying hours, with some pilots flying only five sorties during the same period.

Venom NF.3s of 141 Squadron share the flightline at Coltishall with the Javelins of the All-Weather Wing, West Raynham, during Exercise 'Beware' in September 1955. (*Darryl Cott*)

This predicament for the Coltishall Venom Wing, caused by a lack of tradesmen and exacerbated by the difficulty in obtaining aircraft spares, continued into the new year, which was further marred by the loss of two Venoms in flying accidents in fairly quick succession. On 2 January 1956 WX879 of 23 Squadron crashed soon after take-off at Lilac Farm, Worsted, killing Flg Offs Ian Jarvis and Don Parsons. Two weeks later Flg Off John Pugh was airborne in WX795 of 141 Squadron when it suffered an engine failure and he was forced to belly-land on the site of a disused wireless station on the Scottow–Coltishall road. John Pugh had joined 141 Squadron in November 1955 straight from Cranwell and jet flying training at Driffield:

My colleagues and I were the first products of 'straight-through' on to night-fighter training. Before mid-1955 all night-fighter pilots had done a previous tour on day-fighters. We were 'specially selected' for night-fighters – I seem to recall twelve of us – while about the same number went on to day-fighters.

In those days we trained against a threat of intruders at about 35,000ft. We had only small calibre armament fitted to the aircraft, and we had to get a visual identification before opening fire at night. This involved getting to within 150–200 yd of a target, and if the navigator got you to the right place, the target would be silhouetted above you. But the heating and ventilation system was so poor that when you looked for a visual contact, all you saw was an iced-over canopy! This was compounded on return to base, when the windscreen would also ice-up on descent. If you were small and put the seat right down, you might just see the runway through the bottom 2 inches of the windscreen. The navigators all carried long lengths of extra oxygen tubing, which they attached to the end of the heating pipe by their right ear, and waved it over the windscreen – which was one good thing about side-by-side seating!

There were no Vampire trainers at first, so dual checks were carried out on the Meteor trainer left over from the NF.11 days. The conversion on the Venom involved eleven sorties, but then you entered the much longer period to become fully operational. One peculiar aspect of the latter was that you had to get cine film assessed of a gun attack on a Canberra before you could be classed as 'operational' – but you were not allowed to attack Canberras except on certain exercises, for which you had to be operational!

Overall, the Venom 3 was a nice aircraft to fly, but was no great improvement on the Meteor NF.11; marginally quicker perhaps, but lacking solidarity – and the reassurance of two engines! Other points included the lack of ejection seats, fuel measured in gallons, a pretty useless AI Mk.21 radar, carrying out interceptions at night without lights, unreliable artificial horizons, an 'up-rated' engine that still coughed every time you crossed the coast at night, and the fact that 'bone domes' were optional – we tended not to wear them on air-to-air and combat flying as they kept banging into the hood as we moved our heads around.

My personal memories of the aircraft may be clouded by the engine failure we suffered at low level on 16 January 1956. We force-landed in a field, but unfortunately hit an old wartime air-raid shelter at about 60 knots. My navigator, Flg Off Stan Perry, suffered two broken legs after the AI fell on top of them, and I was knocked unconscious as the GEE box threw me on to the gunsight (I was wearing a helmet!). Three farmers pulled us to safety after the aircraft caught fire – and were subsequently awarded MBEs and a BEM for their bravery. The cause of the accident was a drive failure to the fuel pump, which didn't please the Board of Inquiry who were trying to nail me for running out of fuel!

By the end of 1955 three more squadrons had been re-equipped with Venom NF.3s, each with an establishment of sixteen aircraft. In July of that year 151 Squadron (Sqn Ldr D.B. Ainsworth) at Leuchars began its conversion from Meteor NF.11s. By the following October A Flight was declared operational and took part in two major exercises, 'Beware' and 'Embellish'. It was during the latter that the squadron was able to claim four B-47 Stratojets, four Canberras, and three Valiant bombers, after which the jubilant crews were convinced that the interceptions would not have been possible with the Meteor NF.11s. With a new CO, Wg Cdr I.H. Cosby, the squadron continued to provide the all-weather defence of the Scottish industrial centres and remained the only night-fighter unit to be based north of the border.

On 15 December 1955 89 Squadron (Sqn Ldr J.W. Valentine) was re-formed at Stradishall with an establishment of sixteen Venoms – although it had to wait until the following January for the first aircraft to arrive and was subsequently not declared as operational until the beginning of April. Also in December A Flight 125 Squadron (Wg Cdr R.I.W. Baelz) started to replace its Meteor NF.11s with Venoms, followed by B Flight at the end of January. Both these squadrons constituted the Stradishall All-Weather Wing.

A regular feature of squadron life was the detachment to the APC at Acklington for a period of live gunnery, where the crews improved their shooting skills against drogue, flag and glider targets towed behind Meteor 'tugs'. In September 1957 four aircraft from 89 Squadron were also sent to Leconfield to compete in the annual gunnery competition, which culminated with the award of the Ingpen Trophy to the best overall squadron. Throughout the week-long event the crews from 89 Squadron flew some twenty-four sorties and were unlucky to be narrowly beaten into second place by the Meteors of 33 Squadron.

The delivery of the first Javelin FAW.1s to the RAF in February, followed by the

WX914 was the first Venom NF.3 to be delivered to 89 Squadron at Stradishall in January 1956. By the time this photograph had been taken the following month, the squadron's light and dark blue horizontal bars had been applied. (*via Sqn Ldr Joe Warne*)

Photographed from the tail of a Lancaster in October 1955, this is Venom NF.3 WX796 of 141 Squadron, flown by Flg Offs Warne and Stephens. It had an operational life of just seventeen months, before being placed into open store in February 1957 and eventually scrapped. (*Sqn Ldr Joe Warne*)

The only night-fighter squadron to be based north of the border, 151 Squadron converted from Meteor NF.11s to Venom NF.3s in July 1955. Note the St Andrew's Cross insignia on the tail-booms. WX849 was later passed to 33 Squadron, ending its days as an instructional airframe. (*Squadron Collection*)

improved FAW.4 and FAW.5 in October 1956 and March 1957 respectively, brought a gradual end to Venom operations. The first unit to go was 141 Squadron; in January 1957 it officially operated Venoms for the last time as the conversion to Javelin FAW.4s got under way. On 8 February Wg Cdr Peter Chilton flew the first replacement Javelin into Horsham St Faith and by the beginning of March the Venoms had been dispersed to either 23 Squadron or 27MU Shawbury. In May 1957 two more squadrons were to follow suit, with 23 Squadron relinquishing its Venoms after re-equipping with Javelins in April and 125 Squadron disbanding on 10 May. No. 151 Squadron also received its first Javelin FAW.5 during May and paraded its Venoms for the last time the following June, when HM the Queen visited Leuchars to present the Squadron Standard to 43 Squadron. Later the same day ten Venoms of

151 Squadron (together with four Venom NF.2As of 219 Squadron) flew as the 'E' of the royal cypher 'ER' in a formation salute. The following day the Venoms were flown away for disposal.

With the last of the Venom NF.2A squadrons disbanding at the beginning of September 1957, this left 89 Squadron at Stradishall as the final unit to operate the Venom night-fighter. Its existence as such was to be short-lived, however, for with the delivery of two Javelin FAW.6s on 30 September the squadron was declared non-operational and ordered to begin conversion. Between 15 and 17 October 1957 the last of the Venoms were flown to Shawbury for storage, joining those already waiting to be broken up and sold for scrap. A former staff pilot at Shawbury poignantly recalls the Venoms arriving in early 1957 for scrapping:

I remember 141 Squadron arriving en masse and leaving their Venom NF.3s at the MU there, soon afterwards to be scrapped. There is something very sad about watching twelve serviceable aircraft run in and break, then taxi in and park right where they are to have their radars smashed with sledgehammers because they cannot be exported.

Perhaps the last word on Venom operations should go the CO of 23 Squadron. In March 1957 he wrote in his monthly summary:

As a Venom squadron we became non-operational on 25 March, nearly 3½ years after equipping as the first night-fighter squadron. This has been a period of not unmixed blessings. In its early days the Venom 2 could not be called a reliable aircraft, but it had a spectacular performance for a night-fighter. The technicians had removed the last of the 'bugs' from the aircraft by the summer of 1955, but in November of that year we were re-equipped with the Venom 3, with inferior performance at height but with superior AI Mk.21. Our last night exercise with the Venom 3,

on 21 March 1957, proved to be a highly successful finale, for we 'destroyed' seven Valiants with a total of eight fighters scrambled, at heights of 43–44,000ft and speeds of 0.78 to 0.80 Mach. With the Venom 2 this would have been routine, but with the Venom 3 it showed an excellent coordination between the GCI controllers and the aircrew in getting the ultimate performance out of their aircraft at the critical place, height and time.

Of the 129 Venom NF.3s built, some twelve aircraft were temporarily reprieved and used as ground instructional airframes at various training establishments until early 1964. At least three are preserved, including WX788 (a former company trials aircraft) at the Aero Venture Museum, Doncaster; WX853 (an ex-23 Squadron and instructional airframe at RAF Debden) at the de Havilland Heritage Centre at Salisbury Hall; and WX905 (whose career included service with 23 Squadron, and periods spent as an instructional airframe at RAF Yatesbury and as an ATC airframe at Hendon) at the Newark Air Museum.

A formation of Venom NF.3s belonging to 23 Squadron off the Norfolk coast, soon after delivery in November 1955. The unit was the first to receive the type and its red and blue squadron colours are repeated on the rear of the tip-tanks. (*Flight*)

CHAPTER TEN

SEA VENOM DEVELOPMENT

The early development of the Vampire and Meteor jet fighters had been closely watched by the Admiralty, who were considering the feasibility of operating such types from the decks of aircraft carriers. However, the range and endurance limitations of these jet aircraft were considered by sceptics as too restrictive for effective carrier operations, not to mention the improvements that would have to be made to deck equipment and arresting techniques.

In May 1944 the Aerodynamics Flight of the RAE was asked by the Admiralty to recommend a suitable type of jet aircraft for deck landing trials, for which the Vampire was eventually selected. Although the Vampire's twin tail-boom layout was thought to present problems with catapulting and arresting, the trials went ahead, with the initial deck landing assessment being carried out at Hatfield during May 1945. The result of this assessment concluded that the Vampire would prove satisfactory, subject to a suitable arrestor hook being fitted.

By the following November the Vampire had been duly modified with increased area flaps and air brakes, long-stroke under-carriage oleos and an arrestor hook, and it carried out a series of ADDLs at RNAS Ford in preparation for the first-ever deck landing on an aircraft carrier by a pure jet aircraft. On 3 December 1945 history was made when the CO and chief naval test pilot of the Aerodynamics Flight, Lt Cdr Eric Brown, completed a series of landings with the second prototype Vampire, LZ551/G, on the light fleet carrier HMS *Ocean*.

There followed a brief respite in the test programme while the Ministry of Supply considered whether to persist with the trials to the service acceptance stage. Despite the RAE's doubts as to the Vampire's suitability for deck landings – doubts which were centred on its limited fuel capacity and lack of immediate engine response – the test pilots involved in the trials were all enthusiastic about the aircraft's deck landing potential, with the combination of a tricycle undercarriage and excellent all-round view from the cockpit more than compensating for any inherent deficiencies.

In the spring of 1946 the Admiralty requested a second series of trials, which were conducted by the Naval Test Squadron at Boscombe Down. The pilots recommended improvements to the engine throttle response and a review of the deck landing technique. This was followed by the official service carrier trials during late 1949 and early 1950, which were carried out by a team from the A&AEE and 703 Squadron RN, whose subsequent report was generally favourable to the Vampire but recommended that a more powerful version of the Goblin engine should be installed.

In March 1947 an order for twenty Sea Vampire F.20s was placed with the English Electric Company at Preston, with deliveries beginning from October 1948. The main role for these aircraft was with second-line training and evaluation units, but they were later supplemented with further orders for Sea Vampire trainers for use as jet conversion aircraft and for operational flying training.

The prototype Sea Venom NF.20, WK376, was built at Hatfield and first flew on 19 April 1951. It retained most of the design features of the earlier Vampire NF.10 and was photographed on 15 January 1952. (*de Havilland via Peter Goodwin*)

Although the Admiralty never considered the Vampire to be a front-line fighter, preferring instead to operate both types as a cost-effective means of introducing pilots to jet flying and the development of future carrier deck technology, by 1950 it had begun to take an interest in the de Havilland Venom as a stop-gap between the piston-engined Sea Hornet and the advanced DH 110 all-weather fighter, which was suffering problems with its development programme.

The search for a radar-equipped, night- and all-weather fighter built to naval requirements to replace the Sea Hornet actually began just after the Second World War with the issue in January 1947 of Naval Staff Requirement NR/A.14 under Specification N40/46 and to Operational Requirement 246. Several project studies resulted from

this, the best being the DH 110 from de Havilland's and another project from Fairey Aviation. In March 1949 N40/46 was updated as N14/49 to cover both versions and the following month an order was placed by the Ministry of Supply for a number of DH 110 prototype aircraft. Progress of the DH 110 was slow, however, and in the early autumn of 1950 the Admiralty expressed an interest in a 'navalised' version of the Venom to fill the gap that left the fleet without an efficient night-fighter. It was considered that the Sea Venom's usefulness as a general-purpose fighter aircraft would outlive its night-fighter role and therefore would justify its acquisition.

In the autumn of 1950 an evaluation of the prototype Venom NF.2, G-5-3, which was to include a set of ADDLs and a carrier landing,

This is a later photograph of WK376, now featuring smaller tail bumpers and mass balances under the tailplanes. It also wears the colour scheme that was then applied to the Sea Venoms, namely extra-dark sea grey and sky. (*Darryl Cott*)

was requested to assess its suitability for naval use. Although the aircraft was heavily involved in the company trials programme, it was considered possible to carry out a brief assessment by a team of pilots from the A&AEE.

The results of this 'preview' assessment carried out at Hatfield on 27 October 1950 indicated that the aircraft had potentially very good deck landing qualities, with innocuous stalling characteristics and relatively small changes of trim required when operating the flaps and/or undercarriage on the approach. Both members of the crew commented on the good all-round

view and the roominess of the cockpit for such a small aircraft. They added, however, that it was thought doubtful whether a safe emergency exit could be made in flight without the assistance of ejection seats. It was also determined that the elevator power was inadequate, a feature considered essential for an aircraft intended for night deck landings.

The brief trials were sufficient for Naval Air Requirement NR/A30 to be drawn up, resulting in the issue of Specification N.107D for three prototype aircraft, WK376, WK379 and WK385, to be built to Contract no. 6/Acft/5972/CB.7(a), dated 21 November 1950. As both Hatfield and Chester were extremely busy with production of the Vampire, Dove, Chipmunk and Comet airliner, the design work was allocated to Christchurch under the designation Sea Venom NF.20.

It was decided to build the first two prototypes at Hatfield. In common with the Venom NF.2, the Sea Venom was based on a combination of the design features of the Venom FB.1 and Vampire NF.10, with side-by-side seating for the pilot and observer. Both aircraft retained the fixed wings fitted with boundary layer fences, manual flying controls, a round-top framed canopy hood which was hinged at the rear for crew access, extended tailplane, and the tall, pointed fins and rudders of the Vampire NF.10. Modifications to the basic airframe for naval use included the incorporation of an hydraulically operated arrestor hook, which consisted

of two tubular steel struts forming an A-frame and pivoted from brackets at the root end of each mainplane, with the hook being housed against a rubber pad in a fairing extending above and behind the jet pipe orifice. Non-jettisonable 75-gallon wing-tip drop-tanks, fitted with fins and a fuel-jettison outlet at the rear, were also redesigned with a slight flattening of the inboard sides to decrease airflow interference at high speed, thus delaying the onset of lateral instability at high Mach numbers. Power for the aircraft would be provided by a 4,850lb-thrust Ghost 103 engine.

The first prototype, WK376, flew on 19 April 1951 and was delivered to the Experimental Flying Department of the RAE at Farnborough the following month for arrestor trials with a new hydraulic hook damping installation. On 31 May the aircraft

The second Sea Venom 20 prototype, WK379, pictured at Hatfield in July 1952. It is unpainted and is yet to be fitted with the modified tail assembly. (*MoS via Ray Sturtivant*)

Further deck landing trials were completed by pilots of the A&AEE during May 1952. Here, WK376 is about to pick up the wire on HMS *Eagle*. (*RN Official*)

was transferred to C Squadron of the A&AEE at Boscombe Down for an airfield deck landing assessment, to be followed by initial deck landing trials on board HMS *Illustrious* off Sandown on the Isle of Wight between 9 and 12 July 1951.

The first carrier take-off was made on 9 July with Lt Cdr D. Callingham DSC, RN, as pilot. Within three days a further sixty take-offs and landings had been made by Lt Cdr Callingham and Lts Price and Robertson. The greatest number of take-offs – thirty-four – was recorded on the second day, 10 July. Throughout the trial period the pilots remarked on the excellent view of both the flight deck and the batsman obtainable during the approach. On the fourth day a demonstration was laid on for the C-in-C Coastal Command before the aircraft was

returned to Boscombe Down. From these trials it was considered that, subject to the provision of an aileron trimmer, an increase in both elevator power and hook damping, together with an improvement in escape facilities by the incorporation of a redesigned cockpit and the installation of ejection seats, the prototype should prove satisfactory for both day and night deck landings.

The aircraft was returned to Hatfield on 20 July 1951 and spent the next eleven months on development work at Hatfield and Farnborough, before returning to Boscombe Down in May 1952 for further deck landing assessment and trials. Between 21 and 26 May a second series of deck trials were completed on board HMS *Eagle*, with some forty-nine take-offs and landings being made by two test pilots. The results of this assessment showed a great improvement over the earlier carrier trials, particularly in regard to the A&AEE's previous criticism that the handling characteristics of aircraft fitted with tip-tanks were potentially dangerous owing to the high stalling speed and uncontrollable wing dropping when passing over the bows during take-off from the deck. Other deficiencies had included the lack of an artificial stall warning, a radio altimeter and a 'stick-shaker'. Subsequent modifications included the fitting of fixed-wing leading edge slats. The test pilots considered the aircraft to be excellent for day deck take-off and landing, but again criticised the inadequate hook damping and lack of windscreen wipers.

Following a brief trip to Hatfield, WK376 was returned to Farnborough in July 1952 for a programme of RATO and proofing trials. On 27 August 1952 the aircraft was engaged on catapult trials with Lt Alec Facer RN, who had joined the flight the previous January after graduating from no. 10 Course at the Empire Test Pilots School. Having completed two catapult launches, he was launched for the third time, after which he requested permission to carry out a low run over the airfield. However, as the Sea Venom made a slow turn over Pirbright Camp an elevator spring tab was seen to fall off the aircraft. The Sea Venom then went into a shallow dive. Almost immediately the port rudder broke away and the aircraft crashed out of control at Windmill Hill, Frimley Green. Lt Facer was killed instantly.

Despite the loss of the first prototype, development work continued with the two other aircraft. WK379, which incorporated the original pointed tail and rudder design, had been flown for the first time in June 1952. During an early test flight the pilot experienced severe vibration problems with the Sea Venom's tailplane, resulting in the loss of the port rudder. This time the pilot

was able to land the aircraft safely at Hatfield, enabling a subsequent investigation into the difficulties of rudder buffeting to be carried out.

In September 1952 WK379 was issued to the A&AEE for deck landing trials, which were carried out the following month and, despite a few criticisms, were found to be generally satisfactory. Following a brief trip to Boscombe Down for proofing of the modified arrestor hook damper, the aircraft was returned to Hatfield for the incorporation of the new redesigned tail unit to improve longitudinal stability and control. The change in shape of the fin and rudder was designed to prevent application of excessive yaw and rudder locking at low speeds, which had the additional effect of decreasing rudder power near the stall. Reversed bullet fairings at the intersection of the rudder and elevator were also installed to prevent rapid fore and aft oscillation of shock waves at high Mach numbers, thereby reducing elevator and rudder buffet. The aircraft was sent back to Boscombe Down in February 1953 for handling trials and a further deck landing assessment, following which the official report described it as a great improvement over its predecessor, especially with regard to its handling characteristics.

Between April 1953 and May 1954 WK379 was kept extremely busy with radio and armament acceptance trials, before being passed to the RAE at Farnborough for barrier trials. In October 1955 it was extensively damaged during a landing accident, which resulted in it being written off the following January and broken up for spares.

The third prototype, WK385, was built at Christchurch and made its first flight on 26 July 1952. The aircraft was fully navalised with long-stroke undercarriage legs and power-operated folding wings, which were folded and spread by hydraulic power taken

The third prototype, WK385, was the first to feature folding wings. This photograph, which was taken at Farnborough in July 1953, also shows the part-modified tail assembly and RATO gear fitted to the tail booms. (*DERA*)

directly from the engine-driven pumps; the actual thickness of the wing at the folding position was a maximum of 8in and a single jack, mounted in a reinforced structure between ribs 8 and 9, operated the wing-fold linkage.

An appearance at the SBAC display at Farnborough in September was followed by a period of RATO and catapulting trials at Farnborough between February and May 1953. By June 1953 WK385 had been fitted with the modified tail unit at Christchurch and was transferred to Boscombe Down for a series of deck landing trials in the Solent with the USS *Antietam*, the first US Navy carrier to be converted with an angled deck. On 4 and 5 November 1953 WK385 carried out further landing trials on HMS *Eagle* in Weymouth harbour, returning for the first night landings on the carrier between 10 and 12 November.

With the completion of the company trials programme, the third prototype was issued to Boscombe Down for the development of the emergency arrestor barrier, before being transferred to the NAE at Bedford in June 1955, where it was struck off charge the following January and broken up.

Confident that the Sea Venom would fulfil the requirements of the Royal Navy, Contract no. 6/Acft/6165/CB.7(a), dated 2 January 1951, was issued to incorporate the production of sixty FAW.20s, serialled WM500–523 and WM542–577. The contract was later amended to allow the last ten aircraft (WM568–577) to be built as FAW.21s, and production was shared between Christchurch, which built twelve aircraft (WM500–504, WM507–511, WM515 and WM518) between May 1953 and March 1954, and Chester, which built the remaining thirty-eight aircraft between April 1954 and June

1955. The first production FAW.20 (WM500) was flown on 27 March 1953, with the last (WM567) taking to the air on 6 June 1955.

The production Sea Venom 20s were similar to the RAF's Venom NF.2As. They were fitted with boundary layer fences, repositioned fixed leading edge slats, non-jettisonable 80-gallon wing-tip tanks and a G.45 cine camera contained within a streamlined housing beneath the port wing. Provision was also made for RATO gear consisting of two carrier assemblies on the forward end of each outer side of the fuselage booms, each incorporating two 5in rockets fired by a switch on the engine control box.

To compensate for the lack of ejection seats, the third production aircraft (WM502) was fitted, as standard, with an improved, clamshell canopy with a symmetric wind-

screen, which was capable of being jettisoned under water to improve the otherwise poor crew-escape facilities. Designed by ML Aviation, the canopy jettison mechanism occupied a small compartment at the rear of the cockpit and was designed not only to throw off the canopy in flight but also to force it to open if the aircraft was submerged in deep water.

Radar and radio equipment comprised AI Mk.10 (SCR 720) radar, with the indicator and synchroniser unit arranged in front of the observer's seat and the scanner unit enclosed within a neoprene-covered fibreglass radome. A transmitter-receiver type IFF (ARI. 5679) was installed behind the pilot's seat, together with an AYF (ARI. 5284) radio altimeter and ZBX beacon receiver. A ten-channel TR. 1934/35 VHF radio was also fitted and, for

A production Sea Venom 20 (WM515) during an early test flight from Christchurch in 1954. It is fitted with the clamshell hood. This aircraft later served with 890 and 766 Squadrons and with Merryfield Station Flight, before being sold for scrap in May 1960. (*via Alan Roach*)

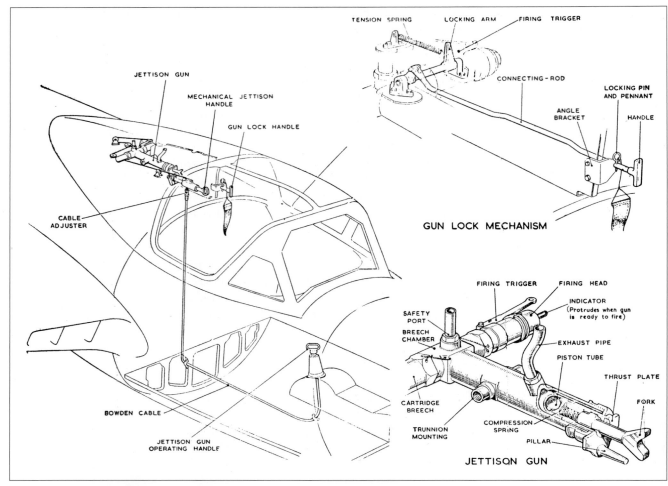

Canopy hatch jettison gun and control. (*de Havilland*)

crew comfort, the cockpit was supplied with facilities for pressure breathing suits and anti-'g' equipment.

The Sea Venom 20 retained the standard armament of four 20mm Hispano Mk.5 cannon mounted in the underside of the nose, with 150 rounds per gun. The type's strike capability was further enhanced following trials conducted at Boscombe Down between October 1954 and April 1955 which approved the carriage and firing of four or eight 3in rocket projectiles fitted with either

25lb, 60lb or flare heads and carried on either single or double tier rails. Two 1000lb bombs or 80-gallon drop-tanks could also be carried under the wings. All of this served to increase the Sea Venom FAW.20's all-up weight to 14,270lb, some 400lb heavier than an equivalent NF.2.

Deliveries to the Controller (Air) began on 8 May 1953, when the first production aircraft, WM500, was issued for company handling trials at Christchurch. In April 1954 the aircraft was issued to C Squadron

A&AEE which satisfactorily carried out the official spinning trials between August and October of that year. The aircraft was later fitted with a new tailplane at Christchurch. Following a period of storage and service with Airworks, it was eventually sold for scrap in March 1960.

With deliveries to the first operational squadron only months away, the responsibility for writing the Pilots' Notes for the Sea Venom was given to the RN Handling Squadron, a small naval flight attached to the RAF Flying College at Manby. On 4 January 1954 WM507 was collected from Hurn by the flight's CO, Lt R.M. Crosley DSC, RN, who made a thorough assessment of the aircraft's handling behaviour and expected performance during a programme of 14 hours' routine flying. His assessment included high-altitude handling, as well as fuel consumption, aileron flutter and stalling tests, all of which were completed satisfactorily. Two minor incidents occurred during January. Due to flutter, the starboard aileron almost disintegrated during a high-speed dive, and on another occasion the wing-fold bolts unlocked in flight. On both occasions the aircraft was able to return safely to Manby. Although the unit moved to Boscombe Down in April 1954, the RN Handling Squadron was briefly attached to Ford to maintain the flying programme. The following month, in a welcome salute on the occasion of the Queen's return from a tour of the Commonwealth, Lt Mike Crosley led a flight of six Sea Venoms as part a formation flypast of five FAA squadrons – including the first Sea Venom squadron, 890 Squadron – over the Solent.

By January 1954 a further eight Sea Venoms had been allocated for use in the company and naval trials and development programme:

WM501: A general CS(A) handling assessment at the A&AEE between March

and October 1954 confirmed the poor lateral and directional control at low speeds, previously criticised during early trials. Failure of a panel of the rear hood fairing resulted in the tests with the aircraft being abandoned and transferred to WM502. In November 1954 the aircraft was returned to de Havilland's to be fitted with a new canopy and was eventually delivered to St David's in September 1956 for use with Airworks Ltd.

WM502: Engaged in trials with a stall-warning device and windscreen wipers at the A&AEE between December 1953 and December 1954. The trials also included a handling assessment for CS(A) release, which found the control effectiveness and response to be adequate except for the rudders, which were considered ineffective. Also criticised was the lack of an adequate stall-warning, the low rate of roll and the aircraft's behaviour at high Mach numbers which rendered it unsuitable as a radar interception platform above 0.78M and as a gun platform above 0.81M. Although its performance on normal runways was acceptable, it was further recommended that consideration should be given to braking on wet runways. Following service with 766 and 781 Squadrons, it was sold for scrap in March 1960.

WM503: Following company flight trials, during which it appeared at the 1953 SBAC display at Farnborough, the aircraft was operated by NAE Bedford and RAE Farnborough between November 1955 and July 1957 on nylon barrier arrestor trials. It ended its days at RNAS Arbroath in October 1957 as an instructional airframe.

WM504: During November 1953, following a deck landing assessment on board HMS *Eagle* by A&AEE pilots (which included the first night landings undertaken by the Sea Venom), it was decided that, owing to poor lateral and directional control, the aircraft was unsuitable in this form. On the basis of the ADDLs, however, the mirror sight technique appeared to be more promising because of the negligible effects of approach turbulence. The system was later fitted with variable ratio aileron gearing, after which a further assessment by A&AEE pilots concluded that it was satisfactory and offered an acceptable improvement in lateral control during deck landings. Between July 1954 and April 1956 the aircraft was employed by the RAE on RATOG jettisoning trials, and the CS(A) release of the Green Salad VHF Homer (ARI. 18049).

WM507: Delivered to the Handling Squadron at Manby in January 1954 for the compilation of Pilots' Notes, before being transferred to A&AEE for acceptance trials with various RP installations between October 1954 and February 1955. It was eventually sold as scrap in March 1960.

WM508: Employed by the A&AEE between February 1954 and July 1955 on navigation, engineering, fuel jettisoning and gun freezing trials. The aircraft was placed into store at the Stretton RDU and eventually sold for scrap in March 1960.

WM509: Between January 1954 and February 1955 this aircraft carried out a series of low-speed buffet trials at Christchurch while fitted with a wooden, part-span sharp wing leading edge extension. Following a period of storage at Abbotsinch, it was eventually relegated for use an instructional airframe A2479.

WM510: Involved in the development of a two-speed aileron stick gearing arrangement to improve lateral control at approach speeds at Christchurch. This was followed in June 1954 with a deck landing assessment and carrier trials on board HMS *Illustrious* by A&AEE and de Havilland's pilots. With the incorporation of a two-pointer open scale airspeed indicator and windscreen wiper, it was recommended to be acceptable for day and night landings with the variable aileron gearing fitted. In December 1954 it was used by the A&AEE on RATOG and air starting trials and experiments with OR.1099 high-performance air-to-surface 3in rockets, before transfer to RAE Bedford in March 1956 for steam catapult trials to measure aircraft speed at the moment of arrest.

THE 'SUPER VENOM'

In June 1948 two designs – the Gloster GA.5 and the de Havilland DH 110 – were submitted in response to Specification F.4/48, which called for a two-seat, all-weather fighter. Although the GA.5 design eventually became the RAF's choice and was ordered with a 'super priority' status as the Gloster Javelin, the navy still had a requirement for a high-performance all-weather strike fighter. Subsequent delays in ordering the DH 110 for the navy led the company to propose a swept-wing version of its Venom design – the DH 116 – which was tendered in response to Specification N.114T issued in January 1951.

The specification called for a two-seat day- and night-fighter, equipped with AI Mk.18 radar, a top speed of 540 knots and a minimum ceiling of 40,000ft. A minimum patrol time of 1½ hours was also required, together with either a Sapphire or RA.7 Avon engine fitted with reheat. Armament would comprise a combination of four Aden cannon, rockets, and air-to-air missiles.

The DH 116 Venom modernisation project – known as the 'Super Venom' – was based on the cockpit and forward fuselage of the Sea Venom combined with a swept-back, thinner wing giving an overall span of 34ft. The design also featured an all-moving tail,

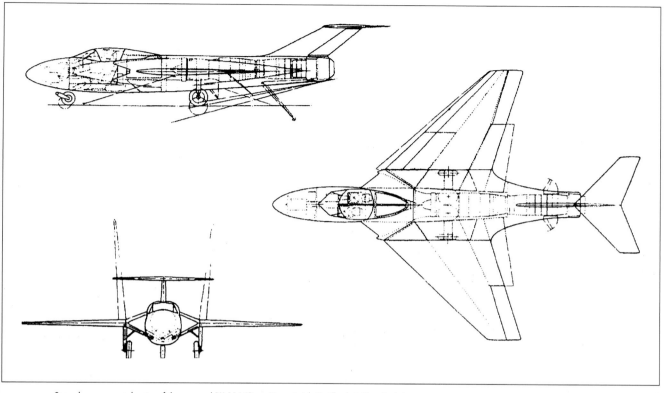

General arrangement drawing of the proposed DH 116 'Super Venom'. (*de Havilland via Tony Buttler*)

powered controls, Fowler flaps, two 30mm Aden cannon and an improved AI Mk.17 or APS Mk.21 search radar to replace the existing AI Mk.10. It was powered by a 9,500lb-thrust Rolls-Royce RA.14 Avon jet engine fitted with reheat, and it was estimated that the maximum speed of the design would be just over Mach 1.0 in level flight at 30,000ft. Two prototypes were ordered in March 1951 to Contract no. 6/Acft/6417/CB.7(a), and these were allocated the serials WT816 and WT822.

Staff Requirement NA.38 and Specification N.131T, issued in March and September 1952 respectively, were both written around the project but in November 1952, before work could commence at Hatfield, the design was dropped because of the firm's heavy workload and it was replaced by the updated navalised DH 110. The opinion within the MoS that the Sea Venom had reached the end of its development life was also a contributory factor in the decision to abandon the DH 116. It was believed that the navy would be better served with a twin-engined fighter. Two years later the DH 110 was ordered into production for the Royal Navy as the Sea Vixen and entered service in 1958.

CHAPTER ELEVEN

INTO SERVICE WITH THE ROYAL NAVY

As production of the Sea Venom FAW. 20 got under way, and deliveries were made to the Controller (Air) at Christchurch for development and trials work, the Sea Venom made its public debut during the Coronation Review of the Fleet Air Arm on 15 June 1953. Led by Cdr D.B. Law MBE, DSC, RN, and operating from RNAS Ford, four company aircraft, including prototypes WK379 and WK385 and the first two production aircraft, WM500 and WM501, formed the 'Prototype Flight' as part of the mass flypast of FAA aircraft over the Solent in salute to HM the Queen, watching from the frigate HMS *Surprise*. By March 1954 the rate of production was sufficient for the RDU at RNAS Stretton to receive its first Sea Venoms, where they were prepared for squadron use.

On 20 March 1954 890 Squadron was formed and commissioned at RNAS Yeovilton as the first naval squadron to operate Sea Venom FAW.20s. Six days later the first aircraft (WM515) was collected from Stretton by the CO, Lt Cdr Alan Gordon-Johnson RN; this was followed by a second aircraft (WM518) on 30 March. Both aircraft were, however, temporarily grounded to incorporate Mod. 281, which called for the strengthening of the rear false spar. The discovery of a small crack in the upper wing skin in the RAF's Venom fleet had imposed short-term restrictions until the problem could be rectified. The modification required a small reinforcing plate to be riveted over the affected area at the rear of the under-carriage bay. This kept both Sea Venoms out of service throughout most of April.

The Sea Venom crews at Yeovilton were also issued with crash helmets, 'g'-suits, pressure breathing waistcoats, string vests and immersion suits. The latter were designed to be worn in the aircraft and were made of porous cloth which sealed itself when immersed. Boots were integral with the suit, with the wrists and neck sealed with rubber glands. The Dunlop Mk.4 pressure suit, which consisted of a vest and leggings to be worn to relieve the effects of 'g' during violent manoeuvres or at extremes of altitude, was considered by the crews as unnecessary, the performance of the Sea Venom rendering its use totally superfluous!

Further deliveries continued throughout April and May, but the squadron's acute shortage of aircraft was not improved with the loss of WM522 at Hurn on 14 May, while being ferried to Yeovilton. The pilot was forced to abandon his take-off and overshot the runway, killing an unfortunate motorcyclist. The squadron eventually received its full complement of aircraft during August 1954 with the arrival of WM520.

The squadron's initial work-up period covered a full range of operational training, including formation flying, navigation and radar interception exercises, and a live gunnery programme at Bracklesham Bay and

Brawdy. Despite a busy training schedule, on 14 May 1954 the squadron was able to contribute eleven aircraft to take part in the flypast of five Fleet Air Arm squadrons to welcome HM the Queen in HMY *Britannia* on her return from the Commonwealth tour.

In the spring of 1954 the CO decided to form and lead a squadron aerobatic team. The other team members were Lts 'Barny' Barron, Ron Davidson and Peter Young. Their first public display was carried out in May 1954, and as the navy's first all-weather jet display team they were soon in demand and made regular appearances at 'Navy Air Days' throughout the south of England during 1954 and 1955. One such memorable display was staged at Yeovilton

on 22 May 1954, when the team laid on a spectacular performance despite a torrential downpour of rain. Fuel was jettisoned from their wing-tip tanks to emulate coloured smoke, as the announcer declared that the aircraft had only been cleared for aerobatics the previous day!

The squadron's work-up period culminated in a programme of dummy deck landings prior to embarkation in HMS *Bulwark* on 16 May 1955 for a period of carrier training. Ten days later the squadron started night flying. After the initial familiarisation and navigational exercises, the first night interceptions were carried out under the control of the GCI stations at Kete and later Hope Cove.

The aircrew of 808 Squadron RAN at RNAS Yeovilton during the work-up period. Back row, left to right: Pete Wyatt, Dave Hilliard, Pete Seed, Geo Jude, Barry Thompson, Alan Cordell, Steve Wilson, Geoff Gratwick. Front row: Ron McIver, Stan Carmichael, Keith Potts, Neil Ralph, Bernie Brennan. (*RAFM*)

Between May and September 1954 the aerobatic team of 890 Squadron laid on many displays, led by the CO, Lt Cdr Alan Gordon-Johnson. It is photographed at the top of a loop in July 1954 while rehearsing for a forthcoming Naval Air Day. (*RAFM via Lt Cdr John Hackett RN*)

On 10 February 1954 a second unit, 809 Squadron (Lt Cdr S.A. Mearns DSC, RN) was re-formed at Yeovilton with an establishment of nine aircraft. Deliveries were slow and the squadron had to borrow Vampires from the station flight to maintain its work-up programme. The first Sea Venom (WM521) was eventually collected from Hawarden by the CO in June 1954.

Tragedy struck the squadron on 4 October when pilot Lt Hobbs-Webber and his observer Flg Off O'Boyle were killed when their aircraft (WM546) crashed into high ground near Charlton Horethorne while attempting to join the GCA pattern at Yeovilton. Three months later, on 31 January 1955, 809 Squadron was detached to Ford for three weeks of armament training; as the Sea Venoms made their stream-landing approach, the senior pilot, Lt Cdr Frank Cawood, was seen to undershoot and strike the branches of a tree. The aircraft (WM542) dived into the ground and both crew members were killed.

A third and final operational Sea Venom FAW.20 unit, 891 Squadron (Lt Cdr S.A. Birrell DSC, RN) was formed on 8 November 1954. Due to a shortage of available aircraft the squadron was initially equipped with only three aircraft (WM548, WM549 and WM552); until regular deliveries resumed in March 1955, it was obliged to operate temporarily with a mixture of Vampire FB.5s and Sea Vampire T.22s. Despite the lack of Sea Venoms, the squadron was still able to participate in a round of spring exercises, especially Exercise 'Short-Lop One' in January 1955, which was designed to test the fleet's radar defences.

Following Australia's decision to purchase the Sea Venom, 891 Squadron's X Flight (Lt Cdr G.M. Jude RAN) was established at Yeovilton in March 1955 as a holding unit and to provide conversion training for the Australian crews with FAW.20s on loan from the Royal Navy. With the formation of 808 Squadron (Lt Cdr G.M. Jude RAN) on 10 August 1955, the RAN's first jet fighter unit's work-up period at Yeovilton was achieved with eight aircraft, most of which had been transferred after the disbandment of X Flight. No. 808 Squadron RAN was declared operational by February 1956, and exchanged its FAW.20s for Sea Venom FAW.53s when the crews embarked on the carrier HMAS *Melbourne* at Glasgow Docks and sailed for Australia the following month.

In the spring of 1955 a series of unfortunate accidents began to trouble 890 Squadron: during the deck landings on board HMS *Bulwark* in Lyme Bay on 18 May the catapult hold-back ring failed during a night launch of Sea Venom WM556. Immediately throttling back and rapidly applying the brakes in a vain attempt to stop the aircraft before it reached the end of the deck, Lt Cdr Alan Gordon-Johnson and Senior Observer Lt Jack Carter felt the aircraft's nose collapse as the nose-wheel hit the catapult shuttle. The aircraft went over the bow and into the sea, where it began to sink rapidly while the crew struggled to release themselves. After an agonising wait to allow the carrier to pass over them, both crew members were able to surface and clambered into a dinghy, from which they were eventually rescued.

On 18 July 1955 the squadron embarked on HMS *Albion* for a two-month cruise of the Mediterranean and lost another Sea Venom (WM558) during a night launch on 5 August. Water from the catapult track entered the intakes and caused an engine flameout. The CO was able to make a controlled ditching ahead of the carrier, before he and his observer, Jack Carter, were rescued by ship's helicopter. Finally, on 22 August Commissioned Pilot Clarke and Lt West were rescued from the sea off Gibraltar when the arrestor hook broke away on landing and their Sea Venom (WM559) went into the sea.

Two days later the squadron disembarked at North Front, Gibraltar, and on 7 September received a signal informing them that its Sea Venoms were prohibited from carrying out further deck landings because of

The third unit to be equipped with Sea Venom 20s was 891 Squadron. WM548 was one of three aircraft initially supplied to the squadron in November 1954. The Kon Tiki insignia can be clearly seen on its nose. (*R.L. Ward*)

Sea Venom 20s of 808 Squadron RAN, photographed off the Dorset coast from a Vampire trainer on 18 August 1955. The tip-tank colours are Oxford Blue with a white lightning flash. (*C.E. Brown*)

a suspected straining of the arrestor hook. The Naval Air Section of the RAE immediately carried out a programme of intensive arresting trials at Farnborough with Sea Venom WM573. Although it was scheduled to carry out 100 runs, the A-frame brackets failed on the 73rd run and the tests were temporarily suspended. On 30 September another Sea Venom, WW198, was flown to Bedford by Lts Blunden and Arbuthnot of 891 Squadron for a further set of runs into the modified Mk.11 gear between 4 and 8 October, which resulted in a hook failure during the 140th run. During a final set of runs carried out at Bedford between 19 and 27 October with WW200 and WW202, both delivered from new and flown during the trials by Lts Blunden and Reynolds, it was decided that if each could successfully complete 250 runs into the arresting gear an official clearance of fifty deck landings per

aircraft could be issued. There were further hook failures at 140 and 150 runs respectively. Severe damage to the wing trailing edge skinning and ribs precluded the completion of the tests, but it was concluded that landing on the ship's centre-line was critical; any deviation could lead to a high stress loading, which would eventually cause the A-frame attachment brackets to fail.

On 12 September 890 Squadron returned to Yeovilton and joined the other Sea Venom squadrons in Exercise 'Beware' at the end of the month, during which they formed part of the Southern Sector Defence and achieved no small measure of success against incoming raids by 'enemy' bombers. The following month Trafalgar Day was commemorated by a flypast over Plymouth in which thirty-four Sea Venoms took part, led by Lt Cdr Sammy Mearns. This was the largest formation of Sea Venoms ever to get airborne at the same time,

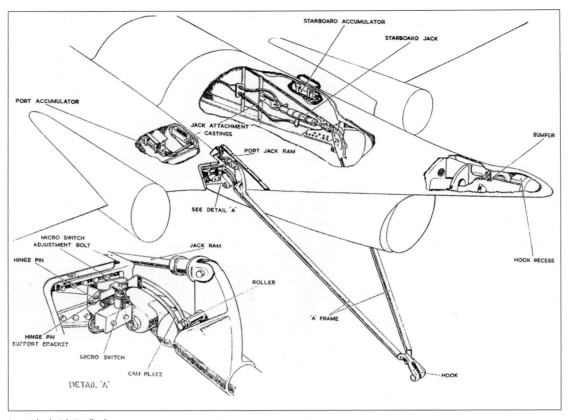

Arrestor hook. (*de Havilland*)

and was a unique occasion when all Sea Venom squadrons, both RN and RAN, were based at Yeovilton on the same day.

On 18 October 1955 890 Squadron was disbanded and absorbed into 766 Squadron at Yeovilton the same day; the task of the new unit was to familiarise crews with the Sea Venom before they eventually joined a front-line, all-weather squadron. Prior to disbanding, 890 Squadron had exchanged some of its FAW.20s during June 1955 for a handful of FAW.21s, passing the earlier aircraft to shore-based second-line units. One such unit was Airwork Ltd at Brawdy/St David's, which provided aircraft exclusively for the Naval Direction School at Kete until withdrawal in September 1958. After re-equipping with FAW.21s, 891 Squadron also gave up the last

of its Sea Venom FAW.20s on 30 June 1955, when four aircraft were transferred to 808 Squadron RAN at Yeovilton.

Only 766 Squadron (Lt Cdr L.A. Jeyes RN), the Royal Navy's All-Weather Fighter Pool based at Yeovilton, continued to operate with an establishment of eight Sea Venom FAW.20s obtained from 890 Squadron. These were retained until March 1956, when the first of the replacement Sea Venom FAW.21s were received from 893 Squadron; the last FAW.20s (WM502 and WM515) remained with the unit until the following December.

A number of Sea Venom FAW.20s were relegated to instructional airframes for use at various naval training establishments. However, the majority were passed to the AHU at Abbotsinch, where they languished in long-

The bright red de Havilland 'Vennet' or 'Fairey Nuff' at the RNAS Abbotsinch Air Day in 1961. The code '12HS' on the nose referred to the fact that it had been designed and built in No. 12 hangar at Abbotsinch, and it was known as the 12 Hangar Special. (*Ted Cottle*)

term storage until they were sold for scrap between 1958 and 1963. A few redundant airframes were also used for fire practice, but several were given a temporary reprieve when they formed the basis of the conversion for the navy's 'top secret, experimental aircraft', the DH 'Vennet' (also variously referred to as the 'Fairey Nuff' or 'Sea Snipe'). Preparing for the 1961 Open Day, the engineers of no. 12 Hangar at Abbotsinch, under the direction of the AEO Lt Ted Cottle, decided to build a spoof aircraft. The conversion involved removing the tail booms and tip-tanks from a surplus Sea Venom, while the rudders of two Fairey Gannets were fixed to the boom attachment points and connected to the rudder pedals by adapting the control

cabling. Dummy missiles were also fitted, together with an extended nose, in which a standard tubular office chair – or 'pilot's seat' – was bolted to the cockpit floor.

The 'Vennet' was described as the Fleet Air Arm's 'latest rocket-powered, high-altitude fighter, capable of flying at over Mach 3', and it was reported that it would be making its maiden test-flight in front of the public during the forthcoming Air Day. As an 'experimental aircraft' it was kept at a discreet distance from the crowd line before the pilot, Lt Paul Stevenson, taxied to the main runway and accelerated away at 90 knots. As smoke and flames poured from the condemned Ghost engine, the bemused public were told that the aircraft had developed an

One of four Sea Venom airframes converted in 1962 to replicate Sea Vixens for the Royal Tournament. This 'Vixette', XJ601/241-H, is seen at RNAS Lee-on-Solent and shows the amount of work undertaken by the engineers at Abbotsinch to produce such a creditable simulation of the navy's latest all-weather fighter. (*via R.C.M. King*)

'engine failure', and that because of repeated trouble with the 'superheat ignition system' the test-flight would have to be abandoned!

The following year the technicians of no. 10 Hangar produced the 'Vennett Mark II' as a successor to the Mk 1 for the 1962 Air Day. With Sea Venom and Gannet airframes again used as the basis for the conversion, the main alterations included the fitting of wing-tip ramjets, modified rudders, a nose-type intake and the addition of two guided weapons. The aircraft was painted white, indicating the strike role, with a yellow 'P' on the fuselage. Unfortunately, the 'ultrasonic version of the previous supersonic world beater' failed to take off for the planned Air Race and was returned to the hangar for further modifications!

In November 1961 Abbotsinch was asked to investigate the conversion of older aircraft into a modern type for the Fleet Air Arm's display in the Royal Tournament, as the service aircraft would prove too heavy for the floor of the Earl's Court Stadium. With the technical expertise behind them from their early conversions, it was decided that the simplest method was from Sea Venom to Sea Vixen. Four Sea Venoms were selected. The work was completed by March 1962 and the airframes were transported to Portsmouth by lighter. Dubbed 'Mini-Vixens' or 'Vixettes', three of the replicas were known to have worn the spurious markings 'XJ601: 241/H', 'XJ602: 247/H' and 'XJ603: 246/H'.

CHAPTER TWELVE

THE SEA VENOM FAW.21

Even before the Sea Venom FAW.20 had entered service with 890 Squadron in March 1954, development work was being carried out by de Havilland's to improve the type. The new variant was equivalent to the RAF's Venom NF.3 and featured powered ailerons, a clear-view jettisonable cockpit canopy, a strengthened long-stroke undercarriage, a variable aileron stick gearing arrangement and an enlarged fuselage nose to accommodate the APS-57 (AI Mk.21) radar. The Sea Venom NF.21 – as it was initially designated – was fitted with a 4,850lb-thrust Ghost 104 (Ghost 48 Mk.2) engine, which featured a redesigned front casing and gearboxes for twin 6kW alternators, while the dual Lucas pump fuel system of the earlier engines was replaced by a Dowty spill-burner fuel system. The FAW.21 also incorporated Maxaret anti-skid brakes, a strengthened arrestor hook, a windscreen wiper and provision for the fitment of RATOG. The radio and radar installation consisted of a TR1934–5 VHF set, ZBX (ARI 5307) navigational aid, AYF (ARI 5284) radio altimeter and IFF identification equipment. Further improvements included longer chord ailerons and elevators, and the deletion of the tailplane extensions on the outboard of the fins.

Although the early examples of the FAW.21 were still fitted with fixed, moulded plastic seats, design work had already been undertaken jointly by the de Havilland military design and development team at Christchurch and the Martin-Baker Aircraft Company at Chalgrove and Denham to install two lightweight MB4A ejection seats. In September 1954 the project was begun and WM569 was flown to Chalgrove, together with a spare fuselage (WW295) which was dispatched to Denham for a detailed study. The work required to fit the new seats was not without its problems, for although the larger MB3B seats had fitted quite comfortably into the side-by-side seating of the Vampire trainer, the cockpit of the Sea Venom was 4in narrower and contained much radar equipment. It was therefore concluded that the cockpit layout would have to be revised and that the seats would have to be specially adapted.

The trial installation of the ejection seats in WM569 at Christchurch found that although it would prove satisfactory in the FAW.20, it would be critical in the FAW.21. The main problem lay in the lack of access to cockpit equipment, particularly the IFF Transponder and the difficulty with fitting the proposed 'Green Salad' VHF Homing set. It was eventually found that the ejection seats could be accommodated, although the most difficult problem concerned the observer's position. This had to be moved 5in forward and arranged so that the back of the seat hinged forward from its base prior to ejection in order to give adequate clearance between the back of the seat and the rear canopy arch. The seat for the pilot was also designed to be adjustable to allow it to be raised for landing, which not only offered a greatly improved view but also required a blister on the port side of the canopy. In October 1954 the first Martin-Baker mock-up was ready and the

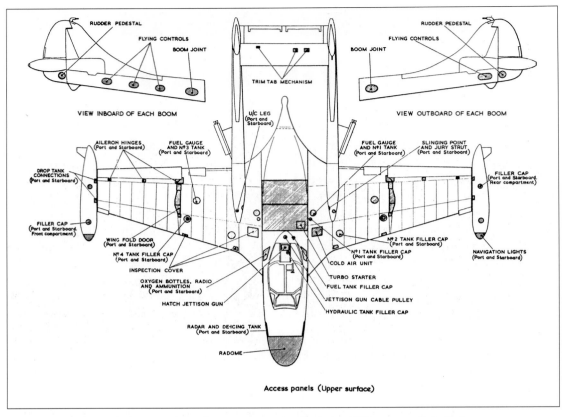

General arrangement drawing of a Sea Venom, showing the various access panels and positioning of RATO equipment. (de Havilland)

company was asked to proceed with the design, which would be incorporated under Mod. N.759. The aircraft and fuselage were returned to Christchurch and work began on the repositioning of the cockpit equipment. The only items left in their original position were the flying and engine controls.

In September 1955 the decision to fit ejection seats was finally approved and they were introduced onto the production line, with the first examples reaching squadron service in the spring of 1956; unmodified aircraft were returned to Chester and RNAY Belfast between March 1956 and September 1958 to be brought up to standard.

Only one prototype, XA539, which was built at Christchurch, was ordered against Contract no. 6/Acft/7062/CB.7(a), dated May

1952. In fact, by the time the prototype had made its first – albeit brief – flight on 6 February 1954, production orders for the FAW.21 were already in place and the last ten airframes of the second batch of Sea Venom FAW.20s at Christchurch (WM568–577) were built to FAW.21 standard. A further ninety-six aircraft (WW137–154, WW186–225 and WW261–298) were ordered in June 1951, with a final production order for a hundred aircraft being placed in June 1954; the first sixty-one airframes of the order (XG606–638 and XG653–680) were built as FAW.21s, the remaining thirty-nine being built as FAW.22s. The construction work of the 167 FAW.21s was shared between Chester (99 aircraft) and Christchurch (68), with the first aircraft (WM568) taking to the air at Christchurch

The first deck landing of the Sea Venom 21 prototype, XA539, on HMS *Albion*, 29 August 1954. The aircraft was flown by the CO of the Naval Test Squadron at Boscombe Down, Lt Cdr S.G. Orr. (*Stan Orr*)

on 22 April 1954. Deliveries took place between May 1954 and October 1956.

Following development work at Christchurch, XA539 was issued to the A&AEE at Boscombe Down in August 1954 for the official handling assessment and deck landing trials. On 29 August, after two weeks of dummy deck landing practice at Boscombe Down, the CO of the Naval Test Squadron, Lt Cdr S.G. Orr, carried out the first deck landing on HMS *Albion* which was on station off the Isle of Wight. Over the next two days Stan Orr and his fellow pilots, Lts Colin Little AFC, Alan Reckell and Jack Overbury, completed twenty catapult take-offs and landings, using the carrier's mirror landing aid and interim angled deck.

These trials proved the Sea Venom 21 to be suitable for both day and night deck landing, subject to the provision of a suitable

twin-pointer open scale airspeed indicator. Although the type's powered ailerons and Maxaret brakes were considered an improvement over the Mk.20, the subsequent A&AEE report criticised the restricted forward vision during final approach and the lack of a low-speed warning and continuous approach speed indicators. The aircraft was also fitted with a variable aileron stick gearing arrangement to improve lateral control by reducing stick movements, especially during the approach and landing. The poor lateral and directional control characteristics had earlier been criticised during the Sea Venom 20's development programme when the new variable gearing system showed a marked improvement during the deck landing trials.

In September 1954 the prototype made a brief appearance at the SBAC display at Farnborough before being transferred to

Damage caused to the rear of a Sea Venom — probably WM573 of the NAS — when the arrestor hook brackets failed during the intensive programme of trials carried out at Farnborough in September 1955. (*DERA*)

Hurn for further company trials. The following March, XA539 was returned to Boscombe for three days of performance trials on board HMS *Bulwark*, after which it was issued to the NAD Bedford for a brief period of barrier trials. It was eventually broken up for spares in May 1956.

SEA VENOM FAW.21 TRIALS AIRCRAFT

WM568: Following a period of company handling trials, the aircraft was issued to the RAE in July 1954 for catapulting, RATOG and arresting proofing trials. It was returned to Christchurch in March 1955 for spinning trials, which were continued at the A&AEE

between May and July 1955. Following the various trial installations of a flowmeter, hydraulic actuator and drop-tanks at de Havilland's, the aircraft was dispatched to RNAY Belfast in March 1957.

WM569: Issued to Martin-Baker's at Chalgrove in October 1954 for the design study of ejection seats, following which it was passed to Christchurch in April 1955 for the seats to be installed. In February 1956 the aircraft was passed to the A&AEE for canopy jettison trials and assessment of the ejection seats, after which it was downgraded to an instructional airframe in March 1956 for use at Arbroath.

WM570: Between January 1955 and February 1956 the A&AEE evaluated this aircraft for radar trials, gun-firing checks, and engine handling and carrier trials. It was dispatched to RDU Stretton in March 1956.

WM572: Dismantled and shipped to Canada on 20 June 1955 for cold-weather trials at CEPE Alberta between July 1955 and July 1956. It returned to Chester for examination before being passed to RNAY Belfast on 16 November 1956.

WM573: Engaged in RP handling trials at Hurn and A&AEE between November 1954 and July 1955, followed by catapult trials with RPs at the RAE. The aircraft was damaged in November 1955 and passed to Chester for repairs.

WM574: Used for development flying with redesigned flaps and flap blowing trials at Christchurch between January 1955 and February 1956, following which it went on board *Ark Royal* in March 1956. It was transferred to RAE Bedford for catapulting and arresting assessment flight trials the following June and was later operated by the ETPS from June to November 1958, before being used to assess the effects of spray agents at Boscombe Down on behalf of the CDEE.

WM575: Allocated for tropical trials on behalf of the A&AEE at Idris in Libya between June and October 1955.

WW193: Airframe used for analysis of Sea Venom mainplanes at RAE between February 1957 and July 1958. It was tested to destruction and later scrapped.

WW198: This aircraft was involved in arresting trials at NAE Bedford from October 1955, but the trials had to be cut short the following month after an accident which necessitated repairs at Chester.

WW200: Used in arresting trials at RAE and NAE from October 1955, after which it was transferred to the A&AEE for RATOG jettison trials at Boscombe Down. It was dispatched to RNAY Belfast on completion of the trials in August 1956.

WW201: Installation and evaluation of angle of attack indicator at Christchurch between June and August 1958, after which it underwent further evaluation at RAE Bedford until November 1958.

WW202: Used in arresting trials at NAE Bedford from October to November 1955, when it was transferred to Chester for repairs after the hook was pulled out.

WW208: Catapulting trials and investigation of acceleration after take-off at RAE Bedford between June and November 1958, following which it was issued to Christchurch to be fitted with AOA equipment. Further deck landing approach aid trials took place at Bedford between August 1959 and March 1960, when it was passed to 700 Squadron at Yeovilton for a service evaluation of the equipment.

WW210: To RAE Bedford in July 1960 for an investigation into hook failures, on completion of which it was passed to Abbotsinch in September 1960.

WW211: IFF.10 flight trials at the A&AEE between September and October 1955, following which it was used for catapult trials at Bedford. It was embarked on *Bulwark* for flight trials between 5 and 16 March 1956, followed by further catapult and arresting trials at Bedford. It was sold for scrap in July 1959.

WW294: This airframe was used for fatigue testing at Hatfield between June 1960 and July 1961, when it was struck off charge and scrapped.

WW295: This airframe was used as a mock-up for an ejection seat conference at Christchurch in September 1954, following which it was fitted with a Ghost 105 engine and later carried out a series of navigation trials. In May 1956 it was passed to the A&AEE for a navigational assessment, before being dispatched to RNAY Belfast the following month.

WW296: Engaged in flight trials of the Ghost 105 engine at the A&AEE between June and October 1956.

Sea Venom 21 XG612 climbing out of Christchurch over Parkstone Bay, Poole Harbour, in April 1956, with company test pilot Ron Clear at the controls. This aircraft was used by the company for engine and catapulting trials. It was later modified to carry out the service evaluation of the Blue Jay air-to-air missile. (*de Havilland*)

XG607: Fitted with Blue Jay AAM modifications this aircraft completed flight trials of associated equipment at Christchurch between March 1957 and June 1958.

XG612: Engaged in flight trials of the Ghost 105 engine at Christchurch from May 1956, before the installation of Blue Jay modifications and subsequent transfer to RAE Bedford for associated catapulting trials in February 1958.

XG613: Used at Christchurch for various trial installations from February 1956 to September 1958. It passed to A&AEE for handling trials of 50-gallon pylon drop-tanks, until eventually being transferred to RAE Bedford in February 1960 for catapulting trials with improved elevator mass balance weights, head-up display development and continuation training. It was passed to the Imperial War Museum in September 1969 for preservation.

XG622: To RAE Farnborough between December 1956 and March 1957 for investigation into mainplane skin cracking.

XG631: Employed with Mk.13 arrestor gear trials at NAD/RAE Bedford in March 1961.

XG632: Fitted with AOA equipment at Christchurch in July 1958, which was evaluated at RAE Bedford between August and November 1958.

XG658: Trial installation of radio cooling modifications at Christchurch between December 1957 and February 1958.

XG659: To Christchurch in May 1958 for investigation of control system aileron locking.

XG662: This aircraft was fitted with Blue Jay AAM modifications at Christchurch and

This photograph was taken at the commissioning ceremony of 809 Squadron at RNAS Yeovilton, September 1956. The CO, Lt R.A. Shilcock, is flanked by the senior pilot, Lt Cdr Manuel, and the senior observer, Lt Hackett. The two RAF navigators are Flt Lt Duncan Watson (on left) and Flt Lt Bob Olding, who was seriously injured during the Suez crisis. (*Lt Cdr John Hackett RN*)

passed to A&AEE in November 1957 for handling and armament trials. It returned to Christchurch in February 1958 for preparation for GW trials, and passed back to A&AEE the next month. Following catapulting and arresting trials at RAE Bedford, it was passed to the A&AEE in June 1958 for preparation for its embarkation on board HMS *Victorious*.

INTO SERVICE

On 3 May 1955 809 Squadron at Yeovilton became the first operational unit to receive the FAW.21 when WW138 was collected from Stretton by the CO, Lt Cdr S.A. Mearns DSC, RN. Further deliveries were slow and the squadron was not up to full

strength until the end of August when a ninth aircraft was accepted. Once it had completed its work-up period, it was intended that 809 Squadron would join HMS *Ark Royal* in the Mediterranean in September 1955. However, continuing problems with the Sea Venoms' arrestor hooks, which required urgent modification work by the engineering staff, delayed the squadron's embarkation. By November nine of the squadron aircraft were able to fly down to Malta and joined the carrier for a period of exercises with units of the French Navy at Hyeres, Toulon and Oran. The deployment culminated with a four-day exercise, 'Cascade', before the Sea Venoms returned to Yeovilton, where the squadron was disbanded on 20 March 1956.

Sea Venom 21 WW223 of 890 Squadron displaying the squadron's witch-on-a-broomstick insignia. Built at Chester, this aircraft had a relatively short career and served with 890 and 893 Squadrons between March 1956 and March 1958, when it was relegated for instructional duties. (*Fleet Air Arm Museum*)

No. 809 Squadron featured a red phoenix on the noses of its Sea Venom 21s, as shown on WW222 at the moment of launch from HMS *Albion* in 1958. The launching bridle is about to fall away as the aircraft leaves the carrier's port catapult. (*R.L. Ward*)

A formation of Sea Venom 21s of 809 Squadron from RNAS Yeovilton during the summer of 1956. The aircraft in the box of the nearest formation (WW138) is currently preserved at the FAA Museum, Yeovilton. (*Lt Cdr S.A. Mearns DSC, RN*)

In June 1955 891 Squadron (Lt Cdr M.A. Birrell DSC, RN) became the second unit to equip with FAW.21s. Following a period of mixed operations with FAW.20s, it was fully equipped by November. The following month, on 4 July, 892 Squadron (Lt Cdr M.H.J. Petrie RN) also re-formed at Yeovilton with eight aircraft.

On 7 May 1956, under the command of Lt Cdr R.A. Shilcock RN, 809 Squadron re-formed again at Yeovilton with nine unmodified Sea Venom FAW.21s. Following its work-up during the summer, which concentrated on the squadron's primary role of air interception, together with a gunnery programme and deck landing practice on HMS *Bulwark*, on 15 September 1956 the unit embarked for the Mediterranean in HMS *Albion* with a new batch of aircraft fitted with ejection seats.

On 6 February 1956 a fourth Sea Venom FAW.21 unit, 890 Squadron (Lt Cdr P.S.

Brewer RN), re-formed at Yeovilton, having received the first of its new aircraft (WW150) on 31 January. Soon after re-forming, the CO re-created the squadron aerobatic team. Practice sessions began in mid-February and the team was declared official by May when it was established with Lt Cdr Bill Brewer and Lts Nigel Anderdon, Peter Young and Nobby Hall.

Joining HMS *Bulwark* in May for a period of deck landing training, the squadron suffered a fatal accident on 31 May when one of the Sea Venoms (WW224) crashed inverted off the carrier's starboard bow following a loss of control during a catapult launch. On 4 June another tragic accident occurred when the commanding officer and his observer, Lt E.E.J. Massee, were killed when their Sea Venom (WW262) stalled short of the round-down of HMS *Bulwark* and crashed into the sea after the wing struck the port safety net.

The crowded — and windswept — aft-deck of HMS *Ark Royal* in early 1956. Awaiting a mass launch are Sea Venom 21s of 891 Squadron, Fairey Gannets of 824 Squadron and the Skyraiders of 849 (B) Squadron. (*Darryl Cott*)

Despite these unfortunate accidents during the squadron's period of deck landing training on board *Bulwark*, it did manage to complete seventy-one landings and returned to Yeovilton on 6 June. In recognition of the hard work put in by the late Lt Cdr Bill Brewer, the aerobatic team immediately began rehearsing again for their planned display at HMS *Aerial* at the end of the month. With a team now comprising the new CO, Lt Cdr Peter Young, Lts Nigel Anderdon and Nobby Hall, together with Sub Lt Bob Hilditch, the display went ahead on 23 June. Two days later, on 25 June, the squadron was disbanded and its aircraft passed to 893 Squadron.

Together with 890 Squadron, 893 Squadron also re-formed at Yeovilton on 6 February 1956 under the command of Lt Cdr M.W. Henley DSC, RN, with six Sea Venom FAW.21s. This figure was increased to nine following the disbandment of 890 Squadron in June. Joining HMS *Eagle* at Malta in August 1956, the squadron spent the next few months deployed alternately between the carrier and its shore base at Hal Far.

This left 891 Squadron. Following the fitting of new arrestor hook brackets to its aircraft at the end of 1955, this unit finally departed on 9/10 January 1956 to Malta via Chateauroux, Istres and Naples to join HMS

Ark Royal for a two-month cruise in the Mediterranean. Included in a busy round of NATO activities, the squadron was involved in Exercise 'Febex', during which the Sea Venoms acquitted themselves well against US aircraft operating from Wheelus Field, Libya. On 7 March a squadron Sea Venom (WW142) disappeared without trace following a night interception of an RAF Shackleton during Exercise 'Cascade'. At the end of March 891 Squadron returned to Yeovilton and disbanded on 19 April 1956.

Lt Cdr Maurice Birrell DSC commanded 891 Squadron during its first commission with Sea Venoms from November 1954 to April 1956. During his time with the squadron it was successively equipped with FAW.20s and FAW.21s, and following his departure he wrote a critical analysis of the Sea Venom and its operational capabilities, a part of which is reproduced below:

After years of admiring the American naval aircraft's sturdy undercarriages, we had at last in the Sea Venom 21 an aircraft which sat down among the wires in a most impressive manner, and was as good as anything seen on the deck. There was never a suggestion of bounce after a hard landing such as could be seen with the Sea Hawks and Gannets.

The large radome got in the way at times on the final approach and it took several shots to learn how to approach the catapult when landing, owing to the off-set driving position, but one soon got used to it. The small bubble in the canopy made a big difference to the pilot's angle of sight.

After landing, two aspects of bad cockpit layout were apparent. First, you barked your knuckles and lost your fingernails scrabbling for the hook lever which was awkwardly placed between the pilot's seat and the cabin pressure wheel and got hidden under the parachute leg strap. Once landed, and with a strong desire to clear the angled deck for your next astern, one struggled to unlock and fold the wings. These levers were also awkwardly placed on the rear cockpit wall and always took too long to find and operate. A long-armed type had to release his straps and lean forward to get at them.

Although not a brilliant performer, the Venom 21's 0.82M in level flight left the day-fighters behind in the climb. Given time and distance, the Venom could make successful interceptions at 40,000ft, both day and night, but time to height varied according to atmospheric conditions. Having reached high altitude, the aircraft was slow to accelerate and required 20 miles or so to reach a reasonable interception speed.

The power controls were excellent. Most people flew with the geared aileron in the mid-position for high-altitude work and for deck landing.

The maximum deck landing weight allowed for 150 gallons of fuel remaining. If you couldn't get your hook down or had to divert for other some reason, you could only travel 60 miles at that fuel state. This figure allowed 20 gallons unusable and 45 gallons for bad-weather circuit at a strange airfield.

The airborne performance of the AI Mk.21 radar was most satisfactory, particularly during Exercises 'Febex' and 'Cascade', when bomber-sized targets were regularly picked up at ranges well into double figures. As always, the ASV mapping capabilities of the radar were outstanding, the aircraft invariably picking up the carrier well before the carrier had picked up the Venoms.

During the autumn of 1956 the looming crisis in the Middle East following the nationalisation of the Suez Canal found the three operational Sea Venom FAW.21 squadrons in place with the two British strike carriers of the Anglo-French Task Force in the Mediterranean. HMS *Eagle* with 892 and 893 Squadrons and HMS *Albion* with 809 Squadron could put up twenty-five Sea Venoms in all, and a fuller account of the preparation and action during this brief conflict can be found in Chapter Four.

Sea Venom 21 WW187 of 892 Squadron about to pick up the wire on board HMS *Eagle* during 1956. (*Fleet Air Arm Museum*)

Following the cessation of hostilities and the withdrawal of the Anglo-French invasion fleet from the eastern Mediterranean, the British strike carriers disembarked their Sea Venom squadrons at Hal Far at the end of November 1956.

On 11 December 1956 892 Squadron joined 893 Squadron on board HMS *Eagle* for a month's cruise in the Mediterranean; eight days later a serious mishap occurred when the guns of an 893 Squadron Sea Venom (WW193) were accidentally discharged while the aircraft was being serviced, causing severe damage to two other squadron Sea Venoms (WW270 and WW282) and a Wyvern of 830 Squadron. No. 892 Squadron disbanded on 26 December, with its crews being absorbed into 893 Squadron.

The following February 893 Squadron joined HMS *Ark Royal* and returned to the UK, temporarily operating from Merryfield while the runways at Yeovilton were being resurfaced. It was joined during March 1957 by 809 Squadron, which returned from the Mediterranean on board HMS *Albion* for modifications to the Sea Venoms' mainplane structure. Subsequent inspections of the aircraft from both squadrons revealed cracks in the wing centre sections from constant catapulting during the Suez conflict, which necessitated their withdrawal for urgent repairs. However, by the time 809 Squadron joined HMS *Albion* the following June, it had been reissued with modified aircraft and successfully took part in the major NATO autumn exercise 'Strikeback', which took place in the north-east Atlantic during September 1957 and involved about a hundred warships, including nine aircraft carriers of the RN and US strike fleets.

The sub-assembly area at Chester in early 1957, with a number of Sea Venom 21s undergoing a variety of modifications as part of the 'Return to Work' programme. Modifications included the installation of ejection seats. (*via Alan Roach*)

ENTER THE SEA VENOM FAW.22

The final Sea Venom variant to enter service with the Royal Navy was the FAW.22, which began life as the proposed Venom NF Mk.5 for the RAF. The type's principal improvement was the installation of a Ghost 105 engine, which was fitted following the withdrawal of MoS support for the projected RAF version. This offered an opportunity for de Havilland's to re-engine some of the later aircraft, including the Venom FB.54s supplied to Switzerland and Venezuela. Originally designated the Ghost 53 Mk.1, the Ghost 105 was basically similar to the earlier 103 and 104 engines. The new engine retained most of the design features of the earlier marks, but positive improvements included a substantial increase in maximum power to 5,300lb static

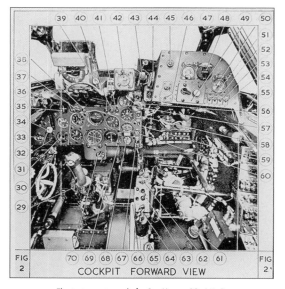

The instrument panel of a Sea Venom 22. (*MoS*)

thrust and a reduction in weight. In addition to an improved take-off, higher rate of climb and increased maximum level speed, the new engine was also seen to restore the climb performance of the later marks of the Sea Venom all-weather fighter which had suffered when a heavier radar installation was adopted for greater operational efficiency. It was also possible to convert some of the earlier engines to the 105 standard.

The Sea Venom FAW.22 also incorporated powered ailerons, Maxaret anti-skid brakes, RATOG, Martin-Baker Mk.4A lightweight ejection seats, AI Mk.21 (ARI 5860) search radar, and Green Salad UHF (ARI 18049). A total of thirty-nine FAW.22s (XG681–702 and XG722–737) were ordered, the first of which (XG681) took to the air on 1 October

1956. With the exception of one aircraft (XG685) which was produced at Christchurch, deliveries from the Chester factory took place between November 1956 and January 1958. In addition, between May 1958 and March 1960 some thirty-nine FAW.21s were also converted to FAW.22 standard at RNAY Belfast.

At least one FAW.22, WW220, was set aside for trials. Following its conversion at Christchurch, it was issued to the A&AEE in August 1959 for an assessment of a new UHF radio installation. Two months later it was fitted with the emergency homing aid known as 'Violet Picture' at Christchurch and returned to Boscombe Down for a brief set of tests before it eventually entered squadron service the following year.

The first operational unit to receive the

A formation of Sea Venom 22s of 894 Squadron in February 1957. The squadron had formed at RNAS Yeovilton the previous month and the aircraft already carry the black and red chequered tip-tanks. (*Flight*)

Sea Venom FAW.22 was 894 Squadron (Lt Cdr P.G. Young RN) at Yeovilton. Commissioned at Merryfield on 14 January 1957, the squadron initially operated with a mixture of FAW.21s and FAW.22s until the following March, by which time it had become established with twelve FAW.22s. A series of air defence exercises with 766 Squadron during February 1957 saw mixed successes while trying to intercept a variety of 'hostile' aircraft. The Valiant bomber proved particularly elusive as it was able to fly some 2,000ft above the Sea Venoms' operational ceiling, and it was not until the last day of Exercise 'KingPin', on 28 February, that one was finally claimed by the squadron.

Continuing problems with radio failures persisted into March, and in an attempt to resolve the situation XG685 was fitted with thermocouples distributed throughout the radio bay. More serious, however, was the temporary grounding of all Sea Venoms on 14 March owing to suspected cracking in no. 2 rib in the vicinity of the arrestor hook. On 5 August 1957 the squadron was at last able to embark on HMS *Eagle* for the first of its regular cruises with the carrier. Two further squadrons were also re-equipped with Sea Venom FAW.22s: 891 Squadron (Lt Cdr W.G.B. Black) at Merryfield in December 1957 and 893 Squadron (Lt Cdr E.V.H. Manuel) at Yeovilton in January 1959.

All four front-line Sea Venom squadrons were at sea during the latter half of 1957, but had returned to Merryfield by late November after a period of varied and rewarding exercises in the Mediterranean and North Atlantic. One of the last units to return to Merryfield was 891 Squadron, command of which had been assumed by Lt Cdr George Black on 5 December. The following day he had the distinction of becoming the first pilot to successfully eject

from a Sea Venom (XG727) when a problem in the fuel system caused the engine to fail during night ADDLs. His aircraft crashed at Ashill in Somerset. His successor, Lt Cdr J.F. Blunden RN, took command of the squadron on 9 December.

The year 1958 would prove to be an eventful one for the Royal Navy's Sea Venom squadrons. During the early months of the year a series of crashes occurred in almost identical circumstances following night catapult launches; some of them had fatal consequences. On 17 January a FAW.22 of 891 Squadron (XG735) crashed into the sea off HMS *Bulwark*, killing the pilot and RAF observer. Over the next few months at least four more aircraft from 891 and 893 Squadrons suffered a similar fate when they were seen to pitch up and roll to starboard after launch, before crashing into the sea.

As this was clearly an anxious time for all the embarked squadrons, this tendency to stall after night launches was a serious problem which needed to be urgently resolved. Therefore, on 23 April de Havilland's test pilot Ron Clear arrived on board *Ark Royal* to investigate the possible cause. An interrogation of squadron pilots revealed their disconsolation at having no external visual references during the night launch, and their habit of increasing the nose-up trim more than was recommended in the Pilots' Notes. Later flying with the CO of 893 Squadron, Lt Cdr John Elgar, Ron Clear could find no aerodynamic reasons for the pitch-up, but did notice his habit of anchoring his right elbow against his hip before launch to ensure that the acceleration did not force his arm and therefore the stick back. He also noticed that the rate of climb indicator fluctuated during the launch, and that the artificial horizon displayed misleading pitch indications when the acceleration of the

On 5 February 1960 894 Squadron joined HMS *Albion* for a ten-month cruise of the Mediterranean and the Far East. XG723 was the first of the unit's Sea Venoms to embark on the carrier, and it is seen here at the point of picking up the wire. The aircraft were adorned with shark's teeth markings, while the 'Hypogriff' (winged sea horse) insignia can just be seen on the fin fillet. (*Fleet Air Arm Museum*)

catapult (especially the older catapults in use at the time) caused the gyro to precess and demonstrate a nose-up attitude.

Following the recommendations in Ron Clear's subsequent report, de Havilland's eventually instigated modifications to the aircraft's mass balances, as well as to the pitot static system and artificial horizon. Ron also emphasised the precise need for aircrew to fly to the Pilots' Notes, which were rewritten to include special provision for night launches. Following the advice given in his report, no further pitch-up and stall problems were reported by the operational Sea Venom squadrons.

Ron Clear's report had also suggested the installation of the Kelvin and Hughes angle of attack (AOA) indicator, which would provide the pilot with an attitude for reference during night catapult launches. Three Sea Venom

21s (WW201, WW208 and XG632) were allocated for the trials and were fitted with the instrument at Christchurch during July 1958. The following month an evaluation of the AOA equipment was carried out at RAE Bedford, which recommended that it should be installed in all operational aircraft as soon as possible. With the completion of the assessment, WW201 was returned to Christchurch for the removal of the equipment, while XG632 was passed to 700 Squadron at Yeovilton for service trials.

In October 1958 the third Sea Venom (WW208) involved in the AOA evaluation was passed to 894 Squadron, and the crews were instructed to comply strictly with the readings supplied from the attitude indicator until the aircraft had climbed to a 'safe' operational height and airspeed. Squadron crews recalled the 'exciting' early daylight

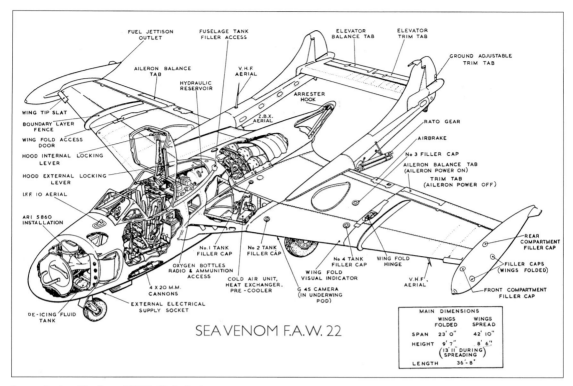

Cutaway drawing of Sea Venom FAW.22. *(de Havilland)*

experiments with the AOA-fitted aircraft, as adhering to this instruction produced an exceptional rate of climb – especially when it involved straying into the path of other aircraft in the airfield circuit!

On 7 April 1958 891 Squadron joined HMS *Bulwark* off Gibraltar for an eleven-month cruise and sailed with the carrier for Hong Kong. By the end of July the ship had arrived at Aden and disembarked its Air Group at Khormaksar, where it was held in operational readiness for the trouble in Oman and the possible Iraqi invasion of Kuwait.

After several weeks of routine exercises with the Aden Protectorate Levies, 891 Squadron (together with the Sea Hawks of 801 Squadron) was called upon to take part in the ground-attack operation in the Jebel Akhdar, a range of desert mountains in central Oman. It was here that the rebel leader Talib and his

dissidents had taken up position. Despite determined attacks by RAF aircraft to dislodge him, he was busily waging a protracted terrorist war against the government.

On 9 September *Bulwark* sailed for Muscat, and three days later the two squadrons flew their first armed strikes. A total of forty-four operational sorties were flown during the day, including twelve by the Sea Venoms. More sorties were flown early the following day, but further operations were suspended when the carrier was called to the assistance of the stricken Liberian tanker *Melika*, which had collided with another tanker off Masirah Island. Having taken the tanker safely in tow to Muscat, *Bulwark* was able to launch its squadrons for one last strike against the rebel positions on 21 September before sailing to Cyprus to relieve HMS *Eagle*.

For a further three weeks 891 Squadron was able to participate in several air defence and army cooperation exercises over Cyprus until the carrier sailed for Malta on 22 October. The following day the Carrier Air Group was flown off to Hal Far, from where 891 Squadron returned to Yeovilton, arriving on 28 October 1958.

In March 1959 the Sea Venom squadrons were at sea again in the mid-Atlantic for Exercise 'Dawn Breeze IV', which was designed to test the air defences of a carrier attack force. Up to fifty ships took part in the exercise, including the carriers *Centaur*, *Eagle* and *Victorious* which comprised 'Blue Force'; their brief was to 'attack' targets in the south of England. These strikes were opposed by the 'enemy' or 'Orange Force', who also attacked the ships with aircraft such as V-bombers, Canberras and Shackletons.

The following month 891 Squadron embarked on HMS *Centaur* for a cruise of the Far East. On 26 May the carrier left Brest harbour for a NATO exercise with the French Navy, but it all got off to an unfortunate start when a Sea Venom (WW289) suffered a brake failure after landing and went over the side after hitting a parked aircraft. Although the Observer, Sub Lt Adams, was rescued unhurt, the squadron's senior pilot, Lt Cdr C.R. Bushe, was not found and was presumed to have drowned. The following month another Sea Venom (XG696) bolted during a heavy landing and struck two parked Sea Hawks of 804 Squadron. Despite losing the tip-tank from the starboard wing, the Sea Venom was able to climb away and both crew members were able to eject to safety ahead of the carrier.

By January 1960 *Centaur* had reached Singapore and the squadron went ashore at Seletar for an air defence exercise with RAF and RAAF Canberra bombers. A further exercise at Trincomalee saw the squadron providing CAPs against aircraft of the Royal Ceylon Air Force.

Sailing up from Mombasa to Aden the following April the opportunity for *Centaur*'s Air Group to assist the RAF in ground-attacks against rebels in the Radfan area of the Aden Protectorate was quickly accepted. Between 12 and 14 April the Sea Venoms of 891 Squadron and the Sea Hawks of 801 Squadron continuously attacked terrorist hideouts in the mountains with rockets and cannon fire during Operation 'Damon'. Some 400 rockets and thousands of 20mm rounds were fired into the mountainous terrain by the Sea Venoms during the operation, the aircrew taking part in the operation being subsequently awarded the Naval General Service Medal. On 25 April 891 Squadron was flown off and returned to Yeovilton.

After 893 Squadron's embarkation on HMS *Victorious* for trials with the Firestreak missile in the Mediterranean during late 1958 (*see* Chapter Thirteen), and its subsequent re-equipment with Sea Venom FAW.22s during January 1959, the squadron was to spend the rest of the year either at Yeovilton, on Front Line Armament Practice at Brawdy during May and October, or on board HMS *Victorious*. In July 1959 the squadron crossed the Atlantic and spent the next six weeks on the eastern seaboard of the USA, operating from Norfolk, Virginia, up to Boston, Massachusetts, together with a short spell in New York.

One of the aims of the visit to the USA was to demonstrate the carrier's new, computerised air defence radar system – the Type 984 – which was able to detect aircraft at considerable range and could show their position simultaneously in range, bearing and height. The efficiency of the radar controllers of '984 Squadron' had been successfully tested during earlier attacks by RAF bomber aircraft and, as the carrier drew nearer to the

HMS *Albion* during its final cruise of the Far East in 1960. The Carrier Air Group comprised the Sea Venom 22s of 894 Squadron, the Sea Hawks of 806 Squadron and the Skyraiders of 849 Squadron. A Ship's Flight Whirlwind helicopter is airborne on 'plane guard' duties. (*Bob Hillman*)

United States, 893 Squadron's Sea Venoms, guided by the resident 984 Direction Officer acting as controller, were able to intercept nineteen of the twenty-three F-8 Crusaders – the USN's latest supersonic fighter – sent up against them from NAS *Oceana*.

Three days of further operations with the American fleet during Exercise 'Rip Tide' included a cross-operating exercise with the Crusaders and Skyrays from the carrier USS *Saratoga* on 16 July, and a simulated 'strike' against the cruiser USS *Boston*.

No. 893 Squadron's final cruise with Sea Venoms began in January 1960 and climaxed with an exercise in the North Sea with Norwegian coastal forces off the Skaggerak. After this, the squadron returned to Yeovilton and disbanded on 29 February 1960.

No. 894 Squadron also went to sea for the last time in February 1960 when HMS *Albion* departed for a ten-month cruise of the Mediterranean and Far East, visiting Gibraltar, Aden, Mombasa, Karachi, Singapore, Hong Kong, the Philippines, South Korea and Japan. An eventful and demanding cruise saw exercises with the Pakistan Navy, the RAAF and RAF Venom units in Aden and Hong Kong. A severe thunderstorm off Singapore resulted in the squadron's aircraft recovering to various airfields with smashed radomes, and a Chinese controller at Kai Tak strained international relations to the limit when he refused to allow the Sea Venoms to land following an earlier accident on the runway, and was forced to confront the rage of the squadron CO, Lt Cdr Bain. Although four squadron aircraft had been lost in flying accidents during the embarkation, the high standard of flying achieved was attributed to the improved carrier launching instrument technique and the professionalism of the crews. Returning to Yeovilton, the squadron was disbanded on 17 December 1960.

A farewell cruise for 891 Squadron on board HMS *Centaur*, which included visits to the Norwegian bases at Bodo and Sola, began on 12 June 1960. Following its return to Yeovilton in October, the squadron's final months were spent on exercises and formation aerobatics by the display team, the 'Kon Tikis'. Initially commanded by the CO, Lt Cdr Brown, the display team comprised Lts Borrowman, Jones and Layard, and throughout its brief existence the team put up creditable performances at numerous 'Air Days' and 'Navy Days'. The final display was on 8 July 1961, by which time the squadron was in the process of being run down, with the last operational flight taking place on 26 July 1961 when Sea Venom XG680 was delivered to RNAS Abbotsinch by Lt Layard for disposal. The squadron was finally disbanded at Yeovilton on 27 July 1961.

ELECTRONIC SEA VENOMS: THE ECM.21 AND ECM.22

The disbandment of 891 Squadron left 831 Squadron at Culdrose as the only front-line unit to operate Sea Venoms, six of which had been inherited when the unit had been renumbered from 751 Squadron in May 1958. On 13 May 1958 changes within the unit saw its Gannets being allocated to A Flight and the Sea Venom Flight being renamed B Flight. As an ECM unit the squadron made frequent overseas detachments: in February 1959 four ECM.21s, led by Lt Cdr Wilcox, went to Malta with the object of 'selling' electronic warfare to the Mediterranean fleet. The detachment demon-

strated the effectiveness of 'jamming' against a variety of naval and shore-based target radars, with the Sea Venoms being directed at designated radar targets in support of air strikes within the operational range of the aircraft. Two periods on board HMS *Eagle* and *Victorious* were also made during the six-month visit, with regular 'jammex' runs for the carrier-based squadrons. The detachment returned to Culdrose on 5 November.

Although originally not considered ideal for the task of electronic warfare, the Sea Venom ECM.21 was modified to incorporate Naval Service Modification (NSM) 3020, which was installed by NAIRU at Lee-on-Solent from March 1957. The NSM introduced a lightweight UHF (PTR170) radio, in addition to the ARC52 UHF radio already in place, to provide normal communications while the ARC52 was being used for jamming. The PTR170 used the upper and lower boom aerials and a further aerial was installed for the ARC, located on the underside of the port wing. The ECM.21 was also fitted with three Lend-Lease units:

- **APR-9 (Airborne Pulse Receiver)**: a 'tuneable' RF receiver with TN-129 and TN-131 tuner units to cover the frequency bands of the ships' radars.
- **APA-69 (Airborne Pulse Analyser)**: an adjunct to the APR-9, it comprised a high-speed rotating dish antenna feeding the APR-9, the output of which was displayed on a cockpit-mounted display unit as a radial 'spoke' on the bearing (relative to the aircraft's heading) from which the signal was received.
- **ALT-6 (Airborne Jamming Transmitter)**: a high-powered jammer that covered the same frequency bands as the APR-9.

In the ECM.21 the ALT-6 and its forward-facing antenna, plus a rather crude left–right antenna unit to replace the APA-69's rotating antenna, were mounted in the nose radome instead of the AI Mk.21 radar. The four 20mm cannon were also removed, which resulted in ballast blocks having to be bolted to the forward cockpit wall to restore the aircraft's centre of gravity.

The original trials of the ECM equipment were carried out in Sea Venom 21 XG608 at NAIRU and the RAE at Bedford between June 1956 and November 1957, by which time further aircraft had been modified and delivered to the navy. By the time the last aircraft was delivered to 831 Squadron in June 1964 a total of seven ECM.21s and seven ECM.22s had been converted at NAIRU.

As most of the unit's training was undertaken at low level, the resultant lack of range was also a problem but the delivery in April 1960 of the first of five ECM.22s fitted with additional long-range, under-wing drop-tanks resolved some of the ECM.21's shortcomings. Also in 1960 831 Squadron was deservedly awarded the annual Boyd Trophy for efficiency in training with the fleet. Lt Cdr Jesse Hanks commanded both 751 and 831 Squadrons:

I was appointed to command 751 Squadron on 10 March 1958. We quickly became 831 Squadron the following May since by that time there was increasing interest in Electronic Counter Measures, and it was intended that we should embark on the carriers for fleet exercises.

ECM was a tender art in those days and it needed enthusiasts to get everyone involved, even though it was many years before one saw the improved capabilities as demonstrated in the Gulf War. However, in the late 1950s we were accepting Buccaneer aircraft into the FAA to attack surface targets and the 'under the lobe' technique was being exploited. Maintaining radar silence, aircraft could approach a target ship at altitude and using a passive receiver be able to detect (and identify at times) the target ship's air warning radars. The passive warning receiver should give the attacking aircraft an advantage, since the target ship would not yet have detected the attacking aircraft on its prime radar.

The attackers could now descend quickly to remain outside the target ship's radars and since the aircraft passive receiver would have given the target bearing, it could continue to use that bearing as the track to the target. Keeping 'below the lobe' it could then remain undetected unless the defenders had airborne early warning patrols; during fleet exercises you knew they would have AEW Skyraiders or Gannets airborne. Eventually at 20–30 miles from the target, the attacker must be detected by the target ship's radars, but by that time it would be very difficult to get defending fighters to intercept and the Buccaneers could go into a loft-bombing or toss-bombing technique to deliver their weapons.

Against that background, our ECM squadron had been given Sea Venoms to practise the techniques and provide the fleet with opportunities to evolve defensive tactics. The Sea Venom had been chosen because it was already 'in service', with ease of spares and serviceability, and qualified pilots from the NF squadrons were available. The ECM installations in the Sea Venoms (and Gannets) were designed and fitted by NAIRU at Lee-on-Solent. The APR-9 was a beautifully engineered piece of American equipment; it had very good sensitivity, and when properly set up it was highly accurate in terms of the frequency it was tuned to – so much so that we learned each ship's 'frequency signature'. It could detect ship's radars long before they could see us coming – usually at 200–300 nautical miles at 25,000ft.

Further detachments included trips to Bodo in Norway for long-range passive ECM searches, RAF Ballykelly for exercises with the Joint Anti-Submarine School, Valkenburg in Holland to participate in Exercise 'Matador II', and BAN Lann-Bihoue, near Lorient, for NATO's Exercise 'Dawn Breeze'.

One of three Sea Venom 21s (XG607) modified at Christchurch for trials with the Firestreak missile, seen with 700 Squadron – the trials unit based at RNAS Ford – in June 1958. It carries a dummy round under the wing. (*Arthur Pearcy*)

In July 1963 831 Squadron was transferred to RAF Watton for closer cooperation with its RAF counterparts.

Between 2 and 13 May 1966 a final squadron detachment, comprising two aircraft, was made to Sola in Norway for Exercise 'Bright Horizon'. No. 831 Squadron was disbanded on 16 May 1966, with the squadron personnel transferring to 360 Squadron RAF for joint RAF/RN trials and training in ECM work. On 1 June 1966 the last Sea Venom (XG694) left the unit when it was flown to RNAY Belfast for storage.

SECOND-LINE UNITS

700 Squadron. Re-formed at Ford on 18 August 1955 with a variety of aircraft types, the unit received its first Sea Venom FAW.21s (WW147 and WW191) on 11 January 1956. As a Trials and Development Squadron, it was responsible for the acceptance procedure for new aircraft, equipment or operation type before issue to the service. Although only two or three Sea Venoms were ever on strength at any one time, they were kept extremely busy with a variety of operational trials, including weapon firing, ejection seat backpad installation, and deck trials on board HMS *Albion* and the Dutch carrier *Karel Doorman*. The unit also performed target-towing duties for the operational squadrons; after the temporary grounding of the Sea Venom 21s in March 1957 it was loaned an FAW.20 (WM523) to maintain its commitment. With the closure of Ford, the squadron moved to Yeovilton in September 1958 and extended its duties with the service flying trials of the angle of incidence indicator to improve catapult launches (February 1959), audio and miniature binocular equipment (May 1959), and a low-level map installation (February–June 1960). The squadron also carried out a brief evaluation of the Firestreak missile, which culminated in one of the three modified Sea Venoms (XG612) being embarked on board HMS *Victorious* during June 1958 for Exercise 'Blue Jay'. It was disbanded on 30 June 1961.

738 Squadron. Following basic and advanced flying training provided by the RAF, potential all-weather student fighter pilots transferred to 738 Squadron at Lossiemouth for a further twenty-one weeks of operational and armament training, flying Sea Venom FAW.21s without an observer. The delivery of the first Sea Venoms in November 1957 enabled AWF students to be trained on type without first converting on the Sea Hawk. The first course to be trained on the Sea Venom, 64 AWS, ran from January to June 1958, with a syllabus including air-to-air camera gun firing and RP practice during some 79 hours day and 11 hours night flying.

In late 1958 the school was renamed the Naval Air Fighter and Strike School, with 738 Squadron becoming the Sea Venom Operational Flying School, Parts 1 and 2, providing refresher conversion and instrument flying training. The initial 50-hour syllabus covered the full fighter-training course before students progressed to the weapons phase for an additional 45 hours, which included air-to-air and air-to-ground firing, navigation and instrument exercises, and formation flying.

With the return of the Sea Hawks from 736 Squadron, the Sea Venoms were withdrawn following the graduation of 82 Course in September 1960.

750 Squadron. On 1 July 1960 the first two of an eventual establishment of four Sea Venom FAW.21s (WW274 and XG627) arrived at Hal Far, with the unit assuming 766 Squadron's task of observer basic jet training. The first course began on 3 October, with observers for all-weather fighters being provided with an initial 30-hour jet familiar-

A Sea Venom 22 (XG699) of 750 Squadron (the RN Observer School) banking away from the camera. The unit transferred from Hal Far to Lossiemouth in June 1965, having received its first FAW.22 some four years earlier. (*Fleet Air Arm Museum*)

Sea Venom 21 XG565 of 700 Squadron was loaned to the SME Flight at Farnborough to assess the efficiency and safety of the catapult bridle. Between 17 and 20 September 1957 the aircraft made a number of launches and arrested landings, including the last from the BH5(1) catapult on Jersey Brow on 20 September by Lt Freddie Hefford RN. (*DERA*)

isation course over seven weeks on high-speed navigation and radar instruction. The observers then proceeded to the Operational Flying Training Course at the Naval Fighter School ahead of the pilots, during which they were introduced to more advanced radar-interception training.

The squadron training syllabus saw the Sea Venoms being used for medium- and low-level navigational exercises, including frequent long-range trips (or Land-Away Navexes) to such airfields as Cyprus, Libya, Copenhagen, Oslo and Amsterdam. Replacement Sea Venom FAW.22s arrived in August 1961 and the unit transferred to Lossiemouth on 23 June 1965. One of the final duties of the squadron was to provide jet familiarisation to observers destined for Buccaneer and Sea Vixen squadrons. The last Sea Venoms (WW151, XG692 and XG734) were withdrawn on 24 March 1970.

751 Squadron. A radio warfare unit based at RAF Watton, this squadron operated a small,

exclusive naval element responsible for the development and trials of radio counter-measures and electronic warfare. The unit worked in conjunction with the RAF, installing electronic equipment in aircraft for exercises with the fleet and providing radio jamming capability and pulse analysis of ground-based and seaborne radars.

In June 1957 A Flight began to equip with Sea Venom FAW.21s, although B Flight retained its Grumman Avengers. The flight's first task was a 'windows' trial in association with a Meteor night-fighter. In August 1957 the first two ECM.21s (WW294 and XG628) were collected from NAIRU at Lee-on-Solent, and the unit had five aircraft on strength (including the first of its ECM.22s) by the time it moved to Culdrose on 2 October 1957. The following month four Sea Venoms embarked on HMS *Eagle* for homing exercises against RAF Coastal Command Neptune MR.1s during Operation 'Phoenix II'. In March 1958 751 Squadron was renamed the Electronic Warfare Unit and was

Following service with 894 Squadron, Sea Venom XG698 was converted to an ECM.22 and issued to 831 Squadron at Watton in February 1964. The tip-tank colours are red with a yellow lightning flash. It later served with Airworks Ltd and was burnt at RNAS Culdrose in 1970. (*Geoff Cruickshank*)

eventually granted front-line status when it was renumbered as 831 Squadron on 1 May 1958.

766 Squadron. On 18 October 1955 766 Squadron was re-formed at Yeovilton as an All-Weather Fighter Pool from the simultaneous disbanding of 890 Squadron. Equipped with eight Sea Venom FAW.20s, the unit provided a reserve of trained AWF crews for the front-line squadrons. Because of work to extend the runways at Yeovilton, 766 Squadron moved to Merryfield in November 1956, and from October 1957 it operated as the Naval All-Weather Fighter School (NAWFU), taking over the task of training pilots and observers previously undertaken by 228 OCU and 238 OCU respectively. No. 766 Squadron returned to Yeovilton in January 1958.

With the arrival of the AI ground trainer at Yeovilton in February 1958, the RAF Brigand Course could be eliminated and 3 Course became the first to train both pilots and observers at the NAWFU. Under the new

scheme, observers first completed a seven-week course at Culdrose before crewing-up with a pilot at Yeovilton, then began a further fourteen-week all-weather training syllabus with exercises including navigation and air interception training, before finishing the course with a period of tactical training. The school's other commitments included refresher courses for experienced crews, short courses for COs and SPs Designate, and occasional trials.

The first of the replacement Sea Venom FAW.21s (WW208) was delivered during March 1956, and the unit was able to complete its conversion from the FAW.20 by the following August. The squadron was also able to participate in Exercise 'Vigilant' during May 1957, but there were few 'targets' and the Fairey Gannets intercepted over the south coast were considered 'easy meat'.

In May 1959 the unit became the All-Weather Fighter Training Squadron and during the following August was able to put together a display team comprising four Sea

Sea Venom 21s of 766 Squadron outside the AWF School, RNAS Yeovilton, in June 1959. The stylised heron insignia on the noses of the aircraft was adapted from the station badge. (*Author's Collection*)

Sea Venom 22 XG729 of the Air Directors School, RNAS Yeovilton, in the static display at RAF Chivenor's International Air Day, 23 August 1969. Finished in an attractive extra dark sea grey and white scheme, the tip-tanks were adorned with 'day-glo' fabric strips. (*Author*)

Venoms, crewed by available instructors. The team's existence was tragically cut short at RAF Chivenor's Air Day on 19 September following a collision during a high-speed descending approach to the main runway. Both crews ejected from their aircraft (WW297 and XG617), but unfortunately the parachutes of one crew failed to deploy, and both men were killed.

The first Sea Vixen FAW.1s which arrived in October 1959 were issued to the newly formed 766 (B) Squadron for type conversion training. By this time the requirement for Sea Venom courses had considerably decreased, with the last (18 Course, comprising just three crews) being held between 27 June and 12 October 1960. The 120-hour course – of which a third was flown at night – included deck landings on HMS *Victorious*, practice interceptions, rocketry and formation flying exercises. With the completion of the course, the establishment's twelve Sea Venoms were quickly withdrawn from service, with the last two aircraft (WW212 and XG631) being ferried away on 14 October 1960.

787 Squadron. As the Naval Air Fighting Development Unit, 787 Squadron, based at West Raynham, was responsible for the tactical trials of aircraft and equipment in association with the RAF. The first Sea Venom 21 (WW147) was delivered on 26 May 1955, and was joined by two more (WW148 and WW191) on 6 September. Trials began in mid-September with an evaluation of the AI Mk.21 radar unit and a familiarisation programme with the night interception technique. These were followed by manoeuvre boundary, flow meter and 'weapons release conditions determination' trials.

Between October and November 1955 the Sea Venoms were used to investigate the 'diving interception' technique against a variety of aircraft, including Venoms, Sea

Certificate presented to graduates of the Sea Venom All-Weather Fighter Course at RNAS Yeovilton – in this case, the last to be completed by 766 Squadron in October 1960. (*Admiral Sir Michael Layard KCB, CBE, RN*)

Hawks and a Canberra bomber. The 'swoop and plunge' procedure was employed during the trial, and although 135 intercepts were carried out only 50 per cent were considered to have been successful.

With the future of the unit under review and the tactical trials of present aircraft completed by the end of 1955, the Sea Venoms were withdrawn between 11 and 13 January 1956. The unit disbanded on 16 January 1956.

Airwork Ltd. This unit, based at St David's airfield in Pembrokeshire, was managed and staffed entirely by Airwork personnel, with flying duties exclusively for the Naval Direction School at Kete, close to Milford Haven. The first Sea Venom 20s were received in October 1955. With an establishment of nine aircraft, six pilots and a manager (who also helped out as a pilot), the unit performed a variety of duties for the

The final sortie. On 6 October 1970 Bill Slade flew Sea Venom 22 XG683 of the ADS from RNAS Yeovilton to RNAS Culdrose for eventual scrapping. He was escorted by a Hunter trainer, flown by Peter Williams. (*Peter Williams*)

Admiralty, including air traffic control and interception training. There were four launches per day, each launch consisting of three pairs of aircraft, and flights generally comprised practice interceptions controlled by the trainee directors. Each session would consist of five or six interceptions, followed by a GCA descent to base during an average sortie time of 1 hour and 20 minutes.

In February 1957 the FAW.20s were gradually replaced with Sea Venom FAW.21s. The unit returned to Brawdy in September 1958 but continued to use St David's as a satellite airfield. On 21 January 1959 the unit suffered a tragic accident when two Sea Venoms (WW150 and XG678) collided in cloud during a pairs GCA exercise, and crashed 10 miles west of Strumble Head.

In January 1961, following the closure of Kete, the unit transferred to Yeovilton and operated as the Air Direction School, receiving Sea Venom FAW.22s the same month to replace the FAW.21s. The unit continued to supply aircraft for the courses, providing naval direction officers with practice in controlling aircraft, together with occasional 'targets' for CAP exercises. Tragedy struck the unit again on 25 July 1961 when Sea Venom XG672 failed to get airborne and crashed into Yeovilton village, destroying a cottage and killing the pilot. (Coincidentally, the cottage was owned by a former Sea Venom pilot, Lt Cdr Nigel de Winton.)

Throughout the summer of 1970 the Sea Venoms were gradually withdrawn and replaced with Hunters. On 5 September 1970 the Sea Venom made its last public appearance at the Yeovilton Air Day flypast when Peter Williams flew the unit's last remaining aircraft (XG683) at the head of a formation of twenty-six naval aircraft over the airfield. On 6 October, the last official Sea Venom sortie was made by Airwork contract pilot Bill Slade, when he flew XG683 from Yeovilton to Culdrose for fire-fighting duties.

Miscellaneous Use: The following units all used Sea Venoms for various duties at one time or another: 736 Squadron, Lossiemouth; 781 Squadron, Lee-on-Solent; 787 Squadron, West Raynham; Merryfield Station Flight; Yeovilton Station Flight; Flag Officer Flying Training, Yeovilton; Maintenance Test Pilots School, Abbotsinch.

CHAPTER THIRTEEN

PROJECT 'BLUE JAY'

Shortly after the Second World War it was recognised by the Air Staff that conventional armament for fighter aircraft was inadequate, and that a more accurate and lethal weapon system was required to produce a greater probability of target destruction. Existing knowledge of missile guidance systems at the time was based upon radar techniques. However, by early 1951 the Radar Research Establishment at Malvern was undertaking research on the design of an air-to-air missile incorporating an infra-red guidance system. The aim was to develop a weapon with a guidance system that would enable it to engage a high-speed bomber aircraft at great heights and, after a careful comparative study the infra-red system was eventually chosen. Both the RAF and Royal Navy recognised the need for such a missile, and on 31 December 1951 Joint Naval/Air Staff Requirement OR.1117 was issued to develop an 'air-to-air, infra-red homing weapon for fighter aircraft'.

The design requirement called for a weapon incorporating a detector eye sensitive to the infra-red rays emitted from an aircraft and capable of intercepting high-performance manoeuvring targets at altitudes ranging from sea level up to at least 45,000ft, and at speeds of 0.95M. By using the infra-red radiation from the engines of the target aircraft as the homing source, the firing range 'bracket' for an attack was considered to be between 4,000 and 20,000 yd. The missile would be in six main sections: guidance, power supply, a solid propulsion motor, a proximity fuse system to detonate the 50lb warhead, and a contact fuse system in order to ensure target

destruction in the event of a hit. The components would be housed within an aerodynamic body fitted with four wings and four control fins. The parent fighter would carry the missile on an under-wing launching shoe, the weapons being fired singly or in pairs, and with provision also being made for jettisoning in the event of an emergency.

The following February the missile, code-named Blue Jay, was given official approval by the Defence Research Policy Committee, who further recommended that the contract to design and develop it should be given to de Havilland (Propellers) at Hatfield. Initial trials to establish the detection and lock-on ranges of the guidance system were carried out against a Meteor target, using an AI-equipped Mosquito B.35 (TH988) flown by the company's chief test pilot Desmond de Villiers. Following these early experiments, the Blue Jay systems were designed and built for ground test-firings at the Larkhill ranges on Salisbury Plain. The first successful test-firing took place in April 1952, and was conducted at night against a large wire frame which carried heaters to simulate the radiation from an aircraft.

By early 1953 work had progressed sufficiently to warrant the start of air-launched trials. Initial airborne telemetry trials over the Aberporth range between September and October 1952 had already been conducted with a Meteor NF.11 operating from RAF Valley. In December 1952 a Venom NF.2, WL813, was acquired by de Havilland (Propellers) for the air trials of the Blue Jay missile, with the intention of

Venom 2 WL813, with dummy Blue Jay missile rounds, in July 1953. It was one of two Venom night-fighters modified to operate the missile. (*DERA*)

carrying out the firings by flying direct from Hatfield; the range of the Venom was considered sufficient for this when operating at 25,000ft. From June 1954 the airfield at Broughton was also used for refuelling and as a diversion facility should the weather over the range be unsuitable.

The air trials were preceded by ground launches from the wing of the Venom, which had been transported to Pendine Sands, near Aberporth, for the test. The nose of the aircraft was pointed out to sea and jacked up, and an anti-blast door was fitted over the undercarriage. With Desmond de Villiers and an engineer in the cockpit, the missile was successfully fired without causing any damage to the aircraft. At the same time jettison tests were carried out from the underwing position on a Venom model in a 24ft tunnel at Hatfield.

On 16 April 1953 the first air-launched, unguided round was successfully fired. Further air launches of the missile continued and in June 1953 a second Venom NF.2,

WL820, was obtained by the trials team to assist in the development programme. On most occasions a test-firing 'formation' normally consisted of the two Venoms (a primary and secondary firer) and a Meteor, which acted as the 'chase' aircraft.

The climax of the trials came on 5 September 1955, when the first firing of a fully guided and controlled round took place over the Aberporth range. The missile was launched from WL813, flown by the new chief test pilot of de Havilland (Propellers), M.P. 'Mike' Kilburn, against an unmanned, radio-controlled Fairey Firefly from Llanbedr. The target was totally destroyed.

At this stage of the development of the missile, flight trials also began in Australia. It had always been recognised that the Aberporth range was too limited in size to allow high-speed target aircraft to be used; moreover, as every firing yielded valuable information, they needed to recover both the target and the missile, and retrieving them from the sea was practically impossible. In

December 1954 12 Joint Services Trials Unit (JSTU) was formed with personnel drawn from the RAF and Royal Navy to carry out joint MoS/service acceptance checks, and subsequently the unit moved to Woomera in 1956 to take advantage of the greater range facilities and better weather. Equipped with Sabre and Canberra aircraft, the unit carried out its first live firing in September 1957 against an unmanned Jindivik target aircraft.

By January 1957 the missile was considered sufficiently developed to be tested against Operational Requirements and an extensive series of acceptance trials was begun, initially by the contractors, then by the A&AEE. In February 1958 the Blue Jay missile was officially renamed 'Firestreak'. Between December 1957 and May 1958 fourteen Firestreak rounds (without warheads) had been fired at unmanned Firefly targets. By this time, however, a Canberra had replaced the Venoms as the firing aircraft; Venom WL820 was declared surplus in February 1958, followed by WL813 in March 1959. In December 1957 a further Venom FB.1, WR370, from the A&AEE was recorded as being briefly used in the development programme for 'making smoke trails'.

The in-service trials of the Firestreak weapon system were conducted by 1 Guided Weapons Trials Squadron (GWTS), which had formed at Valley in September 1959 from 1 Guided Weapons Development Squadron. Operating under the aegis of the CFE, the GWTS received the first of its Javelin FAW.7 aircraft the same month and carried out its first live missile launch on 21 December.

In December 1958, following its re-equipment with Javelin FAW.7s, 25 Squadron at Waterbeach became the first to fly the Firestreak operationally. The following August the missile was 'partially released' to the service, and on 2 June 1960 Fighter Command was able to carry out its first live

firings with the Javelin FAW.7s of 23 Squadron at Coltishall.

At the same time the Royal Navy began its own service trials of the missile. To gain sea experience in the maintenance of the missile and to provide pilot familiarisation in its application by carrier-borne aircraft, three Sea Venom FAW.21s – XG607, XG612 and XG662 – were modified at Christchurch in early 1957 to carry two Firestreak Mk.1 missiles. To accommodate this modification (SOO Mod. N.923, to Contract no. 6/Acft/14132/CB(a)), the four 20mm Hispano guns, rocket wiring and associated gear were removed, together with the 50-gallon underwing drop-tanks. The G.45 camera gun was repositioned in a fairing beneath the port front fuselage, the local wing structure at the pylon position was strengthened, fuel bag tanks were slightly modified and an additional pitot head was fitted to the starboard fin. In the cockpit a special control panel was installed in the centre of the pilot's instrument presentation. A switch at the bottom left-hand corner of the panel energised the missile from the aircraft's power supply, and a warning light was then extinguished after two minutes when the missile was warmed-up and armed. As the pilot maintained the initial phase of the interception by means of the AI radar, the heat-seeking eye in the nose of the missile became active; after lock-on and range indication, the interception continued until the acquisition light showed that the missile's infra-red homing system was locked on to the target and the pilot could press the firing button to complete the circuit. The missiles could be selected to be fired singly or in pairs, and were launched after 0.4 seconds. The firing ranges were between 2,000 and 4,000 yd at 55,000ft, and 1,000 and 2,000 yd at sea level.

Following the initial development flying at Hatfield and Christchurch, together with a

Ratings prepare Sea Venom
21 XG607 of 893 Squadron
for a sortie during the service
evaluation trials of the
Firestreak missile on board
HMS *Victorious* in January
1959. (*Royal Navy*)

brief period of catapulting and arresting trials at Bedford, XG662 was dispatched to C Squadron A&AEE at Boscombe Down in November 1957 for the official service clearance trials. A total of eighteen target acquisition flights were carried out over the Aberporth range with a Meteor T.7 being used as the target aircraft. The last firing sortie was completed on 17 February 1958. Despite minor criticism of the lighting of the gunsight and the comment that no live rounds were carried throughout the trials, the resultant A&AEE report cleared the Sea Venom for the carriage and firing of the Firestreak missile.

By June 1958 two of the modified Sea Venoms, XG607 and XG612, were passed to 700 Squadron, a trials unit based at Ford, where they underwent four weeks of acceptance checks before being delivered to the first – and only – operational Sea Venom unit to be equipped with Firestreak missiles: 893 Squadron at Yeovilton. Both aircraft were collected from Ford on 10 July, with XG662 joining the squadron on 22 September.

In order to provide a greater continuity of reporting it had been decided to restrict the flying within the squadron to four nominated pilots. The pilots selected included the CO, Lt Cdr Eric Manuel, Lt Cdr Derek Matthews (Senior Pilot) and Lts Robbie Robertson and Leslie Dudgeon (the squadron AWI), together with their observers, Lts Pete Matthews, Harry Hicks and David Mather, and Sub Lt Patrick Mountain. Following a short course for the aircrew at the navy gunnery school at Whale Island in September, the pre-embarkation period soon followed, with Sun Acquisition and Radiation Hazard flights, together with catapult launches and deck landings to confirm the missile's stress loading. Lt Cdr Eric Manuel also carried out the first catapult launch and arrested landing with two missiles fitted. Although no

handling difficulties were encountered it was found that owing to its altered centre of gravity the aircraft was incapable of aerobatics, and could not be flown un-ballasted.

On 25 September 1958 893 Squadron embarked in HMS *Victorious* and sailed for the Mediterranean with all three guided-weapon aircraft included in its normal complement of Sea Venom FAW.21s. The squadron's three-month task was to employ the aircraft in a series of trials to obtain data on the acquisition phase of guided weapon interceptions, and to work up the standard of flying and missile preparation to enable *Victorious* to launch guided-weapon aircraft capable of attacking pilot-less drone targets; and for this purpose it was provided with the full back-up of on-board specialist workshops and test laboratories for the maintaining, testing and checking of the weapons.

HMS *Victorious* arrived in Malta on 16 October 1958 to begin its work-up period, which was directed towards an armament and around-the-clock flying programme, together with the sea trials of the Type 984 Carrier-Controlled Approach Radar. The initial flying trials of the Firestreak missile were carried out with training rounds. This simulated flying was intended to familiarise the pilots with the acquisition phase of a missile attack, with other squadron Sea Venoms acting as target aircraft.

By 10 November sufficient simulated flying had been carried out to enable the firing trials to begin against radio-controlled Fairey Firefly U.9s of 728 (B) Squadron, based at Hal Far. As the Firestreak was an infra-red homing weapon, some additional source of heat other than that normally produced from the piston-engined Firefly was required to simulate the radiation pattern of jet aircraft, and this was achieved by fitting electrical lamps in the faired end of

37

FROM H.M.S. VICTORIOUS.

11th Dec. 1958   Time carried forward :— 729 | 05 || 169 | 35

Date	Time of Take Off	Aircraft Type and No.	Pilot	Duty	Remarks	Day Hrs.	Day Mins.	Night Hrs.	Night Mins.
2nd December	0940	Sea Venom 21	Lt. Dudgeon	R/P	- Delimara from Hal Far		15		
	1505			R/P	" "		20		
10th	1005			H.L. Intex.	at 40,000	1	05		
	1930			H.L. Intex	with C.C.A.			1	10
11th	0845			R/P	Splash target & mutuals		45		
11th December	1210	Sea Venom 21	Lt. Dudgeon	FIRESTREAK G.W. Trial.	First successful firing from a ship-borne a/c		40		
13th	0645			Strike	- on Filfla directed by Skyraider		50		
	0845			Low Cap	- 1 Sea Devon!		45		
15th	1045			Cap & Army Co-op	- 1 USAF Super Constellation. Target struck	1	00		
	1700			Glowworm & Intex	- two runs. & C.C.A.		30		35
	2100			Glowworm & Intex	- two runs & C.C.A.			1	05
16th	0900			Low Strike	- on Victorious - bounced by CAP	1	00		
	2200			Glowworm, R/P	and Intex			1	05
18th	1200			Test Flight	after M.C.5.		35		
19th	0300			H.L. Intex	- two runs L0 & C.C.A.			1	05
	0500			L.L. Intex	- five runs on Skyraider			1	05
	1900			L.L. Intex	- five runs - lights out - Skyraider direction			1	05
	2100			Med. lev. Intex	- target & C.C.A.			1	05
						7	45	8	15
Harry Hicks		Lt. RN	J.S.R. Hicks	893 SQN	TOTAL TIME	736	50 || 177	50

Page from the logbook of Lt Harry Hicks recording the first successful firing of a Firestreak missile from a carrier-borne aircraft on 11 December 1958. (Harry Hicks)

the camera pods mounted on the drone's wing tips. Radar coverage of the Filfla range, some 15 miles from Malta, would be provided by the Douglas Skyraider airborne early warning aircraft of 849 (B) Squadron.

Once the drone was airborne it was shepherded by a manned Firefly to the range, where it was flown on a racetrack pattern of 25-mile-long legs, at 10,000ft and 175 knots. The Sea Venom was then launched from the ship and vectored to a run-in point some 12 miles away. Once visual contact was established, the shepherd aircraft was ordered to break away and the planned missile launch was carried out. To ensure safety in the event of a direct hit, the breakaway range for the fighter was established at approximately 1,500 yd.

On 11 December 1958 the first live missile firing by 893 Squadron was carried out on the Filfla range by Lt Leslie 'Dudge' Dudgeon and his observer, Lt Harry Hicks, when a Firefly U.8 was successfully destroyed. Harry Hicks recalled:

Basically there were three types of the weapon. Dummy rounds (or 'inerts') were used for both initial aircraft handling tests and for naval airmen practising moving and loading. Acquisition rounds were the mainstay of the trials and comprised the weapon proper, but minus its warhead. The third was the real missile itself, of which I think only six rounds were provided.

Three crews were allocated for the trials and altogether some forty sorties were flown. The vast majority were acquisition sorties – supplementing data from ashore and confirming that the weapon was standing up to the rigours of life on-board. The crews had to familiarise themselves with the vagaries of acquisition and even lock-on and practise the firing and follow-up evasive routine. It could often be infuriating when after what seemed to be a good acquisition and even lock-on to have the weapon suddenly decide it preferred the sun instead!

The trials, intermingled with normal flying, continued through October and November 1958 until the date of the planned 'great day' was announced; it was to be on 11 December 1958, at half an hour past local noon. The day was perfect, and the three crews, including the CO, the senior pilot, and 'Dudge' and myself, sat in the front row of the briefing room which was packed with boffins and technicians. (By our reckoning 'Dudge' and I were there just to make up the numbers and we had been through the day's procedures enough times between ourselves so we could relax – rather like the 12th man when the skipper comes in to announce the batting order!)

A summary of the briefing was as follows. The drone (and its 'shepherd' – its airborne radio-controller) would be flying at 10,000ft and would have an endurance of one hour on range. Take-off order, at approximate 20 minute intervals, would be the CO, the senior pilot and then Lt Dudgeon. Individual time on range was also 20 minutes. Then it was on deck, aircraft checks, man aircraft, strap in, cockpit and weapon checks, sit and wait. Meanwhile, the 'Boss' called for start-up clearance, the ship turned into wind and off he went.

We listened in. First run . . . no go! Second also. We prick up our ears. The senior pilot starts up and is off. His first run. Bloody hell! Also a no go! We begin to think about the possibility of actually getting to fly! Repeat checks . . . The 'Boss' was heard asking for circuit clearance for land on in five minutes. Then . . . the senior pilot's second run was also no go!

We looked at each other, then, on intercom only, we both agreed that the CO would attempt to 'pinch' our aircraft. This was unless we . . . 'Dudge' called for a start-up. An unwitting Flyco agreed. 'Dudge' pressed the 'tit', the catapult officer gave a green, and whoosh, we were airborne with a live missile.

As we climbed away the ship's fighter directors kept me up-to-date of the drone's location and I gave 'Dudge' a course and speed. First we had to ensure the missile made a steady acquisition of the heat source . . . could be at around 4 or 5 miles . . . and run in on it with just a little overtaking speed, get a lock-on at 3,000 yd. Then the tricky bit. The firing bracket was only 600–400 yd.

Things went well. We repeated all the final checks according to calls we had devised: I called 'Lock! Bracket! Fire! Hold!' – and there was a minor shudder as I screamed 'Pull! . . . Shepherd!'

And that was that. Neither of us saw the missile impact, though there was a bit of a shock wave as it exploded. All we knew about the actual success was the shepherd pilot calling 'Splash! – one Firefly!' There was a helluva party that night – and two days later we were back on the Filfla range firing plain old concrete-head practice rockets!

Despite irritating delays caused by drone unserviceability and bad weather, the requisite number of firings were completed a week later on 18 December, when Lt Robbie Robinson and Sub Lt Patrick Mountain (flying XG607) successfully destroyed another Firefly drone.

The trials were officially completed on 20 December. Cameras fitted in the attacking aircraft showed missile bursts within a few

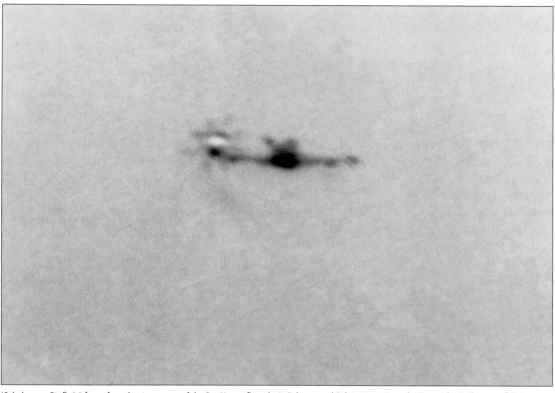

'Splash – one Firefly.' A frame from the cine camera of the Sea Venom flown by Lt Robinson and Sub Lt Mountain as the Firestreak missile successfully impacts on a Firefly drone on the Filfla range on 18 December 1958. (*Patrick Mountain*)

feet of the drones on all but one occasion, which was sufficient for the trials to be declared a success. Thereafter, further guided-weapon flying throughout January 1960 was restricted to a handful of sorties to enable graphs to be completed and to carry out a brief, salt-water attenuation trial.

On 13 January, with the conclusion of an exhaustive period of AI, army cooperation and Glow-worm firing exercises, HMS *Victorious* returned to the UK and disembarked 893 Squadron at Yeovilton, where the following month it began to re-equip with Sea Venom FAW.22s. The three modified

aircraft were sent to various RNAYs and restored to their original configuration. In February 1960 893 Squadron was disbanded at Yeovilton, re-forming with Firestreak-equipped Sea Vixen FAW.1s in the following September.

The trials and development of the first British air-to-air missile to go into service were considered a great achievement, and for the next thirty years the Firestreak was to form the main defensive armament for the RAF's Gloster Javelins and BAC Lightnings, together with the Royal Navy's all-weather strike fighter – the de Havilland Sea Vixen.

CHAPTER FOURTEEN

BLOWN-FLAP TRIALS

By early 1954 various aircraft manufacturers were showing considerable interest in the possibilities of boundary layer control in the form of flap blowing. Such a system, which basically consisted of blowing high-pressure air over the top surface of a lowered flap, prevented separation of the boundary layer and a rapid rise in drag. The chief benefit was a large increase in the lift coefficient leading to a reduction in stalling speed. This was clearly an important potential advantage for aircraft such as naval types in which low approach and stalling speeds were of great significance.

With their experience in this field through the laminar flow wings of the Spiteful and Attacker, Vickers Supermarine Ltd received a contract to equip and evaluate its prototype Type 525 (from which evolved the N113 and Scimitar) with a flap blowing system – or 'super circulation' as the company preferred to call it. The system comprised a series of nozzles along the upper surfaces of the flap to which surplus air was ducted from a late engine compressor stage to energise the boundary layer and prevent flow breakaway. Used for catapult take-offs and landings, the effect of the blow, coupled with an increased flap area, was seen to reduce approach speeds by more than 10 per cent, utilising some 5 per cent of the engine mass flow.

Notwithstanding the obvious advantages to be gained from the flap blowing system, the trials showed lack of lateral stability and control and high longitudinal trim changes, which limited its usefulness. The importance of lateral stability and control during the landing approach had always been recognised, and had been given as the major factor in deciding the minimum usable approach speed on high-performance aircraft. Similarly, poor longitudinal control and the strong nose-down change of trim were shown to make the aircraft pitch down, especially during catapult launches.

In order to assess the flight measurements of boundary layer control by flap blowing, the de Havilland Aircraft and Engine Companies were asked by the MoS during 1954 to undertake a design study in order to 'explore the advantages of this system and gather knowledge under practical working conditions'. In January 1955, following wind-tunnel experiments, a standard Sea Venom FAW.20, WM574, was modified and issued to the Controller (Air) at Christchurch to gain air experience of the installation. As a type, the Sea Venom did not need lift augmentation, but being already established in carrier service it offered itself as a convenient test-bed. The modifications included the standard Sea Venom split flaps being replaced by plain flaps of an increased chord, with blowing slots (0.10in inboard and 0.08in outboard) situated in the nose of each flap, the wing leading edge being drooped over the whole span to prevent flow separation. The greatest change, however, was to the aircraft's Ghost 104 engine, which allowed air to be tapped from the elbow of each of the ten combustion chambers and carried to an annular collector ring at the rear of the engine. This collector ring supplied blowing air to the insides of the hollow

'Blown-flap' Sea Venom 21 WM574 during trials at RAE Bedford. The enlarged flaps and markings on the nose and tail fin for sighting measurements can be clearly seen. (*RAE Bedford*)

torque tubes, which operated the flaps. The two torque tubes were joined in the middle by a flexible coupling (due to 'man plane' dihedral) and each had a butterfly valve to control the blowing air flow. Early test flights by the company's test pilot Ron Clear showed that, although the stalling/approach speeds were reduced by about 15 knots (from 92 to 77 knots), the longitudinal trim changes were very high.

In June 1955 the aircraft was transferred to the A&AEE at Boscombe Down for further flap blowing assessment, before being passed to the RAE at Bedford to continue the rigorous flight-test programme. This would include dummy deck landings, overshoots and accelerated take-offs from a ground-installed steam catapult, followed by carrier trials from HMS *Ark Royal*. Cdr Geoffrey Higgs RN was the naval test pilot at RAE

Bedford's Naval & Aerodynamics Flight at this time. He commented:

The 'blown' Sea Venom, WM574, arrived at RAE Bedford in early March 1956; my first flight was on 5 March. So far as I can see from my logbook my last flight was on 11 March 1956, involving a demonstration at Hatfield, before returning to Bedford. The aircraft was then passed to the manufacturers as we had completed the carrier evaluation and research.

The aircraft's arrival at Bedford proved to be a very busy time for me, coinciding, within two or three days, with that of the prototype DH 110 (Sea Vixen) and N113 (Scimitar) for catapulting and arresting trials.

After carrier trials on HMS *Ark Royal* between 6 and 12 April 1956 (where I completed six arrested deck landings and a good number of touch and goes) I returned the aircraft to Hurn on

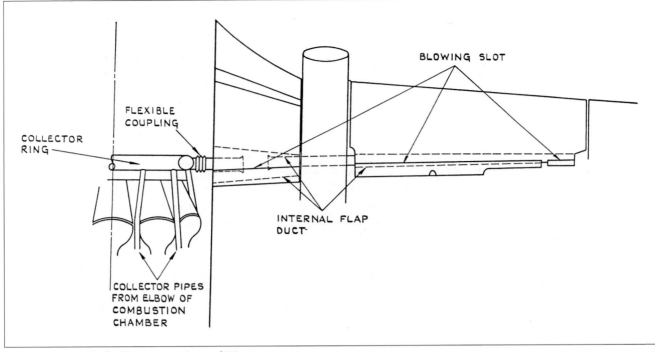

COLLECTOR
RING

FLEXIBLE
COUPLING

BLOWING SLOT

COLLECTOR PIPES
FROM ELBOW OF
COMBUSTION
CHAMBER

INTERNAL FLAP
DUCT

Layout of the flap blowing system. (*Courtesy of RAE*)

20 April 1956. The following September it was back at Bedford again for two flights only.

Altogether, I made twenty-seven flights in WM574, including twelve catapult tests at Bedford and a further eight catapult take-offs and deck landings. So far as I am aware, no one else flew the blown-flap Sea Venom off the catapult at Bedford or carried out the carrier trials.

Apart from the catapult and carrier tests, we evaluated partial climbs and trim tests, with and without blow, to establish power/drag relationship. The tests showed that a reduction of plus or minus 10 knots could be achieved on a standard carrier approach using the blown flaps; a significantly – to the pilot, at least – reduced angle of attack on the approach, owing to the aft movement of the centre of pressure; a noticeable increase in induced drag that resulted in reduced power available on the approach and hence was the governing factor in establishing the minimum safe approach speed.

However, at the blown approach speeds, lateral control worsened so that corrections to line up on the final stages of carrier landings became difficult unless well anticipated. With ship movement in poor sea conditions, this would have been an inhibiting factor and very likely resulted in curtailing the benefit from blown flaps.

The movement of the centre of pressure had little effect on the stability of the aircraft – for practical purposes – except that longitudinal control was less responsive. This was particularly noticeable during catapult launches at Bedford owing to ground effects, which tended to make the aircraft pitch nose down.

As a final point, it is of interest that while a true reduction in strict stalling speeds of 15 knots was obtained throughout the trials, because of other factors such as longitudinal and lateral control, overshoot procedure during a carrier landing, as well as downdraught and turbulence effects astern of the ship, the full benefit of the system was not effective in producing a reduced recommended approach speed.

Additional flight testing of the lateral stability of the aircraft at Bedford between April and June 1957, which comprised some thirty-four flights, showed that adverse aileron yawing movements would make the holding of an instrument approach path difficult, and that the effects of blowing over part-span flaps (on a Sea Venom at least) were small. For the purpose of the trials, the tip-tanks were filled with varying amounts of liquid ballast to test the rolling power of the ailerons.

Further development of boundary layer control by both Vickers Supermarine and Blackburn Aircraft was encouraging and was eventually incorporated into their respective strike fighters produced for the Fleet Air Arm, the Scimitar and Buccaneer. It must be considered, however, that both aircraft were designed and built to accommodate the effects of their respective blowing system. In practice, combined with other factors, both aircraft suffered adverse control problems when the blowing system was switched on.

Prior to being transferred to the ETPS at Farnborough in June 1958 at the completion of the trials, the blown-flap Sea Venom WM574 was flown briefly by Geoff Higgs' successor, Lt Cdr Ian Normand RN, who also recalled that this form of boundary layer control produced a reduction of some 15 knots in the approach speed because of the smoother wake and more stable airflow over the trailing edges. In November 1958 the aircraft was briefly used for tests with chemical sprays at Porton Down, following which it was sold for scrap in October 1959.

CHAPTER FIFTEEN

VENOMS IN SERVICE OVERSEAS

ROYAL AUSTRALIAN NAVY

On 3 July 1947 the Australian government approved the formation of the Royal Australian Navy's Fleet Air Arm within a defence programme that included a plan to purchase two aircraft carriers and newer aircraft, and the establishment of two shore bases at Nowra and Schofields in New South Wales. The first carrier, HMAS *Sydney* (formerly HMS *Terrible*) was commissioned into RAN service in February 1949. A second carrier, HMAS *Melbourne* (formerly HMS *Majestic*), was delayed to incorporate a number of developments to improve deck operations, including a half-angled deck, steam catapult and deck-landing mirror sight, and was not commissioned until October 1955. Deliveries of large quantities of Hawker Sea Fury fighter-bombers and Fairey Firefly anti-submarine aircraft began in 1949, and both types served with distinction during the Korean War while operating from HMAS *Sydney*.

In July 1951, as part of a RAN modernisation programme, the Australian Minister for the Navy announced a decision to order the de Havilland Sea Venom all-weather fighter to replace the Sea Fury (in preference to the much cheaper Hawker Sea Hawk single-seat fighter, on the grounds that it lacked radar). The order for forty-nine Sea Venom NF.21s (WZ893–911 and WZ927–956) was formalised the following December, with production planned at the Hawker de Havilland factory at Bankstown, NSW, where the aircraft would be manufactured under licence.

However, this plan was eventually abandoned following a large-scale order for Vampire trainers for the RAAF, and following an amendment to the original order which cancelled the final ten aircraft (WZ947–956) the Sea Venoms were built at de Havilland's Christchurch factory to the export type designation FAW.53.

The Australian version differed primarily from its British equivalent in the installation of the improved AI Mk.17 search radar, together with a Blind Predicting Gunsight System (BPGS). Criticism that the original layout of the pilot's gunsight and radar presentation restricted the view of the instrument flying panel and constituted a flying hazard at low altitudes, especially when the gunsight was in use, resulted in a modified cockpit layout. The new layout comprised a BPGS head mounted with a small 'para-visual' angle of attack indicator – or collimator – forward of the GGS Mk.5 gunsight on a transverse sliding carriage extending the width of the cockpit; when in use, the collimator could be locked into the required position to display a locked-on radar target blip in front of the gunsight. Although not considered a great improvement over the original layout, the modifications ensured that the essential blind flying instruments remained in view for accurate flying during blind aiming.

The Sea Venom Mk.53 was powered by a 5,300lb-thrust Ghost 104 engine. Originally it lacked ejection seats, but a two-year modification programme by de Havilland's at Bankstown saw Martin-Baker Mk.4A

The first production Sea Venom FAW.53 (WZ893) for the RAN was used for company trials at Christchurch before departing for Australia. While later serving with 805 Squadron in July 1963, it was involved in a mid-air collision over Sydney harbour. The airframe was repaired and eventually scrapped in May 1967 following service with 724 Squadron. (*de Havilland*)

lightweight seats being eventually installed. The first modified aircraft (WZ897) was test-flown on 9 October 1957.

Deliveries began on 15 September 1954 when WZ893 was issued to the manufacturers for trials and development work. In March 1955 it was transferred to the A&AEE at Boscombe Down for radar release trials, which included an assessment of the radar absorbent material fitted to the undersurfaces of the radome to improve low-altitude range performance. A second aircraft, WZ894, was issued for development work on 14 January 1955. Following a brief period of trials work at Christchurch, it was delivered to the NAD at Farnborough during March for catapulting and arresting trials. Having been granted preliminary clearance

for deck landing trials on HMS *Bulwark*, it was joined by WZ893 between 21 and 24 March when four crews were selected to prove the radar fit for duty at sea. On 1 July 1955 both aircraft were flown out to Idris in Libya for tropical trials: it was a notable flight out, in the course of which Lts Jack Overbury RN and Garvin Kable RAN were able to establish a new capital-to-capital record of 534mph during the 422-mile leg from Ciampino in Rome to Luqa in Malta. After the completion of the trials, both aircraft were briefly based at Malta between 6 and 11 August for a series of humidity trials, returning to Boscombe Down on 13 August 1955. Following further hot-weather trials at Idris during the first two weeks of September, the aircraft were flown to AHU

Abbotsinch in February 1956 for preparation for their voyage to Australia.

Four further aircraft from the batch of Australian Sea Venoms were selected for development work: WZ895 was issued to Christchurch between April 1955 and February 1956 for the trial installation of ejection seats; WZ934 was briefly loaned to the A&AEE, Boscombe Down in October 1955; WZ941 was also issued to the A&AEE during November and December 1955 for high-speed gun-firing tests to assess the strength of the radome; while WZ944 was operated by both Christchurch and Boscombe Down for the trial installation and assessment of radio and armament equipment.

The crews selected for the first RAN Sea Venom squadron were required to undertake training for the night-fighter role; the observers went to 238 OCU at Colerne in August 1954, completing their standard night-fighter course on Brigand radar navigational trainers in October. The pilots had earlier received an initial jet conversion course at 2 (F) OTU, RAAF Williamtown, NSW, and had been attached to various operational Royal Navy Sea Hawk squadrons and training establishments in the UK before joining the observers at 228 OCU Leeming in November 1954 for crew training on Meteor NF.11s. Their training was completed in February 1955, with the newly qualified crews joining 891 Squadron at Yeovilton the following month.

On 1 March 1955 891 Squadron's X Flight (Lt Cdr G.M.C. Jude RAN) was formed at Yeovilton for type/conversion training with eight Sea Venom FAW.20s and two Sea Vampire T.22s loaned from the Royal Navy. Over the next few months an intensive training programme was carried out, which included ADDLs, instrument training and GCA exercises, airborne interceptions and rocket-firing practice at targets in Bracklesham Bay.

The flight disbanded on 10 August 1955 with the formation of 808 Squadron RAN (Lt Cdr G.M.C. Jude RAN), which had received the first of its establishment of eight Sea Venom FAW.20s at Yeovilton in June. Later in the month the squadron flew to Culdrose where it was officially commissioned on 23 August in a ceremony that also included two other RAN squadrons, equipped with Fairey Gannets. A busy work-up period, which included deck landing training with HMS *Bulwark* in November 1955 and a period of armament practice training at Lossiemouth, was quickly followed by a brief participation in NATO's Exercise 'King Pin'.

On 5 January 1956 the squadron suffered a tragic accident when a Sea Venom FAW.20 (WM551) struck a chimney of a house in Yeovilton village during a take-off in bad weather and plunged onto two caravans at Castle Farm, Ilchester, killing Lt P.H. Wyatt RAN (the squadron IRE) and Commander G.F.S. Brown (Staff Officer [Aviation] at Australia House), together with a woman and a baby in one of the caravans.

Work-up was completed by the middle of February 1956 and the squadron personnel embarked on HMAS *Melbourne*, together with thirty-nine cocooned Sea Venom FAW.53s, which were loaded on at Glasgow's King George V Dock after being taken on RAN charge at Abbotsinch AHU on 27 February 1956. The crowded carrier (which also contained twenty-two Fairey Gannets of 816 and 817 Squadrons RAN, three Sycamore HR.50 helicopters for 723 Squadron RAN, a Meteor NF.11 destined for Woomera and an Avro 707A research aircraft) sailed for Australia on 11 March 1956. Its departure from UK waters was marked by twelve Sea Venoms drawn from 890, 893 and 766 Squadrons at Yeovilton, which made a farewell salute over the carrier as it sailed into the English Channel, 10 miles south of the Needles.

Sea Venom FAW.53 WZ939 of B Flight, 816 Squadron RAN, at Air Station Nowra. Later reserialled N4-939, it is preserved at Parafield Airport, Adelaide. (*via R.L. Ward*)

HMAS *Melbourne* eventually arrived at Sydney on 9 May 1956, having previously unloaded the aircraft and equipment at Jervis Bay, NSW, for delivery by road to RNAS Schofields and Hawker de Havilland at Bankstown, where the Sea Venoms were de-preserved and prepared for service. No. 808 Squadron reassembled at RNAS Nowra, NSW, in May 1956 and began flying the following month. After three months ashore the squadron re-embarked on 6 August for its first operational cruise on board HMAS *Melbourne*, from which it took part in numerous exercises with foreign and Commonwealth air forces and navies in SEATO waters. Although the Sea Venoms were temporarily grounded in March 1957 when cracks were found in the arrestor hook mountings, the squadron maintained a good flight safety record with only four aircraft (WZ896, WZ933, WZ936 and WZ942) lost in flying accidents during almost three years of operations.

On 1 December 1958 808 Squadron was disbanded at Nowra, with the RAN's all-weather task being passed on to 805 Squadron (Lt Cdr G.E. Beange RAN), which had earlier re-formed with six Sea Venom

FAW.53s on 31 March 1958. No. 805 Squadron went to sea with HMAS *Melbourne* the following October, and for the next four years formed part of Australia's Far East Strategic Reserve. Prior to its disbandment on 30 June 1963, and subsequent incorporation into 724 Squadron, 805 Squadron was able to form an aerobatic team called the 'Checkmates'. Originally commanded by the CO, Lt Cdr Beange, the team's polished performances almost ended in disaster when two aircraft collided at the top of a formation loop, causing one aircraft (WZ940) to crash into Sydney harbour. The other (WZ893) managed to return to Nowra with a large part of its tailplane missing.

The disbandment of 805 Squadron effectively brought the RAN's front-line Sea Venom operations to an end. As early as November 1959 the government had announced that the Fleet Air Arm would cease operations by 1963 when the Sea Venoms and Gannets had reached the end of their service lives. It was also considered that the cost of modernising HMAS *Melbourne* to operate modern aircraft would be too great. However, a further review of defence requirements and a decision to extend the life of

HMAS *Melbourne* as an anti-submarine carrier granted a new lease of life for the Sea Venom, with four aircraft being issued to 816 Squadron's B Flight at Nowra in July 1964, which was normally equipped with Fairey Gannets. The squadron was able to complete five carrier deployments and at least one major SEATO exercise before being disbanded at Nowra on 25 August 1967.

Primarily a second-line unit, 724 Squadron had re-formed at Nowra on 1 June 1955 and was responsible for operational flying training and aircrew conversion. The squadron was equipped with a variety of aircraft types and operated its Sea Venom FAW.53s as all-weather fighter trainers. In 1958 724 Squadron became an all-jet unit with Sea Venoms and Vampire trainers and was tasked with jet conversion and all-weather training courses, together with fleet requirement duties.

In January 1961, despite having only four Sea Venoms on strength, the squadron's CO, Lt Cdr Norman Lee RAN, was given the task of re-forming the 'Ramjets' aerobatic team for a display at the International Air Convention at Avalon airfield. The team had originally formed in 1959 under the leadership of Lt Cdr Ian Josselyn RAN, and had been sponsored by the Golden Fleece fuel company (whose emblem was a Merino ram) to produce a short film about Australian jet aerobatics. Following its display at Avalon, the team gave its final performance on 10 March 1961 before members of a visiting parliamentary committee and was disbanded soon after.

At about this time the RAN adopted type identification codes for its aircraft, with the Sea Venom serials being prefixed with 'N4-'; although the prefix was not always used, the aircraft remaining on RAN strength became N4-(WZ)897, N4-(WZ)901, N4-(WZ)903, N4-(WZ)904, N4-(WZ)910, N4-(WZ)930, N4-(WZ)935, N4-(WZ)939 and N4-(WZ)944. Between July and October 1964 four of

Following conversion to target-towing configuration, Sea Venom FAW.53 WZ943 was issued to 724 Squadron. It is seen here at RANAS Bankstown in December 1964, painted silver with black and yellow stripes on the undersurfaces. It was one of the last Sea Venoms to be withdrawn from RAN service in 1973. (J.M. Gradidge)

Taxiing in at RANAS Nowra, Sea Venom FAW.53 WZ905 of 724 Squadron was used as an all-weather fighter trainer, following service with 805 Squadron. It was later placed into storage at Bankstown and scrapped in May 1967. (*via R.L. Ward*)

724 Squadron's dwindling number of Sea Venoms (WZ930, WZ935, WZ943 and WZ944) were converted for use as target-towing aircraft, using the Delemar system. In October 1967 further modifications to WZ897 and N4-935 included the installation of IKARA (code-named 'Blue Duck'), an anti-submarine torpedo weapons system.

Following an earlier decision by the Australian government to purchase Douglas A-4G Skyhawks and Grumman S-2E Trackers to replace its Sea Venoms and Gannets, during 1969 724 Squadron was renamed VC-724 in order to conform with current US Navy practice. In June 1973 the last two Sea Venoms (N4-935 and WZ943) were officially withdrawn from RAN service and put up for disposal the following October. Eleven aircraft had been written off in flying accidents, but at least fifteen

airframes are still thought to be in existence somewhere in Australia.

Especially worthy of interest is the Sea Venom held by the Naval Aviation Museum at Nowra. WZ895 has undergone a protracted restoration programme intended to return the aircraft to flying condition. It saw service with 808, 805, 724 and 816 (B) Squadrons before being withdrawn in May 1966 following the discovery of skin cracking. The airframe was relegated to an instructional role at the training school at Nowra, before transfer to the Naval Aviation Museum in December 1978 for static display as 870/NW of 724 Squadron. In 1981 a team of dedicated volunteers began to restore the airframe. The first successful ground run of the engine was carried out in September 1982 and taxiing trials took place in the following February. The Australian civil registration

VH-NVV was originally allocated in 1990, but was subsequently transferred to another aircraft when the Sea Venom's overhaul was discontinued. The airframe was dismantled and placed into long-term storage at Nowra, where its future remains uncertain.

SUD-EST AQUILON

With the failure of the French aircraft industry to develop successfully its postwar fighter projects for the expanding Aero-nautique Navale (Naval Air Arm), in August 1951 the French government stated its intention, without further delay, to buy foreign two-seat, radar-equipped aircraft to replace its elderly fleet of Grumman Hellcat fighters. Interest was shown in the Sea Venom, and the Secretary for Air showed a preference to buy the licence for 150 fighters, which they hoped would be financed by the United States with funds from MDAP. The contract to build the airframes would be given to SNCASE, which was already producing Vampire and Mistral fighters under licence at Marignane, and was scheduled to start building Venom FB.1s in the near future. Although the US government refused to supply funds for the arrangement, the French decided to proceed with their purchase of the Sea Venoms, and on 5 December 1951 authorised a contract for 146 Sea Venom NF Mk.52s, together with a quantity of Ghost 48 engines which would be produced by FIAT in Italy.

In the spring of 1952 the contract was extended to include four prototype aircraft to be assembled at Marignane from components supplied by de Havilland's; these would be joined by a Sea Venom fuselage mock-up to assess the cockpit layout arrangement for the installation of ejection seats. In September 1952 the first prototype, '01', was rolled out and made its first flight on 31 October, with test pilot Jacques LeCarme at the controls. It was followed by a further four pre-pro-duction aircraft, '02'–'05'. Two of these aircraft – '03' with the original tail unit and '01' with a modified tail and rudder assembly – made their first public appearance at the Paris Air Salon at Le Bourget in 1953. The following year, on 6 February 1954, the type was officially named the SE.20 'Aquilon', or 'North Wind'.

The first twenty-five SE.201 Aquilons ('1'–'25') were produced at Marignane between March 1954 and January 1955. This variant was built to Sea Venom 20 standard, with fixed seats, a clam-shell hood and four 20mm Hispano cannon. It was also capable of carrying four Matra-type 21 rocket launchers, four 5in HVAR rocket launchers or eight 100mm rockets, a Dervaux range finder and a FACINE cine camera. Its Vampire-type landing gear, however, made it only suitable for operation from shore bases.

The SE.202 Aquilon was the first of the carrier-capable variants and was fitted with SNCASE E-86-241 and E-86-242 ejection seats for the pilot and observer respectively, under a rear-sliding hood which was normally slid back for take-off and landing. It was also equipped with Westinghouse AN/APQ-65 radar and a guidance system for its primary armament of two MATRA 511 air-to-air missiles. On 16 July 1954 the fourth pre-production aircraft '05' took to the air as the prototype Mk.202 and twenty-five further aircraft ('26'–'50') were built, with deliveries commencing in April 1956.

The single-seat SE.203 also featured a sliding hood, but was fitted with an AN/APQ 94 radar installation in a di-electric nose and a radar turbo alternator in the vacant observer's position. Armament comprised MATRA 511 air-to-air missiles, but the guidance system was later adapted for the type to carry Nord 5103 missiles as well. '05' was again converted as the prototype, and some forty Mk.203s ('51'–'90') were

In October 1954 Aquilon 201 '05' was issued with a temporary civilian registration and was flown from Bretigny to Farnborough for combined catapulting and RATO proofing trials, as depicted in this sequence of photographs. (*DERA*)

eventually built with deliveries between April 1956 and June 1958.

The final model was the SE.204 two-seat, all-weather fighter trainer, fitted with dual controls but lacking the standard cannon installation mounted in the fuselage belly. Only five aircraft ('91'–'96') were produced, being extensively modified from former Aquilon 20 airframes '8', '11', '15', '16', '18' and '24'. The incorporation of a short-stroke undercarriage restricted its use to shore bases, and deliveries to Escadrille 59.S at Hyeres took place between March 1957 and January 1958.

On 28 July 1954 deliveries to the Aeronautique Navale began when two Aquilon 20s ('2' and '3') were issued to the Aquilon Trials Flight at Hyeres Naval Air Base. Commanded by Lt de Vasseau Claude Hurel, the flight had been formed the previous May from the night-fighter flight with radar-equipped Grumman F6F-5N Hellcats to provide familiarisation training. By the end of September 1954 the flight had four Aquilon 20s ('2', '3', '5' and '6') and six Hellcats on strength.

In October 1954 Aquilon 201 '05' was issued with the temporary civilian markings F-WGVT and was flown to the Royal Aircraft Establishment at Bedford, where it completed the combined catapult and RATO clearance trials. The following June work began on achieving the first deck landing, for which three pilots and two aircraft ('27' and '28') were allocated. After completing a period of ADDLs at Istres, the pilots and technicians were sent to Boscombe Down in July for a deck landing assessment, before joining the aircraft carrier HMS *Bulwark* for the initial trials later in the month. On 13 July 1955 LV Georges Picchi made the first-ever carrier landing in an Aquilon ('28'),

Aquilon 20 12 of Flotille 11.F at Hyeres, shown with folded wings, served with the Aeronautique Navale between December 1954 and June 1964. (*Flotille 11.F*)

Twenty-five Aquilon 202s were built, being the first French variant to be able to operate from carriers. This aircraft, 27, was delivered in June 1955 and served with Flotille 16.F. (*via R.L. Ward*)

which was successfully repeated by his two colleagues over the next two days, thereby clearing the way for future carrier operations.

Earlier that year, on 3 January 1955, the Aquilon Trials Flight at Hyères was disbanded and absorbed into the first operational squadron, Flottille 16.F, commanded by LV Georges Picchi. The first aircraft ('4', '6', '10', '11' and '13') were delivered in November 1954, and the unit quickly reached its establishment of sixteen aircraft, eight Mk.20s and eight Mk.202s. The following June the squadron made its public debut at the Paris Air Show at Le Bourget when a formation of twelve aircraft flew over the public enclosure area in the shape of an anchor. Once fully operational, the squadron took part in many demonstrations and exercises, including the NATO exercise 'Medflex Dragon' in April 1956, when eight aircraft were detached to Hal Far for ten days. In March 1957 the squadron was transferred from Hyères to a new permanent home at Kouraba Naval Air Base in Bizerte, where it carried out 'policing operations' for the security forces.

On 4 April 1955 a second squadron (Flottille 11.F) was re-formed at Hyères under the command of LV Henri Perrin. The

squadron had previously flown Grumman F6F-5 Hellcats in Tunisia and had been disbanded in January 1955 to re-equip with Aquilon Mk.20s, the first of which was delivered in May. The following month the squadron embarked eight aircraft (four Aquilon 202s and four Aquilon 203s) for three days of carrier qualification training on board HMS *Ark Royal*. A successful programme of launching and recovery, together with a further series of exercises with the carrier's air squadrons, was overshadowed by the loss of Aquilon '83' which crashed into the sea after launch on 13 June, killing the pilot.

In July 1956 the first of the radar-equipped Aquilon 203s was issued to the squadron, and in September 1957 the unit joined 16.F at Lann-Bihoué for Exercise 'Parasol', when a large number of RAF and American 'intruders' were successfully intercepted during four days of realistic operations.

Although qualification training and the familiarisation of the French crews with equipment and techniques had been previously carried out on Royal Navy carriers, in September 1959 the French aircraft carrier *Clemenceau* joined the fleet and began her deck flying trials in the following March. On 30 March 1960 the CO of 11.F, LV Gaultier de la Ferriere, landed the first Aquilon on board the carrier, clearing the way for the first embarkation of 16.F in August. Between that date and the final detachment of an Aquilon unit in June 1962, both squadrons spent regular periods afloat, both in the North Atlantic and in the Mediterranean.

By the mid-1950s fighting had broken out again between the various groups in Algeria seeking independence from France. The most extreme of these groups was the Front for National Liberation (or ALN), which was the military wing of the Muslim Liberal Democratic movement. Ground-attack operations against rebel positions in villages and mountainous strongholds were usually in support of army units. In 1958 a change in tactics and strategy saw a greater use of air power to eliminate the ALN, and in July 1958 11.F was transferred to Maison-Blanche for three months of ground-attack operations; 16.F followed in October. Between September 1958 and May 1961 both squadrons took part in the operations in Algeria, when detachments were maintained on a rotational basis at Maison-Blanche, using their rockets and 20mm cannon to

great effect. After the collapse of the revolt, a cease-fire was announced in March 1962, followed by independence in July.

In February 1958 further trouble flared up when the President of Tunisia demanded the withdrawal of French forces from the base in Bizerte following attacks on local villages by the French Air Force; he agreed, however, to suspend the demand until the war in Algeria was over. In July 1961 he again protested at the extension of the runway at Karouba naval airfield, and on 17 July announced a blockade of the base. The French parachuted soldiers into the base, after which the Tunisians shelled the bases in Bizerte. The French responded by bringing cruisers into the harbour; in addition, Aquilons of 11.F and 16.F were detached to Bizerte from July to September 1961, attacking Tunisian positions with rockets and cannon fire over a three-day period following a mortar attack on Sidi-Ahmed on 20 July. Pressure from the UN forced a cease-fire on 22 July, and later in the year the French began their withdrawal, leaving Bizerte in Tunisian hands in June 1962. One aircraft ('74') was known to have been lost during the operation in Bizerte when it crashed into rising ground during a night sortie on 21 July 1961. Following the

The white flash on the tip-tank identifies this Aquilon 202 on the flightline at Gibraltar as belonging to Flotille 11.F. It was struck off charge in June 1963 and relegated for use as an instructional airframe at Rochefort. (Geoff Cruickshank)

end of the fighting in Bizerte, 11.F was disbanded on 18 April 1962, re-forming the following year with Dassault Etendard IV M strike fighters.

Routine operational training continued for the remaining Aquilon squadron, including a period of cross-operations with HMS *Victorious* during Exercise 'Dawn Breeze VII' in March 1962 and a series of trials on board *Clemenceau* with its MATRA 511 missiles. In September 1963 16.F was ordered to join the carrier *Foch* as she sailed for the Indian Ocean. A week earlier an Etendard had been involved in a serious crash, which resulted in the type being grounded – leaving the carrier without effective air cover. However, following a fatal crash involving Aquilon '90' on 25 September, during a period of ADDL training at Hyeres, the Aquilons were also temporarily grounded and the deployment was cancelled.

With newer, improved types of carrier-based fighter aircraft entering service with Aeronautique Navale, notably the Dassault Etendard and the supersonic F-8E (FN) Crusader, the service life of the Aquilons of 11.F was drawing to a close. On 27 March 1964 the final operational sortie was carried out by the squadron commander, LV Magnan de Bornier, and five days later, on 1 April 1964, 16.F was disbanded as an Aquilon squadron at Hyeres, passing its remaining aircraft to 59.S and re-forming with Etendard IV.P reconnaissance fighters.

Additional Aeronautique Navale units operating the SE Aquilon, included:

Escadrille 2.S. Based at Lann-Bihoue, the unit was responsible for checking the currency of desk-bound jet pilots. It flew at least four Aquilon Mk.20s between July 1957 and December 1961, when the Aquilons were replaced by Fouga CM 175 Zephyrs (a navalised version of the two-seat Magister jet trainer).

Escadrille 10.S. The primary role of this unit was to carry out various trials and experiments specified by the Commission d'Etudes Practiques d'Aviation (CEPA). Between May 1957 and March 1965 at least two Aquilon Mk.20s and one Mk.203 are known to have completed the evaluation and service testing of the DRAA-7B, Thompson and APQ-94 radar installations, the 68mm rocket installation, and Sidewinder, NORD 5103, and MATRA 310 and 511 air-to-air missiles. The unit was based at Hyeres.

Escadrille 54.S. This was a shipboard qualification school based at Hyeres and commanded by LV Bernhard Waquet. The unit had an establishment of six Aquilon Mk.20s, the first of which was delivered in January 1956. The unit was disbanded on 1 May 1958 and its aircraft transferred to 59.S.

Escadrille 59.S. This unit was formed as an all-weather fighter training and shipboard qualification school at Hyeres on 1 February 1957. The unit's role was to train pilots to fly the type, and it was initially equipped with four Aquilon Mk.203s. These were joined by four Mk.204s, and later supplemented with six Mk.20s from 54.S in May 1958. The unit was also tasked with occasional trials, and in 1956 it evaluated an experimental wire pick-up installation fitted to the underside of an Aquilon. During October and November 1959 four of the unit's aircraft were detached to Cazaux to take part in ground-attack operations alongside 16.F. The Aquilons were withdrawn in March 1965 and transferred to the Aquilon Flight at Cuers-Pierrefeu.

Centre d'Essais en Vol (CEV). A government agency equivalent to the British Empire Test Pilots School and based at Istres, it was responsible for the testing and development of all French military and civilian aircraft, together with the operation of a test-flying

The first of the fifteen Venom FB.50s built at Chester for the Royal Iraqi Air Force, 352 was delivered by George Thornton in April 1954. The camouflage scheme for the Iraqi aircraft was dark earth and sand upper surfaces, with light blue undersurfaces. (*Darryl Cott*)

school. Between November 1955 and February 1960 the unit flew a mixture of Aquilon Mk.20s, Mk.202s and Mk.203s.

Aquilon Flight. This unit was formed at Cuers-Pierrefeu on 5 April 1965 to evaluate Sidewinder and MATRA 310 missile trials for the Etendard and Crusader fighters on behalf of CEPA. Following a final contribution to an air defence exercise at Brest naval port, the unit was disbanded on 30 June 1966 at a ceremony that also marked the retirement of the Aquilon from service. Three of the final aircraft were present at the event ('34', '53' and '57'), which was attended by many former personnel associated with the type.

At least twenty Aquilons were written off as a result of flying accidents during the type's eleven years of service with the Aeronautique Navale, and following their withdrawal some were passed to the School for Air Mechanics at Rochefort as training airframes, while others languished on various airfields waiting to be scrapped. At least one Aquilon is known to have survived: Mk.203 '53' first flew in April 1956 and was delivered to the Aeronautique Navale the next month. Following service with 16.F, 11.F, 59.S and the Aquilon Flight between May 1956 and July 1966, it was withdrawn in August 1966 and was initially issued for display at the naval base at Lann-Bihoue. It is currently preserved at the French Naval Aviation Museum at Rochefort-Soubise. One further aircraft, '8', was on display for many years at the French naval training base at Hourtin during the 1960s.

IRAQ

Iraq's decision to place an order for fifteen Venom ground-attack fighters in 1954 was a logical step after a successful period of Vampire operations, and was undoubtedly influenced by the presence of similarly equipped RAF units based in the Middle East. In June 1954 the Venom FB.1s of 6 Squadron RAF moved from Amman to Habbaniya to join 73 Squadron RAF, and during the next two years both units formed a close working relationship with 5 and 6 Squadrons of the Royal Iraqi Air Force (RIAF), the former operating Vampire FB.52s purchased from Britain in 1953.

The order for the fifteen Venom FB.50s (352–366) was completed at Chester, with the aircraft being transferred to Hatfield between March and November 1954 for onward delivery to Iraq. The first aircraft (352) was delivered to Habbaniya by production test pilot George Thornton on 9 April 1954 via Marseilles, Malta and Nicosia in a total flying time of 6 hours 23 minutes. One of the Venoms (357) was written off during its ferry flight in September 1954, after crashing at Luqa during a local test flight; a replacement machine (370) was transferred from Chester to Hatfield in May 1955 for onward delivery.

The aircraft were initially delivered to 5 Squadron RIAF (Lt Col Sadiq al-Azawi) at Habbaniya, which briefly became a jet conversion squadron for the Iraqi pilots until the first Venom squadron was created the following year. Assisted by RAF pilots seconded from 6 Squadron RAF, the conversion programme included weapons training and instrument flying, with most of the work being carried out in a batch of Vampire trainers that had been delivered from the UK a few months earlier.

No. 6 Squadron RIAF was formed at Habbaniya on 15 March 1955 under the command of Lt Col Arif Abdul Razzak.

Deliveries began the following month and the squadron commander, assisted by his flight commander Maj A.L. Mahmood (who was appointed as temporary commanding officer in August 1955), was able to bring the unit up to operational status by the time the last Venom was delivered in February 1956.

Both RIAF fighter units participated in joint exercises with 6 Squadron RAF, including Exercise 'Desert' in October 1955 and Exercise 'Nisir' in March 1956, which provided the Iraqi pilots with valuable experience in air defence and ground-attack operations. Following the signing of the Baghdad Pact with Turkey in April 1955, Britain agreed to the termination of the Anglo-Iraqi Treaty, which resulted in the withdrawal of British forces from the area. The following month Habbaniya was handed over to RIAF and 73 Squadron moved to Cyprus. In April 1956 6 Squadron RAF also moved to Cyprus, leaving the RIAF wholly responsible for the air defence of the region. Occasional joint exercises were still held with RAF units, including Exercise 'Alert' in June 1956; together with a joint APC with the Sea Fury Wing and regular detachments to Mosul, Rashid and Amman, these exercises served to maintain the operational efficiency of the RIAF Venom squadron.

In May 1957 a further six reconditioned Venom FB.1s (WE459, WK392, WR278, WR286, WR292 and WR349) were acquired from the RAF as attrition replacements; in Iraqi service they were possibly reserialled within the 400 to 600 numbers.

A bloody internal coup and the overthrow of the Iraqi monarchy in July 1958 resulted in the prefix 'Royal' being removed from the air force title, and with the delivery of Soviet equipment during the early 1960s the Venoms were withdrawn from service and scrapped.

Several of the squadron's Venoms were alleged to have been lost during an escort trip for King Faisal's visit to Jordan in the autumn of 1954, when a dust storm forced the aircraft to put down in the desert between Amman and Damascus. Further reported accidents were also known to have later occurred on 17 May 1958 when a Venom swung off the runway during take-off and was seriously damaged, fortunately without injury to the pilot; and on 18 January 1959 another Venom flown by the IAF Commander, Col Mamoud Aziz, crashed on landing and burst into flames, again without causing serious injury.

Very little is known about the Iraqi Venoms after the revolution except that none were present at Habbaniya during a visit in September 1961, although there is a suggestion from within Iraqi circles that some may have been included in a batch of surplus Vampires which had earlier been presented to the Moroccan Air Force. One aircraft, '370', is currently held in open storage at the former horse racing track on the outskirts of Baghdad at Al Abied, the site of the Military Museum of Iraq.

ITALY

As part of the process of rebuilding its postwar air force, the Aeronautica Militare Italiana (AMI) sought permission from Britain to licence-build large numbers of jet-engined day-fighters to replace the war-surplus American aircraft it had received following the withdrawal of the Anglo-American forces of occupation. Plans were made for the de Havilland Venom and the American Republic F-84 to become the standard NATO fighter-bombers, and a scheme was formulated for a sizeable number of Venoms to be built on the continent to form a united defence system.

On 24 October 1949 the Director-General of FIAT signed a licensed production and development agreement at Hatfield. This agreement included orders for Vampire day- and night-fighters to be built both in the UK and in Italy, as well as a quantity of Venom fighter-bombers and night-fighters, and Goblin and Ghost engines. At the same time France also signed a contract to build Vampires, Mistrals and later Venom FB.1s and Aquilon naval fighters at its SNCASE factory at Marignane, with the engines being produced by Hispano Suiza in Spain.

The licence to manufacture the Vampire and Venom aircraft in Italy was given to FIAT and Macchi, with the Ghost 48 Mk.1 engines being built by Fiat Motors in Turin and Alfa Romeo in Pomegliano D'Arco near Naples. By the end of 1950, however, the USA was already expressing doubts about the manufacture of the Vampires in Italy, pointing out that they were already obsolescent and did not conform to United Nations defence plans; alternatively, more F-51 Mustang fighters could be provided to Italy from surplus stocks, together with a further offer to supply F-84G Thunderjet fighter-bombers by the following spring. In the summer of 1951 the Italian government offered to provide a large number of training aircraft built with Italian money for NATO use in exchange for the financing of first-line types for the Aeronautica Militaire. The Venom was chosen as the operational type and American representatives from the Atlantic Congress paid a special visit to Italy to make it clear that any order for Venoms to be produced for its European partners could not be paid for from Mutual Defence Aid Programme (MDAP) funds, but would have to be funded by the Italian government.

The Italian government realised there was little hope of the US financing day-fighter Venoms so they decided instead to order the Venom night-fighter, knowing that there was a great need for this type in Europe and that the Americans had none to supply. At a meeting of the NATO Congress, the British government set out its plans to mass-produce 1,100 Venom night-fighters in various European countries, together with 1,000 Ghost engines, in order to guarantee unified, round-the-clock, all-weather fighter protection. It was also proposed that funds would come from NATO and any European country interested in purchasing the fighter; hence the Italian industry should benefit from an extra 120 Venom night-fighters for the united defence system project.

Paradoxically, the worst blow to this European project came from the British government itself following the election of the Conservative Party in October 1951. Its introduction of new inflationary policies required a drastic reduction in military spending. As the early Venom trials at the CFE had been disappointing, the government decided to cancel orders for 750 aircraft, giving the US an opportunity to call for a further reduction of 300 aircraft for the NATO air forces.

At a further meeting of the NATO Congress, held in Lisbon in February 1952, a proposal was put forward to abandon the Venom project and concentrate on the production of 300–400 Vampires and to investigate the development of more advanced aircraft technology. By the spring of 1952 the AMI was still insistent on buying Venom night-fighters for air defence purposes. In October 1952 the USA took advantage of the failure of the English and Italian governments to reach an agreement to licence the project and blocked the plan; the USA further suggested that the Venom was obsolete by modern standards and submitted a proposal to supply the NATO air arms with more advanced aircraft built under licence, which included fifty F-86K Sabre all-weather fighters to be assembled by FIAT at Turin.

In November 1952 the US representatives at the NATO Congress confirmed that the Venom night-fighter programme would not be financed by either NATO or Off-Shore funds. It did, however, view the absence of an all-weather fighter from the projected equipment of the NATO air forces with concern, and proposed that if the trials were successful it would consider an off-shore contract for the Gloster Javelin all-weather fighter to be produced by the FIAT company in Italy. In an attempt to save the Venom project, an Italian representative flew to London to meet with the British government, but neither party was able to find an alternative to the plan, subsequently missing out on an opportunity to produce the Gloster Javelin as a result.

The deal to build Ghost engines for the French and Swiss Air Forces at FIAT Motors still went ahead, however, together with the French contract to build the Sud-Est Aquilon. As a result the first Venom was built under licence in France and powered by a Ghost 48 engine made by FIAT Motors.

With the negotiations between Italy and Britain terminated two Venom FB.50 aircraft (MM6153 c/n 12566 and MM6154 c/n 12567) were purchased by the AMI for trials and experimental purposes. Both aircraft were collected from Chester and flown to Hatfield on 19 January 1953 by Lt Col Romano Palmera and Capt Umberto Bernardini. Finished in a metallic blue colour scheme, the two Venoms were flown to Rome-Ciampino on 29 January, where one was delivered to the Sezione Velivoli a Reazione of the Reparto Sperimentale Volo (RSV), while the other was transferred on 30 January to the Scuola Aviogetti at Foggia-Amendola. On 10 April 1953 the second aircraft was returned to the Sezione Velivoli a Reazione. Both aircraft subsequently had limited flying careers because of problems in keeping the aircraft fully serviceable, which resulted in MM6154 being withdrawn in July 1954.

The surviving Venom (MM6153) served with the Reparto Sperimentale at Rome-

One of the twenty-two Venom FB.54s built for the Venezuelan Air Force during an early test flight from Chester in late 1955. (*BAe plc*)

Ciampino until March 1957, when it was finally struck off charge. It is currently stored at the Museo Nazionale della Scienza e della Technica at Milan.

In 1953 an unusual proposal was made to use one of the Venoms for a record-breaking high-altitude parachute descent by Signor Sauro Rinaldi, who planned to jump from a special container fitted to the starboard side of the aircraft. The project was eventually abandoned in February 1953 when another parachutist claimed the record by jumping from a Breda transport aircraft.

VENEZUELA

Following a service evaluation at Hatfield by two air force officers, in July 1955 Venezuela announced its intention to buy twenty-two Venom FB.54s (the export version of the Venom FB.4), fitted with Ghost 105 engines, to equip Escuadron de Caza 34 of the Fuerza Aerea Venezolana (FAV). Serialled 1A-34–8C-34, these aircraft were among the last of the type to be completed at Chester, with the first aircraft (1A-34) being delivered to the packers on 3 December 1955 and the last (8C-34) on 17 August 1956.

The Venoms were delivered by sea to Maracay in Venezuela and were distributed between three flights of 34 Squadron 'Caciques' at Maiquetta, which had formed on 20 December 1955 under the command of Maj Roosevelt Adriana Galvis, supplementing the Vampire FB.5s that had been delivered a few years earlier to 35 Squadron at Boca de Rio as part of the FAV's modernisation programme.

Soon after receiving the last of its Venoms the FAV decided to create a formation aerobatic team – 'Los Caciques' – to replace the earlier Vampire team which had disbanded in December 1956. A mid-air collision involving four of the Venoms during a display routine at El Liberator air base on 7 September 1967 was a tragic blow to the team. Astonishingly, three of the pilots were able to safely eject, but Capt Nestor Luis Guerrero Hernandez was unfortunately killed when his parachute failed to open.

In December 1960 34 Squadron was transferred from Maiquetta to El Liberator air base, to join 35 (Vampire FB.52s) and 36 (F-86F Sabres) Squadrons, and on 12 July 1961 the three FAV fighter squadrons came under the control of the newly formed 12 Fighter Group. In 1968 further changes saw the former squadron code letters changed to four-digit serials: known serials being 0099, 0325, 5232, 7090, 7125, 8331 and 9418.

In February 1972 the Fighter Group was re-equipped with Northrop CF-5A/Ds and the Venoms were withdrawn from service with the FAV the following year. Little is known of their subsequent fates, but at least one aircraft (8C-34) is preserved at the Museo de la Fuerza Aerea Venezolana at Maracay, while another (8176) is to be found at the Escuela de Aviacion Militair at Mariscal Sucre AFB.

Further Venom accidents are known to have happened: on 19 August 1958 one crashed at Barquisimeto, killing Sub-Tte Luis A. Blanco Abreu, and on 7 May 1969 another crashed near El Liberator air base, killing Sub-Tte Freddy S. Pereira Bracho.

SWITZERLAND

A review undertaken by a government commission in 1950 to determine the future requirements of the Swiss Air Force (Flugwaffe) discussed the replacement of the de Havilland Vampire. A considerable number of these proven and versatile aircraft had been built under licence at Emmen and had entered service with the Swiss combat squadrons during the summer of 1949. Several aircraft types were considered as replacements, including the Dassault Ouragan, the Hawker Sea Hawk and both the de Havilland Venom day- and night-fighter variants.

With current production of the Vampire being taken into consideration, an extensive evaluation of the Venom as a fighter and ground-support aircraft was undertaken, both in Switzerland and in England. In December 1950 the Venom was finally chosen as the most likely to fulfil the requirements of the air force and the results were forwarded to the Chief of the Swiss Armed Forces for his approval. At SFr 730,060 each, including the engine, the Venom was considered a simple, low-cost aircraft with excellent aerodynamic qualities. It also demanded 'sensitivity, attention and self-control' by those who flew it – which was thought to present no major problems for a well-trained Swiss pilot! Also taken into account was the continuity of production at Emmen, with assembly rigs for the Vampire already in place and the prospect of spares compatibility a practicable expectation. To provide a brief engineering appraisal and carry out a series of demonstration flights to representatives of the Swiss Air Force, a standard Venom FB.1 (WE280) was also flown from Hatfield to Emmen by DH development test pilot George Thornton.

On 12 April 1951 an order worth SFr 175 million was placed for 150 Venom FB.1s (J-1501–J-1650) to be built under licence by the consortium of F+W Emmen, Doflug Altenrhein and Pilatus AG at Stans following completion of the Vampire contract. Concurrent with the manufacture of the Venom airframes, the contract to licence-build 410

de Havilland Ghost 48 Mk.1 turbine engines was awarded to the firm of Gebr Sulzer Brothers Ltd of Winterthur. However, the firm's lack of practice in building jet engines could hardly compare with the consortium's vast airframe manufacturing experience, and the first thirty-five engines had to be procured from de Havilland (Engines) in the UK to achieve a simultaneous output; Swiss-built engines were installed in the thirtieth and subsequent aircraft. Production soon reached an output of six aircraft per month, and in July 1953 the first aircraft were transferred to the government procurement agency at Emmen – the Kriegstechnische Abteilung – for acceptance. A number of structural defects in the initial airframes were quickly resolved and during March 1954 the first combat squadrons were issued with Venom FB.1s, including Fliegerstaffeln (Fl.St.) 3, 4 and 16. A further four squadrons had been equipped by the time the last aircraft had been delivered in April 1956.

As the progression from day- to all-weather flying operations was considered the most important step for the air force, all combat squadrons were required to complete a blind-flying training course. During 1956 ninety-six pilots had achieved blind-flying stage 8, the highest flight qualification relating to instrument flying regulations.

An outstanding event in the Swiss Venom's career occurred on 5 May 1953, when Max Mathez, a test pilot at Emmen, was able to establish a new Swiss altitude record of 51,378ft while flying J-1501. The record was later verified by the Swiss Aero Club at Zurich.

On 5 February 1954 a second order for a hundred improved FB.4s (J-1701–J-1800) was placed with the Swiss aircraft manufacturing consortium. Deliveries were scheduled between August 1956 and March 1958, replacing the P-51D Mustangs of Fl.St. 18, 19, 20 and 21. The first aircraft, J-1701, was delivered to the Flugwaffe on 27 August 1956.

Further problems were encountered as the original Venoms began to reach the end of their service lives, with the metal structure showing signs of fatigue. Delays also in the selection of new combat aircraft by the Swiss Air Force prompted a team from F+W at Emmen to carry out an extensive fatigue testing programme, which resulted in the whole Venom fleet undergoing various structural reinforcement modifications to the wings. Coupled with a planned maintenance programme and constant monitoring of the remaining aircraft, the imposition of load restrictions was also avoided, which effectively more than doubled their service lives.

Between December 1971 and April 1975 at least thirty of the surviving original fleet of Venom fighters, especially those with fatigue fractures, were withdrawn and their various component assemblies fitted into the batch of second-hand Hunters recently purchased from the UK. The withdrawal of such a large number of Venoms also resulted in the disbandment of four combat units, Fl.St. 4, 7, 18 and 19.

As a result of the valuable experience gained from its ageing fleet of P-51D Mustang reconnaissance aircraft, the Swiss Air Force was convinced that a suitable replacement should be found as soon as possible. By removing two of the 20mm cannons and installing three oblique 100mm Vinten 360 automatic cameras in modified, fixed underwing drop-tanks, and a vertical Eastman Kodak 180mm K-24 camera in the nose of the Venom (which was sighted by means of a periscope in the cockpit), the last twenty-five aircraft of the original production batch were built as the Mk.1R reconnaissance version. The order was eventually reduced to twenty-four aircraft (J-1626–J-1649), with deliveries to Fl.St. 10 between March and September 1956.

The Venom FB.1Rs continued to provide an important contribution to the Military

The cockpit of a Venom FB.1 of the Swiss Air Force. (*Swiss Air Force*)

Surveillance Wing until 1969, when Fl.St. 10 was re-equipped with the Dassault Mirage IIIRS and the number of operational FB.1R aircraft was reduced to eight for use in the training role; the remaining Venoms were returned to their original FB.1 standard in 1970.

During the 1970s the allocation of new UHF-band radio frequencies for military aircraft meant that the avionics and IFR equipment had to be housed in a longer and more pointed nose, together with a new 'bombing computer' system. Although the modifications were installed towards the end of the Venom's military life, this more favourable aerodynamic form served to increase the aircraft's stability, and with the new UHF-radio system the instrument capability was also improved. At the same time the remaining Venoms were also fitted with an improved LAR S-17 bomb-aiming

With cameras mounted in the drop-tanks and the small fairing under the fuselage, J-1638 was one of twenty-four Venom FB.1Rs built for use with the Military Surveillance Wing. It carries the insignia of Fl.St.10 on the nose. This aircraft was destroyed in a take-off accident in 1973. (*Swiss Air Force*)

sight, which was used in conjunction with the S-108 bombing computer.

Flown by the country's unique mix of professional, militia and Swissair pilots, the Venoms were usually dispersed between a number of bases, including Alpnach, Emmen, Dubendorf, Payerne and Sion. In the event of war the aircraft were also capable of operating from autobahns or from pre-assigned self-contained 'cavern' bases in central Switzerland. Between 1954 and 1983 fifteen Fliegerstaffeln were equipped with the Venom: Fl.St. 2 (1955–82), Fl.St. 3 (1954–80), Fl.St. 4 (1954–74), Fl.St. 6 (1960–78), Fl.St. 7 (1963–74), Fl.St. 9 (1967–82), Fl.St. 10 (1963–7), Fl.St. 13

A selection of the underwing stores carried by Swiss ground-attack Venoms, including sixteen unguided 8cm air-to-ground rockets, and a combination of 50kg, 200kg and 400kg bombs. (*Swiss Air Force*)

A cartridge start for two Venom FB.1s of the Swiss Air Force, which ordered 150 of the type. They entered service in March 1954. (*Swiss Air Force*)

(1955–83), Fl.St. 15 (1955–79), Fl.St. 16 (1954–62), Fl.St. 17 (1955–67), Fl.St. 18 (1957–72), Fl.St. 19 (1957–72), Fl.St. 20 (1957–79) and Fl.St. 21 (1957–9).

Fliegerstaffeln 2 operated the type for advanced operational training until 1982, when trainee jet pilots reverted to being trained solely on Vampires before graduating to the Hunter and the Northrop F-5E Tiger II for air-to-air and air-to-ground training respectively. With the completion of the last training course, the remaining Venoms were 'officially' withdrawn from service and joined the large numbers already placed into 'open store' at Stans. Approximately sixty of these Venoms were kept in operational reserve in case of an emergency, with each aircraft undergoing a periodic inspection and being test-flown every three months.

The official retirement of the Venom from the Swiss Air Force was marked during an 'Open Day' at Interlaken on 15 October 1983, the last combat unit being Fl.St. 13. On 17 December 1984 the remaining ten Venoms were finally withdrawn from operational service.

During the type's twenty-nine years of operational service, fifty-six Venoms (forty Venom FB.1s, three FB.1Rs and thirteen FB.4s) were lost in flying accidents. The most tragic loss occurred on 27 August 1962 when a formation of three FB.4s (J-1759, J-1782 and J-1784) flew into a rock face of the Schwarzorn, killing all three pilots.

In June 1984 sixty-five Venoms were offered for sale at Dubendorf in non-flying condition at a price of SFr 8,000, including the engine. Forty-two were sold to private buyers in Switzerland and eleven were used for Swiss military exhibitions and museums. A further twenty-four were sold to foreign buyers, and some of these later found their way to the USA. In addition, Venom FB.4 J-1704 was presented to the Cosford Aerospace Museum on 23 June 1979 for permanent display.

Initial disposals to foreign buyers were:

United Kingdom. Venom FB.1: J-1523/G-VENI, J-1601/G-VIDI, J-1605/G-BLID, J-1614/G-BLIE, J-1616/G-BLIF (to the USA as N202DM), J-1632/G-VNOM and J-1634/

Swiss Air Force Venom FB.1s operating from an autobahn at Oensingen, outside Zurich, during the early 1970s. These mobility exercises were carried out in the event of a national emergency. (*Swiss Air Force*)

ZK-VNM (to New Zealand). Venom FB.4s: J-1730/G-BLIA (sold to buyer in USA as N402DM), J-1747/G-BLIB (to USA as N747J, ex-N5471V), J-1756/G-BLSD/ N203DM, J-1763/G-BLSE (to USA as N902DM), J-1790/G-VENM/G-BLKA, J-1799/G-BLIC/ZK-VNM (to New Zealand, ex-N502DM).

France. Venom FB.1: J-1544. Venom FB.1R: J-1636.

Israel. Venom FB.1: J-1516 (Air Force Museum, Hatzerim).

West Germany. Venom FB.1: J-1603. Venom FB.1R: J-1628, J-1635. Venom FB.4: J-1797, J-1798.

United States of America. Venom FB.1: J-1527/N9196M. Venom FB.4: J-1727, J-1742

(to La Storia del Volo Museum, Compignago, Italy.)

Austria. Venom FB.4: J-1733.

Of the large number of airframes purchased by private buyers in Switzerland, three are now displayed at the Fliegermuseum in Dubendorf, including FB.4 J-1753, and the nose sections of FB.1 J-1580 and FB.4 J-1751. In July 1984 Venom J-1630/HB-RVA was passed to its new owner, HALOS AG, in eastern Switzerland following refurbishment by a team from Flugzeugwerke Altenrhein. During a four-year restoration programme the Venom was returned to flying condition and took to the air again on 22 June 1988. The aircraft is currently owned by Pegus AB/Wilbur Sammlung and is operated by the Swiss Flying Museum at Altenrhein. Another Swiss-registered Venom

FB.1, J-1631/HB-RVC, is owned and operated by Aeronautique FMPA at Sion.

SWEDEN

In 1948 the Swedish government purchased a batch of refurbished Mosquito XIX night-fighters to equip the F1 Wing at Vasteras. It was planned that these Mosquitos would remain in service with the Flygvapnet (Royal Swedish Air Force) until at least 1955, when they would be replaced by SAAB J32B Lansen jet fighters. However, in the early 1950s the Mosquito's high accident rate and dated technology brought about the decision to replace the Mosquitos with either Meteor NF.11s or Venom NF.2s. Both types were evaluated, and although the air force showed a preference for the Meteor NF.11 the government decided to opt for the Venom, doubtlessly influenced by its earlier purchase of Vampire jet fighters. On 2 January 1951 an order was placed for thirty-five Venom NF.51s (33001–33035), with an option to buy a further twenty-five aircraft, at a cost of £26,500. The price included a 30-minute test flight. In service the Venom would be redesignated the J.33, with the first deliveries scheduled to begin in May 1952. As part of the contract agreement, the aircraft would be fitted with 5,000lb-thrust RM2A Ghost engines, which were to be built under licence by Svenska Flygmotor in Sweden and shipped to the UK for installation; the Hispano 20mm cannon would also be manufactured under licence by the Gevarsfaktoriet at Eskilstuna. The Venoms would, however, be flown to Sweden without the AI Mk.10 radar and radio equipment fitted, as these items would be taken from the Flygvapnet's remaining Mosquito aircraft.

The initial order was later amended to thirty aircraft (33001–33030), and to fulfil the Swedish contract the airframes were diverted from the RAF Venom NF.2 allotment, which were fitted with framed canopies and the original tail assembly. The majority of the aircraft were built at Chester, with a further three (33028, 33029 and 33030) being constructed by Fairey Aviation at Ringway and transferred to Chester for completion between September and October 1953. The Swedish order was delayed slightly as a result of production being transferred to Hatfield following suspension of work on the Comet airliner. The Venoms were flown from Chester and Ringway,

Venom NF.51 33010 at Chester in May 1953, awaiting delivery to Sweden. In service the type was known as the J.33 and was equivalent to the RAF's Venom NF.2. The initial order for thirty aircraft was completed in January 1954. (*via Alan Roach*)

Venom J.33 of F1 Wing, with Stage 2 modifications. These aircraft were modified to Venom NF.2A standard with additional navigation and radar installations. The Sword antennae mounted on the upper wings are for the PN-50/A navigation radar equipment. (*Mikael Forslund*)

which was considered as their initial test flight.

On 20 December 1952 Capt Bengt Floden, the CO of 1 Squadron F1 Wing, delivered the first J.33 (33001) to Vasteras. Further deliveries continued during the spring of 1953, but of the thirty aircraft originally ordered only twenty-nine were eventually delivered to Sweden, 33014 having been lost on 12 August 1953. One of five being ferried to Vasteras, it developed a fuel leak and caught fire soon after take-off from Hawarden; it then dived into the ground at Bee's Nursery in Sealand Road, Chester, killing Lt Olof Hedman and Cpl Bengt Elis Knut Andersson. The Flygvapnet accepted the last of the unmodified aircraft in January 1954.

In order to provide jet conversion training for the pilots of F1 Wing, a handful of Vampire trainers were transferred to Vasteras, while the navigators were given radar training in Junkers Ju86Ks (B3s) and Hunting Pembrokes (Tp83s) equipped as radar

classrooms. By the summer of 1953 the Venom Wing at Vasteras was declared operational. It was divided into three flying squadrons, each being withdrawn in turn for training. In June 1953 the Swedish Venoms made their first public appearance at F1 Wing's 'Flight Day' at Vasteras.

The Flygvapnet had been keen to obtain its J.33s as quickly as possible, and before the aerodynamic problems and structural weaknesses of the RAF's Venom NF.2s were resolved, so a number of operating restrictions were imposed upon the Swedish aircraft until a series of modifications could be installed. Despite these restrictions the J.33s are known to have performed well during their first major air defence exercise in August 1953, and it is worthy of note to record that of the twelve aircraft lost in flying accidents between August 1953 and October 1959 none was due to structural failures.

In late 1953 the second batch of Venoms (33031–33060) was delivered to Sweden. These aircraft were modified to NF.2A standard and were accepted by the Flygvapnet between December 1953 and August 1954. As the first order had been equivalent to the NF.2, in September 1953 a further modification programme to up-date the remaining twenty-eight aircraft (33021 had crashed near Tilberga railway station in October 1954) began at CVV in Vasteras to incorporate the revised tail assembly from kits supplied from de Havilland's. In addition, the navigation and radar equipment was upgraded with the installation of PS-20/A search radar, the temporary incorporation of PN 53/A navigation radar and the mounting of Sword antenna on the upper surface of the inner wings in readiness for PN-50/A navigation equipment, which would be installed during the second phase of the modifications. The first phase of the programme was completed by December 1954.

In March 1955 the second phase of the modification programme on the original twenty-eight aircraft began. This included the installation of clear-view jettisonable cockpit canopies and the fitting of Ministop anti-locking brakes, the regulator for which was mounted in the armament cavity. Further work incorporated PH-10/A height-measuring radar and PN-50/A navigation radar, wing leading edge slats and an additional pair of stall fences over the wing roots. At the rate of five aircraft a month, it was estimated that the programme would be completed by November 1956, and it was not unusual during the period between the first and second modification programmes to see some of the J.33s flying with the old-style framed canopies and the new tail assembly fitted.

A further addition to the Venoms' target acquisition capability was the introduction of an infra-red (IR) homing sight. Used in conjunction with the aircraft's standard gunsight, the IR sight was of tubular construction, with an illuminated lens system (or C-scope) mounted above the nose of the

Venom J.33 33052, red N of 1 Squadron, F1 Wing, Vasteras. This particular aircraft served with the Flygvapnet between August 1954 and October 1960. (*Geoff Cruickshank*)

aircraft and bearing on the outside of the windscreen; it was also supplemented with a heating device to eliminate icing. The maximum range of the IR sight was about 3 miles and it picked up the jet pipe glow of a target, which was presented on the operator's screen as a slightly diffused spot of light that became more clearly defined as the range was reduced. In August 1954, following successful trials with the IR sight mounted in a Mosquito and a Venom (33056), it was decided to install the device in the J.33s. The work was carried out between September 1956 and June 1957.

In February 1957 two RAF officers were attached to F1 Wing at Vasteras for a three-month exchange visit. They held the Swedish pilots and groundcrew in high regard and were impressed with the general standard of flying. In their subsequent report it was noted that the tactics and training of the NF All-Weather F1 Wing were identical to those of RAF squadrons in a similar role. For training purposes the year was divided into two periods: the winter programme's emphasis was placed on practice interceptions (PIs), while the summer programme was devoted to day tactics, navigation and weapons training. Although PIs formed the largest single part of training during the winter programme, it was considered that it had not progressed beyond the OCU standard of training. It was also noted that the NF squadrons were not equipped with training aircraft and that the Swedish pilots much preferred dogfighting and aerobatics. There were slight variations in the flying characteristics between the Venom NF.2 and the J.33, while the additional modifications and equipment fitted to the J.33 were considered to be beneficial in its all-weather role.

In May 1958 a flying display at Vasteras was attended by 75,000 people. One of the highlights of the programme was an event billed as 'The Waterfall', staged by the F1 aerobatic team. The team had been in existence for two years; led by Lt Charlie Lingren, it consisted of Ernst Moberg, Bengt Lindwall and Ragnvald Johansson. The display at Vasteras took place in total darkness, and to heighten the effect of the team's routine the Venoms' tip-tanks were removed and replaced by canisters of magnesium powder; when ignited the powder would burn for two minutes – sufficient for the team to perform two loops and two rolls. Other effects carried out by the F1 Venoms during the event included the firing of modified rockets from the wing-tips and elaborate smoke trails created by some of the aircraft which had generators installed in the equipment space by the navigator's seat.

The following year proved to be a bad one for the Swedish Venoms, with eight aircraft being lost in a series of unrelated flying accidents between March and October 1959. Fortunately there were no fatalities.

During 1959–60 the Venoms of F1 Wing were gradually replaced by the SAAB J32B Lansen, a two-seat, all-weather attack fighter, with 2 Squadron being the first to convert. By the spring of 1960 the last squadron had been re-equipped, and the last official Venom flight was made on 15 March 1960. The aircraft were officially withdrawn from Flygvapnet service on 24 October 1960 and the remaining Venoms were scrapped, except for four which were retained as target aircraft for the Swedish Flight Service at Vidsel in northern Sweden, on contract to the Flygvapnet. The first two J.33s, 33015 (SE-DCA) and 33022 (SE-DCB), were transferred to Forsoks Centralen at Linkoping for modification into target tugs in 1958, with pylons from which targets could be streamed being installed under the port wing root. In order to give the J.33 the same climbing capabilities as the Jindvik unmanned target aircraft, the IR sight, cannon and various aerials were also removed and the resultant holes faired over. The aircraft were painted in an overall gloss yellow scheme to enhance visibility over the ranges. In 1960 two further J.33s, 33025 (SE-DCD) and 33041 (SE-DCE), were also converted; all four aircraft continued to use military markings until they were officially struck off charge in January 1960 and transferred to the civil register. The J.33s continued to be used as target tugs and missile simulators on the proving grounds at Vidsel until 1968–9, when they were finally replaced by SAAB J32Bs. The details of their cancellation from the civil register are: SE-DCA, 23 July 1969; SE-DCB, 31 March 1971; SE-DCC, 24 January 1969; and SE-DCD, 24 January 1969. SE-DCD was subsequently flown to the RSwAF Museum in Linkoping in 1968 and has been restored to its original colour scheme as 33025 blue E of F1 Wing. It is currently on display at the Flygvapenmuseum Malmen at Malmslatt. The RSwAF Museum also acquired the hulk

of SE-DCA, which was rescued from the Vidsel dump in the 1980s. The other two aircraft were scrapped.

Of interest was the short-lived plan to obtain a further thirty Venom NF.51s, to be used as maritime reconnaissance aircraft under the designation S33. The intention was to purchase the aircraft without radar and then to install the sets taken from the SAAB S18As which the S33s were intended to replace. The plan was cancelled in late 1953, for financial reasons.

The Swedish authorities originally wanted the Venoms to be painted in the current Swedish colours of olive green and light blue, but eventually accepted the aircraft in the standard RAF scheme of overall medium sea grey and dark green. Markings consisted of a yellow Wing number (1) and squadron markings in the colour of the squadron with a white outline (red for 1 Squadron, blue for 2 Squadron and yellow for 3 Squadron). Aircraft assigned to the Wing Staff used white letters with a black outline.

CHAPTER SIXTEEN

WARBIRDS AND SURVIVORS

In December 1984 the Venom was officially withdrawn from service with the Swiss Air Force following a career that had lasted just over thirty years. A comprehensive maintenance and modification programme had ensured that the last Venom squadron remained operational until the end of 1983. Approximately sixty Venoms had been placed in operational reserve at Stans in case of an emergency, and during their time in storage each aircraft was flown once every three months and examined for possible deterioration arising from inactivity. Most of the aircraft had logged over 1,800 flying hours and their engines had been subjected to an average of ten overhauls.

After successfully auctioning its redundant Vampire aircraft in early 1981, the Swiss Federal Office for Military Airports took advantage of the great public interest and offered the Venoms for sale at auction in June 1984. The aircraft were offered in a non-flying condition at a price of SFr 8,000 including the engine, and enthusiasts were also able to purchase Ghost Mk.48 engines separately at SFr 2,000 each. In all, sixty-five Venoms were sold at Dubendorf, forty-two of them to private buyers in Switzerland and eleven to Swiss military exhibitions and museums. A further twenty-four Venoms were sold to foreign buyers, of which thirteen went to the UK, five to West Germany and one each to France, Austria, Israel and New Zealand.

SOURCE CLASSIC JET FLIGHT, BOURNEMOUTH AIRPORT

The Venom and the Vampire have both become popular on the air show circuit and the largest non-governmental display team in the world – Source Classic Jet Flight, based at Bournemouth Airport – specialises in restoring and operating these former Swiss jet aircraft. The first two Venoms, J-1523/G-VENI and J-1601/G-VIDI, were delivered to Source Premium and Promotional Consultants Ltd at Cranfield, owned by Sandy Topen and Don Wood, in June 1984 with the aim of operating the aircraft under the patronage of 11 (Lightning) Squadron at Binbrook. G-VENI was first displayed on the air show circuit in mid-1986, but with the demise of the Lightning and the squadron's subsequent revival as a Tornado unit at Leeming the company lost its military 'umbrella'.

A reorganisation within the company, which resulted in a change of name in December 1989, together with the purchase of three ex-Swiss Vampires, saw Source Ltd moving to its present location at Bournemouth International Airport in 1993. In November 1994 three more former Swiss Venoms (J-1539, J-1573 and J-1611) were acquired, the first of which (J-1573) was registered as G-VICI in February 1995 and was flown back to the UK. The decision to register the original three aircraft to reflect the Latin historian Suetonius's well-known remark 'Veni, Vidi, Vici' ('I came, I saw, I conquered') symbolised Don Wood's search for the aircraft, the problems of getting them onto the British civil register, and his eventual triumph in flying them together as a formation.

Source Classic Jet Flight's policy was to demonstrate that a civilian company could operate former military jets and it flew an

Venom FB.1 G-DHUU (ex-J-1539) of the Source Classic Jet Flight based at Bournemouth Airport, pictured over the Needles, Isle of Wight. The aircraft had served with the Swiss Air Force from May 1954 until it was sold in September 1980. It was acquired by Source in 1994 and, following a six-month rebuild, flew for the first time in July 1996. It is marked as WR410 of 6 Squadron to celebrate the 40th anniversary of the Suez campaign. (*Source Aviation*)

average of a hundred missions per year. The Venoms (and Vampires) were painted in various colour schemes to reflect the contrasting roles and theatres the aircraft assumed during their respective careers. The crews were drawn from current fast jet fighter and former Red Arrows pilots.

In December 2001 Don Wood put his fleet of Venoms and Vampires up for sale, together with a comprehensive engineering and spares support facility. The Venom fleet included:

Venom FB.1 – J-1523/G-VENI. Served with the Swiss Air Force from March 1954 to June 1984. It arrived in the UK by air on 8 June 1984, and was flown to Cranfield the following day. It received its UK permit and first flew on 16 June 1990 as WE402, the aircraft flown by the Wing Leader of RAF Fassberg during the mid-1950s. It was repainted during August 1998 to represent the first Venom prototype, VV612.

Venom FB.1 – J-1539/G-DHUU. Served with the Swiss Air Force from June 1954 to December 1984. It arrived in the UK by road in 1994 (ex-Locarno and G-BMOC ntu). Following a six-month rebuild programme, it flew again on 17 July 1996 and is painted in a sand and brown colour scheme replicating WR410 of 6 Squadron to coincide with the 40th anniversary of the Suez campaign.

Venom FB.1 – J-1573/G-VICI. Served with the Swiss Air Force from January 1955 to December 1984. It arrived in the UK by air in 1995 (ex-Altenrhein and G-BMOB ntu/HB-RVB). Registered on 6 February 1995, it flew again for the first time two months later and is kept in its original Swiss colours.

245

Two of the first four ex-Swiss Venoms for UK buyers arrived at Duxford on 9 June 1984. Both aircraft – J-1601/G-VIDI and J-1523/G-VENI — were passed to Source Aviation at Bournemouth. J-1601 later crashed at Hawarden in July 1996. (*J.M. Gradidge*)

Venom FB.1 – J-1601/G-VIDI. Served with the Swiss Air Force from June 1955 to June 1984. It arrived in the UK by air on 8 June 1984, and was flown to Cranfield the following day. It is painted in a cerulean blue colour scheme to represent WE275, which allegedly flew high-altitude reconnaissance flights over eastern Europe in 1952. It crashed on take-off at Hawarden on 7 July 1996 and was written off.

Venom FB.1 – J-1611/G-DHTT. Served with the Swiss Air Force from February 1956 to December 1984. It arrived in the UK by road in 1994 (ex-Locarno) and was registered on 17 October 1996. It first flew after restoration on 10 July 1997. It is painted in an all-red 'Red

The aircraft of the Source Aviation collection were painted in various colour schemes to reflect contrasting roles or to celebrate anniversaries. G-DHTT (J-1611) was painted in an all-over 'Red Arrows' red to commemorate fifty years of jet formation teams. (*Source Aviation*)

Arrows' colour scheme to celebrate fifty years of jet display teams and is marked as WR421.

Venom FB.1R – J-1626/G-DHSS. Served with the Swiss Air Force from September 1956 to July 1984. It arrived in the UK by road in 1998 (ex-Villmergen) and was registered on 26 March 1999. Repainted by December 1999 as WR360, in the all-white livery of 60 Squadron's aerobatic team at Tengah in 1957, it first flew again on 29 September 2000.

Venom FB.1R – J-1629. Served with the Swiss Air Force from March 1957 to December 1984. It arrived in the UK by road in 1999 (ex-Buochs store). In store.

Venom FB.1R – J-1649. Served with the Swiss Air Force from August 1956 to March 1984. It arrived in the UK by road in 1999 (ex-Bern store). In store.

Venom FB.4 – J-1790/G-BLKA. Originally owned by Sandy Topen of the Vintage Aircraft Team (VAT) at Bruntingthorpe, it has been repainted in a colour scheme to represent WR410:N of 6 Squadron during the Suez campaign. It passed to de Havilland Aviation at Swansea when Jet Heritage went out of business. The registration was cancelled in July 1995 and it was placed into store at Hurn, with its original Venom FB.1 nose being subsequently fitted to G-GONE in 1999. It has been sent on to Martham, Norfolk, in June 2002 for storage on behalf of the de Havilland Heritage Centre.

DE HAVILLAND AVIATION LTD/BOURNEMOUTH AVIATION MUSEUM

De Havilland Aviation was formed at Swansea Airport in 1995 by Gwyn Jones with the intention of preserving de Havilland postwar jets in flying condition. It transferred

Venom G-GONE (J-1542) of de Havilland Aviation at Swansea Airport displaying its new colour scheme in May 2001. It was last flown by the Swiss Air Force in May 1984 and was acquired by the company following the demise of Jet Heritage. (*Paul Harrison*)

the major part of its engineering work to Bournemouth International Airport at Hurn in early 2000 and operates in association with the Bournemouth Aviation Museum, which was established in May 1998. Included in its collection of airworthy vintage jets, the company also owns Venom FB.1 J-1542/G-GONE, which last flew with the Flugwaffe in May 1984 and was sold at auction at Dubendorf the following month. Delivered to Stansted on 15 September 1984 and registered to John Davis of Hawarden, the Venom was operated by Jet Heritage at Hurn in the midnight blue colour scheme of the Royal Navy. Following the demise of Jet Heritage, it was acquired by Gwyn Jones and repainted in a striking yellow and black paint scheme in May 2001 for the forthcoming air show season.

KENNET AVIATION, CRANFIELD/NORTH WEALD

Venom FB.1 J-1614/G-BLIE. Delivered to Stansted on 27 February 1985 (ex-Stans store) and transferred the same day to ACS/Computaplane at Glasgow. The pod only was sold to Russell Dagless at East Dereham. The Venom was re-registered to former US Navy pilot Tim Manna of Kennet Aviation as G-VENM in June 1999 and following a complete two-year refurbishment was painted in 2001 as WK436, flown by the CO of 11 Squadron at Wunstorf in 1954. It took to the air at Cranfield for the first time following refurbishment on 23 November 2001 and joined the rest of Kennet's fleet of classic jets for the 2002 air show season. It moved with the company to North Weald in November 2002.

Venom FB.1 J-1632/G-VNOM. Sold on 9 June 1984, it was flown to Stansted on 3 July 1984 and delivered to Sandy Topen at Cranfield on 5 July 1984. It was struck off the civil register in March 1991 as a spares

source for Kennet, but was transferred on permanent loan to the De Havilland Aircraft Heritage Centre in January 2002 for display.

NEW ZEALAND WARBIRDS . . .

In 1984 former RNZAF pilot Trevor Bland purchased an ex-Swiss Venom FB.1R, J-1634. The aircraft was flown to Stansted in February 1985, where it was dismantled and shipped to New Zealand. Despite damage to the airframe from sea water while in transit to Wellington, it was subsequently transported by road to RNZAF Whenupai for restoration to flying condition. Fitted with the nose of a Venom FB.1 and repainted in the colours of Trevor's former 14 (NZ) Squadron aircraft WE434, the Venom took to the air again on 29 August 1987, becoming the first civilian jet fighter on the New Zealand register as ZK-VNM three months later. Variously owned by Flight Watch Services Ltd at Ardmore in 1990 and Rural Aviation (1963) Ltd in 1991, the Venom was operated under the umbrella of the New Zealand Warbirds Association. On 17 November 1991 it failed to get airborne for a display over Auckland harbour and crashed into an orchard at Ardmore while being flown by John Denton. The airframe was written off and subsequently used for spares.

The following March a replacement Swiss Air Force Venom FB.4 (J-1799) was purchased through Warplanes Inc. of South Burlington. This aircraft had been flown to Britain in July 1984 and was originally registered as G-BLIC before being shipped to Mojave in California, where it became N502DM in June 1985. It was dismantled and shipped to New Zealand, where it was re-registered as ZK-VNM. Owned by Rural Aviation (1963) Ltd of Ardmore, the Venom flew again in January 1993 and is displayed in a distinctive red and white colour scheme.

Following a two-year refurbishment programme by Kennet Aviation at Cranfield, G-VENM (J-1614) was rolled out in October 2001 in the markings of 11 Squadron. It flew again on 23 November 2001, with Rod Dean at the controls. (*Tim Manna*)

The Kennet Aviation team responsible for the restoration of G-VENM (J-1614) pictured at Cranfield. They are Rod Dean, Pete Walker, Tim Manna, Dave Horsfield and John Beatie. (*via Alan Allen*)

. . . AND AMERICAN EAGLES

In Charlottesville, Virginia, former Vietnam War pilot Capt Curtis Farley regularly flies his Venom FB.4, N747J, on the air show circuit as part of a 'Venom/MiG-17 Jet Acro'. He performs aerobatic displays and stages 'head-on conflict dogfights' with a 'Russian MiG-17 Fresco' (actually a former Polish AF Lim-6R). Formerly J-1747/G-BLIB/N5471V, the Venom was subsequently sold to a new owner in the USA in August 1984, and was purchased by Curtis Farley in December 1993. It has since been repainted in an attractive gloss black scheme, complete with red bands on the nose and tail-booms.

Several Venoms are also owned and operated by Dave Van Liere at Huntingdon, Indiana. N402DM (ex-J-1730/G-BLIA, and formerly owned by Aces High at Duxford) was purchased from the late Gene Fisher in

1994 and is located at Salt Lake City, Utah, while former RAN Sea Venom FAW.53 N7022H/WZ944 was acquired from the Amjet Aircraft Corporation of St Paul, Minnesota, in 1999 and is a familiar sight at air shows in the Suez crisis colours of 809 Squadron RN. Dave also regularly flies N202DM (ex-J-1616), which is owned by Merle Maine and operated from its base at Ontario in Oregon. Both Venom fighters are finished in a gloss black scheme and retain their original Swiss markings.

Venom FB.4 N902DM (formerly J-1763/G-BLSE) crashed near Muskogee in Oklahoma in June 1990, while Venom FB.1 N9196M (ex-J-1527), which was last registered to a company in Broomfield, Colorado, has probably since been withdrawn from the register for use as a spares source.

Rod Dean has been displaying civil aircraft since 1984 when he retired from the

Venom FB.4 N747J (J-1747) was purchased by Curt Farley in December 1993. It is painted in an overall gloss black colour scheme with red bands, and is regularly displayed on the US air show circuit as part of a 'Venom/MiG-17 Jet Acro' act. (*Curtis E. Farley*)

Operated by the NZ Warbirds Association and flown by Trevor Bland, Venom FB.4 ZK-VNM (J-1799) wears the distinctive red and white colour scheme developed not only to make the aircraft look good in the air but also to retain its Swiss identity while making it highly visible in the busy Ardmore circuit. (*Qwilton Biel*)

RAF as a squadron leader with over 4,500 flying hours in his logbook on Hunter and Jaguar fighters. In addition to instructing and flying various light aircraft, Rod has displayed a wide variety of Second World War and immediate postwar piston fighters such as the Mustang, Corsair, Wildcat, Sea Fury, Hurricane and, favourite among them all, the Spitfire. He is current on a number of vintage jet aircraft such as the Meteor, Vampire, Venom and Hunter, and is currently Head of the General Aviation Department of the CAA. On 23 November 2001 Rod flew Kennet Aviation's Venom G-

VENM for the first time following its two-year restoration to flying condition:

The first impression of a Venom is that it is something of a 'kiddy-car', sitting so low to the ground and apparently with very little structure. However, this impression is very wrong. The Venom is a meaty aeroplane and, for its time, a very capable little fighter. The cockpit is, as usual for a British fighter, compact – which is a euphemism for being small, cramped and virtually impossible to strap into without either assistance or running the risk of severe damage to the elbows. The cockpit ergonomics (a word that had clearly not been invented in the 1940s) leave something to be desired with some lovely 'gotcha's' such as undercarriage and flap levers being side by side on the same quadrant – which is buried in the bowels of the cockpit and almost impossible to see! It is important to be <u>absolutely</u> sure which one has hold of when making a selection, for obvious reasons.

The fun really starts when it comes to starting the engine – the engine start cartridge is only 2ft behind your head and it goes off with a surprisingly loud 'woomph' and masses of black smoke. Taxiing is straightforward, despite the lack of nose-wheel steering, with the normal British system of differential braking. Care must also be taken with engine handling. These early engines had only rudimentary fuel control systems and moving the throttle too rapidly, particularly at low RPM, could quickly overfuel them. Monitoring the JPT closely is therefore mandatory.

The take-off is easy provided the nose-wheel is straight on when lining up on the runway. If it is not, the initial roll might be a bit of a gyration until the direction is sorted out. The normal procedure is to line up on the runway, with the nose-wheel straight, and stop. Power is then gently brought up to full against the brakes. This does two things: enables the pilot to check that the engine RPM and JPT are correct and also that the brakes are functioning correctly.

Acceleration is quite sprightly for a jet, and gentle use of differential brake might be needed to keep straight, particularly in a crosswind, up to 50 knots when the rudders become effective. The nose-wheel is eased off the ground at about 80–85 knots, but not with the nose too high; it is possible to get airborne too early with the consequent risk of tip stall. At about 110–120 knots, depending on weight, the Venom 'levitates' into the air without any apparent change in attitude – a real weird feeling.

Once the gear and flaps are cleaned up the aircraft accelerates quite well towards 300–350 knots and the controls, even in the FB.1 with manual ailerons, are quite pleasant at this speed.

The roll rate with the long wings, however, is none too bright and at high speeds the manual ailerons can require both hands on the stick to get any decent deflection and roll rate. Aerobatics are fun and the 'g' suit helps with pilot fatigue – I believe that the Venom was the first regular RAF aircraft to be so fitted. Limitations on the aircraft mean that a low-level display is likely to be started with internal fuel only and consequently one eye is firmly glued to the fuel gauge as the other is watching the JPT gauge; three eyes are a distinct advantage! Cross-country flying is limited by the fuel and about 50 minutes at low level at a range speed of 250 knots is the norm.

The Pilots' Notes describe the landing as 'straightforward' and this is correct. Maintaining a minimum of 5,000rpm is recommended until the landing is assured because of slow engine response and the danger of overfuelling. The Venom shares a distinctive feature with the Vampire: application of full flap causes a very marked nose-up change of trim requiring firm forward movement of the stick. The stick loads are not high and this very quickly becomes instinctive. Major retrimming of the aircraft does not seem to be necessary, as the speed reduction following the full flap appears to equal things out, eventually. Speed control is important and, in common with most jets, a fairly shallow final approach is more comfortable and assists with keeping the engine rpms up. A gentle round out at the recommended threshold speed of 110 knots usually produces a clean arrival with little or no float – popping the airbrakes after throttling back can also help. This view over the nose and the short undercarriage gives the distinct feeling of thundering down the runway headfirst and nose down on a runaway wheelbarrow!

What is the overall impression: cramped cockpit, funny forward view, not much gas (what's new with British fighters?), ergonomically challenged, high control loads on the FB.1, and some very quirky handling characteristics – BUT great fun to fly despite all that. I love the Venom and always look forward to the next time we get together.

VENOM SURVIVORS

Australia: Sea Venom FAW.53

WZ939	Preserved	Classic Fighter Jets Museum, Parafield Airport, Adelaide. Display.
WZ943	Preserved	Australian Naval Aviation Museum, Nowra, NSW. Displayed on pole in town. (NB: this aircraft made the last operational sortie with the RAN.)
WZ944/N7022H	Airworthy	Amjet Aircraft Corporation, Blaine, MN. Re-registered N7022H in May 1993 and restored to airworthy condition in the markings of 809 Squadron RN. To D&J Aviation, Huntingdon, IN, in September 2000. Flown and operated by Dave and Chris Van Liere.
WZ895/VH-NVV	Preserved	RAN Historical Flight, Nowra, NSW. Long-term storage.
WZ897	Preserved	Camden Aviation Museum, Narellan, NSW. Fuselage only.
WZ898	Preserved	Queensland Air Museum, Caloundra. (Booms from WZ910.)
N4-901	Preserved	Moorabin Air Museum, Melbourne, Victoria.
WZ903/N7022H	Spares	Amjet Aircraft Corporation, Blaine, MN. Registered to Amjet in February 1998 and used as a spares source for WZ944.
N4-904	Preserved	Aviation & Military Museum/Syd Becks Museum, Townsville, Queensland. Display.
WZ907	Preserved	Camden Museum of Naval Aviation, Narellan, NSW. Display.
WZ909	Wreck	Australian Naval Aviation Museum, Nowra, NSW.
WZ910	Preserved	Queensland Air Museum, Caloundra. Dismantled.
WZ911	Wreck	Brisbane, Queensland.
WZ930	Preserved	Tocumwal & District Historical Society/Bill Riley Collection, NSW. Derelict.
WZ931	Preserved	South Australia Historical Society, Nowra, NSW. Display.
WZ935	Preserved	Australian Naval Aviation Museum, Nowra, NSW. Display.
WZ937	Preserved	Australian Naval Aviation Museum, Nowra, NSW. Display.
WZ945	Preserved	Camden Museum of Aviation, Narellan, NSW.
WZ946	Preserved	Ex-display, Chieftain Aviation Services, Bankstown, NSW. To Murrundi, NSW; now in USA.

France: Aquilon 203

53	Preserved	Musée de Tradition de l'Aeronautique Navale, Rochefort.

Iraq: Venom FB.50

370	Preserved	Military Museum of Iraq, Al Abied, Baghdad.

Italy: Venom FB.50

MM6153	Preserved	Museo Nazionale della Scienza e Della Technica, Milan.

Sweden: Venom NF.51

33015	Spares	Flygvapenmuseum, Malmslatt.
33025/Blue E	Preserved	Flygvapenmuseum, Malmslatt.

Switzerland: Venom FB.50

J-1503	Stored	Niederbipp, Switzerland.
J-1512	Stored	Ulrichen, Switzerland.
J-1516	Preserved	Israeli Air Force Museum, Hatzerim, Israel.
J-1523/G-VENI/ VV612	Airworthy	Source Classic Jet Flight, Bournemouth.
J-1526	Stored	Neuchatel, Switzerland.
J-1527/N9196M	Stored	Broomfield, CO.
J-1535	Stored	Niederbipp, Switzerland.
J-1539/ G-DHUU/WR410	Airworthy	Source Classic Jet Flight, Bournemouth.
J-1542/G-GONE	Airworthy	De Havilland Aviation, Bournemouth.
J-1544	Preserved	Grandvillard, Switzerland.
J-1545	Preserved	Savigny les Beaune, France.
J-1559	Displayed	Herisau, Switzerland.
J-1564	Stored	Kussnacht, Switzerland.
J-1573/G-VICI	Airworthy	Source Classic Jet Flight, Bournemouth.
J-1578	Displayed	Rickenbach, Switzerland.
J-1579	Stored	Rickenbach, Switzerland.
J-1580	Displayed	Swiss Air Force Museum, Dubendorf.
J-1584	Preserved	Payerne, Switzerland.
J-1596	Stored	Stans, Switzerland.
J-1601/G-VIDI/ WE275	Dumped	Hawarden. Written off in a flying accident on 7 July 1996.
J-1603	Preserved	Auto und Technik Museum, Sinsheim, Germany.
J-1605/G-BLID	Preserved	Gatwick Aviation Museum, Charlwood.
J-1611/G-DHTT/ WR421	Airworthy	Source Classic Jet Flight, Bournemouth.
J-1614/G-VENM/ WK436	Airworthy	Kennet Aviation, Cranfield.
J-1616/N202DM	Airworthy	Merle Maine, Ontario, OR.
J-1624	Displayed	Dulliken, Switzerland.

Former Swiss Air Force Venom FB.1R, J-1627 was sold at Dubendorf in June 1984 and transported to Bex the following August for display, where it was photographed in August 2002. (*Alan Allen*)

Switzerland: Venom FB.50(R)

J-1626/G-DHSS/ WR360	Airworthy	Source Classic Jet Flight, Bournemouth.
J-1627	Displayed	Bex, Switzerland.
J-1628	Preserved	Auto und Technik Museum, Sinsheim, Germany.
J-1629	Stored	Source Classic Jet Flight, Bournemouth.
J-1630/HB-RVA	Airworthy	Pegus AB, Altenrhein, Switzerland.
J-1631/HB-RVC	Airworthy	Aeronautique FMPA, Sion, Switzerland.
J-1632/G-VNOM	Displayed	De Havilland Heritage Centre, Herts.
J-1635	Displayed	Museum fur Luftfahrt und Technik, Wernigerode, Germany.
J-1636	Stored	Musée de l'Air et de l'Espace, Le Bourget, France.
J-1639	Stored	Dussnang, Switzerland.
J-1640	Stored	Largenthal, Switzerland.
J-1641	Displayed	Hobbyrama Garden Centre, Dubendorf.
J-1642	Stored	Dubendorf.
J-1643	Stored	Niederbipp, Switzerland.
J-1646	Displayed	Munsingen, Switzerland.

| J-1648 | Displayed | Schupfart, Basle, Switzerland. |
| J-1649 | Stored | Source Classic Jet Flight, Bournemouth. |

Switzerland: Venom FB.54

J-1704	Preserved	RAF Museum, Cosford.
J-1709/'J-1700'	Displayed	Emmen, Switzerland.
J-1712	Preserved	Botany Bay Village, Chorley, Lancs.
		Pod only.
J-1717	Preserved	Italy.
J-1719	Instructional	Scholtz, Switzerland.
J-1727	Stored	Ulrichen, Switzerland.
J-1729	Preserved	Verkehrshaus der Schweiz, Luzern, Switzerland.
J-1730/N402DM	Airworthy	Salt Lake City, UT.
		Operated by Dave Van Liere.
J-1733	Preserved	Ostereichisches Luftfarht Museum, Graz/Thalerof, Austria.
J-1734	Stored	Payerne, Switzerland.
J-1739	Instructional	Jegensdorf, Switzerland.
J-1741	Stored	Ulrichen, Switzerland.
J-1742	Preserved	La Storio del Volo Museum, Comignago, Italy.
J-1747/N5741V	Airworthy	Curtis E. Farley, St Petersburg, FL.

The ultimate Venom enthusiast's den? In February 1994 Christian Noetzli acquired the nose section of former Swiss Venom FB.4 J-1775 and modified it for use as a personal flight simulator in the living room of his apartment in Zurich! (*Alan Allen*)

J-1751	Preserved	Swiss Air Force Museum, Dubendorf.
J-1753	Preserved	Swiss Air Force Museum, Dubendorf.
J-1756	Displayed	Hochstetten, Switzerland.
J-1758/G-BLSD	Stored	North Weald.
J-1766	Displayed	Diepoldsau, Switzerland.
J-1775	Privately owned	Zurich, Switzerland.
J-1776	Stored	Ulrichen, Switzerland.
J-1778	Displayed	Herisau, Switzerland.
J-1790/G-BLKA	Stored	De Havilland Heritage Centre, Herts.
J-1797	Preserved	Flugausstellung L & P Jnr, Hermeskell, Germany.
J-1798	Preserved	Auto und Technik Museum, Sinsheim, Germany.
J-1799/G-BLIC/ ZK-VNM	Airworthy	Rural Aviation (1963), Ardmore, NZ. Operated by NZ Warbirds Assoc.

United Kingdom: Venom FB.1

WK394	Displayed	Aero Venture, Doncaster, S. Yorks. Cockpit only.

United Kingdom: Venom NF.3

WX788	Preserved	Aero Venture, Doncaster, S. Yorks.
WX853	Preserved	De Havilland Aircraft Heritage Centre, Herts.
WX905	Preserved	Newark Air Museum, Winthorpe, Notts.

United Kingdom: Venom FB.4

WR539	Preserved	De Havilland Aircraft Heritage Centre, Herts.

United Kingdom: Sea Venom FAW.21

WW217	Preserved	Newark Air Museum, Winthorpe, Notts.
XG613	Preserved	Imperial War Museum, Duxford.

United Kingdom: Sea Venom FAW.22

WM571	Preserved	Hall of Aviation, Southampton.
WW138	Preserved	Fleet Air Arm Museum, Yeovilton, Som.
WW145	Preserved	Museum of Flight, East Fortune, Scotland.
XG629	Privately owned	Alan Simpson, Stone, Staffs.
XG680	Preserved	North East Aircraft Museum, Sunderland.
XG692	Preserved	Midland Warplane Museum, Atherstone, Warks.
XG730	Preserved	De Havilland Aircraft Heritage Centre, Herts.
XG731	Derelict	Tain ranges, Invergordon.
XG737	Preserved	Jet Aviation Preservation Group, Long Marston.

Venezuela: Venom FB.54

8C-36	Preserved	Museo Aeronautica de la FAV, Maracay AFB.
8176	Preserved	Escuela de Aviacion Militair, Mariscal Sucre AFB.

CHAPTER SEVENTEEN

FROM THE COCKPIT

Air Cdre Bill Croydon was a flying officer with 28 Squadron during the mid-1950s. He had previously flown Hornet fighters with 80 Squadron at Kai Tak, before transferring to 28 Squadron to fly both Vampires and Venoms.

The squadron's firing range was at Port Shelter, a few minutes' flying time away from Kai Tak, with the targets being built into the face of a small spur of land jutting out into a large bay. Chinese junks and sampans frequently sailed too close to the range, and on one occasion a most persistent junk-master who repeatedly endangered the lives of his crew and jeopardised the firing programme had to be given a drastic warning:

There was always a small flotilla of sampans and junks waiting to move into the area, and a safety launch stood by to warn off those that came too close. As soon as the day's firing was finished, the occupants of those vessels would dive into the water to retrieve the shells from the 20mm ammunition. The valuable bit was the small copper ring around the base of each shell.

From time to time they would venture on to the range before we had finished firing, and on one occasion in September 1956, the sampans were persistent and the safety launch was involved elsewhere. I was due to start my firing run and was invited by the range safety officer to 'buzz' the offender. As I passed over it, I pulled up sharply and applied full power. When I turned to see whether the sampan was departing from the range area, I was horrified to see the sampan virtually upside down, its sail in the water, and with pots, pans, and

men, women and children swimming around. The range safety launch came to the rescue.

It turned out that the boat had entered Hong Kong illegally from Communist China and the police had arrested the crew and fined the captain.

Air Cdre Max Bacon joined 73 Squadron at Nicosia in May 1955. The following year he was appointed as a squadron flight commander. He left in April 1957, when 73 became a Canberra squadron at Akrotiri.

In 1955 the Venom had settled into RAF service, having had earlier structural wing failures in Germany. However, they remained unreliable, particularly with their electrical and radio systems.

The Venom's nose could be raised too high on take-off and this prevented acceleration. In addition if one became airborne too early the aircraft could flick. This happened to a 32 Squadron pilot at Nicosia. His aircraft was flying without its IFF set in the nose (meaning that the centre of gravity was further back than usual) and the elastic bungee cord which provided resistance to pulling the stick back was missing. As a result the pilot raised the nose too high and flicked over his leader into the ground.

All Venoms were started by a cartridge and formation start ups were an interesting spectacle with a plume of black smoke from each fuselage. Furthermore a long flame often came from the jet pipe so an asbestos blanket was normally hung over the tailplane to protect it from the heat. Two cartridges were fitted to each engine and it was not unknown for the first cartridge to fire the second. If the safety valve did not work properly the starter disintegrated!

Despite some idiosyncrasies and obsolescence, the Venom was a popular aircraft with pilots and the day-fighter/ground-attack role was interesting as it involved visiting and low flying over large areas of the Middle East.

When seeking a successor to the Venom, the RAF conducted a trial in Aden called the Venom Replacement Trial when the Gnat, Jet Provost and Hunter were pitted against each other. The Gnat scored highly with its manoeuvrability and difficulty of spotting, but the Hunter carried much more weaponry and was already in service as a day-fighter. The Hunter won the competition, as the Jet Provost was no match for potential air defence fighters. I later commanded 20 Squadron with Hunter FGA.9s in the Far East operating over Borneo and northern Malaysia and would not have been happy with Gnats, which I later flew as Chief Instructor at Valley.

Between November 1952 and March 1960 a total of 155 single-seat RAF Venoms were lost as a result of flying accidents, mainly through engine or structural failures. Although some of the accidents had tragic results, twenty-one pilots were able to abandon their stricken aircraft successfully with the assistance of the Martin-Baker ejection seat. This is the story of just one of them.

Tom Lecky-Thompson is probably best known for setting the fastest overall time in the East–West leg of the Daily Mail Transatlantic Air Race in a Harrier in May 1969. Thirteen years earlier, on 11 June 1956, he was a flying officer with 249 Squadron at Amman when his Venom (WR380) suffered an engine flame-out and he was forced to eject 6 miles from base:

I was fortunate in that it was one of the days that the flight commanders had decided that we would simulate 'Operational Turn Rounds', i.e., pilots would just accept the aircraft to fly without looking at the Form 700 or doing any external

checks. On 'normal' flying days we always recorded the amount of fuel left after each flight, and the two previous flights showed that the fuel put in against fuel 'left' meant that the fuel gauge over-read by some 75 gallons! I was returning to the airfield in a wadi, about 500ft above surrounding ground level, when the engine flamed out and I noticed that the fuel gauge read 72 gallons. So no blame attached!

I pulled up from 300 knots and made about 2,000ft of extra height, called the tower and ejected. The seat was the Mk.1 version, taking five seconds before I would be automatically kicked out of the seat. I saw the ground coming up each side and was about to start the manual override separation when I heard the timer click and was pushed out of the seat. The 'chute opened with a jerk as I entered the wadi, and a few seconds later I hit the ground with a wallop about 50 yd from the crashed aircraft. I was soon picked up by a Sycamore helicopter and returned to base.

In 1960 Bob Hillman was an exchange pilot with the Pakistan Air Force, flying Lockheed T-33 jet trainers at Mauripur. In the November of that year he accepted a chance to fly in a Sea Venom . . .

During November 1960 I was attached to HMS *Albion* from PAF Mauripur as an observer to a CENTO exercise. I can't remember why; it was probably just a good skive or Captain McLeod (the Naval Adviser) thought it might improve my education. It was quite a big exercise with a large US carrier and a number of other vessels.

During a lull in the exercise, I accepted an opportunity to fly in a Sea Venom (XG694) of 894 Squadron. The flight lasted about two hours and everything went as normal. What I really remember about the flight was the take-off and landing. This was my one and only carrier sortie and I wanted to savour every moment. The launch was very dramatic; I instinctively closed my eyes during the very rapid acceleration, which was accompanied by a great deal of noise. I very quickly opened them when all went quiet and my vestibulary organs indicated that we were looping; needless to say that we were flying quite normally.

The landing was equally dramatic. The touchdown was quite firm, and some power was kept on in case the wire was missed and one had to execute a 'bolter'. There was a massive deceleration, throttle to idle, brakes left off to allow the aircraft to run back, signal to raise the hook, hit wing fold and turn starboard to taxi into Fly 1 [the area forward of the island]. When the Australian pilot attempted to turn to port, we trundled straight on as the port brake had failed and the aircraft went over the side and into the rigging on the deck edge, which was designed to catch bodies. The aircraft came to rest on the nose-wheel door and was only slightly damaged. I just sat there wittering 'That was great', and 'Thank you very much', when all I could see was the Indian Ocean rushing by. After that I just stayed strapped in until I was helped out by one of the deck handlers. We were later shown a trail of hydraulic fluid from where we had turned to starboard.

Following a period of storage and repairs, the Sea Venom was relegated for use as an instructional airframe at RNAS Lee-on-Solent in September 1964. In a surprising turn of events the airframe was returned to operational flying in December 1965, serving with 831 Squadron at RAF Watton until the following June. It was eventually broken up after use at the Fareham Technical College.

And finally . . . Early postwar Germany was once described as a virtually unrestricted low-flying area. As such, many former 2TAF pilots claimed to have flown *under* the major railway bridge of the Kiel Canal, the canal being in the official low-flying area. This is just one of those stories.

In the late summer of 1956 a low-level battle formation of four Venoms from 145 Squadron at Celle, led by Flg Off 'Ginger' Bradshaw, flew under the bridge. They might have got away with the incident except for the fact that an inspection party from the Deutsches Bundesbahn was on the bridge carrying out an inspection at the time. The leader of the party managed to get the number of one of the aircraft and noted that the leader of the flight was wearing a bright red 'bone dome' ('Ginger' Bradshaw had a penchant for red, apparently, and his newly acquired flying helmet was painted in that colour).

The Wing Commander Flying at Celle was the former Battle of Britain pilot Wg Cdr Don Kingaby DSO, DFC (US), AFC, DFM and 2 Bars, who probably admired the spirit shown by the pilots and restricted their punishment to an extra seven days as Orderly Officer. 'Ginger' Bradshaw went on to become a Concorde captain with British Airways!

AIRCRAFT SPECIFICATIONS

	FB.1/4	NF.2	NF.3	FAW.20	FAW.21	FAW.22	FAW.53	Aquilon
Span	41ft 8in	42ft 11in	42ft 11in	42ft 10in	42ft 10in	42ft 10in	42ft 10in	42ft 10in
Length	31ft 10in	33ft 1in	36ft 7in	36ft 4in	36ft 8in	36ft 8in	36ft 8in	36ft 4in
Height	6ft 2in	7ft 7in	6ft 6in	7ft 7in	8ft 6in	8ft 6¼in	8ft 6¼in	7ft 7in
Wing Area	279.75sq.ft	279.75sq.ft	279.75sq.ft	279.75sq.ft	279.75sq.ft	279.75sq.ft	279.75sq.ft	279.75sq.ft
Normal AUW	13,228lb	13,838lb	14,544lb	14,410lb	15,227lb	15,800lb	15,800lb	15,035lb
Maximum Speed	640mph	630mph	630mph	630mph	630mph	575mph	587mph	630mph
Ceiling	48,000ft	44,000ft	45,000ft	44,000ft	49,200ft	50,000ft	49,200ft	49,000ft
Range	1,075 miles	1,000 miles	1,000 miles	1,000 miles	1,000 miles	950 miles	1,000 miles	1,000 miles

POWER PLANTS
Venom FB.1 and FB.4; NF.2; Sea Venom FAW.20: one 4,850lb-thrust de Havilland Ghost 103.
Venom NF.3; Sea Venom FAW.21; FAW.53: one 4,950lb-thrust de Havilland Ghost 104.
Sea Venom FAW.22: one 5,300lb-thrust de Havilland Ghost 105.
Sud-Est Aquilon (all marks): one 4,850lb-thrust de Havilland Ghost 48 Mk.1.
Venom FB.50: one 4,850lb-thrust Ghost 48 Mk.1 (Ghost 103).
Venom FB.54: one 4,850lb-thrust Ghost 48 Mk.1 (Switzerland); one 5,300lb-thrust Ghost 53 Mk.1
    (Ghost 105) (Venezuela).
Venom NF.51/J.33: one 4,850lb-thrust Ghost 48 Mk.1/RMA.2.

MANUFACTURERS

De Havilland Aircraft Co. Ltd, Hatfield, Herts.
De Havilland Aircraft Co. Ltd, Broughton, Chester.
De Havilland Aircraft Co. Ltd, Christchurch, Hants.
Fairey Aviation Co., Ringway, Manchester.
Marshall's of Cambridge (Engineering) Ltd.
Société Nationale de Constructions Aéronautiques de Sud-Est, Marignane, France.
A combine formed by the Swiss Federal Aircraft Plant at Emmen; Flug und Fahrzeugwerke AG,
    Altenrhein; and Pilatus Flugzeugwerke AG, Stans, Switzerland.

VENOM PRODUCTION

BROOKLANDS AVIATION LTD, SYWELL, NORTHANTS
5 Venom FB.1: deliveries between March and July 1954.
WE469, WK395, WK423–425.
Total Venom production: 5.

FAIREY AVIATION CO., RINGWAY, MANCHESTER
19 Venom FB.1: deliveries between February 1954 and March 1955.

WE464, WK389, WK390, WK418–422, WK492, WK493, WK496, WR276–278, WR294, WR295, WR311, WR337, WR338.

Note: WK390 was not delivered – crashed 22 April 1954. WR276 to Chester for completion; WR294 and WR295 to Hatfield for completion.

15 Venom FB.4: deliveries between May 1955 and April 1956.

WR375, WR405, WR421, WR438, WR444, WR493–496, WR535–540.

Note: WR421 and WR493 to Chester for completion.

3 Venom NF.51 for RswAF: deliveries to Chester for completion between September and October 1953.

33028, 33029, 33030.

Total Venom production: 37.

DE HAVILLAND AIRCRAFT CO., BROUGHTON, CHESTER

285 Venom FB.1: deliveries between July 1952 and April 1955.

WE270–274, WE276–294, WE303–332, WE340–389, WE399–414, WE416–438, WE444–460, WE470–483, WK393–394, WK396–410, WK429–437, WK468–483, WK489–491, WK494–495, WK497–500, WR273–275, WR279–293, WR296–299, WR312–315, WR321, WR334–336, WR344–373.

Note: WE381 is listed in DH documents as a first production FB.4, but has been retained in this list for the continuity of the airframe build sequence. WR347 crashed before delivery near Whitby, Ellesmere Port, Cheshire, on 20 October 1954.

To Hatfield for completion and delivery: WE308/309/323/326/329/369/370/371/383/384/386/401/404/423/424/425/428/435/451/453/454/458/474/479; WK410/435/437/478; WR353

To Marshall's of Cambridge for completion and delivery:
WE364/365/399; WK473/479/481/489/490/491/494/495; WR285/286/288/289/290/291/292

To Christchurch for completion and delivery: WR284

51 Venom FB.4: deliveries between March and August 1955.

WR374, WR377–383, WR397, WR404, WR422–429, WR439–443, WR445–446, WR460–463, WR471–473, WR483–492, WR502–509, WR530.

52 Venom NF.2: deliveries between December 1952 and April 1955.

WL811, WL813–833, WL845–874

Note: At least twenty-three airframes were partially or fully modified to NF.2A standard before delivery, with a further batch later converted at Brooklands, Sywell. To Hatfield for completion and delivery: WL822/827/828/829/830/845/846/847/861*/862/863/864/865/866/867*/868/870*/872/873/874. Aircraft marked * returned to Chester for delivery.

To Marshall's for completion but returned to Chester for delivery: WL832/833/849

WL871 crashed before delivery on 1 January 1955.

30 Venom NF.2: deliveries between June 1954 and March 1955.

WR779–808.

Note: Originally ordered as NF.2s, these airframes were modified to NF.2A standard before delivery.

56 Sea Venom FAW.20: deliveries between 8 May 1953 and 6 June 1955.

WM505–506, WM512–514, WM516–517, WM519–523, WM542–567.

To Christchurch for completion and delivery: WM506/513/514/519/522/523/542/551/553/555.

Note: WM522 crashed on take-off while on delivery to Yeovilton 11 May 1954; WM544 crashed on test-flight at Hawarden, 16 July 1954.

86 Venom NF.3: deliveries between May 1955 and May 1956.

WX797, WX800, WX805–806, WX808, WX810, WX837–862, WX866–871, WX878–883, WX903–907, WX913–922, WX929–949, WZ315–320.

Flown to Christchurch for completion: WX843/844/855.

Flown to Hatfield for completion: WX856/859/860/862/938/947/948 and WZ316.

113 Sea Venom FAW.21: deliveries between April 1955 and October 1956.

WM577, WW137, WW139, WW141–142, WW148, WW150, WW152, WW154, WW187, WW189, WW191–192, WW194, WW200–208, WW212–218, WW221–225, WW264–273, WW275–294,

XG625–638, XG653–662, XG664–665, XG668, XG670–671, XG673, XG675–676, XG678, XG680.
Note: Twenty-one aircraft later converted to FAW.22 standard. Some aircraft also later modified by RN to
   incorporate ECM equipment.
38 Sea Venom FAW.22: deliveries between November 1956 and January 1958.
XG681–684, XG686–702, XG721–737.
2 Venom FB.50: to Hatfield on 19 February 1953 for onward delivery to Italy.
MM6153–6154.
57 Venom NF Mk.51: deliveries to Hatfield for completion between December 1952 and June 1954 and
   onward delivery to Sweden.
33001–33027, 33031–33060.
Note: 33014 crashed on delivery flight, 12 August 1953.
15 Venom FB.50: deliveries to Hatfield for onward delivery to Iraq between March and November 1954.
352–366.
Note: 357 crashed on delivery at Malta.
1 Venom FB.50: attrition replacement for '357'. To Hatfield in May 1955 for onward delivery to Iraq.
370.
22 Venom FB.54: delivered to packers for shipment to Venezuela between December 1955 and August
   1956.
1A-34–7A-34, 1B-34–7B-34, 1C-34–8C-34.
Total Venom production: 808.

DE HAVILLAND AIRCRAFT CO., CHRISTCHURCH, HANTS

1 Sea Venom NF.20: prototype aircraft. First flew 26 July 1952. Retained for company and service
   trials.
WK385.
12 Sea Venom FAW.20: deliveries between May 1953 and March 1954.
WM500–504, WM507–511, WM515, WM518.
39 Sea Venom FAW.53: deliveries for Royal Australian Navy between September 1954 and January 1956.
WZ893–911, WZ927–946.
1 Venom NF.3: prototype aircraft. First flew 22 February 1953. Retained for company and service trials
   of APS 57/AI Mk.21 radar.
WV928.
20 Venom NF.3: deliveries between September 1953 and June 1955.
WX785–796, WX798–799, WX801–804, WX807, WX809.
1 Sea Venom NF.21: prototype aircraft, later redesignated FAW.21. First flew 6 February 1954.
   Retained for company and service trials.
XA539.
68 Sea Venom FAW.21: deliveries between May 1954 and July 1956.
WM568–576, WW138, WW140, WW143–147, WW149, WW151, WW153, WW186, WW188,
   WW190, WW193, WW195–199, WW209–211, WW219–220, WW261–263, WW274,
   WW295–298, XG606–624, XG663, XG666–667, XG669, XG672, XG674, XG677, XG679.
Note: Eighteen aircraft later modified to FAW.22 standard. Some aircraft also later modified by RN to
incorporate ECM equipment.
1 Sea Venom FAW.22: delivered to RDU Stretton, 4 December 1956.
XG685.
Total Venom production: 143.

DE HAVILLAND AIRCRAFT CO., HATFIELD, HERTS

Two Vampire FB.5 airframes built at Preston and transferred to Hatfield in February 1949 for
conversion to Vampire FB.8 standard. Both aircraft later became prototypes for the Venom FB.1 and
were retained for manufacturers and service trials.
VV612, VV613.

1 Venom NF.2: prototype aircraft. First flew 22 August 1950. Retained for company and service trials. G-5-3 (later renumbered WP227).

2 Sea Venom NF.20: prototype aircraft. Later redesignated FAW.20. First aircraft flew 22 February 1953. Retained for company and service trials.
WK376, WK379.

16 Venom FB.1: deliveries between June 1951 and July 1955.
WE255–269, WE275.

51 Venom FB.4: deliveries between October 1954 and July 1955.
WR406–420, WR430–437, WR464–470, WR474–482, WR499–501, WR525–529, WR531–534.

8 Venom NF.2: deliveries between March 1952 and February 1953.
WL804–810, WL812.

Note: Some aircraft later fitted with interim tailplane modification. WL804 crashed while with de Havilland.

23 Venom NF.3: deliveries between July 1955 and January 1956.
WX863–865, WX872–877, WX884–886, WX908–912, WX923–928.

Note: Airframes assembled at Hatfield from completed kits transferred from Chester. WX924 crashed near St Albans on 8 November 1955 while on delivery flight to 48MU Hawarden.

Total Venom production: 103.

MARSHALL'S OF CAMBRIDGE (ENGINEERING) LTD

50 Venom FB.1: deliveries between October 1953 and June 1955.
WE415, WE461–463, WE465–468, WK391–392, WK411–417, WK426–428, WK484–488, WK501–503, WR272, WR300–310, WR316–320, WR339–343.

Note: WK427 crashed on test-flight near Chelmsford, 4 March 1954.

33 Venom FB.4: deliveries between June 1955 and March 1956.
WR376, WR398–403, WR497–498, WR541–564.

Note: Fuselage pods of these airframes were equipped at Chester and taken by road to Cambridge for completion.

Total Venom production: 83.

Total UK production: 1,179.

LICENSED PRODUCTION

SNCASE, MARIGNANE, FRANCE

4 SE.20 Aquilon: prototype aircraft. Assembled from components supplied by DH Hatfield. Deliveries between September 1954 and August 1956.
01–04.

1 SE.201 Aquilon: prototype aircraft. First flew on 16 July 1954 and retained for company trials, including conversions to Mk.202 and Mk.203 prototypes. Delivered in October 1958.
05.

25 SE.201 Aquilon: deliveries between June 1954 and February 1955.
1–25.

Note: Five aircraft later converted to SE.204 standard and renumbered 91–96.

25 SE.202 Aquilon: deliveries between April 1955 and July 1956.
26–50.

40 SE.203 Aquilon: deliveries between April 1956 and June 1958.
51–90.

Total Venom production: 95.

F&W EMMEN, DOFLUG ALTENRHEIN, & PILATUS AG STANS, SWITZERLAND
126 Venom FB.1: deliveries between July 1953 and August 1956.
J-1501–J-1625, J-1650.
24 Venom FB.1R: deliveries between March and August 1956.
J-1626–J-1649.
100 Venom FB.4: deliveries between August 1956 and February 1958.
J-1701–J-1800.
Total Venom production: 250.

Total Licensed production: 345.

VENOM SERIALS

Venom FB.1
WE255–294   8.7.49   200   6/Acft/3627/CB.7(a)
WE303–332
WE340–389
WE399–438
WE444–483
First production order for the Venom single-seat fighter-bomber built by the de Havilland Aircraft Co., Hatfield, Chester and Christchurch, following the first prototypes. Originally the type was ordered as the 'Thin Wing Vampire', but after adopting the name 'Venom' in September 1949 all were built under the general designation DH 112. Deliveries ranged from June 1951 to December 1953. WE381 was later converted to the FB.4 prototype and first flew on 29 December 1953.

Sea Venom NF.20
WK376/379/385 21.11.50 3 6/Acft/5972/CB.7(a)
Prototype aircraft of the naval version of the DH 112 Venom, built to meet Specification N.107. WK376 first flew on 19 April 1951, WK379 in July 1952; both aircraft built at Hatfield. WK385 (the first example to be fitted with folding wings) first flew on 26 July 1952 at Christchurch. The designation was later changed to FAW.20 to encompass the fighter all-weather role.

Venom FB.1
WK389–437   5.12.50   85   6/Acft/6062/CB.7(a)
WK468–503
Continued production of the Venom FB.1 to follow on from WE483, with construction at Hatfield, Chester, Ringway, Marshall's of Cambridge and Brooklands Aviation, Moulton. Deliveries between March 1954 and March 1955.

Venom NF.2
WL804–833 21.12.50 60 6/Acft/6137/CB.7(a)
WL845–874
First production order for the Venom NF.2 night-fighter for the RAF, built at Hatfield and Chester. Deliveries between July 1953 and April 1955. Conversions to NF.2A standard included: WL805–811/814–819/821–822/824–827/831/845 –847/851–852/854/858/866/868.

Venom FB.1
WL892–935 21.12.50 120 6/Acft/6139/CB.7(a)
WL954–999
WM109–138
Projected large-scale sub-contracting of the Venom FB.1 with the Bristol Aeroplane Co. Ltd. However, de Havilland's decided to transfer its main facility from Hatfield to Chester and the need to sub-contract became unnecessary. This apparently led to the cancellation of the contract.

Sea Venom NF.20/21
WM500–523   2.1.51   60   6/Acft/6165/CB.7(a)
WM542–577
The initial contract for the NF.20 variant accounted for 156 aircraft (which also included allocations in the WW– range) but NF.20 (later FAW.20) production was limited to only fifty aircraft. All were built at Chester and Christchurch for the Royal Navy. WM500 first flew on 27 March 1953, following the three prototypes, WK376/379/385. WM567 was the last FAW.20 to be built, WM568 and subsequent allocations relating to the NF.21 (later FAW.21). WM568 first flew on 22 April 1954. WM571/573/575 were later converted to FAW.22 by the Royal Navy.

Venom NF.2
WP227   9.2.51   1   6/Acft/6323/CB.7(a)
Private venture Venom 2 night-fighter built at Hatfield and first flew on 22 August 1950 as G-5-3. It was later serialled as WP227 for evaluation purposes as NF.2 prototype. It was also assessed by

the RN for possible carrier operations, which led to an order for three prototypes (WK376/379/385) to be built under Specification N.107.

Venom FB.1/4

WR272–321   28.2.51   400 6/Acft/6400/CB.7(a)
WR334–383
WR397–446
WR460–509
WR525–574
WR586–635
WR650–699
WR715–764

The original contract called for 400 Venom FB.1s (to follow on from WK503) but this was amended in May 1954 and subsequently 90 airframes, WR272–373, were built as FB.1s and the remaining 150 airframes, WR374–564 as FB.4s. WR565–574/WR586–635/WR650–699/WR715–764 were cancelled in August 1953. Deliveries were between April 1955 and March 1956.

Venom NF.2

WR779–820   2.3.51   100   6/Acft/6401/CB.7(a)
WR835–880
WR897–908

Continued production of the Venom NF.2 (to follow WL874) at Hatfield and Chester. In December 1952 the order was drastically reduced to thirty airframes, WR779–808. The aircraft were modified on the production lines with clear-view canopies and modified fin and rudders against Contract no. 6/Acft/10129 and were unofficially designated NF.2As. Deliveries were between July 1954 and January 1955. WR809 onwards were subsequently cancelled.

F.4/48 Trainer

WT816/WT822 12.3.51 2 6/Acft/6417/CB.7(a)
Two prototype aircraft contracted to de Havilland, Hatfield, as DH 116 to meet Specification F.4/48 and as a naval jet fighter to N.114T. The swept-wing modernisation project was dropped in favour of updating the DH 110 and neither aircraft was built. Project sometimes called 'Super Venom'.

Venom NF.3

WV928   5.6.51   1   6/Acft/7006/CB.7(a)
Prototype Venom NF.3 built at Hatfield and originally ordered as a 'modified NF.2'. It first flew at Christchurch on 22 February 1953 and was used for trials of the APS.21 radar installation at TRE Defford and CFE West Raynham.

Sea Venom NF.21

WW137–154   18.6.51   96   6/Acft/6165/CB.7(a)
WW186–225
WW261–298

The second part of the first production order for the NF.21 (later FAW.21) to follow on from WM577. All were built at Chester and Christchurch and delivered between March 1955 and February 1956. WW137/138/145/147/151/186/187/188/199/200/202/205/207/209/210/213/215/217/220/221/263/268/273/276/278/286/289/292/293/296 were later converted to FAW.22 at RNAY Belfast.

Venom FB.1

WW669–710 10.7.51 42 6/Acft/7142/CB.7(a)
Contracted to Bristol Aeroplane Co. at Filton, but were all subsequently cancelled in August 1953.

Venom FB.1

WW715–751 10.7.51 299   6/Acft/7143/CB.7(a)
WW766–815
WW833–877
WW895–944
WW956–990
WX103–145
WX161–199

Continued production of the Venom FB.1 was projected with this order. All were subsequently cancelled in August 1953, before construction could begin.

Venom NF.2

WX695–740 17.7.51 193 6/Acft/7162/CB.7(a)
WX761–810
WX837–886
WX903–949

Continued planned production of Venom NF.2 was drastically altered in December 1952 and the initial allocations (WX695–740/WX761–784) were cancelled. The remaining airframes, WX785–949, were built to NF.3 standard at Christchurch, Chester and Hatfield, with deliveries between September 1953 and March 1956.

Venom NF.3

WZ315–348 17.9.51 34 6/Acft/7339/CB.7(a)
The final contract for Venom aircraft for the RAF originally accounted for thirty-four NF.2 airframes to be built at Chester and Hatfield. However, production was terminated at WZ320 and the remaining allocations were cancelled in December 1952. WZ315–320 actually emerged as the NF.3

variant. All were built at Chester and delivered between March and April 1956.

Sea Venom NF.21
WZ893–911 18.1.52 49 6/Acft/7622/CB.7(a)
WZ927–956
Sole order for forty-nine Sea Venom NF.21 airframes to be built for the RAN at Christchurch. WZ947–956 were subsequently cancelled while WZ893–911 and WZ927–956 (c/n 12750–12788 respectively) were completed as FAW.53s. WZ893 was transferred to Contract 6/Acft/9673 and initially retained for CA work. All thirty-nine aircraft were delivered to the RAN during March 1953.

Sea Venom NF.21
XA539 29.5.52 1 6/Acft/7062/CB.7(a)
Prototype aircraft built at Christchurch. First flew on 6 May 1954 at Christchurch.

RAF SQUADRONS

5 Squadron
Venom FB.1: November 1952–August 1955
Wunstorf (March 1952)–October 1955
Venom FB.4: July 1955–October 1957
Fassberg, October 1955–October 1956
Wunstorf, October 1956–October 1957
Began to re-equip with Venoms during November 1952. Because of technical problems and the need for a full establishment of aircraft in readiness for the intended visit to southern Rhodesia, most of the squadron's Venoms were passed to 266 Squadron in April 1953; a handful of Vampires were therefore retained to remain operational. Venom conversion began again in May 1953. The squadron disbanded as a Venom unit on 12 October 1957 as part of the White Paper defence cuts.

6 Squadron
Venom FB.1: February 1954–August 1955
Amman, February–June 1954
Venom FB.4: June 1955–June 1957
Habbaniya, June 1954–April 1956
Akrotiri, April 1956–June 1957
First MEAF squadron to receive Venoms, completely replacing Vampire FB.9s by the following May. Canberra B.2s arrived during July 1957, by which time the last of the Venoms had been withdrawn.

8 Squadron
Venom FB.1: March–October 1955
Khormaksar.

Venom FB.4: October 1955–February 1960
(Dets Akrotiri, October–December 1956; Sharjah, July 1957–January 1959).
Venoms delivered in March 1955, gradually replacing Vampire FB.9s. Ground-attack operations and policing duties were carried out in the Western Aden Protectorate and Oman until January 1960, when the Venoms were replaced by Hunter FGA.9s.

11 Squadron
Venom FB.1: August 1952–September 1955
Wunstorf (August 1950)–September 1955
Venom FB.4: August 1955–December 1957
Fassberg, September 1955–October 1956
Wunstorf, October 1956–November 1957
First RAF squadron to receive Venom single-seat fighters, replacing its Vampire FB.5s. Serviceability problems with the early Venoms meant that the Vampires had to be retained until August 1954. The squadron disbanded on 15 November 1957.

14 Squadron
Venom FB.1: June 1953–July 1955
Fassberg (November 1950)–May 1955
Oldenburg, May–July 1955
First Venom delivered in June 1953 to replace the squadron's Vampire FB.5s. Unit began to re-equip with Hunter F.4s in May 1955.

16 Squadron
Venom FB.1: January 1954–June 1957
Celle.
Re-equipped from Vampire FB.5s by June 1954. The squadron was disbanded on 3 June 1957.

23 Squadron
Venom NF.2: November 1953–November 1954
Coltishall (July 1952)
Venom NF.2A: August 1954–March 1956
Horsham St Faith, May 1957
Venom NF.3: October 1955–June 1957
First squadron to be equipped with Venom night-fighters, which were operated until replacement Javelin FAW.4s were delivered during April 1957.

28 Squadron
Venom FB.1: February 1956–November 1959
Sek Kong, December 1955–June 1957
Venom FB.4: November 1959–June 1962
Hong Kong, June 1957–(June 1962)

In January 1956 the unit's Vampire FB.9s were gradually exchanged for Venoms, sixteen of which were on strength by the following August. In December 1957 the squadron was reduced to a cadre basis and was re-equipped with Venom FB.4s in November 1959. Replacement Hunter FGA.9s arrived in May 1962 and the squadron made its – and the RAF's – last Venom sortie on 27 June 1962.

32 Squadron
Venom FB.1: September 1954–January 1957
Kabrit, September 1954–January 1955
Shaibah, January–October 1955
Ta Kali, October 1955–September 1956
Amman, September–October 1956
Mafraq, October 1956–January 1957
Nicosia, January 1957
Conversion to Venoms began in September 1954, but because of technical problems a handful of Vampire FB.9s were retained until January 1955 to enable the squadron to remain operational. Replacement Canberra B.2s were delivered in January 1957.

33 Squadron
Venom NF.2A: November 1955–July 1957
Driffield.
Formed on 1 November 1955. Its brief career as Venom unit lasted until 31 July 1957, when it was disbanded.

45 Squadron
Venom FB.1: September 1955–December 1957
Butterworth.
Began to re-equip with Venoms in September 1955, although Vampire FB.9s were retained until May 1956. Re-equipped in November 1957 with Canberra B.2s, which were flown out to Tengah from the UK the same month.

60 Squadron
Venom FB.1: April 1955–April 1957
Tengah.
Venom FB.4: April 1957–November 1959
First Venom arrived in April 1955 to replace Vampire FB.9s, but the squadron was not fully equipped until the following September. During 1959 the squadron assumed an all-weather role and was equipped with Meteor NF.14s, which were flown out to Tengah in October. Although most of the Venoms were scrapped, a small number were transferred to 28 Squadron in November 1959.

73 Squadron
Venom FB.1: July 1954–December 1956
Habbaniya, April 1954–May 1955
Venom FB.4: December 1956–March 1957
Nicosia, May–October 1955
Amman, October–November 1955
Nicosia, November 1955–July 1956
Khormaksar, July–December 1956
Akrotiri, December 1956–March 1957
First Venoms delivered in July 1954, but Vampire FB.9s retained until the following October. Replacement Canberra B.2s delivered to unit during March 1957.

89 Squadron
Venom NF.3: January 1956–October 1957
Stradishall.
Formed on 15 November 1955, although the first Venoms were not delivered until the following January. Began to re-equip with Javelin FAW.2/6s in September 1957 and the Venoms were flown to Shawbury for disposal.

94 Squadron
Venom FB.1: January 1954–September 1957
Celle.
Venom FB.4: March–September 1957
Re-equipped from Vampire FB.5s by June 1954. Venom FB.1s supplemented with a handful of FB.4s before disbanding as a result of defence cuts on 16 September 1957.

98 Squadron
Venom FB.1: August 1953–April 1955
Fassberg.
Re-equipped from Vampire FB.5s by November 1953. The squadron's Venoms were replaced by Hunter F.4s, the first of which was delivered in April 1955.

118 Squadron
Venom FB.1: September 1953–July 1955
Fassberg.
Re-equipped with Venoms in September 1953, although some Vampire FB.5s were retained until the following June. Replacement Hunter F.4s delivered to Jever in April 1955.

125 Squadron
Venom NF.3: December 1955–May 1957
Stradishall.
The squadron began conversion from Meteor NF.11s during December 1955, but was disbanded on 10 May 1957.

141 Squadron
Venom NF.3: June 1955–March 1957
Coltishall (September 1950)–October 1956
Horsham St Faith, October 1956–March 1957
As the first RAF squadron to receive the Venom NF.3, it began its conversion from Meteor NF.11s in June 1955. It was briefly detached to Horsham St Faith in October 1956 because of runway repairs and began to receive replacement Javelin FAW.4s in February 1957. Most of the Venoms had departed by March 1957.

142 Squadron
Venom FB.4: February–April 1959
Eastleigh.
It was originally intended that the unit would form at Khormaksar as a back-up squadron for 8 Squadron. Following a change in operational policy, the squadron was formed at Eastleigh, Nairobi, on 1 February 1959 as DFGA unit. Its existence was short-lived; disbanding on 31 March 1959 it became 208 Squadron the following day.

145 Squadron
Venom FB.1: March 1954–October 1957
Celle.
First Venom was delivered in March 1954 and the squadron had completely re-equipped from Vampire FB.5s by the following September. Squadron disbanded on 15 October 1957 as part of that year's infamous defence cuts.

151 Squadron
Venom NF.3: July 1955–June 1957
Leuchars.
First Venoms delivered in July 1955, gradually replacing the Meteor NF.11s. Venoms relinquished in June 1957 and squadron rearmed with Javelin FAW.5s at Turnhouse.

208 Squadron
Venom FB.4: April 1959–March 1960
Eastleigh.
Formed at Eastleigh on 1 April 1959 with aircraft transferred from 142 Squadron. Disbanded on 28 March 1960.

219 Squadron
Venom NF.2A: September 1955–July 1957
Driffield.
Formed on 5 September 1955. Another short-lived Venom night-fighter unit, it disbanded on 31 July 1957.

249 Squadron
Venom FB.1: October 1954–December 1955
Amman June 1954–August 1956
Venom FB.4: July 1955–October 1957
Akrotiri, August 1956–March 1957
El Adem, March–May 1957
Ta Kali, May–June 1957
El Adem, June–July 1957
Eastleigh, July–October 1957
Began conversion from Vampire FB.9s to Venoms in October 1954. Disbanded as a Venom unit on 15 October 1957.

253 Squadron
Venom NF.2A: April 1955–September 1957
Waterbeach.
Formed at Waterbeach on 18 April 1955, but detached to Stradishall between 1 June and 20 July 1955 while work was being carried out on the runway. Squadron disbanded on 4 September 1957.

266 Squadron
Venom FB.1: April 1953–August 1955
Wunstorf (July 1952)–October 1955
Venom FB.4: July 1955–December 1957
Fassberg, October 1955–October 1956
Wunstorf, October 1956– November 1957
Re-equipped from Vampire FB.5s by June 1953 to enable the squadron to take part in a goodwill tour of Rhodesia. Disbanded 15 November 1957.

A&AEE, Boscombe Down
CFE/AFDS, West Raynham: Venom FB.1: April 1952–June 1955
CFE/AWNW: Venom NF.3: June 1955–March 1957
CFE/RIDS: Venom NF.2: May 1953–May 1954
Central Flying School, Little Rissington: Venom FB.1: September 1953–May 1954
Central Signals Establishment, Watton
Central Gunnery School/Fighter Weapons School, Leconfield: Venom FB.1: February 1954–October 1957
RAF Handling Squadron, Manby/Boscombe Down: Venom FB.1, NF.2, NF.3, FB.4: February 1952--June 1955
RAE Farnborough
Radar Research Establishment, Defford
Station Flight Coltishall
Station Flight Driffield
Station Flight Eastleigh
Station Flight Stradishall

Wing Leader Celle
Wing Leader Fassberg
Wing Leader Habbaniya
Wing Leader Wunstorf

FLEET AIR ARM SQUADRONS

Although fuller details of the squadrons that flew the Sea Venom can be found in the respective chapters, the brief histories of the units are included here for completeness.

700 Squadron
Sea Venom FAW.20: March–May 1957
Sea Venom FAW.21: January 1956–June 1961
A trials and requirement unit, it re-formed at Ford on 18 August 1955 and moved to Yeovilton on 19 September 1958. Disbanded 3 July 1961. Tip-tank colours: None.

738 Squadron
Sea Venom FAW.20: September 1958–January 1960
Sea Venom FAW.21: November 1957–September 1960
Sea Venoms replaced Sea Hawks at Lossiemouth for the training of All-Weather Fighter pilots in the day and strike roles, with a syllabus comprising weapons training, formation and instrument flying, and navigation exercises. In 1958 the unit was renamed the Naval Air Fighter and Strike School, with 738 Squadron becoming the Sea Venom OFS Parts I and II and providing refresher conversion and instrument-flying training. With the completion of 82 AWS Course in August 1960, the Sea Venoms were in turn replaced by Sea Hawks, which had returned from 736 Squadron. Tip-tank colours: None.

750 Squadron
Sea Venom FAW.21: July 1960–October 1961
Sea Venom FAW.22: September 1961–March 1970
As the Observer School, the squadron trained crews in the fast-jet navigation role at Hal Far, with first observer jet course beginning in October 1960. The squadron moved to Lossiemouth on 23 June 1965 and latterly provided jet familiarisation for observers destined for Buccaneer and Sea Vixen squadrons. Tip-tank colours: None.

751 Squadron
Sea Venom ECM: 21: June 1957–May 1958
A radio warfare unit based at Watton, it was responsible for the development and trials of radio counter-measures and electronic warfare. A Flight re-equipped with Sea Venoms in June 1957, moving with the unit to Culdrose on 2 October 1957 as the Electronic Warfare Unit. Granted front-line status and renamed 831 Squadron on 1 May 1958. Tip-tank colours: None.

766 Squadron
Sea Venom FAW.20: October 1955–September 1956
Sea Venom FAW.21: March 1956–October 1960
Re-formed from 890 Squadron at Yeovilton on 18 October 1955 as the Royal Navy's All-Weather Holding Unit, moving to Merryfield on 24 November 1956. Became the Naval All-Weather Fighter School in October 1957, with course training beginning the same month. Returning to Yeovilton on 20 January 1958, it became the All-Weather Training Squadron during May 1959. Last Sea Venom OFS course completed in October 1960. Tip-tank colours: black and yellow checks.

781 Squadron
Sea Venom FAW.20: May–June 1957
One aircraft reported as being used by the Junior Air Officers' Course at Lee-on-Solent.

787 Squadron
Sea Venom FAW.21: May 1955–January 1956
Unit operated as the Naval Air Fighting Development Unit of the CFE at West Raynham and was responsible for the tactical trials of aircraft and equipment. Disbanded on 16 January 1956.

809 Squadron
Sea Venom FAW.20: May 1954–May 1955
Sea Venom FAW.21: May 1955–March 1956 and May 1956–August 1959
Formed at Yeovilton on 10 May 1954 with Sea Venom FAW.20s, but re-equipped with Sea Venom FAW.21s the following year. Disbanded on 20 March 1956, it re-formed again on 7 May 1956 and embarked on HMS *Albion* from September 1956 to October 1957, during which time it re-equipped with modified aircraft in June 1957. Based at Merryfield, the squadron re-embarked on *Albion* during July 1957 and transferred to Yeovilton later the same month. After a flight down to Hal Far it boarded *Albion* again for an eastern Mediterranean cruise from August to September 1958, when it returned to Yeovilton. It was back on board *Albion* in October 1958 for another Far East cruise and was disbanded at

Yeovilton on 17 August 1959. Tip-tank colours: black with horizontal white flash on FAW.21s.

831 Squadron

Sea Venom FAW.20: May 1960–March 1964
Sea Venom ECM.21: May 1958–October 1964
Sea Venom ECM.22: April 1960–May 1966
Re-formed from 751 Squadron as an electronic warfare squadron at Culdrose on 1 May 1958. The Sea Venom Flight was renamed B Flight and was detached to various stations and aircraft carriers. On 26 July 1963 the squadron moved to Watton and was absorbed into 360 Squadron in May 1966. It was officially disbanded on 26 August 1966. Tip-tank colours: red with yellow lightning flash.

890 Squadron

Sea Venom FAW.20: March 1954–October 1955
Sea Venom FAW.21: January–June 1956
Formed at Yeovilton on 20 March 1954 as the first Sea Venom squadron, and embarked on board HMS *Bulwark* in May 1955 for a period of deck landing training. Following another embarkation on board *Albion* between July and August, the squadron returned to Yeovilton and was disbanded into 766 Squadron on 18 October 1955. It re-formed again on 1 February 1956, and following an unfortunate time on board *Bulwark* in May/June 1956 it was disbanded into 893 Squadron on 25 June 1956. Tip-tank colours: black and yellow checks carried on FAW.21s.

891 Squadron

Sea Venom FAW.20: November 1954–April 1956
Sea Venom FAW.21: June 1955–April 1956
Sea Venom FAW.22: December 1957–July 1961
Re-formed at Yeovilton on 8 November 1954, and between March and August 1955 provided work-up training for RAN Sea Venom crews under the aegis of X Flight. The squadron briefly embarked on board *Ark Royal* in January 1956, only to disband on 17 April 1956. Re-formed again on 3 September 1956, but operated from Merryfield from November 1956 until January 1958 because of work being carried out on the runway at Yeovilton. Between June 1957 and September 1960 the squadron carried out numerous embarkations on board *Bulwark* and *Centaur* during cruises in home waters and the Far East. The squadron disbanded at Yeovilton on 27 July 1961. Tip-tank colours: red and yellow checks carried in 1958.

892 Squadron

Sea Venom FAW.21: July 1955–December 1956
Re-formed at Yeovilton on 4 July 1955 and embarked on board *Albion* in January 1956 for a cruise of the Mediterranean and Far East. Joining *Eagle* in June 1956, the squadron was absorbed into 893 Squadron on 26 December 1956 following the Suez operations. Tip-tank colours: white with horizontal blue flash.

893 Squadron

Sea Venom FAW.20: November 1957–February 1960
Sea Venom FAW.21: February 1956–January 1959
Sea Venom FAW.22: January 1959–February 1960
Re-formed at Yeovilton on 6 February 1956 with six Sea Venoms, later increased to nine following the disbandment of 892 Squadron in December 1956. The squadron carried out service trials of the Firestreak guided missile on board *Victorious* between September 1958 and January 1960. Disbanded at Yeovilton on 29 February 1960. Tip-tank colours: None.

894 Squadron

Sea Venom FAW.21: January–March 1957
Sea Venom FAW.22: January 1957–December 1960
Re-formed at Merryfield on 14 January 1957 as the final unit to be equipped with Sea Venoms. From August 1957 to April 1959 the squadron spent several periods embarked on board *Eagle* in the Mediterranean, before transferring to *Albion* in February 1960 for a final cruise in the Far East. The squadron transferred to Yeovilton on 15 December 1960, disbanding there two days later. Tip-tank colours: red and black checks.

Airwork

Sea Venom FAW.20: October 1955–September 1958
Sea Venom FAW.21: February 1957–April 1961
Sea Venom FAW.22: January 1961–October 1970
A civilian-operated unit run by Airwork at Brawdy, it provided aircraft for the Aircraft Direction School at Kete. In September 1951 the unit moved to St David's but returned to Brawdy in October 1958. With the closure of Kete, the unit moved to Yeovilton in January 1961 and operated as the Air Direction Training Unit. Replacement Hunters arrived on unit during the summer of 1970 and the last official Sea Venom flight was made on 6 October 1970.

808 Squadron RAN

Sea Venom FAW.20: June 1955–February 1956
Formed at Yeovilton on 10 August 1955 to provide operational training for the crews prior to their departure to Australia in February 1956 with Sea Venom FAW.53s. Tip-tank colours: Oxford Blue, divided by white lightning flash.

OTHER UNITS

Station Flights, Abbotsinch, Brawdy, Merryfield, Yeovilton
Maintenance Test Pilots School, Abbotsinch

MAINTENANCE AIRFRAMES

Between July 1953 and January 1974 eighty-one Venom and Sea Venom airframes were allocated for use as ground training airframes at various RAF technical training schools, naval training establishments and ATC squadrons. A small number also became gate guardians or were used for fire/crash rescue training. While most of the airframes had seen previous service, others had languished in storage in Maintenance Units since their original delivery flight from the manufacturer. Although not all of the allocations were taken up, the airframes were renumbered in a numerical series suffixed with M for the RAF and A for the Royal Navy:

7098M/WP227	7115M/WE417	7133M/WE257	7134M/WE262	7135M/WE278
7136M/WE273	7137M/WE270	7138M/WE276	7139M/WE263	7140M/WE274
7157M/WE259	7162M/WE264	7187M/WE255	7189M/WV928	7190M/WE267
7211M/WE266	7228M/WE256	7352M/WE455	7358M/WE272	7363M/WE315
7392M/WE284	7393M/WE293	7394M/WE332	7395M/WE345	7396M/WE349
7443M/WX853	7444M/WX866	7448M/WX912	7452M/WX792	7453M/WX938
7454M/WX857	7455M/WZ318	7456M/WX922	7457M/WX847	7458M/WX905
7459M/WX801	7547M/WX922	7549M/WX843	7565M/WX849	7638M/WR433
7639M/WR493	7640M/WR412	8399M/WR539		
A2327/VV613	A2398/WM505	A2399/WE279	A2411/WM564	A2417/WM569
A2429/WL806	A2447/WM503	A2448/WW148	A2449/WW219	A2453/WW223
A2455/WM514	A2456/WW261	A2457/WW269	A2458/WM570	A2461/WW146
A2464/WW285	A2475/WM557	A2476/WM520	A2477/WM513	A2478/WM512
A2479/WM509	A2480/WM553	A2486/WM543	A2488/WW194	A2491/WW275
A2492/XG616	A2498/XG621	A2504/XG622	A2506/XG655	A2508/WW218
A2512/XG637	A2513/WW267	A2518/WW189	A2520/WW270	

Airframes not allocated A numbers were: WM518, WM573, XG694 and XG736.

INDEX